DATE DUE

DEMCO 38-297

Critical Essays on William Faulkner: The Sartoris Family

William Faulkner in World War I uniform. Copyright © Jack Cofield.

Critical Essays on William Faulkner: The Sartoris Family

Arthur F. Kinney

G. K. Hall & Co. • Boston, Massachusetts

Library of Congress Cataloging in Publication Data

Main entry under title:

Critical essays on William Faulkner — the Sartoris family.

(Critical essays on American literature)
Includes bibliographical references and index.
1. Faulkner, William, 1897–1962 — Criticism and interpretation —
Addresses, essays, lectures. 2. Sartoris family (Fictitious characters —
Addresses, essays, lectures.) I. Kinney, Arthur F., 1933– II. Series.
PS3511.A86Z778   1985   813'.52   85-764
ISBN 0-8161-8690-1

CRITICAL ESSAYS ON AMERICAN LITERATURE

This series seeks to anthologize the most important criticism on a wide variety of topics and writers in American literature. Our readers will find in various volumes not only a generous selection of reprinted articles and reviews but original essays, bibliographies, manuscript sections, and other materials brought to public attention for the first time. This volume on William Faulkner's Sartoris family is a welcome addition to our list. It contains not only five selections by William Faulkner on the Sartoris clan but an entire section of resource materials by and about members of the Falkner family as related to the development of the Sartoris family. In addition, there are reprinted essays by the leading scholars in the field, including Willard Thorp, Alfred Kazin, Jean-Paul Sartre, and Carvel Collins. Arthur F. Kinney has written an important new study of the Sartoris family for his introduction, and he has included eleven original essays on the subject by Howard L. Bahr and William K. Duke, Donald P. Duclos, Nancy Belcher Sederberg, Franklin E. Moak, Francois L. Pitavy, Bruce Kawin, Sherrill Harbison, Esther Alexander Terry, M. E. Bradford, Judith Bryant Wittenberg, and Andrea Dimino. We are confident that this volume will make a permanent and significant contribution to American literary study.

Northeastern University

James Nagel
GENERAL EDITOR

For the Charles Roswell Mudge Family:
Florence, Robert P., Linda M.,
and in memory of Charles R. and Charles R., Jr.

and for
Tommy Covington of Ripley
and J. M. Faulkner and Evans and Betty Harrington of Oxford
for local history rich with the mellow splendor like wine,
gallant and finely tragical

"Q. Sir, what book would you advise a person to read first of yours?

A. . . . If you are asking me to give an objective answer I would say maybe *The Unvanquished*.

Q. Do you think that there's a particular order in which your works should be read? Many people have offered a sequence. Do you think there's a particular sequence . . . ?

A. Probably to begin with a book called *Sartoris* that has the germ of my apocrypha in it. A lot of the characters are postulated in that book. I'd say that's a good one to begin with."

William Faulkner to classes at the University of Virginia on
15 February 1957 and 23 May 1958

CONTENTS

INTRODUCTION

"What is it? something you live and breathe in like air? a kind of vacuum filled with wraithlike and indomitable anger and pride and glory at and in happenings that occurred and ceased fifty years ago? a kind of entailed birthright father and son and father and son of never forgiving General Sherman, so that forevermore as long as your childrens' children produce children you wont be anything but a descendant of a long line of colonels killed in Pickett's charge at Manassas?"

"Gettysburg," Quentin said. "You cant understand it. You would have to be born there." (*Absalom, Absalom!*)

"Yesterday wont be over until tomorrow and tomorrow began ten thousand years ago. For every Southern boy fourteen years old, not once but whenever he wants it, there is the instant when it's still not yet two o'clock on that July afternoon in 1863, the brigades are in position behind the rail fence, the guns are laid out and ready in the woods and the furled flags are already loosened to break out and Pickett himself with his long oiled ringlets and his hat in one hand probably and his sword in the other looking up the hill waiting for Longstreet to give the word and it's all in the balance, it hasn't happened yet, it hasn't even begun yet, it not only hasn't begun yet but there is still time for it not to begin against that position and those circumstances. . . ." (*Intruder in the Dust*)

In "The Golden Dome," William Faulkner's Sartoris family precedes the Compson family on the abbreviated list of exalted Mississippi names;[1] throughout the body of his work, the Sartorises remain his chief touchstone for the glorious past of the Old South and for its diminished present — in *Sartoris/Flags in the Dust*, *Sanctuary*, *Absalom, Absalom!*, *The Unvanquished*, *The Hamlet*, *The Town*, *The Mansion*, in the short stories, collected and uncollected, such as "Ad Astra," "All the Dead Pilots," "With Caution and Dispatch," "A Return," "There Was a Queen," "A Rose for Emily," "Ambuscade," "Raid," "Retreat," "Vendée," "Skirmish at Sartoris," "My Grandmother Millard and General Bedford Forrest and The Battle of Harrykin Creek," "The Bear," "Knight's Gambit," and the unpublished "Drusilla" and "Rose of Lebanon," and even his film script for

1

War Birds. In every instance, however, with bold declaration or subtle insinuation, what distinguishes the Sartorises from the other great families of Jefferson's past — from the Greniers, Habershams, Compsons, Sutpens, and McCaslins — is their heroic, tragic involvement in the War Between the States. And it is this that secures their pride of place in the history of Jefferson and Yoknapatawpha, which makes them central in Faulkner's own imagination: when he came to create his own little world in northern Mississippi, he began by transforming his own noteworthy family — the William C. Falkners — into the Sartorises, beginning with their exploits during the Civil War. For as Quentin Compson tells Shreve McCannon, Gavin Stevens tells Chick Mallison, and the Old Colonel Falkner told the Young Colonel who told his grandson William Faulkner, this was the great, determining watershed of history. Sooner or later, in the South, everything in fact or fiction turns on it.

Indeed, "The Civil War is probably the most significant single experience in our national existence," Bruce Catton claims. "It was certainly the biggest tragedy in American history and, at the same time, probably did more to shape our future than any other event."[2] The grim statistics still bear him out. One out of every five participants in the Civil War died in service: while 126,000 Americans died in World War I and 407,000 in World War II, more than 618,000 Americans were victims of the Civil War.[3] Moments of the greatest promise and heroism had ways of becoming occasions for horror and holocaust. The Battle of Shiloh, Tennessee, for instance: Henry Steele Commager quotes the autobiography of Sir Henry Morton Stanley (1909) who recalls that despite the Confederates' surprise attack, their superior organization, their knowledge of landscape and climate, their ability to back the Federal troops against the bluffs of Pittsburgh Landing on the Tennessee under the leadership of generals Johnston and Beauregard, Polk and Breckinridge, Bragg and Gilmer and Hardee, nevertheless the calculations of Grant, the forcefulness of Sherman, the tenacity of Union forces holding their ground at the Hornet's Nest, and the arrival of reinforcements under the cloak of night turned a potential rout into an experience of agonizing terror.

> It was a terrible period! How the cannon bellowed, and their shells plunged and bounded, and flew with screeching hisses over us! Their sharp rending explosions and hurtling fragments made us shrink and cower, despite our utmost efforts to be cool and collected. I marvelled, as I heard the unintermitting patter, snip, thud, and hum of the bullets, how anyone could live under this raining death. I could hear the balls beating a merciless tattoo on the outer surface of the log, pinging it vivaciously as they flew off at a tangent from it, and thudding into something or other, at the rate of a hundred a second. One, here and there, found its way under the log, and buried itself in a comrade's body. One man raised his chest, as if to yawn, and jostled me. I turned to him, and saw that a bullet had gored his whole face, and penetrated into his

chest. Another ball struck a man a deadly rap on the head, and he turned on his back and showed his ghastly white face to the sky. . . .

We gained the second line of camps, the rush through them, and clean beyond. [Exhausted, losing my company, I rested a half-hour by a tree.] Feeling renovated, I struck north in the direction which my regiment had taken, over a ground strewn with bodies and the débris of war.

The desperate character of this day's battle was now brought home to my mind in all its awful reality. While in the tumultous advance, and occupied with a myriad of exciting incidents, it was only at brief intervals that I was conscious of wounds being given and received; but now, in the trail of pursuers and pursued, the ghastly relics appalled every sense. I felt curious as to who the fallen Greys were, and moved to one stretched out. It was the body of a stout English Sergeant of a neighboring company, the members of which hailed principally from the Washita Valley. . . .

Close by him was a young Lieutenant, who, judging by the new gloss on his uniform, must have been some father's darling. A clean bullet-hole through the centre of his forehead had instantly ended his career. A little further were some twenty bodies, lying in various postures, each by its own pool of viscous blood, which emitted a peculiar scent, which was new to me, but which I have since learned is inseparable from a battle-field. Beyond these, a still larger group lay, body overlying body, knees crooked, arms erect, or wide-stretched and rigid according as the last spasm overtook them. The company opposed to them must have shot straight. . . .

It was the first Field of Glory I had seen in my May of life, and the first time that Glory sickened me with its repulsive aspect, and made me suspect it was all a glittering lie. . . . Under a flag of truce, I saw the bearers pick up the dead from the field, and lay them in long rows beside a wide trench; I saw them laid, one by one, close together at the bottom.[4]

Such new witnessing (and such new testaments) was far from unique; many a lad, at first young and easy under the apple boughs, swiftly saw his own fields and landscape laid waste. Fourteen months later to the southwest where Grant began to lay siege to Vicksburg, his troops, Allan Nevins writes, found

the wholesale removal of Negroes southward, and the ravages of armies and guerillas, had stripped the country bare. The British officer Lieutenant-Colonel Fremantle of the Coldstream Guards . . . found Mississippi and Alabama in an extremity of anguish. He saw boys of fifteen and sixteen badly wounded, and sometimes vain over a missing limb. He visited farmhouses where the women had scarcely any clothes, nothing but the coarsest side meat and cornbread to eat, and sweet-potato coffee to drink; they were in miserable uncertainty as to the fate of their relatives and their own future. When he ate with Johnston and his staff the only cooking utensils were a battered coffee pot and frying pan, and they shared a one-pronged fork among them.[5]

Such wholesale theft and destruction make sense when we remember that there were two theaters (not one) in the Civil War and that the Western theater centered on the broad triangle formed by Memphis, Nashville, and New Orleans; then "The fact that half of the Confederacy lay in the wide Mississippi Valley," Nevins reminds us, "was always in men's minds."[6] And that land could be got at by Federal forces, could be rapidly conquered, if they controlled the Father of Waters, splitting the Confederacy in half and eliminating supplies and foodstuffs from Arkansas, Louisiana, and Texas, and if they could control the east-west railroad line that hugged the Tennessee-Mississippi border, especially where it met the one coming south towards Holly Springs and Tupelo — if, that is, they conquered the Mississippi cities of Vicksburg and Corinth. So Union forces invaded northern Mississippi and trampled her down; the soil Faulkner was born on and born to, like the Falkners before him, was land Grant had encamped on, Sherman had marched over, land where the romantic VanDorn had his irregular romantic escapades and Forrest (and Old Colonel Falkner) had made their daring raids.

General Johnston foresaw this, as other military leaders on both sides quickly did. Halting briefly at Corinth before the fateful march to Shiloh in early April 1862, each regimental colonel read orders to the Confederate troops that were not so much pious, events would show, as prophetic — and fatally optimistic.

> Soldiers of the Army of the Mississippi:
> I have put you in motion to offer battle to the invaders of your country. With the resolution and disciplined valor becoming men fighting, as you are, for all worth living or dying for, you can but march to a decisive victory over the agrarian mercenaries sent to subjugate and despoil you of your liberties, property, and honor. Remember the precious stake involved; remember the dependence of your mothers, your wives, your sisters, and your children on the result; remember the fair, broad, abounding land, the happy homes and the ties that would be desolated by your defeat.
> The eyes and hopes of eight millions of people rest upon you. You are expected to show yourselves worthy of your race and lineage; worthy of the women of the South, whose noble devotion in this war has never been exceeded in any time. With such incentives to brave deeds, and with the trust that God is with us, your generals will lead you confidently to the combat, assured of success.
>   A. S. JOHNSTON, General[7]

These were not professional soldiers but raw recruits, after all, homemade troops for a homemade war where Mississippi, the second state to secede following South Carolina, wished only to be left alone, insuring regional peace, human dignity, individual liberty, and family solidarity. This unusually youthful and personal war cut close along every Southern bone, and heart.

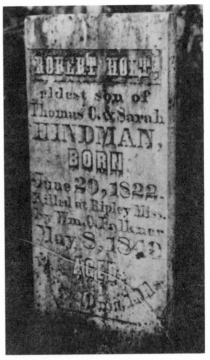

Contemporary portrait of Colonel W. C. Falkner, the prototype of Colonel John Sartoris. *Photograph courtesy of Donald Philip Duclos.*

The Hindman grave; note line on stone "Killed by W. C. Falkner." *Photograph courtesy of Donald Philip Duclos.*

West side of courthouse square, Ripley, in 1890s, the site where Thurmond shot Colonel Falkner and the setting for a closing scene of "An Odor of Verbena"; Thurmond's office is the small building on the left. *Photograph courtesy of Ripley Public Library.*

Contemporary portrait of R. J. Thurmond (prototype of Ben Redlaw/ Redmond). *Photograph courtesy of Tommy Covington and Ripley, Mississippi, Public Library.*

Contemporary portrait of John Wesley
Thompson Falkner I (the "Young Colonel"),
probable basis for Old Bayard; note a similar
wen on the cheek. *Photograph courtesy of
Faulkner Collection, Alderman Library,
University of Virginia.*

Cedar Hills Farm, the probable model for Sartoris; note the iron railings. Faulkner's description parallels this building and is in the location of Sartoris on Faulkner's map, although it lies a few miles west of the location in the novels. The house is presently owned by Faulkner's nephew, but Faulkner knew it as the Wiley House. *Photograph by Arthur F. Kinney.*

Parlor of the John Falkner house, Oxford, probable model for the Sartoris parlor described as a key setting in *Sartoris/Flags in the Dust*. *Photograph by Eva Miller.*

Farmhouse at Greenfield, probable model for the MacCallum place. Off the highway to Tupelo about eight miles northeast of Oxford, this indicates the path Young Bayard took in his flight from Jefferson. Faulkner places the MacCallums here on his map; a short time after writing *Flags in the Dust*, he purchased the property. *Photograph by Arthur F. Kinney.*

Hurricane Creek (locally pronounced Harrykin Creek), eight miles north of Oxford and site of a Civil War skirmish as well as the setting for "My Grandmother Millard and General Nathan Bedford Forrest and the Battle of Harrykin Creek." Faulkner took Boy Scouts here for encampments in the 1920s. *Photograph by Arthur F. Kinney.*

Vicksburg battlefield; Federal gravestones are marked, but Confederate stones are unmarked. *Photograph by Arthur F. Kinney.*

Grave of W. C. Falkner and similar to Colonel Sartoris' grave described in a closing passage of *Sartoris/Flags in the Dust*. *Photograph by Arthur F. Kinney.*

Gravestone of Dean Falkner, the author's youngest brother. Faulkner carved here the same epitaph he had given Young John Sartoris despite his mother's disapproval. *Photograph by Arthur F. Kinney.*

The "Christmas Bullet," probable model for the plane in which Young Bayard is killed during a test flight at the end of *Sartoris/Flags in the Dust. Photography courtesy of* Popular Mechanics.

And, in Mississippi particularly (as with Virginia in the Eastern theater, where the Southern Cavalier way of life had begun), the true story of the War Between the States is also the story of its women and its children in direct and brutalizing ways. The Battle of Shiloh, for example, was the desperate attempt by the Confederates to preserve the two major railroad arteries that joined at Corinth some twelve miles south; and it was to Corinth that the hordes of wounded fled in retreat. Thus we can pick up Sir Henry Stanley's account of war by turning to the sequel recorded by Kate Cumming, until then an unidentified woman from Mobile, who records in her journal having taken up in willing heartache the job of untrained volunteer nurse.

> The men are lying all over the house, on their blankets, just as they were brought from the battle-field. They are in the hall, on the gallery, and crowded into very small rooms. The foul air from this mass of human beings at first made me giddy and sick, but I soon got over it. We have to walk, and when we give the men any thing kneel, in blood and water; but we think nothing of it at all. There was much suffering among the patients last night; one old man groaned all the time. He was about sixty years of age, and had lost a leg. He lived near Corinth, and had come there the morning of the battle to see his two sons, who were in the army, and he could not resist shouldering his musket and going into the fight. I comforted him as well as I could. He is a religious man, and prayed nearly all night. . . .
>
> I have been told by a friend that the night of the first day's battle [my brother] passed by a wounded Federal, who requested him to bring him water from a spring nearby. On going to it, he was much shocked to see three Federals lying with their heads in it. They had dragged themselves to the spring to slake their thirst, and there they had breathed their last. There is no end to the tales of horror related about the battle-field. They fill me with dismay. . . .
>
> I was going round as usual this morning, washing the faces of the men, and had got half through with one before I found out that he was dead. He was lying on the gallery by himself, and had died with no one near him. These are terrible things. . . .
>
> We have had a good deal of cold, wet weather lately. This is the cause of much sickness. Dr. Hereford, chief surgeon of Ruggles' brigade, has just informed me, that nearly our whole army is sick, and if it were not that the Federals are nearly as bad off as ourselves, they could annihilate us with ease. . . .
>
> Everyone is talking of the impending battle with the greatest indifference. It is strange how soon we become accustomed to all things; and I suppose it is well, as it will do no good to worry about it. Let us do our duty, and leave the rest to God.[8]

Another stunning mixture of courage, fortitude, compassion, endurance, and despair — but in a very different key; it is a kind of model for a character like Drusilla Hawk — characterizes Cordelia Lewis Scales at

Oakland, an estate at Holly Springs, less than forty miles southwest of Corinth and nearer by that much to Faulkner's hometown of Oxford. In a letter some eight months later (27 January 1863) to "My Dear Sweet little Friend" Lou Irby and sent, she says, from "Destruction Hollow," she describes life there under Grant's forces.

> The day the army came to Holly Springs, & when the waggon trains were passing thirty & forty of the Yankees would rush in at a time, take everything to eat they could lay their hands on, & break, destroy & steal everything they wanted to — all of our mules, horses & waggons were taken, 42 waggons were loaded with corn at our cribs, & a good many more after. I'll tell you what I thought we would certainly starve. One thousand black republicans, the 26th Ill., camped in our groves, for two weeks. We did have such a beautiful grove & place too, but you ought to see it now, it looks like some "banquet hall deserted" — all the gates and pailings are torn down & burnt & as for a rail it is a curiosity up here. Col. Gilmore was in command of the 26th. He made our house headquarters; he use to let his men go out foraging every day & one day while some of them were out stealing chickens & hogs about four miles from here at Thompsons' place, a company of our "guerillas" overhauled them — killing two & wounding two. I never saw such enraged men in my life as they were when those that were taken prisoners & paroled came in camp with the news.
>
> The Col. took Pa's room for a hospital; when they were bringing the wounded in, I never heard men groan as they did in my life; all our sick & wounded in the hospital did not make as much noise as those two did. Gilmore searched our house for arms & I wore my pistol (a very fine six shooter) all the time & stood by my saratoga, would not permit them to search it. One said, "She's a trump."[9]

Later still, when Grant had moved on to Vicksburg from the west and south and, with Sherman forming a pincers movement from the north, laid a prolonged siege to the city on the bluff — to be as decisive a battle in the Western theater as Gettysburg was to be in the Eastern — Confederate men slowly starved while the women and children fled to caves within the walls of the fortified city. There Mary Ann Loughborough, who had been determined to follow her soldier-husband to Vicksburg from Jackson, wrote in her journal,

> The caves were plainly becoming a necessity, as some persons had been killed on the street by fragments of shells. The room that I had so lately slept in had been struck by a fragment of a shell during the first night, and a large hole made in the ceiling. I shall never forget my extreme fear during the night, and my utter hopelessness of ever seeing the morning light. Terror stricken, we remained crouched in the cave, while shell after shell followed each other in quick succession. I endeavored by constant prayer to prepare myself for the sudden death I was almost certain awaited me. My heart stood still as we would hear the reports from the guns, and the rushing and fearful sound of the shell as it came

toward us. As it neared, the noise became more deafening; the air was full of the rushing sound; pains darted through my temples; my ears were full of the confusing noise; and, as it exploded, the report flashed through my head like an electric shock, leaving me in a quiet state of terror the most painful that I can imagine — cowering in a corner, holding my child to my heart — the only feeling of my life being the choking throbs of my heart, that rendered me almost breathless. As singly they fell short, or beyond the cave, I was roused by a feeling of thankfulness that was of short duration. Again and again the terrible fright came over in that night.[10]

And such journals and letters, by men at the front and by families back of the eternally fluid and sometimes invisible lines of combat, must have been numerous since so many exist in archives now. Faulkner knew and inscribed at least one such memoir — John Milton Hubbard's *Notes of a Private* — which was bought upon publication and carefully autographed by the Young Colonel himself,[11] and which apparently remains in family hands.[12] Other Confederate memorabilia were at hand in the Falkner households in Ripley, New Albany, and Oxford long before William Faulkner settled himself down to chronicling Yoknapatawpha by way of the Sartorises. And if Aunt Jenny (Sartoris) DuPre seems forever wandering back to Jeb Stuart and General Pope at Second Manassas, this singular memory locking her into an obsession in *Flags in the Dust* (1973; first published in a shortened form as *Sartoris*, 1929), her predecessors in a later work, *The Unvanquished* (1938), are forever caught in the crosscurrents of Faulkner's references, coming thick and threefold, to First *and* Second Manassas, Shiloh, Corinth, Memphis, Vicksburg, Atlanta, Chattanooga, and (more subtly) Brice's Cross Roads and Cumberland Gap, to Davis and Lee and Forrest, to Grant and Sherman. Of this, the anonymous reviewer of the British edition made much in the *Times Literary Supplement* for 14 May 1938.

> The violence that stalks his pages never leaves the reader; the atmosphere is thick with the smell of war, the passions of the South, the tension of negro longings and loyalties. All through the book one carries a vision of negro crowds marching to freedom, waiting for Sherman to lead them across Jordan. Mr. Faulkner's subtlety brings its reward. The sense of the chasm makes him oracular and labyrinthine where plain speech might have served him well, but it also conjures from him an odd and startling power to communicate the actuality of sensation. (333)

Mr. Faulkner's subtlety brings its reward: if we think of *The Unvanquished* as so distanced in space, the events of *Flags in the Dust* so distanced in time that the terror and anguish of the War are safely subdued or diminished, we have lost the force and pain behind these novels (and all the Sartoris-related stories that spin out of them from the sheer power and influence of the War). We miss their deeper meaning as well — and the primary significance, for Faulkner, of the Sartoris family.

For we seem always confronted with staunch Sartoris attempts, both direct and indirect, to submerge or evade the fact of the War's destruction and defeat of the Old South, even as we are reminded of its terrific and terrible costs wherever we turn. Despite the camouflage of childhood escapade, Bayard's first memory of War—of his own life—is the invasion of Yankee troops onto his land, into his home. His personal sanctuary is violated. Yet this very boyhood awareness—however dimly voiced—allows him to retain with a kind of painful pathos the Yankees' final destruction of nearly all the Sartorises have, much as in Holly Springs they had destroyed much of Cordelia Scales's Oakland. Bayard remarks with disarming simplicity, "The wagon went on; we passed the ash pile and the chimneys standing up out of it; Ringo and I found the insides of the big clock too. The sun was just coming up, shining back on the chimneys; I could still see Louvinia between them, standing in front of the cabin, shading her eyes with her hand to watch us." Joby's cabin is the Sartoris version of the Vicksburg caves; here they have huddled in a curtained-off portion of their slaves' quarters, where Granny has written urgent letters in pokeberry juice because their initial attempt to escape to Memphis with the dripping roots and bits of earth they tried to preserve was blocked by the Federal troops gathering force through their land. Such continuous events of violation, destruction, and containment constitute a cumulative lesson of defeat, so that the once proud, boisterous Bayard can say of himself and Ringo that they

> had seen Father (and the other men too) return home, afoot like tramps or on crowbait horses, in faded and patched (and at times obviously stolen) clothing, preceded by no flags nor drums and followed not even by two men to keep step with one another, in coats bearing no glitter of golden braid and with scabbards in which no sword reposed, actually almost sneaking home to spend two or three or seven days performing actions not only without glory (plowing land, repairing fences, killing meat for the smoke house) and in which they had no skill but the very necessity for which was the fruit of the absent occupations from which, returning, they bore no proof—actions in the very clumsy performance of which Father's whole presence seemed (to us, Ringo and me) to emanate a kind of humility and apology, as if he were saying, "Believe me, boys; take my word for it: there's more to it than this, no matter what it looks like. I can't prove it, so you'll just have to believe me."

It is strange, Kate Cumming had written at Corinth, *how soon we become accustomed to all things.* Continual humiliation wears some down to acceptance, like Bayard, but it causes others like Granny to retaliate, like Drusilla to fight. And to still others like Miss Jenny it engraves deep scars of bitterness. "Do you think," she says scornfully to Narcissa in *Flags in the Dust,*

> Do you think a man could sit day after day and month after month in a house miles from anywhere and spend the time between casualty lists

tearing up bedclothes and window curtains and table linen to make lint and watching sugar and flour and meat dwindling away and using pine knots for light because there aren't any candles and no candlesticks to put them in, if there were, and hiding in nigger cabins while drunken Yankee generals set fire to the house your great-great-grandfather built and you and all your folks were born in? Dont talk to me about men suffering in war.

Her remarks reveal more than she may realize, for her deprivation, which she seems to make as great or greater than that of "men suffering in war" was actually prompted by filling those random, interminable periods "between casualty lists" when those "men suffering" were pronounced permanently maimed (*boys of fifteen and sixteen badly wounded, and sometimes vain over a missing limb*), missing (*in long rows beside a wide trench*), or dead.

Such obvious outcroppings of references to the war and such obvious descriptions of its wounded and battered survivors are only part of Faulkner's portrait of the War for which the Sartoris family serves as chief metonymy, since Faulkner is, as the reviewer in *TLS* noted, really after the *sensibility* of those who have suffered. We have to search and sense carefully to find hints to what the Sartorises have for so long learned to evade, secrete, leave *un*voiced. Thus Aunt Jenny's fond memories of the recklessness of Jeb Stuart, for example, when he accompanies the Carolina Bayard at Second Manassas, is meant to demonstrate her accommodation by confusion and subterfuge. For Stuart was not at the Battle of Second Manassas. He was, rather, at the *First* Manassas — and there his reckless advance was prompted when he mistook the New York Fire Zouaves in their baggy trousers for an Alabama outfit and so rode into the midst of Federal forces, risking the lives of a Virginia infantry regiment that went forward to save him. We tend to forget that, however, even though it predicts Stuart's glamorous endrun at Gettysburg, which probably cost Lee the battle and perhaps the War.[13] What we remember instead about the fierce battles at First Manassas (besides Stonewall Jackson's indomitability) is the battle of Henry Hill (which suggested to Faulkner the names of Sutpen's children, for Sutpen was also there) in which the leading character was the near-double of Granny Millard:

> Over the crest and down the hill, high on the western leg of the X [that marked the major routes joining at Manassas Junction], the battle raged around a small frame house where the eighty-year-old widow Judith Henry lay dying. When the Union troops came pounding south from Sudley Springs her invalid sons carried her on a mattress to the shelter of a ravine, but she begged so piteously to be allowed to die in her own bed that they brought her back, and there she had her wish. A shell killed her the instant they laid her down, and her body was riddled with bullets as the house began to flame.[14]

Manassas is one metonymy; Shiloh — the word is Hebrew for "place of peace"; it was the name of the church where Sherman and McClernand

first dug in against the C.S.A. — is another. The first major battle of the
Western theater (nearly 24,000 were killed), Shiloh was the scene of the
sacrifice and slaughter of the 6th Mississippi regiment, at the head of the
Confederate advance, which lost all but 100 of their 425 men by the time
they made their fifth straight assault. Eventually, most of them and their
fellow slain were piled seven deep, their identities lost, in one of five
Confederate trenches because Grant refused Beauregard's request to
suspend fighting until they were properly buried. Apparently Gavin
Breckridge is one of these anonymous dead — his name still another
allusion, to General John C. Breckinridge[15] — since his fiancée Drusilla
Hawk, John Sartoris's cousin by marriage and later his wife, left "widowed" at twenty-two, seems not to know where he is interred. The one
bright spot for the Southern forces in the Shiloh campaign occurred on
Sunday morning, when, on the offensive, they raided the half-finished
breakfasts of retreating Union officers. This may be the basis for Aunt
Jenny's story of the raid of Jeb Stuart and the Carolina Bayard Sartoris,
which, otherwise, has no historical precedent; but, if so, given the grim
context of Shiloh, their boyish spirits are doomed and her story grotesque.
It is Faulkner, like Poe, revealing the skull behind the grin. Such references, too, expose the grief and terror, just barely hidden beneath the
surface of fictional events in *The Unvanquished*, that serve to inform and
direct the early generations of Sartorises and remain the legacies to which
later Sartoris generations must forever reconcile themselves. So Grant's
plundering around Holly Springs and Oxford — "For a time he sustained
himself by collecting supplies from the district about Oxford. He sent out
scores of wagon trains, heavily guarded, for twenty-five miles on every
side. They stripped the country bare of livestock, grain, and forage, and
when the inhabitants begged for enough to live on, Grant sternly bade
them to move further south"[16] — provides a model of action for Ab Snopes
and Major Grumby as well as Granny and Ringo, while General A. J.
Smith's retaliatory burning of Oxford (" 'Where once stood a handsome
little country town,' an Illinois correspondent wrote, 'now only remain the
blackened skeletons of houses, and smouldering ruins' ")[17] finds its parallel
in the destruction of Sartoris and Hawkshurst and much in between.
Grant's rather elaborate five-stage siege of Vicksburg (investment, initial
attack, construction of approach, breaching of defenses, final assault) has
its dim analogue in Bayard's and Ringo's slow tracking of Grumby, on
whom they lay their own personal siege (the "riposte in tertio" suggesting
the elaborateness of their offensive) while the state of that city as Grant
discovered it on 4 July 1863 ("Not a single pane of glass remained
unbroken in any of the houses, a journalist noted")[18] makes Ringo's and
Bayard's representation of Vicksburg by using *scattered* wood *chips* a
bone-chilling symbol. Alongside this, Bayard's respect of the doomed
Pemberton is a mockery; earlier, in May, Mary Loughborough noted in her

journal that when she inquired their situation in Vicksburg in May 1863 from harbored Confederate troops,

> "It is all General Pemberton's fault," said a sergeant. "I'm a Missourian, and our boys stood it almost alone, not knowing what was wanted to be done; yet, fighting as long as possible, every one leaving us, and we were obliged to fall back. You know, madam, we Missourians always fight well, even if we have to retreat afterward."
>
> "Oh!" spoke up an old man, "we would ha' fit well; but General Pemberton came up and said: 'Stand your ground, boys. Your General Pemberton is with you'; and then, bless you, lady! the next we see'd of him, he was sitting on his horse behind a house – close, too, at that; and when we see'd that, we thought 'tain't no use, if he's going to sit there."[19]

Bayard's false vision of Pemberton – who historically was as misguided as Stuart at Gettysburg, torn between the contrary orders of Grierson and Lee – is as delusive as Loosh's stillborn sense of liberty and the blacks' belief, on reaching the Tennessee River in northern Alabama, far from the Mason-Dixon Line, that they have reached their Jordan, which will transport them into the Promised Land of the Union.

Yet what else but delusion could we expect from a beleaguered people who must have at some time been aware of some of the hopeless statistics – that with the border states of Maryland, Kentucky, and Missouri, the North outnumbered the South twenty-three states to eleven, with 20,700,000 people to the South's 5,450,000 (plus 3,654,000 black slaves); and that the North had a 10 to 1 superiority in manufacturing firms, a 3 to 1 superiority in railroad mileage, a 2 to 1 superiority in manpower, and a 30 to 1 superiority in arms production[20] – and who were constantly subjected to the scorn of someone like Sherman, who described the Confederate troops as "the young bloods of the South: sons of players and sportsmen, men who never did work and never will"?[21] In Faulkner's Sartoris fiction – which in its depiction of Confederate sensibility hews so close to ascertainable truth that some historians have used it to document their work – a deliberate romanticism becomes the means for communal salvation, the fact of political and physical defeat subjugated to remaining unvanquished spiritually and emotionally. In Faulkner's Sartoris fiction, Roman names like Drusilla and French names like Bayard lead to thoughts of Roncevaux, where death itself is a kind of glory and immortality, a deathlessness. If they are doomed, like Roland (or like Achilles or Patroclus or Turnus) then they will be epic heroes like their glorious predecessors, turning moments of near-defeat – as when Colonel Sartoris is trapped in his home by Yankees or Drusilla threatens to kill Bobolink or Bayard faces Grumby – into moments of epic greatness. Indeed, Bayard's and Ringo's search for Grumby takes on overtones of an epic quest; and they are overtones which, if adolescent and sentimental as well as dangerous on the surface, are profoundly needed psychologically, both for the self and for the South. To this respect and admiration for the beleaguered and the near-vanquished—we remember how fondly Old Bayard fondles Confederate weaponry in *Flags in the Dust* when he pays homage to the family chest of relics in the attic—the Sartoris family, descended from Cavalier stock (as the name *Virginia* DuPre is surely meant to suggest), also manages to retain its courtliness: its civilized sense of style. It is this cherishing of what is civilized that fuses Colonel John Sartoris's courtliness in killing carpetbaggers with Aunt Louisa's demands for a proper wedding between John and Drusilla and so makes a unified episode of "Skirmish at Sartoris"—and it is this same sense of ancien régime that characterizes the Thanksgiving Day ritual in *Flags in the Dust*. (It is also a precise measurement of all that Young Bayard has lost by Christmas Day.) Indeed, it is the preservation of style as the basic remnant of humanity and community that initially causes Aunt Jenny to attack Young John for his careless, thoughtless death and allows her, later in *Flags in the Dust*, to defend the surviving Bayard while scolding Simon: "Do you reckon that when my Bayard came back from The War, he made a nuisance of himself to everybody that had to live with him? But he was a gentleman; he raised the devil like a gentleman, not like you Mississippi country people. Clodhoppers." By referring to World War I as "The War," she collapses it into the War Between the States—still The War for most Southerners—and so anneals any ruptures of principle that subsequent Sartoris history might have been thought to include.

For it is Aunt Jenny's particular function to protect and preserve Sartoris courage and heroism by preserving Sartoris dignity and civility. In "An Odor of Verbena," this means supporting Bayard in his attempt to end the carnage that so threatened the Sartoris family earlier by ending a path of bloody revenge and retaliation that took the life of his father; and it also means correcting (without directly punishing or embarrassing her) the previously courageous Drusilla. In *The Unvanquished*, this means correcting (without openly scorning) Granny Millard, her predecessor at Sartoris, who betrayed the ancien régime when she chose Ringo's methods of survival (stealing, cheating, lying) as the novel encodes them, over Bayard's, and when—in becoming selfish, or uncivilized, in wanting more money and goods than she intended to give the needful of her community[22]—she made an unholy marriage between a Sartoris and Ab Snopes, destroying herself and any further chance she might have had for helping her family or their retainers. Indeed, Granny's growing greed for goods and money (for mules and cash) anticipates Colonel John Sartoris's greed when he takes over the railroad and becomes one of Jefferson's more entrepreneurial businessmen. Bayard's alternate course, to study law and to serve its civil practices, is more in keeping with Aunt Jenny's way. Unfortunately, it is not the way of John or Drusilla. And in time, when Bayard turns from law to the bank, when Young Bayard turns from the farm to self-exile and suicide in an airplane (turning down the chivalric token offered him and so divorcing himself from the original Sartoris claims to glory), and when his widow, Narcissa, giving birth to the last of the Sartoris line, prostitutes herself in a way that makes a mockery of all that is civilized and decent, then Aunt Jenny has no further cause to espouse—and no one to espouse it to. Her death *is* the vanquishing, at last, of this Sartoris spirit: there *was* a *queen*.

But Aunt Jenny is only one member of the Sartoris family, and while she clearly has Faulkner's respect, she remains only one strand of his complicated presentation of Southern aristocracy. Colonel John Sartoris, with his attempted bravery in the face of utter futility, and Drusilla with her constant (if at times equally reckless) courage are other strands. And Young Bayard, the last of that name, with his awesome sense of guilt, wider and deeper even than his namesake's, is still another. For if Faulkner uses the Sartoris family to analyze the need for, and value of, traditional aristocratic behavior, then he also shows us, simultaneously, why that kind of behavior cannot—and perhaps never could—work. One explanation of the Confederate defeat, after all, is that a large, landed aristocracy reliant on slave labor was inimical to a country characterized by democracy and progress. Believing in the immortality of a plantation like Sartoris was a little like Jeb Stuart fighting at Manassas or at Gettysburg as though he were at Roncevaux, or Agincourt. Thus Aunt Jenny's fundamental analogy between World War I and the War Between the States—one that Faulkner was examining himself as early, at least, as the composition of *The Wishing-Tree* in 1927—was a false one, leaving its proponent with the impossible task of making an epic triumph out of an Eliotonian wasteland (something Joyce found he could only burlesque, in the character of Leopold Bloom).[23] Daniel Joseph Singal has recently seen this bifocalism of Faulkner not so much in Young Bayard and Aunt Jenny as in Young Bayard and Young John.

> *Flags in the Dust* may be seen as Faulkner's initial skirmish against the Cavalier myth—with the myth still far from vanquished. In Bayard Sartoris he was attempting to portray how the weight of such a perplexing, violence-ridden heritage pressed down on southerners of his class and generation, leading to possible further violence and self-destruction. The element of compulsion that had entered into the Cavalier tradition is graphically illustrated by means of Bayard's crippling neurosis. At the same time, in John Sartoris, Faulkner was trying to keep the romantic tradition alive. Wistfully he wrote of these swashbucklers as resembling "prehistoric" creatures "too grandly conceived and executed either to exist very long or to vanish utterly when dead from an earth shaped and furnished for punier things."[24]

Faulkner suggests from the first, in *Flags in the Dust*, that Young Bayard, brooding over his heritage as his forebears do, is somewhat more of a realist: he spurns coming home from war by way of the Sartoris railroad, but instead takes a route through the family cemetery where the dead of war and peace are alike interred. It is of a piece with the "cold, arrogant sort of leashed violence" that Narcissa recalls distinguished him from John even as a boy, the coldness that will also characterize his courtship of her and their marriage, his memories and his nightmares. When he·makes an attempt to return to Cavalier manners, as he does in serenading Narcissa, it becomes burlesque; his later and more successful confrontation with this sense of Sartoris is when he reexamines his brother's childhood treasures — and burns them. Withered bear paws, stained hunting coats, and pictures of Princeton eating clubs have no place in a world where cavalry adventures have been displaced by dogfights and the treachery of sneak attacks by the Krauts. *His* civilization is personified by the Horace Benbows who escape war service by serving the YMCA, the Harry Mitchells who wind up servicing prostitutes in Chicago bars, and the Belle Mitchells who sell *their* bodies to the Horace Benbows. Knowing this, Young Bayard is more grimly prepared for Narcissa's act of betrayal, after his death, in naming their son neither John nor Bayard, but Benbow, giving the child a bastard name that recalls the other open act of bastardy — by the MacCallums, who mate a dog with a fox and so wind up with neither.

Yet that is not all we are to make of the name of Benbow Sartoris, the very last of the line. Narcissa suggests as much by calling the boy "Bory": as she may know (and as Faulkner surely did) that too was the nickname of General Pierre Gustave Toutant Beauregard,[25] the Confederate leader at Shiloh upon the death of Johnston. He was a Creole, himself of mixed blood, but it was precisely his Creole excitability and daring that inspired the men at Shiloh to go on against Grant's superior forces (particularly when Buell's reinforcements arrived) and so prevent disgrace even in defeat. Does Narcissa's act of naming her only child, then, mean she is returning to the Cavalier tradition of the Sartoris family? that she means to redefine it in her own terms? that she wants to mock it? How are we to read the conclusion of *Flags in the Dust* (and *Sartoris*)? Indeed, how are we to define morality in *The Unvanquished*? Buddy McCaslin could be taken as Bayard's first teacher of a pragmatic morality, by showing how slaves may be freed without the loss of an aristocratic society, yet we learn in a later work that the McCaslins bought their slaves from General Nathan Bedford Forrest, the voice of authority and source of Cavalier continuation in "My Grandmother Millard," who was in real life a notorious slave-trader before the War Between the States and who was, said Sherman, "the most remarkable man our Civil War produced on either side,"[26] the "Wizard of the Saddle," who, after it was all over, during Reconstruction, became the first Imperial Grand Wizard of the Ku Klux Klan. Is this continuation of the Cavalier tradition — one Buck and Buddy McCaslin would spurn — meant to measure its decline or to expose its potentially rotten roots? What Faulkner is surely saying with the Sartoris family is that they can never escape their connection to the Confederacy and, in a fiction that continually draws energy and significance from historical fact, that the Sartorises, like the ancien régime of the Old South, was at heart paradoxical: civilized and intolerant, awesomely daring and recklessly brave; serving a grand tradition and so backward-looking. Elnora, another bastard because she was sired out of wedlock by John Sartoris, nevertheless has the prescience to sing *"All folks talkin' 'bout heaven aint gwine dere"* and the wisdom and compassion to succeed Aunt Jenny upon her death. She too, then, is a glorious symbol of Sartoris humanity — complex, confused, struggling against impossible odds and thereby gaining what measure of respect and even fame humanity is ever able to earn from itself. If the decline of the Compson family is the decline of Christian morality, as I argued in the first volume in this series, then the decline of the Sartoris family is the decline of Old Southern culture itself — of a whole civilization that could not adjust to changing times and could not forget the memory of what was past.

"Beginning with *Sartoris* I discovered that my own little postage stamp of native soil was worth writing about and that I would never live long enough to exhaust it,"[27] William Faulkner told Jean Stein vanden Heuvel in 1956 for a *Paris Review* interview: it is his most-quoted remark. His friend Phil Stone, an Oxford lawyer, may have contributed to this in his "lectures" to Faulkner on the Civil War,[28] but surely the Young Colonel Falkner's — his grandfather's — study of that war, and his "reasonably diffuse and catholic library,"[29] had much to do with it too. But the most important influence — and a source of much of the early mastery and power of the Sartoris fiction — was his great-grandfather, the Old Colonel, William Clark Falkner on whose life that of Colonel John Sartoris is closely modeled, as Faulkner wrote Malcolm Cowley in 1945.

> My great-grandfather, whose name I bear [actually he was William *Cuthbert* Faulkner] was a considerable figure in his time and provincial milieu. He was prototype of John Sartoris: raised, organized, paid the expenses of and commanded the 2nd Mississippi Infantry, 1861-2, etc. Was a part of Stonewall Jackson's left at 1st Manassas that afternoon; we have a citation in James Longstreet's longhand as his corps commander after 2nd Manassas. He built the first railroad in our county, wrote a few books, made grand European tour of his time, died in a duel and the county raised a marble effigy which still stands in Tippah County. The place of our origin shows on larger maps: a hamlet named Falkner just below Tennessee line on his railroad.[30]

Indeed, this historic profile accords well with the fictional biography of Colonel Sartoris[31] supplied us in "The Jail."[32] The name of Falkner (Faulkner, Falkiner, Falconer, Fauconer, Fauconier) has been traced back to the time of Edward II of England, when a coat of arms was given to the original holder because of his love of or proficiency in falconry — in the medieval sport of hunting.[33] Company F, Colonel Falkner's "Magnolia Rifles," was mustered into state service on 4 March 1861, and he requested uniform buttons for them on 13 April; inexplicably, according to official government records, he did not himself enlist until 30 April.[34] As a leader, he seems to have had a sense of form rather than of discipline, but when told of this by his superiors, mended his ways and became something of a martinet, like Miss Jenny. His chaplain, Dr. Dwight Witherspoon, recalled a rather intricate formation of Falkner's design which he enjoyed practicing with his troops.

> The regiment was formed in column of fours and moved right in front, the head of the column describing the circumference of a circle, just large enough to allow the head and rear of the column to overlap each other a little. The head of the column at the point of overlapping was deflected a little to the left so as to come alongside the rear of the column, and thus moving forward, keeping just within touch of the moving column on the right, the whole regiment was "wound up" like the mainspring of a watch or the coil of a serpent, until the head of the column reached the center and the whole command stood completely coiled around.
>
> When the time to "unwind" came, the order was given to "about face," the column moved left in front, reversing the movement until the coil was unwound. This was the movement executed by him when he wished to address his men and to bring them all within easy hearing.[35]

When he was voted out of command (like Sartoris), he organized a troop of Partisan Rangers which in April 1863 drove a detachment of Federals back to Memphis. Establishing his regiment in Hernando, twenty-five miles south of Memphis, Falkner suffered heavy losses in a cavalry attack under the Union leader Grierson: the defeat was so severe that he was again replaced and in time resigned from service. There is no parallel of this incident in the Sartoris family, but the original name of Hernando, scene of the infamous Falkner battle, has been preserved in Yoknapatawpha: it was Jefferson.[36] There is no clear record concerning Falkner's subsequent activity — blockade-running has been suggested, which would have kept him near Memphis or Vicksburg — but the "Knight of the Black Plume," as he was called at First Manassas, passed on many legends. His descendant Sue Price has written in a letter about one of them.

> One of the most interesting stories that he told me, and IF ONLY I had the foresight to write it down, with all the facts and dates, etc, was about the Confederate spy who stole the 2 Arabians. To begin with, Dad said the Arabian government had presented our government, (the Union, that is) with a mare and a stallion. At the outbreak of the war, they were presented to a Union general (who, I don't remember.) This Confederate spy, (it was a simple name, like Tracy White or Stacey White, or something) was acting as a company clerk to a Union officer. He came into possession of some information about a surprise attack on our

forces; so he slipped away in the middle of the night and was in the act of stealing the Arabian stallion (since it was the fastest horse in the stable) when the mare began to nicker. So he was forced to take her along too. His mission was accomplished, but his usefulness as a spy was ended of course, so he gave one of the horses to a Confederate General, and the other to my great-grandfather. This story is entirely useless except as a legend, of course, since I have no substantiating facts, but I just thought you would be interested.[37]

After the Civil War, when land values plummeted, the Old Colonel acquired a 1,200-acre plantation, a dozen small farms, a grist mill and a cotton mill, making him a local baron, according to his early biographer A. L. Bondurant.[38] His character at this stage of his life can be pretty well established through two letters of 1887, only recently discovered, in his hand; the second is on the stationery of his railroad, the Ship Island, Ripley, and Kentucky. Both are addressed to one Ira South.

When it rains So you Cant work out, fix the press Complete. Have the lint room Cleaned out, and Clean out the Gin house. Drive the hoops on all of those barrels, and put them in the water. Put Mart Stanford to work, and Make him work like hell. Take those barrels off of the top of the Gin house, and get them So they will holid [sic] water. You May hire hands to help You at 60 Cts per day. Fix the Gin Belt, and the press belt, and Make evry [sic] thing ready for gining [sic]. Tell Elbert Smith, that I am out of Corn, and he Must bring Me Some immediately. Send pattern for the key to the (prep [?]). Any thing You need Send for it. Get hands to tear down the old engine house So we Can put it up Over the New engine. Move things aheaid [sic] as fast as You can. Falk-ner.

I Send Counsel to help You. Cover the engine house. I will Send him out evry day. let him Start Home half hour before Sun down of evenings. Make him put his horse in the pasture. If You want Huston to fire the engine, You Can get Some other reliable Man to take charge of the Mules. and Wagon. If you want More Nails, Counsel Can bring them out Saturday Morning. Try to have all the Cotton geathered as Soon as You Can.   W C Falkner.[39]

By this time the shrewd landowner had also become a shrewd partner in a railroad that he built from Middleton, Tennessee, to Pontotoc, Mississippi; the initial contract, signed by the secretary, R. J. Thurmond, on 5 June 1872, allows him and all of his immediate family and their descendants in perpetuity "a first class seat on a first class passenger car at all times over the entire length of the Ripley Railroad with as much as one hundred pounds of baggage."[40]

His death at the hands of his former business partner Thurmond was, as for Redlaw/Redmond and Sartoris, expected but sudden. The first document reporting the event is a telegram to his son the Young Colonel, J. W. T. Falkner, in Oxford, from Judge Anderson: "Thurmond shot Col

Falkner this evening—badly shot Come Walker (?) here with handcar."[41]
That evening (6 November 1889), the *Ripley Advertiser* reported,

TEE [*sic*] FALKNER SHOOTING.
His Wounds Not Necessarlly Fatal.[sic]
The Election

New Albany, Miss., Nov., [*sic*] 6.—Col. Falkner, who was shot at
Ripley, yesterday, is resting somewhat easier this afternoon. Dr. W. B.
Rogers of Memphis was sent for. He examined the wounds and pronounced them not necessarily fatal, unless he should have another
hemorrhage [*sic*] which would undoubtedly cause his death.

There is a great deal of excitement over the matter in Ripley.
Thurmond is in jail, guarded by a large number of Ripley's best citizens.

Col. Falkner is a generous and public spirited man, and has done
much to develop the county in which he resides, and if he should die
Ripley and Mississippi will lose a citizen whose place cannot be filled
[*sic*]

Col. Falkner was the Democratic nominee for the Legislture, [*sic*]
and was elected by a large majority.

Our county election here passed off quietly, all the Democratic
nominees being elected without opposition.

The same page announces that W. C. Falkner had received 1,313 votes for
state representative.[42] A fuller account appeared the following day in the
Southern Sentinel.

Terrible Affair.

On Tuesday evening last near five o'clock, the heavy report of a
pistol was heard on the west side of the square, a crowd soon gathered in
front of Alexander & Co's., store, where lay prostrate the form of brave,
noble, generous and manly Wm. C. Falkner, Representative-elect of
Tippah county, Pres. of the G. & C. R. R. and one of the biggest hearted
men that ever lived. He had been shot by a ball from a 44 calibre pistol
in the hands of Mr. R. J. Thurmond. Col. Falkner is in a very critical
condition; the ball entered his chin ranged around his jaw bone and
lodged in the neck; he bled profusely and is very weak. There is a slight
hope of his recovery and if the prayers of the people are heeded, he will
still live.

Mr. Thurmond is in jail and for fear of any out break from the
people, has been well guarded. Col. Falkner and Mr. Thurmond have
not been on very friendly terms for a year or two; but as to the cause of
the shooting we can give no details in advance of a trial; besides we
know none.

Col. Falkner is one of the ablest business men of the state and by
hard work and well directed energy has acquired a fortune of considerable proportions. He is noble, brave and generous and has many friends
because he deserved them. He is about 63 years of age.

Mr. Thurmond is a shrewd business man of about 60 years of age,
and is one of the wealthiest citizens of North Mississippi. He also, has
many friends.

The sad affair is greatly deplored by our whole people.

LATER: — Since the above was in type, the soul of Col. Wm. C. Falkner has taken its flight to the God who gave it.

One of nature's noble men has passed from the stage of action — his place can not be filled. There is a void where the noble Falkner stood — his manly form will be seen no more forever, his generous deeds to the poor and needy, will close; a life devoted to the interest of the people of his county and state, a soul that ever burned with patriotism and loyalty to his people, a man who has arose from the bottom to the top by his own exertions, is cut down in old age and the strong body lies mouldering in the cold damp ground.

The people mourn for their lost friend; this is right. A leader on the battlefield, a leader at the bar of our courts, a leader in the business world, a leader in the political field — a born leader of men — his followers and friends deeply grieve that he is no more: But fellow citizens, let not your love for your lost leader prompt you to rashness, let the law take its course — let justice be done to the living and the dead.[43]

One week later, on 14 November, the *Southern Sentinel* ran another story, "At Rest."

On Friday morning last beginning at 11 o'clock, the funeral services of the late Col. W. C. Falkner were held. There were about 1000 people present to do honor to the remains. The funeral services were under the direction of the Masonic order, of which Col. Falkner was an honored member. The funeral address was delivered by Rev. W. T. Lowery [sic] in the Presbyterian church, not half the people who desired to hear it could secure even standing room in the church building. Mr. Lowrey's address was very eloquent words to the great worth of the lamented Falkner. Capt. J. E. Rogers assisted Mr. Lowrey. The vast throng then proceeded to the Ripley Cemetery where with the beautiful and expressive burial service of the Masonic Fraternity, all that was mortal of the noble Falkner was laid in the tomb. Flowers were heaped upon the metalic [sic] casket until there was room for no more; strong men wept as they looked upon the face of their friend for the last time; the children cried as they cast a flower upon the tomb, while noble women with wreathes [sic] of flowers watered with tears stood at the tomb and gently placed their token [sic] of love and sorrow within its confines. Never in the history of Ripley has such a throng of sorrowing people gathered together to honor the dead. All felt that a friend was gone forever. Dry eyes were few. And so passes away the noblest man that ever honored Tippah County with his citizenship.[44]

C. Kendrick's poem "Faulkner," written on 1 December, confirmed such sentiments. He wrote, in part,

Honored he lived, and bravely died,
Beloved of all who knew him well,
For years and years to come his friends,
Of his good deeds will often tell.

> The Legislature, too, will miss
> A statesman true and wise and great.
> And many a time will they be sad,
> When thinking of our Falkner's fate.[45]

The courts, however, moved slowly; the following notice, under "Circuit Court," did not appear in the *Southern Sentinel* until 26 February 1891:

> Circuit Court adjourned last Saturday night at about 11 o'clock, the grand jury having [finished] its work on the previous day. The term just closed was one of a great deal more than ordinary interest. Wednesday morning the case of R. J. Thurmond charged with manslaughter, was taken up and the court House was jammed with interested spectators from that time until Friday night when District Attorney Spight closed the argument. Aside from the prominence of the defendant and Col. Falkner, who was slain, there was a great array of legal talent representing both sides of the case, which added somewhat to the general interest manifested. Mr. Thurmond was defended by Hon's C. B. Mitchell, of Pontotoc; Z. M. Stephens, of New Albany, and Ira D. Oglesby, of Senatobia; while the prosecution was represented by Hon's J. A. Blair, of Tupelo; J. D. Fontaine, of Pontotoc, and District Attorney Thos. Spight. Hon. John Allen was employed in the case was prevented from being present by the recent death of his only son and the present serious illness of his wife. The whole of Wednesday and Thursday were spent in examining the numerous witnesses, and Friday was devoted principally to the argument of counsel. The case was given the jury Friday night and a verdict of "Not Guilty" rendered at about 12 o'clock on Saturday. While great interest was manifested both by the Attorneys and the vast throng of spectators, there was no excitement and not a single "scene" during the progress of the trial, and even the verdict was silently received by all.[46]

All records of that trial, with its grounds for acquittal, are missing. Falkner's imposing statue — described in accurate detail at the close of *Flags in the Dust* — still stands in the Ripley Cemetery, looking out on the railroad.[47] It was designed from a model by Chancey Joseph Rogers of Grand Junction, Tennessee, who sent the pattern to Italy to be carved there of marble. But more than the statue remains. On 10 August 1966, Daniel Hunt of Tacoma wrote in a letter,

> The reason I mention the Falkner-Thurmond affair is because it had a great effect upon my young life. I was the only one related to both sides. Even as a baby I must have noticed it because I would not talk until I was three years old even though I understood as much as a child of that age was supposed to. From four to six the occurrences are still vivid in my memory — a mother pulling her child back to prevent him or her from playing with me; as if to say he has Thurmond blood or is Falkner tainted. As a consequence until my father died in 1895 I played by myself or with little colored children."[48]

Little wonder so forceful a man also had such a profound influence on William Faulkner.

As the Old Colonel served as the model for Col. John Sartoris, so other members of the Falkner family sat for the other Sartorises. The Young Colonel, John Wesley Thompson Falkner, the author's grandfather, a banker and student of the Civil War, is the basis for Old Bayard—even down to the wen that shows on contemporary portraits made of him.[49] In turn, Faulkner's father Murry—generally thought to be pointedly absent from the Sartoris saga—is also represented, if only by insinuation: it is in his livery stable, on Van Buren Street, around the corner from South Lamar's Buffalo Cafe, that Buddy and Young Bayard find the wild stallion. And as for the Sartoris women, Aunt Jenny is thought (and said by living members of the family) to be a composite of the author's great aunt Bama (Mrs. Walter McLean, daughter of the Old Colonel) and Auntee Holland (Mrs. J. Porter Williams, daughter of the Young Colonel) with, perhaps, a touch of Miss Maud, Faulkner's stern, disciplinarian mother, while Granny Rosa Millard is likely a composite of Lizzie Vance Falkner, the Old Colonel's second wife, and Lelia Dean Butler, Maud Falkner's mother.[50] As for Young John and Young Bayard, they are, in some profound ways, projections of Faulkner himself, drawing on his old balloon rides and possum hunts as a child;[51] they are both Faulkner's love for risk and for airplanes and his sense of failure when he was unable (because of his size) to join the U.S. Army and unable (because he enlisted too late) to go with the RAF of Canada to Europe and so missed the action of World War I. Perhaps more importantly, Young John seems to have been drawn on Faulkner's youngest brother Dean, as his daughter, Dean Faulkner Wells, points out in a master's thesis at the University of Mississippi (1975). She notes that the description of John closely resembles a self-photograph of Dean (19–20) and that their natures are similar. Dean, she says,

> found it difficult to work training regulations and practices into his otherwise informally structured existence, and when people (family, teachers, coaches, or friends) approached him or criticized him for his lackadaisical attitude, he responded with a wide grin and perhaps an invitation to play yet another game. Being alive, for Dean Faulkner, was a game, and he enjoyed every minute of it. He also had the unusual gift of being able to show the people close to him the best way to go about living. By the time he finished high school, these characteristics were formed, and they enabled Dean to lead an almost completely worry-free existence for the rest of his life (69).

Like Young John Sartoris, Dean Falkner was a talented hunter (49), a daredevil—"The olympic sized concrete pool [of his friends the Calloways, which he frequented] had a swing, and one of his favorite stunts was to stand up in the swing, pump until 'he was going as high as he could go.

Then, timing it exactly, he would let go of the rope and dive off the swing into the water. It was perfect every time,' his friends remember" (46)[52] — and interested in knight errantry. Despite Dean's "cocksure, flippant attitude toward academics" and his carelessness in assignments, one of his essays nevertheless was chosen as the best theme for the week ending 12 February 1927 (one year before *Flags in the Dust*). It was titled "In the Good Old Days":

> If I could have chosen the age in which I was to spend my life, it would have been in the good old days when everybody was a knight of some sort. Then I could have had a shiny iron suit, and have ridden about on a big black horse fighting everybody I met. I could have fought on horseback with a long pole spiked at the end, without being in danger of getting hurt, until my horse got tired. Then the friend I was fighting with and I could have got off our horses and fought with swords, or else have had a good crap game, until our chargers got rested. I should never have had any trouble finding somebody to fight, for there was never much danger of getting hurt. I have heard that people in those days could manage a whole war so that only 3 or 4 men would get killed. Those were the good old days. (85)[53]

Dean also loved planes and, encouraged by his brother William, earned his living by giving lessons and joy rides; he died in a plane crash between the composition of *Flags in the Dust* and that of *The Unvanquished*; in abject grief, William Faulkner had carved as his epitaph the same words he had put on the tombstone of Young John Sartoris in the earlier novel: "I bare him on eagles' wings and brought him unto Me."

Like people, places are likewise based on reality — on historical reality, such as Shiloh and Vicksburg, Holly Springs and Oxford, and family realities, such as the MacCallum house, based on Faulkner's own farm Greenfield, and the Sartoris parlor, drawn with surprising exactitude after the parlor of Lucille Falkner. Even the exterior, and the property of Sartoris, is based on Cedar Springs Farm, an antebellum house that still stands proudly, as if to prove the point, just (as in the fiction) four miles north of Oxford (Jefferson) and close to the battlesite of the skirmishes at Harrykin (Hurricane) Creek. Originally the land was taken from the Indian O Nah Mock Tubby (a name approximating Faulkner's Ikkemotubbe) and sold by federal grant to Thomas Pettis (in 1837); while Faulkner was growing up, it was known as the Wiley House (Mary Wiley inherited the property in 1880). Coincidentally, it now belongs to Faulkner's nephew J. M. Faulkner and his wife, Nancy.

In many ways, then — including the ways of culture, history, and family — the Sartoris saga was keenly felt by Faulkner at every step of his realization of it. How close to his bone it was is clear in a statement he made while visiting Japan.

> A hundred years ago, my country, the United States, was not one economy and culture, but two of them, so opposed to each other that

ninety-five years ago they went to war against each other to test which one should prevail. My side, the South, lost that war, the battles of which were fought not on neutral ground in the waste of the ocean, but in our own homes, our gardens, our farms, as if Okinawa and Guadalcanal had been not islands in the distant Pacific but the precincts of Honshu and Hokkaido. Our land, our homes were invaded by a conqueror who remained after we were defeated; we were not only devastated by the battles which we lost, the conqueror spent the next ten years after our defeat and surrender despoiling us of what little the war had left.[54]

Such scars, for those invaded, like the Sartorises and the Falkners, do not heal easily; and sometimes they do not heal at all. The visit to Japan occurred in 1955; the last work to deal with the Sartorises, *The Mansion*, appeared in 1959, three years before Faulkner's death.

The critical reception of William Faulkner is a well-known story, often told. Despite early support from Sherwood Anderson (who helped Faulkner to publish his first two novels, *Soldiers' Pay* and *Mosquitoes*, and advised him to write about Mississippi for his third, *Flags in the Dust*, shortened by his agent Ben Wasson for publication as *Sartoris* in 1929), most of his early recognition came from scattered reviews. These were uneven; Faulkner's work was often thought derivative, tangled, obscure, or morbid. *Sanctuary* (1931) was his first successful novel — but because it was thought sensational, not serious; Faulkner himself called it a "pot-boiler." Indeed, throughout the 1930s, when Faulkner was publishing much of his finest fiction, he was more admired in Europe than in his own country; Jean-Paul Sartre's acclaim for *Sartoris* is a representative example. In the United States, the first important critical reception came in 1939, and with two essays: Conrad Aiken's "William Faulkner: The Novel as Form" and George Marion O'Donnell's "Faulkner's Mythology." This was also the year of Faulkner's election to the National Institute of Arts and Letters. Yet he had to wait until 1946, and the publication of *The Portable Faulkner* edited by Malcolm Cowley, for a growing, serious audience. It was Cowley's anthology — coupled with the 1949 Nobel Prize for Literature (awarded in 1950, the year Faulkner's *Collected Stories* won the National Book Award) — that led directly to his present popularity with readers, students, critics, and scholars. Now Faulkner is the subject of more criticism in English than any other author except Shakespeare. Detailed examinations of the public response to Faulkner's work from his earliest days have been conducted, in differing perspectives, by Frederick J. Hoffman, Robert Penn Warren, John Bassett, O. B. Emerson, and Thomas L. McHaney and need not be summarized here.[55] There are also excellent bibliographies of his work and of work on Faulkner's fiction available.[56]

This present work shows the centrality of the Sartoris family to

Faulkner's whole conception of Yoknapatawpha; it serves as the backbone for much of his mythical kingdom. Perhaps because of this, it is complex — especially because, as we have seen, it deals simultaneously with the cultural history of the antebellum South, the events and effects of both the War Between the States and the subsequent period of Reconstruction, and with the cultural, historical, and psychological importance and relevance of World War I: tracing the Sartorises, we trace much of America. It also deals with Faulkner's own family — and with Faulkner himself. And understanding the Falkners is no easy matter, for the records of their lives mix facts with legends and interpretations that are always being questioned or challenged, as with the Sartorises themselves.

The first section, "Materials," draws together accounts Faulkner may have known when conceptualizing the Sartoris family. As a boy, Faulkner spent time with the Young Colonel, who told him legends and accounts of the Old Colonel and of the War. Although stories of women taking up arms were commonplace, the portrait of Drusilla may also owe something to *The Spanish Heroine*, the Old Colonel's first novel; even as a child, Faulkner told an elementary schoolteacher, "I want to be a writer like my great-granddaddy." We do not know what accounts of Falkner, Hindman, and Thurmond the family kept, but we do know A. L. Bondurant was a dean at Ole Miss when Faulkner was young and that he took special interest in the boy. The Young Colonel bought *Notes of a Private* in 1909 and inscribed it on "Nov. 2nd." Faulkner later inscribed it too: "Rowan Oak, 1933," as he did only with very special books. (The family still retains that copy.) Faulkner himself got a copy of Fletcher Pratt's *Ordeal by Fire* from his New York publisher in 1935, when he was at work on *The Unvanquished*, and that novel takes on fresh meaning when we can measure how far from fact the Sartoris' understanding of the Confederates' situation is. This was as timely, doubtless, as the article in *Popular Mechanics* on a new biplane, the Christmas "Bullet," which seems to have suggested the conclusion of *Flags in the Dust*. Important family documents are reprinted in the appendix of Donald Philip Duclos "Son of Sorrow" (Diss. Univ. of Michigan, 1961), many of them incorporated by Joseph Blotner in his two-volume biography of Faulkner (New York, 1974), but readers should also consult the definitive treatment of the Old Colonel's wartime experience in Andrew Brown, "The First Mississippi Partisan Rangers, C.S.A." in *Civil War History*, 1, No. 4 (January 1956), 371–89. William R. Taylor is helpful on the notion of the cavalier in the Old South, and Miss Jenny's ideas can be profitably compared to *Cavalier and Yankee: The Old South and American National Character* (New York, 1961), pp. 146–48, 169–76, 340–41. At the other extreme, John B. Cullen has said that Grumby bears a relationship to Old John Murrell (*Old Times in the Faulkner Country* [Chapel Hill, N.C., 1961], pp. 66–68). Specific accounts of World War I that may have influenced

Sartoris/Flags in the Dust are examined by Richard T. Dillon in "Some Sources for Faulkner's Version of the First World War," *American Literature*, 44, No. 4 (January 1973), 629-37. Limitations of space prevented including other relevant accounts, such as Joseph Blotner's overview in "The Faulkners and the Fictional Families," *Georgia Review*, 30, No. 3 (Fall 1976), 572-92. J. B. Miskelley's account of the Old Colonel's "Doodle Bug railroad" and Paul R. Coppock's "General Hindman: A Feisty Little Son of the South" appeared in the *New Albany Gazette* for 31 May 1980, p. 4, and the *Memphis Commercial Appeal* for 9 Sept. 1979, p. G7; a further memoir of the Hindman family is in the *News and Journal* of the Tippah County Historical and Genealogical Society No. 4 (December 1982), pp. 76-82. For overviews of the War, see Mrs. Calvin Brown, "Lafayette County, 1860-1865: A Narrative," Matthew Callender O'Brien, "William Faulkner and the Civil War," and John Cooper Hathorn, "A Period Study of Lafayette County from 1836 to 1860 with Emphasis on Population Groups," all unpublished papers or theses in the Mississippi Collection at the University of Mississippi Library, and see also the standard histories of the Civil War by Bruce Catton (New York, 1961 et seq.), William C. Davis (New York, in progress), Shelby Foote (New York, 1958 et seq.), and Allan Nevins (New York 1947 et seq.); cf. the account of the burning of Oxford in the *New York Times*, 10 Sept. 1864, p. 2; James W. Garner, *Reconstruction in Mississippi* (New York, 1901); Medford Evans, "Oxford Mississippi," *Southwest Review* 15 (1929); Bell Irwin Wiley, *The Life of John Reb: The Common Soldier of the Confederacy* (Baton Rouge, 1943; 1978), Albert Dillahunty, *Shiloh* (National Military Park, Tenn., n.d.) and two essays by Elmo Howell — on the Andrews raid (*Georgia Historical Quarterly*, 49, No. 2 [June 1965], 187-92) in connection with the railroad race in "Raid" and on General Forrest (*Tennessee Historical Quarterly*, 29, No. 3 [Fall 1970], 287-94). Specific sources for Sartoris fiction are found in James Branch Cabell's "The Wen on Grandfather's Neck," columns in the *Oxford Eagle* collected by Jay Jeffrey Folks in "Plot Materials and Narrative Form in Faulkner's Early Fiction" (Diss. Indiana 1977), pp. 203-04, 212-18, and in Thomas Nelson Page's *Two Little Confederates* as noted by Edward Stone in *Ohio University Review* 4 (1962), 5-18. E. A. Muir discusses sources for Young Bayard's test plane in "A Footnote on *Sartoris* and Some Speculation," *Journal of Modern Literature*, 1, No. 3 (March 1971), 389-93.

The first Sartoris fiction, *Flags in the Dust*, began, Joseph Blotner writes,

> with old Bayard Sartoris musing in the attic over a Toledo blade and Mechlin lace which pushed the Sartoris genealogy back to the Plantagenets. In revision Faulkner condensed this material, deleting Aylmer Sartoris and the Bayard Sartoris who had fought at Agincourt. But he retained other relics of old Bayard's son, John, wounded in the Spanish-

American War; of his son John, killed in World War I; and of Old Bayard's father, Colonel John Sartoris, whose mementos recalled his service in both the Mexican War and the Civil War.

Faulkner had thus set up a direct equivalency between the four generations of Falkners and Sartorises. ("The Falkners and the Fictional Families," pp. 582–83)

Included in this volume is an even earlier version in which John is named Evelyn; it tells of his crucial meeting with Young Bayard and the latter's marriage, providing details for *Flags in the Dust* and "With Caution and Dispatch." Faulkner's first work of prose, "Landing in Luck," is his first treatment of flying, while "The Hill" is his first prose treatment of the young man aloof and isolated; he will eventually become Young Bayard. Both of these works first appeared in Faulkner's school newspaper at Ole Miss. The bleak European environment recalled by Young Bayard is also the subject of an early poem, "We sit drinking tea," included here, as is Faulkner's own early commentary on *Sartoris*. All remaining treatments of the Sartorises can be found in *Collected Stories* and *Uncollected Stories* where readers may also wish to read another story of the effect of the War Between the States in "A Return" and "Nympholepsy," Faulkner's first prose treatment of the eternal dreamer with an obsessive vision. Finally, the script for *War Birds* may be found in *Faulkner's MGM Screenplays*, ed. Bruce F. Kawin (Knoxville, Tenn. 1982).

The section on "Early Reviews" reprints four reviews each for *Sartoris* and *The Unvanquished*; the one from the *Oxford Eagle* is the only review I know of one of Faulkner's works in his hometown newspaper and is reprinted here for the first time. Generally, reviewers were not kind to *Sartoris*;[57] an exception is Henry Nash Smith in the Dallas *Morning News* who admired the style as "eloquent," "remorseful," delicate and rich, although he found the vision "a little chill and disturbing" (17 Feb. 1929, amusements, p. 3). Considerably more notice was paid to *The Unvanquished*. Clifton Fadiman told readers of the *New Yorker* that Faulkner "has made an art out of the elaborate induction of tedium; he is tirelessly tiresome" (19 Feb. 1938, p. 60); John Chamberlain, in *Scribner's*, found the book "almost laughable" and yet accurate in its "unmitigated Grand Guignol of the Deep South" (103, No. 4 [May 1938], p. 83). But in England, the anonymous reviewer for the *Times* (*London*) praised the *The Unvanquished* for its "extraordinary vividness and excitement," contributing to the important growth of American literature (13 May 1938, p. 10) while Brian Howard wrote in the *New Statesman and Nation* for 14 May 1938, "*The Unvanquished* is one of those small, violent and itself somewhat frightened works of art which read so much more easily, nowadays, than Gorki and Herr [Thomas] Mann" (p. 844). Earle Birney, in Canada, was less complimentary: " 'The Unvanquished,' like Faulkner's other books, is a timepiece with a number of tiny jewels and delicate wheels, oiled and sparkling and ingeniously fitted; but there is no mainspring and the watch doesn't tick" (*Canadian Forum*, 18, No. 209 [June 1938], 85).

The Sartoris fiction is still undergoing important scholarly investigation and critical analysis; only a small, if representative, portion is included here in "Previous Commentary." Serious readers will also want to consult the pioneering essay by George Marion O'Donnell, "Faulkner's Mythology," *Kenyon Review*, 1, No. 3 (Summer 1939), 285–99; the important chapter on *Sartoris* as "the making of a myth" by Olga W. Vickery in *The Novels of William Faulkner: A Critical Interpretation* (Baton Rouge, La., 1959); Elmo Howell, "William Faulkner and the Concept of Honor," *Northwest Review*, 5, No. 3 (Summer 1962), 51–60; the view of Colonel John Sartoris as a classic tragic hero in John Lewis Longley, Jr., *The Tragic Mask: A Study of Faulkner's Heroes* (Chapel Hill, N.C., 1963), pp. 182–91; T. H. Adamowski's psychological reading of Bayard in "Bayard Sartoris: Mourning and Melancholia" in *Literature and Psychology*, 23, No. 4 (1973), 149–58; an essay on the origin of the Sartoris name by Carter W. Martin (*South Carolina Review*, 6, No. 2 [April 1974], 56–59) and Lyall H. Powers' commentary on the various families in *Sartoris* in *Faulkner's Yoknapatawpha Comedy* (Ann Arbor, 1980), Chap. 1. In addition serious readers should consult James Gray Watson, " 'The Germ of My Apocrypha': *Sartoris* and the Search for Form," *Mosaic*, 7, No. 1 (Fall 1973), 15–33 on Faulkner's method, and Faulkner's own comments on the Sartorises in *Faulkner in the University*, ed. Frederick L. Gwynn and Joseph L. Blotner (Charlottesville, Va., 1959), pp. 42, 249–56. For overviews, see Frederick J. Hoffman, *William Faulkner* (New York, 1961), pp. 46–48, 82–83, and Edmond L. Volpe, *A Reader's Guide to William Faulkner* (New York, 1964), pp. 66, 68–87. For the use of the Falkner family in the Sartoris saga, see Robert Coughlan, *The Private World of William Faulkner* (New York, 1954), pp. 27–38, which was historically influential if somewhat inaccurate and, more reliably, Walter Taylor, *Faulkner's Search for a South* (Urbana, Ill., 1983), pp. 27–35, 90–98. Useful treatments of the Sartoris family and the Civil War and Reconstruction include M. E. Bradford, "Faulkner's *The Unvanquished*: The High Costs of Survival," *Southern Review*, NS 14, No. 3 (July 1978), 428–37; James B. Meriwether, "Faulkner and the South," in *The Dilemma of the Southern Writer*, Institute of Southern Culture Lectures, Longwood College, 1961 (Farmville, Va., 1961), pp. 143–63; Douglas T. Miller, "Faulkner and the Civil War: Myth and Reality," *American Quarterly*, 15, No. 2 (Summer 1963), 200–09; John Pilkington, " 'Strange Times' in Yoknapatawpha," in *Fifty Years of Yoknapatawpha*, ed. Doreen Fowler and Ann J. Abadie (Jackson, Miss., 1980), pp. 71–89; and Frank Wilsey Shelton, "The Family in the Novels of Wharton, Faulkner, Cather, Lewis, and Dreiser" (Diss. North Carolina 1971), pp. 99–113. For the strengths and weaknesses of the Sartoris tradition, see Mary Elizabeth Smith, "Faulkner's Myth" (Thesis Rhode Island 1957); for ironies in the tradition see Lawrance Thompson, afterword to *Sartoris* (New York, 1964) pp. 304–16; for the Sartoris family and the Oedpial complex, see John T. Irwin, *Doubling and Incest/Repetition and Revenge* (Baltimore, 1975), pp. 56–59; for Faulkner's failure to make the Sartoris condition real enough, see Irving Howe, *William Faulkner: A Critical Study* (Chicago, 1975), pp. 10–12, 33–45. Bayard's name is discussed by Marta Powell Harley, *American Notes and Queries*, 18, No. 6 (February 1980), 92–93; his relationship to Horace is examined by Melvin Backman, *Modern Fiction Studies*, 2, No. 3 (Autumn 1956), 95–100; and Young Bayard's and Young John's reembodiment of the conflict of Cain and Abel is located by Ralph Page, *Arizona Quarterly*, 23, No. 1 (Spring 1967), 27–33. Robert Scholes sees parallels between the Sartorises and the MacCallums in "Myth and Manners in *Sartoris*," *Georgia Review*, 16 (1962), 200; Albert J. Devlin has an important rereading of the MacCallum episode in *Twentieth Century Literature* 17, No. 2 (April 1971), 83–90. Arthur F. Kinney argues that Young Bayard can be understood through his relationship with other characters in *Faulkner's Narrative Poetics* (Amherst, Mass., 1978), pp. 123–39. *The Unvanquished* is read in light of the Greek *Oresteia* by Gorman Beauchamp, *Mississippi Quarterly*, 23, No. 3 (Summer 1970), 273–77; in light of the Roman values of *pietas, integrites, virtus,* and *gloria* by Charles Anderson in *Études Anglaises*, 7; No. 1 (January 1954), 48–58; and is compared to *A Fable* by Andrew Nelson Lytle in *Sewanee Review*, 63, No. 1 (January–March 1955), 130–37. For studies of black characters in the Sartoris fiction, see Thadious M. Davis, *Faulkner's "Negro": Art and Southern Context* (Baton Rouge, 1983), pp. 66–69, 241, 243; Lee Jenkins, *Faulkner and Black-White Relations: A Psychoanalytic Approach* (New York, 1981), pp. 110–33; and Charles H. Nilon, *Faulkner and the Negro* (New York, 1965), pp. 59–66, 70–73. *War Birds* is the starting point for Douglas Day, "The War Stories of William Faulkner," *Georgia Review*, 15, No. 4 (Winter 1961), 385–94; Max Putzel discusses both "Rose of Lebanon" and "There Was a Queen" in "Faulkner's Memphis Stories," *Virginia Quarterly Review*, 59, No. 2 (Spring 1983), 259–62, 264–68. For the latter, see also Melvin E. Bradford, "Certain Ladies of Quality: Faulkner's View of Women and the Evidence of 'There Was a Queen,' " *Arlington Quarterly*, 1, No. 2 (Winter 1967–68), 106–39, and Philip Castille, " 'There Was a Queen' and Faulkner's Narcissa Sartoris," *Mississippi Quarterly*, 28, No. 3 (Summer 1975), 307–15. The Sartoris saga has given rise to numerous creative projects, too; Colonel Falkner's life is captured in a romantic pageant based on the legends by Raymond Allen Hagood, *Ripley Rebel* (Ripley, Miss., 1972), while the problem of race in the Sartoris family is approached by way of burlesque in a musical comedy by Evans Harrington and Andrew Fox, *The Battle of Harrykin Creek*, housed in the Mississippi Collection at the University of Mississippi Library.

The problem of the texts of both novels that deal with the Sartoris family is an especially thorny one. When Faulkner failed to secure a publisher for his manuscript of *Flags in the Dust* (1927), he agreed to allow his friend Ben Wasson to cut it and publish it as *Sartoris* (1929), although he remained equivocal about the shorter version. Two accounts are in Blotner's biography *Faulkner* (I, 582–86) and Wasson, *Count No 'Count: Flashbacks to Faulkner* (Jackson, Miss., 1983), pp. 89–90; but see also *Selected Letters of William Faulkner*, ed. Joseph Blotner (New York 1977), pp. 39–43. Near the end of his life, Faulkner proposed publishing the original work. *Flags in the Dust* (1973) was reconstructed for posthumous publication by conflating earlier versions at the University of Virginia; the process is described by the editor, Douglas Day, in his introduction (pp. vii–xi). Strong exception to the text was taken by Thomas L. McHaney who entered into a debate with Albert Erskine, Faulkner's editor at Random House (see the *Faulkner Concordance Newsletter*, No. 2 [November 1973], pp. 7–8 and No. 3 [May 1974], pp. 2–4); a fuller treatment is provided by George F. Hayhoe in *Mississippi Quarterly*, 28, No. 3 (Summer 1975), 370–86. These works, of which the Hayhoe essay is especially revised for this collection, constitute Part V of the present volume. Additional observations are made by Richard P. Adams in "At Long Last, *Flags in the Dust*," *Southern Review*, N.S. 10, No. 4 (October 1974), 878–88; Stephen Neal Dennis, "The Making of Sartoris: A Description and Discussion of the Manuscript and Composite Typescript of William Faulkner's Third Novel" (Diss. Cornell 1969); and later refinements still in Melvin Reed Roberts, "Faulkner's 'Flags in the Dust' and 'Sartoris': A Comparative Study of the Typescript and the Originally Published Novel" (Diss. Texas 1974), and Merle Wallace Keiser, "Faulkner's 'Sartoris': A Comprehensive Study" (Diss. New York University 1977). A critical comparison of the two novels by Judith Bryant Wittenberg has been written for this volume.

A new batch of previously unknown Faulkner manuscripts and typescripts was discovered at his home, Rowan Oak, in 1971 (see Arthur F. Kinney and Doreen Fowler, "Faulkner's Rowan Oak Papers: A Census," *Journal of Modern Literature*, 10, No. 2 [June 1983], 327–34.) A large percentage of this material is a series of manuscripts, typescripts, and printer's copy for the episodes of *The Unvanquished* which enable us to reconstruct some of the composition of that novel. Some discussion of changes may be found in the textual notes to the various stories in *Uncollected Stories*; a convenient summary of some of the expansions, particularly as they affect style and characterization, is in John Pilkington, *The Heart of Yoknapatawpha* (Jackson, Miss., 1981), pp. 194–97. Two earlier but still useful studies are Joanne V. Creighton, *William Faulkner's Craft of Revision* (Detroit, 1977), pp. 73–84, and Edward M. Holmes, *Faulkner's Twice-Told Tales: His Re-Use of His Material* (The Hague, 1966), pp. 46–57, which is particularly concerned with Faulkner's reshaping separate stories to fashion a "composite" text.

The task of assembling the materials concerning Faulkner's Sartoris family has been a long and difficult one, but it has been made considerably easier and more pleasant by the cheerful help of a number of colleagues. I have mined the collections of Faulkner materials at the Alderman Library, University of Virginia; the Mississippi Collection, University of Mississippi; and the records at Rowan Oak; and, for materials on the Falkner family, the collections of the Tippah County Historical and Genealogical Society and the Ripley Public Library. To the staffs of all these collections, I am deeply indebted. A number of persons knowledgeable and conversant in historical matters of Lafayette and Tippah Counties were also generous with time and information, and I would like to thank especially Howard Bahr, John and Martha Cofield, Tommy Covington, Donald Philip Duclos, J. M. Faulkner, Mrs. John Faulkner, Evans Harrington, James Hinkle, Thomas L. McHaney, Franklin E. Moak, Noel Polk, Bobby Towery, and Thomas Verich. I am also grateful to the Center for the Study of Southern Culture, University of Mississippi, to its directors, William Ferris and Ann J. Abadie, and to its staff for arranging two extended visits to Oxford. In pictorial matters, I am indebted to the archival research and work of Edmund Berkeley, L. D. Brodsky, John and Martha Cofield, Tommy Covington, Joan St. C. Crane, Robert Dann, Donald P. Duclos, Robert W. Hamblin, William Martin, and Eva Miller.

In this volume, citations to journals follow the MLA style sheet, but not necessarily the forms used by the publications themselves.
University of Massachusetts, Amherst   ARTHUR F. KINNEY

Notes

1. *Requiem for a Nun* (New York: Vintage Books, 1975), p. 97.

2. *Reflections on the Civil War*, ed. John Leekley (New York, 1982), p. 3.

3. James I. Robertson, Jr., *The Concise Illustrated History of the Civil War* (Harrisburg, Penn., 1979), p. 61.

4. Commager, *The Blue and the Gray: The Story of the Civil War As Told by Participants*, rev. and abrid. (New York: New American Library, 1973), pp. 363–65.

5. Nevins, *The War for the Union* (New York: Charles Scribner's Sons, 1960), VI, 423.

6. Ibid., VI, 65.

7. Shelby Foote, *The Civil War: A Narrative* (New York: Random House, 1958), I, 327.

8. *A Journal of Hospital Life in the Confederate Army of Tennessee from the Battle of Shiloh to the End of the War* (Louisville, Ky.: John P. Morton & Company, 1866), rept. *Heroines of Dixie*, ed. Katharine M. Jones (St. Simons Island, Ga.: Mockingbird Books, Inc., 1974), I, 117–24.

9. "The Civil War Letters of Cordelia Scales," *Journal of Mississippi History*, 1 (July 1939), quoted by Jones, I, 217–18.

10. *My Cave Life in Vicksburg, with letters of trial and travel* (New York: D. Appleton & Company, 1864), quoted by Jones, II, 10–11.

11. "J. W. T. Falkner/Oxford/Miss/Nov. 2nd, 1909." *William Faulkner's Library – A Catalogue* (Charlottesville, Va.: Univ. Press of Virginia, 1964), p. 37. Hubbard was attached to Co. E, 7th Tennessee Regiment, Forrest's Cavalry Corps, C.S.A.

12. The curator at Rowan Oak conjectures the volume is now with Faulkner's daughter, Mrs. Jill Summers, since it is no longer in the library at his Oxford home.

13. Stuart was both romantic and heroic, "a man who was both an unconscionable show-off and a solid, hard-working, and wholly brilliant commander of light horse. He wore an ostrich plume in his hat, he had a gray cloak lined with scarlet, and he kept a personal banjo player on his staff, riding off to war all jingling with strum-strum music going on ahead" (Bruce Catton, *The Coming Fury* [New York: Pocket Books, 1967], p. 447). But his chivalric methods with cavalry were outdated; lances, for example, were no good against the infantry the Federals advanced. See Catton, *Reflections*, p. 131.

14. Foote, *Civil War*, I, 79.

15. Defeated at Shiloh, he was successful at New Market on 15 May 1864.

16. Nevins, *War For the Union*, VI, 381.

17. Foote, *Civil War*, III, 518.

18. Ibid., II, 612.

19. Loughborough, *My Cave Life*, Rept. Jones, II, 7–8.

20. These statistics are taken from Robertson, *Concise Illustrated History*, p. 7.

21. Edmund Wilson, *Patriotic Gore* (New York: Oxford Univ. Press, 1962), p. 195.

22. Not that she did not have precedent, even in her son-in-law, Colonel John Sartoris. "As Union trade regulations in Memphis grew stricter, more ingenious methods of smuggling were used. Joseph H. Parks reports several: When one lady attempting to pass the lines was asked to alight from the carriage, the difficulty with which she complied aroused suspicion; a search revealed that beneath a huge girdle she had tied twelve pairs of boots each containing whiskey, military lace, and other supplies. A Negro woman was caught with a five-gallon demijohn of brandy underneath a loose-fitting calico dress and suspended from a girdle at the waist. Dead animals, their bodies filled with packages of quinine and other contraband goods, were dragged by smugglers to the boneyards outside the city. On at least one occasion, the hearse of a funeral procession bore a coffin filled with medicine for Gen. Earl Van Dorn's army" (Charles W. Crawford, *Yesterday's Memphis* [Miami: E. A. Seemann, 1976], p. 34). The morality of smuggling becomes a good symbol, in fact, for the Confederacy under siege.

23. For the importance of Eliot and Joyce to Faulkner's Sartoris fiction, see among others James Gray Watson, " 'The Germ of My Apocrypha': *Sartoris* and the Search for Form," *Mosaic*, 7, No. 1 (Fall 1973), 15–33.

24. Singal, *The War Within: From Victorian to Modernist Thought in the South, 1919-1945* (Chapel Hill: Univ. of North Carolina Press, 1982), p. 166. Cf. Walter K. Everett who is led to define Sartoris as "a man deeply concerned with the death wish, a man seeking an exit from this life, not just a departure but a departure like a shooting star" (*Faulkner's Art and Characters* [Woodbury, N.Y.: Barron's Educational Series, 1969], p. 83).

25. James Hinkle, "Some Yoknapatawpha Names," p. 8 (unpublished).

26. Crawford, p. 35.

27. Rept. in *Lion in the Garden: Interviews with William Faulkner, 1926-1962*, ed. James B. Meriwether and Michael Millgate (New York: Random House, 1968), p. 255.

28. Emily Whitehurst Stone, "Faulkner Gets Started," *Texas Quarterly*, 8 (1965), 142–48.

29. William Faulkner, "Foreword," *The Faulkner Reader* (New York: Random House, 1954), p. ix.

30. *Selected Letters of William Faulkner*, ed. Joseph Blotner (New York: Random House, 1977), pp. 211–12. The name is pronounced with the emphasis on the first syllable.

31. Cf. Frederick S. Kullman, "A Comparison of Yoknapatawpha and Lafayette Counties" (Thesis, Harvard, 1958).

32. *Requiem for a Nun*, pp. 198–200, 205.

33. Carl E. Falkner of Demarest, N.J., to Mrs. William Anderson of Ripley on 1 April 1969; letter now in the Tippah County Historical Society Collection.

34. Donald Philip Duclos, "Son of Sorrow: The Life, Works, and Influence of Colonel William C. Falkner, 1825–1889," Diss. Univ. of Michigan 1961, p. 124.

35. *GN., M. & N. News*, 27 Nov. 1925, p. 10; in the Tippah County Collection.

36. Faulkner later developed a more elaborate reason for calling the county seat of Yoknapatawpha Jefferson; see *Requiem for a Nun*, pp. 16–28.

37. To Judge William Anderson of Ripley on 2 Oct. 1970; in the Tippah County Historical Society Collection.

38. *Publications of the Mississippi Historical Society*, 3 (1900); see Sec. I.

39. My transcriptions; in the Tippah County Historical Collection.

40. Deed Record Book I, Tippah County, p. 797; filed 10 June, 1872.

41. Rept. *New Albany Gazette*, 5 Nov. 1964; Tippah County Collection.

42. Tippah County Historical Society Collection.

43. Tippah County Historical Society Collection.

44. Tippah County Historical Society Collection.

45. Published (?) 2 Jan. 1890; Tippah County Historical Society Collection.

46. Tippah County Historical Society Collection.

47. It was originally designed by the family to be placed in the Ripley town square.

48. To "Duke"; Tippah County Historical Society Collection.

49. Cf. portrait in the Faulkner Collection, Alderman Library, University of Virginia.

50. Emma Jo Grimes Marshall, "Scenes from Yoknapatawpha: A Study of People and Places in the Real and Imaginary Worlds of William Faulkner," Diss. Univ. of Alabama pp. 107, 106. One authority cited is J. M. Faulkner.

51. Faulkner's brother John has executed paintings of these scenes.

52. Citing interview with Kelly Slough, Oxford, January 1975.

53. Another theme, "Why?," is in The Mississippi Collection.

54. *Faulkner at Nagano*, ed. Robert A. Jeliffe (Tokyo, 1956), pp. 185–86.

55. Frederick J. Hoffman, "William Faulkner: An Introduction," in *William Faulkner: Two Decades of Criticism*, ed. Hoffman and Olga W. Vickery, (East Lansing: Michigan State College Press, 1951), pp. 1–31; Hoffman in *William Faulkner: Three Decades of Criticism*, ed. Hoffman and Vickery (East Lansing: Michigan State Univ. Press, 1960), pp. 1–50; Robert Penn Warren, "Introduction: Faulkner: Past and Present," in *Faulkner: A Collection of Critical Essays*, ed. Robert Penn Warren (Englewood Cliffs, N.J.: Prentice-Hall, Inc., 1966), pp. 1–22; John Bassett, "Introduction," *William Faulkner: The Critical Heritage* (London: Routledge & Kegan Paul, 1975), pp. 1–46; O. B. Emerson, "William Faulkner's Literary Reputation in America" (Diss. Vanderbilt 1962); and Thomas L. McHaney, "Watching for the Dixie Limited: Faulkner's Impact upon the Creative Writer," in *Fifty Years of Yoknapatawpha*, ed. Doreen Fowler and Ann J. Abadie (Jackson: Univ. Press of Mississippi, 1980), pp. 226–47.

56. John Bassett, *William Faulkner: An Annotated Checklist of Criticism* (New York: David Lewis, 1972) and McHaney, *William Faulkner: A Reference Guide* (Boston: G. K. Hall and Co., 1976; now being updated). (Earlier, and somewhat outdated, is Irene Lynn Sleeth, *William Faulkner: A Bibliography of Criticism* [Denver: Alan Swallow, 1962].)

57. Truman Frederick Keefer, "The Critical Reaction to the Novels of William Faulkner As Expressed in Reviews Published in American Periodicals up to 1952" (Thesis, Duke 1953), pp. 10ff.

I MATERIALS

[Ellen Fights the Mexicans]

W. C. Falkner*

Henry, Ellen and Pedro soon finished their sumptuous supper, then commenced preparing to start on their nocturnal journey towards Monterey. Henry and Pedro saddled the horses, whilst Ellen arranged her riding dress. She placed a long, flowing skirt, of black cloth, around her slender waist, which was circled with several rows of gold lace, and hung far beneath her feet, as she proudly sat on her beauteous steed; on her brow rested a black velvet cap, from which floated three red ostrich feathers, and her long glossy tresses were platted in two long mazy folds, and hung carelessly around her snowy neck. Henry now lifted Ellen into the saddle, then mounted his noble steed, and Pedro did the same, and soon the party were riding swiftly along the road to Monterey. Ellen rode in the centre, Henry on the right and Pedro on the left, so as to protect the beauteous damsel, in case of an ambuscade by the guerillas, who frequented that part of the country. Each rider had a pair of holsters hanging to the pommel of the saddle, whilst a ponderous sabre hung to each waist, and Pedro and Henry had each a well-charged carbine resting across the saddle before. Thus equipped they rode along at a rapid pace, whilst Ellen's musical voice filled the air with a sweet sound. Her beauteous face, as it shone in the bright rays of the moon, was lovely beyond the power of my pen to describe. With her left hand she held the bridle thong, whilst the other arm rested on Henry's shoulder, and ever and anon she bent over and pressed his lips with a tender kiss. Pedro rode close to her left side, ready, in case of an attack by the guerillas, to lay down his life, if necessary, to protect Ellen from harm or danger. . . .

. . . After riding some ten miles on the Monterey road, by which time the bright moon had arose high in the southern skies, and made all around nearly as bright as day, they came to a short crook in the road, where it made around a large peak of the mountain. They rode slowly around it, and on rising a small mound, they stood in plain view of six armed

*From *Spanish Heroine: A Tale of War and Love. Scenes Laid in Mexico* (Cincinnati: I. Hart & Co., 1851), pp. 123–28. This is the first subsequent publication. The setting is the countryside around Monterey.

Mexicans, evidently the same band who had pursued Henry and Ellen on the day previous morning from Saltillo. Henry did not discover them until he was within thirty yards of them; 'twas vain to attempt a retreat; the only alternative left them was to fight or die. Henry threw himself between Ellen and the foes, who were advancing on them at a rapid pace, and requested her to hide herself behind the hill.

"No, my dear Henry, resolved am I to die by thy side. I have rode where balls of death flew thick around me like falling hail, and think you that I would shrink at this dreadful and critical moment? No, Henry, urge me not to leave you, for determined am I to fight, live and die with you."

By this time the Mexicans were within fifteen paces of Henry and his little party; as quick as thought, and before Henry expected the firing to begin, Ellen drew a pistol from the holster, presented it at the band of Mexicans, and fired. A loud scream of pain, and the foremost of the band fell lifeless to the earth.

Thus the young damsel begun the fight. Simultaneously Henry and Pedro fired and two more Mexicans fell dead from their horses. The three living Mexicans fired, and instantly killed Henry's horse, which dropped heavily to the earth, and hurled Henry against the ground, and wholly disabled him to rise. Pedro and Ellen fired the second time, but did no harm. All their fire-arms being empty, they could do no more; consequently they were seized by the Mexicans, tied fast, and hurried on toward Saltillo, leaving Henry as they thought, dead in the road. And poor Ellen also believed him killed.

Reader, does it not seem that heaven itself is arrayed against these young lovers. Sometimes we behold them in each other's arms, engaging each other's caresses, and filled with buoyant hopes of unending happiness; then in less than two hours we again see them separated, one tied fast on her horse, on her way back to Saltillo, to end her life by a military execution, the other lying lifeless in the public high-way. I say, reader, does it not seem that they have incurred the Divine displeasure of heaven? Are they not pursued by unending misfortunes?

Ellen screamed and tried to throw herself from her horse, but her little feet were tied fast beneath the horse's breast — her hands tied fast to the pommel of the saddle. The tall mountains echoed and re-echoed for miles around with her piteous screams of woe. She screamed Henry's name at every breath. Pedro rode silently by her side, and gave vent to a copious flood of tears.

Soon Henry regained his breath; he sprang quick to his feet, and gazed with an idle stare, his mind was sorely confused, and all seemed but a dream. He saw three dead Mexicans lying in the road, he also saw his own noble horse lying dead by his side. He screamed for Ellen, but, alas! the dreadful reality now rushed to his mind that she was a prisoner, and on her way back to Saltillo. He set off on the road leading back to Saltillo at a rapid pace, after running on fast several miles, until his breath was almost gone, he found a lame steed standing in the edge of the road, he approached and found it to be one of the horses belonging to the Mexicans who were killed. The steed had got the halter tangled around his feet, which held him fast.

Henry mounted the horse quick, put spurs to him, and dashed off at full speed. After dashing over a space of about five miles, he ascended a tall peak of the mountain, and beheld Ellen on a horse, driven on at a rapid pace. Death and hellish vengeance blazed from his eyes as he beheld his tender love tied fast to her horse, and heard her piteous screams. For some time he was at a loss how to manage to rescue her from them. He knew that if he rode up behind they would murder her and Pedro before he could get to them. But at length the following plan entered his mind. He put spurs to his horse, and dashed through the chapparel, and entered a little path about a hundred yards from the road, and running parallel with it, he hurried on till he passed the party who had Ellen confined, then made his way back to the road, and concealed himself in a dense thicket close to the edge of the road; he had not been concealed more than five minutes, when he heard the sound of horse's feet coming down the road, and also heard the mournful sound of Ellen, who had so exhausted herself that she could not be heard but a few yards. Henry grasped his sabre in his right hand, whilst he held the bridle in his left, he turned his horse's head toward the road, and waited till the Mexicans came up. Now he dashed the spurs to his steed, which at a single bound stood in the center of the road, and at a single blow a Mexican's head fell to the earth, and rolled along the dust, leaving a bloody trail behind; both the surviving Mexicans fired at Henry, one ball took effect in his left arm, the other missed entirely. Then they both closed on Henry with sabres, one struck a tremendous blow at his head, he arrested it with his blade, then dashed it through the Spaniard's heart. At this instant the other Mexican gave Henry a heavy blow on the head, which cut him to the skull; exhausted from the loss of blood, Henry fell headlong to the earth; the Mexican leaped off his steed, raised his sabre high above his head to plunge it in Henry's heart, as he lay helpless on his back. Ellen saw his danger, her strength grew tenfold stronger, a desperate effort she made and snapped the cords asunder which bound her hands. Henry was lying near her horse's feet. She seized a sabre, and just as the last surviving Mexican aimed his blow at Henry's heart, and whilst her little feet were still tied fast to the horse's breast, she cleaved the Mexican's head asunder, who fell bleeding and lifeless across Henry's body.

Thus she had slayed two Mexicans, and saved her lover's life; her feet being tied under the horse's breast, she was unable to release herself. So she and Pedro remained fastened to their horses until Henry was sufficiently recovered to release them. With the sabre he cut the cords which bound her little feet, and she fell from the saddle into Henry's extended arms. He strained her again and again to his anxious heart, and kissed her warm lips, whilst again their tears of joy mingle together. For several minutes they remained in each other's arms without speaking. . . . Reader, think not that Ellen was wholly void of modesty—you will recollect that the Spanish ladies are differently brought up from the American. But place yourself in the same situation of Ellen, and you would have done as she did. A dishonest thought had never entered the mind of Ellen or Henry; but their young hearts were wholly filled with pure love and esteem for each other. Each one had often rescued the other from the very jaws of death. And how could Ellen refuse to let his bleeding head—that head, too, which bled for her—I say, how could she refuse to let it rest in her lap, instead of suffering it to rest on the leaves?

[A Letter from Oxford]

Colonel R. F. Lowrey and
Lieutenant D. A. Buie*

Oxford Missi Septb 26 1864

To Maj Genl J. R. Chalmers
    Grenada Miss
Genl.
    We would respectfully represent that during the recent Federal raid to this town private property of every description was almost universally destroyed, pillaged, or carried off, thus leaving a large majority of the citizens of the place without even, bedding, blankets or provisions of any kind, and unless these things can be procured from the Enemy much Suffering must ensue the approaching winter especially among the poorer classes—
    We know Genl the danger of opening Communication with the Enemy to all, in allowing Spies to pass to and fro with impunity, but at the same time we are cognizant of the suffering that must follow in case necessaries cannot be procured from the Enemy, and in behalf of the Citizens we now appeal to you to authorize and empower Some one to barter Cotton for this purpose—
    We would suggest and beleive [sic] that all the Citizens will approve the suggestion, Messrs. Felix R. Hardgrove & Asa. R. Chilton as men well qualified in every respect to Secure and bring to this place the articles So much required—
    They and persons well acquainted with the losses Sustained, think that it will require One hundred Bales of Cotton to Supply the people with

*From "Selected Correspondence of the Adjutant General of Confederate Mississippi," ed. Jerry Causey, *Journal of Mississippi History*, 43, No. 1 (February 1981), 57-58. Reprinted by permission.

absolute necessaries for the winter, and we would therefore request that
you empower them to transport that amount through our lines.
.   We are Genl
        Your ob' Servts[1]
    R. F. Lowrey
        Col P. A. C. S.
    D. A. Buie
        1st Lt P. A. C. S.

Notes

   1. This letter is actually a petition. Following the signatures of Lowrey and Buie are
seventy-five others — presumably the citizens in whose behalf they were writing.

[The History of the
Ripley Railroad Company]   W. C. Falkner*

June 14 1874

John F. Johnson, Esq

Dear Sir,
    Your letter is to hand. In reply to your inquirries, I have to Say, that
while money matters, remain, So depressed as they are now, it is
impossible to build our road further South, but as soon as financial
confidence is restored, we expect to build more road. We will build on the
most direct line, from Middleton Tenn. to Mip City on the Gulf. The
length of our road when Completed will be 318 miles. We expect then to
Consolidate with the Cairo & St. Louis. road which is the same gage of
ours. You ask me to inform you how I managed to build my road so quick
and So Successfully. The road was built by a combination of *"labor &
capital"* gotten up among the people at each end, and along the line of the
Road. I had at one time as many as fifteen hundred private Citizens
working on the road. I have Seen the Sheriff of our County, and all his
depties, in Company with the Circuit & Chancery Clerks all at work
togeather on our road. I have Seen many Preachers engaged at work on
the road. There was a universal Combination here among all Classes, both
black and white, to aid in building the road. The Ladies. Subscribed
liberally to aid in building the road. Large Basket dinners, were given by
the ladies frequently, in order to get Crowds togeather [*sic*] to hear rail

---

*Transcribed from manuscript by Arthur F. Kinney and reprinted with permission of the
curator of the Mississippi Collection, University of Mississippi.

road Speeches. I have Seen widow Ladies, take the last Side of Bacon. from her Smoke House, to feed the laborers on this road. The Cost of the road including equipments, rolling Stock &c was $12000 per mile. The length of the line Completed is 25 miles. Property at each end and along the line has increased in value from 3 to 5 hundred per Cent in value. The weight of the Iron is 35 pounds to the yard and 55 tons to the mile. The passenger Coaches Seat 35 passengers. We Can run 20 miles per hour with ease and Safty. We can do ten times more buisnes than we are able to get. We have been running the road 2 years, and have never had an accident yet. No breakage of any kind. No Man or animal hurt. No Cow, or Engine, injured in any manner, and for the last 15 months have never failed to make a round trip evry day. No other road in the South has done this. Any people who will unite, and act togeather [*sic*] can build a narrow gage road.

> Respectfully
> W C Falkner
> Pres
> R R R Co

[A Profile of W. C. Falkner]   Anonymous*

Col. W. C. Falkner, of Mississippi, has composed an interesting novel entitled *The White Rose of Memphis*. The title of the story is derived from a Mississipi river steamboat of that name, on board of which many of the thrilling scenes are described as having transpired. This excellent work has been running as a serial story in the Ripley *Advertiser* for the last nine months, and has greatly increased the circulation of that paper, proving a real bonanza to the publisher. The work will be published in book form by D. Appleton & Co. at an early day, and, as we think, will meet with a very rapid sale. The successful career of Colonel Falkner as a lawyer, financier, soldier and railroad president has established his reputation as a man of high order of intellect, and will cause his book to be largely sought for by the reading public. We know of no man better qualified to write an interesting romance than the author of the *White Rose*, because we know that his life has been crowded thick with thrilling incidents of a romantic character. Thirty years ago he wrote a little book entitled the *Life of McCannon*, which was published by a company in this city, who trusted to

*Transcribed by Arthur F. Kinney from the Tippah County Historical and Genealogical Society copy of a story in the *Ripley Advertiser*, 16 April 1881; reprinted from the *Memphis Commercial Appeal*, 10 April 1881.

the honor of the author to pay them out of the proceeds of the sale. He sold 2500 of his books in one day, netting $1250, after paying cost of printing. Col. Falkner is an eloquent orator, and the brilliant canvass he made in 1876 as the Tilden elector, is well remembered by all Mississippians. He made the canvass at his own expense, at a cost of near $1000, declining to receive any of it back when his party proposed to re-imburse him. He is one of those public spirited men who are of incalculable advantage to the community in which they live. He founded the Stonewall college, built the first narrow gauge railroad in the United States, and has done as much as any man in Mississippi for the encouragement of the agricultural interests of the country. As a lieutenant in the Mexican war and as a colonel in the Confederate army he distinguished himself and won the approbation of his superior officers. He commanded the second Mississippi regiment at the first battle of Manassas, and it was on that bloody field that General Beauregard pointed to Colonel Falkner who was charging Rickett's battery at the head of his gallant regiment, and asked General Johnston who the officer was who wore the black plume. On being informed who it was, he addressed a new battalion that had just arrived, and as he pointed to Colonel Falkner, he said, "Men, follow yonder knight of the black plume, and history will never forget you!" This occurred late in the evening on that memorable day, when the left flank of our army was being pressed back by a fresh division of Federal reserves. Rickett's battery was pouring grape and canister shot at short range into the Confederate ranks, mowing them down like wheat, and fate seemed on the eve of deciding the day against the south. The battle-field was thickly strewn with the dead and wounded. General Bee was killed, and Colonel Falkner was the only field-officer of the brigade who was not killed or disabled [.] General Johnston, who had been engaged at another part of the field, now came galloping up to the spot to where his presence was so much needed. The general instantly comprehended the critical situation, and said to Colonel Falkner: "That battery must be silenced immediately at all hazards; and, Colonel Falkner, I shall depend on you to do it." ["]If I do not succeed general," the colonel replied, "you will please have my dead body sent home to Mrs. Falkner." Within three minutes afterward Colonel Falkner was quietly seated on one of the captured guns, superintending the collection of the gallant dead and wounded of his command, eighty-two of whom had been shot down while making the charge. It was while Colonel Falkner was making that gallant charge that General Beauregard gave him the complimentary title of the "Knight of the Black Plume." Colonel Falkner has encountered and triumphed over many dangers and difficulties outside of his military career, that would have discouraged and crushed the heart of any but a courageous hero. With all the facts connected with the Hindman feud, which resulted in the death of Robert H. Hindman and Mr. Morris, we are perfectly familiar, as one of the editors of the *Appeal* [Colonel M. C. Galloway — Editor's note] had the good fortune to effect a final reconciliation between Colonel Falkner and General Thomas C. Hindman.

Immediately after Col. Falkner was acquitted for killing R. H. Hindman, whose life he had been compelled to sacrifice in order to save his own, General T. C. Hindman, the brother of the deceased, renewed the difficulty, a street fight ensued, in which Colonel Falkner, while acting purely on the defensive, was forced to take Morris's life, who became involved as the friend of General Hindman.

As soon as Colonel Falkner was tried and acquitted for killing Mr. Morris, General Tom Hindman attempted to shoot him across a table at a hotel, but accidentally dropped his pistol on the floor, when it fired, sending a bullet through the ceiling just above Falkner's head. Falkner instantly presented a revolver at Hindman, and instead of shooting him down, as many a man would have done, he merely required Hindman to let his pistol remain where it was, telling him that he did not want to shed any more blood, and he was determined not to do it when he could avoid it without giving up his own life. By the interference of friends the difficulty was for the time stopped, but soon after renewed, and when Colonel Falkner became convinced that another fight was unavoidable, he consented to go with Hindman to Arkansas, opposite Memphis and settle the matter finally. They had drawn up and signed a written agreement to the effect that at 6 o'clock on the morning of the first day of April, 1851, they were to meet at a point in the State of Arkansas, 400 yards from the bank of the Mississippi river and immediately opposite the front of Jefferson street, in Memphis, Tennessee, each to be armed with two revolvers and no other kind of weapons. No seconds or surgeons were to be present, and no friends of either party except one witness, who had been selected and who was known to be a friend to both parties. The name of that friend had been agreed on and inserted in the written agreement. The party who had been selected as the witness was, by the agreement, only required to take his stand at a safe distance and witness the combat, without any attempt to interfere. The agreement bound the parties to take their places fifty yards apart, and when the word was given they had the right to advance and fire as often as they wished. Now, as luck would have it, the party who had been agreed upon as witness happened to be a man more inclined to prevent the shedding of blood than to encourage hostilities. Consequently, when the parties came to Memphis, on the day previous to that on which the combat was to be fought, he went to work to prevent the meeting, which he succeeded in doing. One of the editors of the *Appeal* was the man they had agreed on, and it has ever been a source of gratification to him to know that he did not only prevent the fight, but that he succeeded in making two bosom friends out of two deadly enemies. We have often heard General Hindman since that time speak of Col[onel] Falkner in the highest terms of praise. He said that through all of those troubles, Colonel Falkner's conduct was that of a brave, honorable man, who only fought in self-defense. When General Hindman was bitterly assailed by political enemies in Arkansas, Colonel Falkner espoused the general's cause, got up a barbecue at Ripley, Mississippi, and invited Hindman to speak, and had resolutions passed indorsing him. Hindman was triumphantly elected to congress, and until his death was a staunch friend to Colonel Falkner. The colonel has resided at his present home for forty years, during which time he has never been involved in any feuds, quarrels, or difficulties, except the unfortunate affair with Hindman and Morris. He is now, and ever has been, regarded as a quiet, peaceable, good citizen, by all who know him, always retaining the love and respect of his neighbors. *The White Rose of Memphis* contains a glowing description of many scenes and incidents that transpired in and near the vicinity of this city, and some of the characters will be readily remembered by many of our citizens, notwithstanding the fact that they appear under *nom de plumes*. The moral of the composition is good, and will, as we think, have a beneficial influence on young people who may read it. It will make a large sized book, and one that will be interesting and instructive. Those who may read the *White Rose* will at once conclude that no man could compose such noble soul-stirring sentiments who was not himself the possessor of a noble soul and generous heart.

[The Falkner-Hindman Feud: A Reply]

C. J. Frederick*

I read with feelings of great pleasure an article in the *Appeal* of the tenth instant, in which Colonel W. C. Falkner was mentioned in terms of highest praise. I, who have known him intimately for many years, am happy to be able to indorse the truth of every line of that article, with one single exception. You have fallen into error as to dates, because it was in 1857 that the feud between General Hindman and Colonel Falkner was finally settled by the generous and timely interference of Colonel M. C. Gallaway [*sic*], one of the present editors of the *Appeal*, who had been agreed on as the one to witness the combat, and if that gentleman knew the high appreciation with which this community regards the noble part he played, which resulted in a reconciliation, I have no doubt it would cause his big heart to throb with pleasure. The *Appeal* was, indeed, correct in the statement that Colonel Falkner was regarded as a man of peace by the community in which he lived, for I do not believe Mississippi,

*Transcribed by Arthur F. Kinney from the Tippah County Historical and Genealogical Society copy of an article in the *Ripley Advertiser*, 30 April 1881; reprinted from the *Memphis Commercial Appeal* (n.d.)

or any other State, could produce a man less inclined to violence, or one who loves peace more. In fact, he established a reputation here as a real peace-maker, and I have often been struck with admiration to see him casting his great influence on the side of peace when there was danger of bloodshed among our own citizens. The father of your correspondent happened to be on one of the juries that tried the two cases against Colonel Falkner. The unfortunate affair, that resulted in the death of Robert H. Hindman, occurred in the eighth day of May, 1849, and Colonel Falkner was put on his trial at the first term of the court after that time, and was defended by Hon. P. T. Scruggs. Two of the main witnesses are yet residing in this county. The Hindman family, as is well known, was composed of brave, fearless, high-strung men. Robert and Thomas C. were aggressive in the extreme, and rather inclined to be reckless, and, I dare say, that no braver men ever lived than those two brothers; and the same may be said about the old man Hindman, the father of Thomas and Robert. The family resided two miles east of Ripley, and up to the day of the unfortunate affair between Colonel Falkner and Robert H. Hindman, the most cordial relations of friendship existed between Falkner and the Hindmans. They were all volunteers in the same company during the war with Mexico, Falkner being first and Thomas C. Hindman second lieutenant, and Robert H. a private. When the war ended Thomas C. Hindman commenced the study of law and was admitted to the bar a short time before the difficulty between Falkner and Robert H., and made his maiden speech against the defendant on the trial, which, though very eloquent, was pregnant with bitter denunciation. The evidence was short, conclusive, and totally free from contraditions, making out a clear case of self-defense, and the jury, after being out ten minutes, returned a verdict of not guilty. The proof showed that some malicious tale-bearers had told Hindman that Falkner had made a speech before the temperance organization against his (Hindman's) admission as a member into the order, when the very reverse of this was true, for Falkner instead of opposing his admission, had made a most eloquent and feeling speech in favor of admitting Hindman. The meetings were held in secret, and when Hindman was informed that Falkner had made a speech against him he flew into a passion and publicly declared that he would kill him, and calling Falkner to where he was, demanded in an angry tone to know why he had opposed his admission. Falkner denied having done so. Hindman replied, "You are a d–d liar," at the same time drawing from his right-hand pants-pocket a small revolver and attempting to shoot. Falkner seized Hindman's wrist with both hands and tried to take the pistol away from him. Hindman, being a very strong man, managed to throw Falkner back against a house and extricated his wrist from Falkner's grasp, when he presented the pistol within two feet of the colonel's breast and pulled the trigger, but the weapon failed to fire. Hindman then cocked the pistol and again attempted to shoot, but the pistol again failed to fire. Falkner then drew his knife, and as Hindman made the third attempt to shoot him he stabbed Hindman, inflicting a wound from the effects of which Hindman died immediately. It does look as if Providence had directly interfered in Falkner's behalf, because a gentleman — Mr. J. R. Moores — took the pistol from the hand of the deceased, who died with it firmly grasped in his hand, and when the gentleman went to discharge the pistol the two barrels that had not been snapped failed to fire, but when it came round to the three barrels that had been snapped at Falkner, every one of the three barrels fired promptly, and when it came round the second time to the two barrels that had not been snapped they fired clear, showing clearly that the caps were too small for the tube, which required one blow of the hammer to drive them on the tube, so that when the hammer struck the caps the second time they exploded promptly. Now, this unfortunate affair was the beginning of a feud here that resulted in the death of Mr. Morris, who became involved as the friend of General Hindman, though he was in no way related to the general except as his friend. This unfortunate feud drew into its vortex a large number of our best citizens, who arrayed themselves on the side of their friends, and it lasted several years, and never did stop until Colonel M. C. Gallaway succeeded in bringing about a final reconciliation. The *Appeal* was correct when it stated that Colonel Falkner never fought only in self-defense, the fact is he begged for peace all the time, and never did fight until all hope of escape was cut off. Mr. Morris was a man of undaunted courage, and when he espoused the cause of General Hindman he determined to wage the war to the bitter end. The difficulty between Falkner and Morris, which resulted in the death of the latter, occurred in February, 1851. The circuit court met on Monday, an indictment was presented on Tuesday, a venire was summoned on Wednesday, Falkner was tried Thursday. Then the feud was renewed with redoubled bitterness by General Hindman and his friends, which kept our town in a constant fever of excitement. Finally, Falkner, in order to keep his friends from becoming seriously involved, being convinced that a fight would be forced on him, in which many others would be likely to get killed, consented to meet General Hindman in Arkansas, as stated in your paper, only that the date was not correctly stated. All the preliminaries had been arranged by correspondence, carried on secretly between General Hindman and Colonel Falkner, and it was especially stipulated that no citizen of Mississippi should know anything about the affair until it was over, and that no one should be present except the parties to the combat and Colonel M. C. Gallaway. This was done in order to prevent the friends of the parties from becoming further involved in the unpleasant affair. They were to take their places fifty yards apart, armed with revolvers, with the right to advance and fire as they pleased. Colonel Falkner has often told your correspondent that he did not intend to advance on General Hindman, and that he was resolved not to fire at all unless the general came within twenty paces of him. Falkner's conduct during the troubles previous to that time clearly go to sustain the truth of his statement in that respect, for on one occasion, just before the meeting had been arranged, Dr. Desoto, a friend of Falkner, became involved in a difficulty with General Hindman, and while Desoto had his pistol presented at Hindman, Falkner seized the pistol at the very instant when Desoto pulled the trigger; the hammer fell, but instead of striking the cap it fell on Colonel Falkner's thumb, that had been thrust under it, thus saving Hindman's life. Colonel Falkner succeeded in wrenching the pistol out of Desoto's hand, put it in his pocket, and quietly walked to his office. After the feud had been settled by the timely interference of Colonel Gallaway, the friendship that existed between Colonel Falkner and General Hindman was of the most cordial sort, and the same good feelings were restored among the many friends of these gentlemen. As regards the *White Rose of Memphis*, I am not so vain as to undertake to criticize it; but I know that all who have read it are exceedingly well pleased with it, and no one more so than your correspondent. There are, as I understand, thirteen chapters of the work unpublished yet, and if that which is to come is equal to the rest, I am sure it will prove a success. I think we have just cause to be proud of Falkner, for the services that he has rendered to this community have been of immense value to the citizens and given him a strong position in their affections. With Jefferson Davis to write up the war, and the reasons that produced it; Claiborne to write up the history of our State; Simmons, the sweet bard of Sardis to write our songs; and Falkner to write our soul-stirring novels, why should Mississippi be behind her literary sisters of the Union? The greatest mystery to me is that Colonel Falkner could find time to compose such a charming novel as the *White Rose*, and at the same time keep up and manage more business than any other man in this community. He is the president of the Ripley Railroad company, and has been for ten years; he runs a farm near this place, cultivating 1200 acres; successfully manages over a hundred tenants; runs a grist-mill, cotton-gin, saw mill, a law office, a dozen small farms, helps to build churches, schoolhouses, and leads in all public enterprises in this county, looking to the improvement of the same, and then has time to compose a novel from every page of which gushes the most charming sentiments. I must confess that this is a mystery that I am not able to unravel. Colonel Falkner never seems to be in a hurry, nor does he ever appear to be pressed for time, and although he is an eloquent orator, he does not often make speeches, and never thrusts himself forward among strangers he is as bashful and timid as a girl of sixteen, but among old and familiar friends he is lively, vivacious and most interesting, possessing a charming disposition and fascinating manner. His large plantation is run on a perfect system, and the improvements are arranged in such a manner as to furnish proof of the great mind that planned them. He seems to be able to measure a man's worth at a single glance, and in the selection of his agents he rarely ever makes a mistake. He makes money by enabling honest, industrious men to make it, and to this trait in his character we are indebted for the production of the *White Rose*. The *Advertiser* office was burned down, the press and material all destroyed, and the owners left without means to take a new start. Colonel Falkner's big heart caused him to advance means to start the paper again, and in order to give her a good "send off" began to write the *White Rose*. The more he wrote the better he got, and the result is the beautiful *White Rose of Memphis*. If any man ever deserved success, the generous, noble-hearted author of the *White Rose of Memphis* deserves it, and so far as Mississippi is able to extend her influence to secure for him that success that he so richly deserves, I assure you it will be done, and I believe, also, Tennessee, on whose generous soil the author of the *White Rose* was born, will do the same. As one of Colonel Falkner's admirers and friends, allow me, in conclusion, through the column of the *Appeal*, to tender to Colonel M. C. Gallaway a renewal of the thanks which I have always felt toward him for settling the feud which probably saved Colonel Falkner's life. I know I state the truth when I say that the same sentiment of regard that dwells in my heart for Colonel Gallaway is felt by the entire community.[1]

Notes

1. This essay is in the form of a letter to the editor and signed "Respectfully, / C. J. F. Ripley, Miss., April 15, 1881."

[Pen Pictures of the War and Its Aftermath]

W. L. Clayton[*]

December 22, 1905

I will this week change the regular course of events, and give my readers a little war incident which I did not myself witness, but the particulars were given me by my brother, J. S. Clayton, one of the actors in the interesting episode.

In the winter of 1864–65, and probably about February of that year, J. S. Clayton and Carroll Mitchener attached themselves to Gambrell's scouts, a kind of independent command, who were at that time hovering round the enemy's outposts a few miles above Memphis, near what is

*From the columns of Washington Lafayette Clayton originally published in the Tupelo, Miss., *Journal*. The text is from *Olden Times Revisited*, edited by Minrose Gwin (Jackson, Miss.: University Press of Mississippi, 1982), pp. 117–20, 147–50, 153–55. Reprinted with permission of the University Press of Mississippi.

called the "Devil's Elbow" on the Mississippi River. The day after they joined that command, about a dozen of that company planned to make a dash on the pickets of the enemy about five miles east of Memphis. They made the dash, succeeded in capturing the vidette and two horses, and drove the reserve back into Memphis. Carroll and James, my brother, were detailed to carry the captured "Blue Coat" and turn him over to General Forrest, who was then in camp not far from New Albany, Mississippi. After having discharged that duty, they started on their return trip to the "Devil's Elbow" to join their command. On the third night out they stayed all night at Will Tate's, a brother of Dr. Rice B. Tate, who used to live at Mooreville, and with whom both Carroll and James were well acquainted. Will Tate lived near Germantown, Tennessee, as my brother's memory serves him. This was in debatable ground, mostly occupied though by the Federals, yet no harm came to them that night, and next morning they moved on their way, aiming to pass through this town, but, as they approached it, they saw a soldier come out of a house something about a hundred yards to their right, mount his horse and ride towards them, saying, "Come by, boys." He had on a blue overcoat—but many of the Confederates were then in that part of the country—and from his familiar salutation, they supposed he was one of their own men. They left the road and went to meet him. When they had approached to within about thirty feet of him, a ravine being between them, he presented his pistol at brother James, and ordered both of them to hold up their hands. But I want to say that neither of the boys had ever contracted to surrender at even numbers, and much less so when the odds were two to one in their favor. James dropped his bridle reins, raised his left hand as though in fulfillment of the command, but attempted to draw his pistol hung in the scabbard. In the meantime, Carroll, who was about ten feet to the right of James, drew his pistol and fired at the soldier, and he at the same time, having changed his pistol from my brother to Mitchener, fired, both pistols going off at the same time. The shot fired by Carroll cut about one half its depth out of the right cheek of the Federal, while his shot glanced the top of Carroll's hat, a new white one, and scorched and powder burned it somewhat. At this both the Southern boys wheeled their horses, and started back in a run the way they had come, having looked to their right a short distance beheld a large number of cavalrymen coming to the aid of their friend. They demanded the surrender of the boys, but instead of complying they only ran the faster. They ascended a long, slanting hill with the enemy in full pursuit, firing at them constantly. The boys could see their bullets cutting up the dirt at their front making impressions like water falling in a puddle. When they had gone about one half mile, they crossed a bridge, and this delayed the enemy somewhat, but while the boys were going up another long hill, brother's hat blew off. Hats were hats in those days, and he could not get his consent to part with the hat and risk getting another. So when they reached the top of the hill and discovered that only a few of the enemy had crossed the bridge, and that they were about the same distance from the hat as the boys were, James said to Carroll, "I must have my hat!" So they raised the rebel yell, as though they had met their command, and dashed back towards the Federals, yelling, shouting as if they had a dozen or more. They, supposing the Confederates were coming in force, fell back across the bridge, and when the boys reached the hat, still yelling, my brother dismounted and recovered his hat, again mounted and both dashed off for dear life as they had been going. The enemy, seeing the ruse, sent about twenty-five men in hot pursuit. The road was straight for about a mile and a half, and Carroll's horse being rather small and not very fleet, they gained on the boys, and poured the shot into them pretty lively. Coming to a creek, whose bridge had been washed away, and to cross the ford one had to go down the creek about thirty feet, and then come up the channel to near the place where the bridge had been to get out on the other side, my brother, being just then in a considerable hurry, did not go down to the place where the road entered the creek, but jumped his horse off the bank just below the bridge and out on the far side. Carroll, fearing his horse might not be able to cross in this manner, turned up the creek on a road leading in that direction. Four of the enemy followed James, while all the others pursued Carroll, and each could hear the firing at the other for some minutes. Brother, being now untrammeled by a slower horse than his own, gave his horse full rein, and in the course of a mile he had so far distanced his pursuers that they turned back. Desiring to learn what had become of his fellow soldier, he turned to the left, and struck across fields and swamps, intending and aiming to intersect the road he had taken. After the separation Carroll was pursued for about a mile, and being fired on all the time, when he came to a small town, and feeling that his only hope of safety lay in a bold move, adopted the same ruse they had used so successfully in relation to the hat, and again raising a rebel yell, dashed back toward his pursuing foes. He, being hidden just then from the Federals, and they thinking he had surely met up with reinforcements this time, and influenced by the noise he made, fled in great disorder, and their peril was at an end for that time. Carroll, instigated by the same motives which prompted brother James to turn to the left, himself turned to the right, and down in some unknown creek bottom, a mile and a half from any road, and about five miles from their first encounter with the would-be familiar "Blue Coat," the friends met again, and you may be sure no two comrades were ever prouder to see each other than they were. Not a wound had either received, and yet the peril was great, and the escape almost miraculous. . . .

November 30, 1906

When the war of 1861 had closed and the survivors of the army returned to their homes, they found many changes had taken place in their absence, and especially was this noticeable in the border land of the country. In the first place, all property in slaves was destroyed, and the supply of horses and mules had been reduced very much. Such a thing as a good saddle horse or a good wagon mule could not be found, unless they had been hidden out, and this was a very dangerous thing to do. Some enemy or slave would be almost sure to point out the hiding place of the stock, and if the enemy came, he took them, and if the friend happened along, he impressed them for service, and in either event, the stock was gone and the owner none the better off, as the scrip given by the friend proved of no more value toward the last than the want of it by the enemy. To the everlasting credit of the negroes it must be said that they were so far loyal to their owners as a general thing that they remained at home and worked faithfully, and in many instances had the care and possession of the entire interests of their master's farms and stock, and were ever ready to do and suffer whatever might be required for the interest of their owners.

After the war in all the thinly settled slave districts, like North Mississippi, they still remained at home and finished the crops before they were turned loose as free. I have often thought that as the slaves assembled round the cabin hearths in the days succeeding the close of the war and before the time of their final release, they had wonderful reasonings among themselves as to what would be the outcome of the war to them. You must remember that they could neither read nor write, and only in a few instances had anyone explained to them that Lincoln had issued his proclamation freeing them, and as we went on with our work as formerly, they must have endeavored often to peer into wonderland to find what it would bring to them. And yet how cautious they must have been, because of the fear of punishment. They had not yet learned that they were no longer in fear of the Patrolers if they failed to carry a pass from their owners, and consequently had not moved about much. I remember very well that our slaves were just as obedient and worked as well during the making of the crop of 1865 as they had ever been and done. So one morning after the crop was completed, I said to my father, "Father, I think we had better tell our negroes they are free and have a right to go where they please." He agreed it was the course to take, and we called them up and told them of their right to go or remain as they might choose, and that they were as free as we were, and I think we might have added, a little freer. And I assure you that the white women had the cooking to do that day, and many women who had never made a biscuit or fried ham and eggs, were forced to look into cook books to learn that which seemed to have come to the old black mammy by instinct.

But I want to tell you it did not take a lifetime for the poor ignorant negroes to learn the extent of their freedom and their rights thereunder. When they ascertained the fact that they had a right to stand and listen to a white man talk, and none dare molest or make them afraid, they took advantage of every opportunity to listen and to learn. And when the reconstruction measures were passed by Congress, they were not long in learning that the bottom rail was on top. I remember and shall never forget the wonderful influence any worthless carpetbagger had on them to the exclusion of all advice any of us might give. Some irresponsible fellow put it into their heads that every slave was to be given forty acres of land and a mule from the lands of the former slave owners, and having once taken root, it spread through the land of the South, and was generally believed.

Once upon a time one of these slick friends of the former slaves, and who had such wonderful influence over them, taking advantage of the ignorance and confidence of an old time darkey, meeting him on his former master's plantation, informing the old ex-slave that he was one of the men whom the government had appointed to measure off the aforesaid forty acres and give him a deed to it, and that another man would be round soon to assign and deliver him his mule with which to work it. So with glad heart and ready hand the old negro assisted the pretended official in making the measurement. When that was done, the old man wanted his deed, which was readily written and delivered on the payment to the swindler of $8.75, being all the money the old man had. Some days after this the old negro seemed more independent than usual, and began putting on airs of ownership when his former master said to him, "Dick, what's the matter with you? For some time you have been putting on airs like you owned the place." "Yes, sar, I does own part of de place." "How's that? What do you mean, you old fool?" "Well, sar, de guberment man jist comed round and measured me off my forty acres offen your land, and gived me a deed to it." Much astonished, but knowing some fraud had been practiced upon the old darkey, the owner asked to see the deed. Thereupon the old man handed out his supposed deed for the inspection of his former master, and the present landlord, and when held up to the light of intelligence, the old man was dumbfounded to hear the words read, "As Moses lifted up the serpent in the wilderness, so have I lifted this old darkey out of eight dollars and seventy-five cents. Selah!" It was said long, long time ago that "a fool and his money are soon parted," and this is especially true where gross ignorance and unbounded confidence on one side and unscrupulousness on the other. But I have thought of all the villains known to mankind it is he who abuses the confidence reposed in him, and swindles under the guise of friendship. It puts me more in mind of the kiss with which our Savior was betrayed than any with which I can compare it.

It was some years before the old darkey ceased saying, "Masser" when addressing a white man. Old Uncle Jim Hussey, a fine old time darkey, who lived and died near Mooresville in Lee county, Mississippi, kept up the habit of calling his old friends Masser till the time of his death. There was another peculiarity about Uncle Jim which I do not think applies to any other ex-slave in all this country, and that is that he always under all circumstances voted the Democratic ticket. In the darkest days of Mississippi, when the colored population marched to the polls in solid phalanx and voted in columns for the Republican party, Uncle Jim always from the very beginning and as long as he voted, put in his vote for the Democrats. He always said that as the colored people were living with the whites and largely dependent upon them, it did seem to him that what was to the interest of one race must be equally so for the other, and that as the white people were the more intelligent, it stood to reason that they would advocate and vote for those principles which would make for their betterment and consequently for the best interests of all.

He was a fine old character, as polite as a Chesterfield, and as kind hearted as any man I have ever met, white or black. He thought nothing of taking off his hat and bowing graciously to anyone whom he met from pure politeness. But those kind are becoming fewer and fewer every year. If we had more such men as Uncle Jim, and fewer of the worthless and law-breaking class, the country would be better off. . . .

December 14, 1906

Many of us remember and will ne'r forget the days from 1865 to 1875, ten eventful years in the history of our Southland. Of course it is impossible to paint in true colors the events of those years. Being under military rule part of the time, and under military power all this time, which means the same thing as military rule practically, we could do nothing openly that would alleviate our condition. What we did in the way of relief measures had to be done on the sly. Young men were growing up who had never been in the war, but whose hands were itching to take hold of something by which they might signalize their entrance into life's arena by some action for the benefit and relief of their country and which might put a feather in their own caps that would in some degree look like they were worthy sons of worthy sires; and so they were ever ready to do anything which might be thought to even tend toward relief, and doubtless would have been guilty of many indiscretions but for the advice of older and wiser heads. But in the meantime the negroes kept moving from bad to worse, led on by unworthy and often trifling white men. Under these circumstances many devices were resorted to to checkmate their political moves. An old friend of mine, just before an election, happened to come into the possession of a Republican ticket. He showed it to some of the Democratic leaders in an adjoining county and they were delighted to get it, saying it was the very thing they had been endeavoring to secure for some time. You see, before the Democrats came into power and passed a law that no picture or device of any kind should be printed on any ballot by which it could be distinguished and that all ballots should be alike, the ignorant negroes knew their Republican ticket by the picture that headed it, and not by the names which were written thereon. You see how easy it was for the "leading politicians" on our side to duplicate the ticket, how easily these bogus tickets could be placed in the hands of the ignorant voters and how the count would show up on our side. Again, men did not scruple to take out the votes which were actually cast and substitute the Democratic ticket therefor, and ease their conscience by the thought that "all things are fair in war," and that the good of the country demanded this. Sometimes one means was used and sometimes others to accomplish such action. It was well known that the most of the leaders of the negroes, both white and black, were quite venal and ready for a bid in money to betray their party. By this means the ignorant voter was often deceived by his pretended friends, and made really to vote the Democratic ticket, when he thought he was voting for the other side. Sometimes the tickets were exchanged by the art of legerdemain, so to speak, and the innocent leader gave out the tickets which had been left in place of the genuine article. You see the picture was there all the same, and it was that by which they judged. But, after a few of such tricks had been played on them, they were more careful and some other scheme had to be resorted to. The rule of the black voter was always to line up in solid column at voting time. This was very distasteful to the white man. Many means were resorted to to break up this custom. Sometimes the whites came to the polls with their cannons on the ground, booming them once and awhile while the white men stood 'round, and some of them occasionally fired off pistols or guns. There was nothing said to the negroes about not voting as they might please, and no intimidation whatever, but all the same the cannons were boomed and guns and pistols fired, and the negroes ran off and left the polls and never came back to vote.

Finally, in 1875, the whites decided they had had enough of it, and it must stop in some way. It was managed differently in different places. In Lee county we had a meeting of prominent workers for the cause and it was decided that everybody should be on a committee to make a general and close canvass of the county one day before the election and press home to the negroes every argument we could to induce them to vote with us. I remember very well to have been in that canvass. We searched out the brother in black and told them one by one in as much as we could, and each squad of whites numbering as many as we well could, and one man talking for awhile and then another. Many agreed to vote with us, but said it in such a way that we knew very well that they did not mean it. Many others were mum. On the next day when the polls were opened the whites were much and early on the ground, and when the negroes came in they did not present that solid black phalanx of column they had formerly done. The truth is they had been informed that it was not good manners. The most of them, though, were very anxious to vote the Republican ticket. No violence was offered, but many whites would surround a negro voter and use all kind of arguments and persuasions to vote the Democratic ticket, and as each voter could be induced to cast his vote in that way, the entire white contingent would raise a yell that would have done honor to the old Rebel soldier's battle cry; and thus one by one the negroes were induced to fall into line, except a few who retired to the rear without voting at all. This took place throughout the state, and the Republican party was put out of business in Mississippi.

[Some Notes of a Private]   John Milton Hubbard*

When we had somewhat recovered from the fatigue and demoralization incident to the Armstrong raid, four companies of the Seventh Tennessee and four of the First Mississippi were ordered to march under the Lieutenant Colonel F. A. Montgomery of the latter regiment in the direction of Hernando, Miss. Colonel Grierson with his Sixth Illinois Cavalry was making a scout from Memphis, and the eight companies were to watch his movements. I remember we passed down through Byhalia and Cockrum and across Coldwater river on the road towards Hernando. Then turning north and marching leisurely along we recrossed the Coldwater at Holloway's bridge, quite a rude affair, about ten miles south-west of Byhalia. The men seemed to think that we were only making one of our usual marches for practice. But when we had reached the foothills on the east side, there was a commotion in the ranks and we were ordered to countermarch, while the word passed down the line that Grierson was in our rear. He had crossed the bridge and was following us. In a few minutes the whole command was in the greatest excitement. As soon as the immediate presence of the enemy was discovered, a company of the Seventh Regiment was thrown front into line, but, unfortunately, very near the enemy, who had advanced on foot and were well concealed in the heavy timber. There were brisk firing from the Federal line, which portended certain death to the men and horses of our front company. There was a bolt to the rear, and what is known to the participants as the Coldwater stampede was on. Nothing could surpass it in excitement. The other companies had been drawn up by company front with Company E next in position to the one so near the enemy. When the latter had reached our front, it had acquired about sufficient momentum to dash through on their excited horses, which seemed to have gotten beyond the control of

*From *Notes of a Private* (Memphis: E. H. Clarke & Brother, 1909), pp. 27–36, 60–61, 122–26, 133–35, 142–44, 149–52, 181–83. Hubbard was a member of Company E, 7th Tennessee Regiment, Forrest's Cavalry Corps, C.S.A., and served on the battlefields used as a setting for *The Unvanquished*. Faulkner's grandfather bought this account in 1909; Faulkner signed his name to it in 1933, before he began writing the episodes of *The Unvanquished*. This book is now quite rare.

their riders. The Federals saw their opportunity and promptly advanced, delivering a galling fire as they did so. The demoralization was imparted from man to man and the scare from horse to horse till it became a rout. Some of the men of Company E spoke encouraging words to one another, when they saw what was coming, and denounced the retreat as cowardly. In some, this was no doubt a manifestation of inborn bravery, in others, of self-esteem or personal pride. From whatever motive, it was a creditable act, for it was one of those occasions when a man can take his own measure to see whether or not he is a brave soldier, or is prompted by other impulses. But however much inclined some were to stand firm, it was only a moment before all were borne to the rear. Concert of action was impossible, and those who at first resolved to resist, were very soon getting away with those who seemed to be making the best time. The command did not exactly take to the woods, but there was no delay in crossing a stout fence which put us into a corn field where the fall crop of crabgrass seemed to be the rankest I had ever seen. We happened to be going in the direction of the rows or we would have played havoc with the crop. As it was, we trampled great paths through the crabgrass and spoiled a fine lot of hay. Everybody seemed willing to halt when we got on the other side and had an open field between us and the enemy. The command was reorganized with dispatch, after which there were various expressions as to the cause of the disaster. Smarting with shame and mortification, a great majority of the detachment would then and there have put up the fight of their lives, had they been coolly led into action. Clearly, we had been outgeneraled by one of the most alert of Federal officers, the first on his side to gain a reputation as a bold raider.

How vividly I recall my own feelings and those expressed by others, when we retired from the scene of the affair just related! Everybody had some incident of the disaster to relate, and the usual funny things were said about how the boys got over that first fence and through that cornfield, though it did look like smiling at a funeral.

When the excitement was at its height and Grierson's men were yelling like demons turned loose, Sherrill Tisdale's horse was running madly to the rear with his rider trying to keep himself in the saddle by holding desperately to the mane. Tisdale fell to the ground and was captured, but his fine young horse, afterward ridden by the late Emmet Hughes, escaped and would have carried his owner to safety.

John Allen, a brother of Dr. Joe Allen, killed only a few days before at Briton's Lane, was shot through the foot before our line was broken. He was riding a splendid mule which carried him out of danger by leaping two big logs, lying one upon the other. Joe and John Allen with their brother Thompson, who served in another regiment, were, like their father, Long John Allen, of Whiteville, noted for their sprightly intellectuality, physical and moral courage and height. John used to turn his six feet four inches to an amusing account when he encountered a citizen with whom he wished to swap horses. Putting his hand to his right ear he would ask his new acquaintance to talk very loud, intimating that he was very deaf. "Old Innocent," usually a man of short stature as compared with John's, who had, on the quiet, plenty of confidence in his own ability as a judge of horseflesh, would tiptoe to John and raise his voice to a high key. John, like a born actor, would turn his right eye down on his unsuspecting subject while he winked with his left to his audience. John Allen's penchant for horse trading caused him sometimes to be mounted on a mule.

Company E now knew that there was work to be done in the immediate future. The Federals had garrisoned many places on the Memphis and Charleston Railroad, and were making incursions into Mississippi. Steps were taken to unite the armies of Price and Van Dorn for the purpose of making an attack on Corinth where General Rosecrans was posted. As preliminary to this attack, Colonel W. H. Jackson was ordered to take his own and the First Mississippi Cavalry under Pinson and make a reconnoisance in the direction of Corinth. At Davis' bridge on Big Hatchie river Jackson somewhat unexpectedly came upon Ingersoll's Eleventh Illinois Cavalry and some regulars just going into camp. The vidette, who had just taken post, was taken in and the rest was very easy. Pinson in front charged across the bridge and into the camp of the enemy, who were largely engaged in gathering corn from a field to the right of the road, while the Seventh Tennessee brought up the rear and waked the echoes with the rebel yell. The firing was promiscuous, but there were few casualties. Pinson was the only Confederate wounded. He manifested the spirit and courage of the hero, as we bore him to the Davis residence on a cot secured for the purpose. He had very good reason to think that the ball had penetrated the intestines, but he, nevertheless, spoke cheerfully to anxious enquirers as "boys," and said that it was only "a small matter" and that he "was all right." Happily he was.

The spoils were great, considering the few minutes the battle lasted, consisting of one hundred and eighty fine Illinois horses with their accoutrements and arms. We captured only fifty or sixty prisoners, as it was just at nightfall, and most of the enemy took refuge in the timber. I always thought that those fine horses and accoutrements should have been distributed among the boys where most needed and their inferior articles taken up. This might have been done under a board of survey in such a way as not only to increase the efficiency of the command, but also to stimulate it for future enterprises. But we didn't get a halter. All went to supply the demands of other commands. There was one particularly fine horse in the captured lot which had been thoroughly trained and was evidently something of a pet, as we say, of his former owner. Jim Weatherly of Somerville, was not long in discovering his fine points and "smart tricks," and soon had him "going his way." The beautiful brown with two white feet had to be turned in, and Weatherly was disconsolate.

Thereafter, when any legitimate capture fell in the way of the boys, mum was the word. It was now September, 1862, and Price and Van Dorn were ready to move on Corinth. This movement was made from Ripley, Miss., in two divisions commanded by Price and Lovell, with Van Dorn as chief. The army was well equipped, well fed and in fine spirits. It had not rained for many weeks, and the dusty roads and scarcity of water made the marches, which were necessary to effect the concentration of the two armies, severe ones for all branches of the service. But the prospect of making a successful assault on the works at Corinth and capturing Rosecrans and his army buoyed up the spirits of the soldiers. Ten miles out on the Chiwalla hills the cavalry encountered a small Federal force which was easily swept back. Company A of the Seventh Tennessee, was active in this affair as Jackson's escort and lost the first man killed on the expedition. I was with a detachment of Company E that had been ordered forward and deployed as skirmishers. I came upon the corpse of the soldier, which had, for the moment, been left where he had fallen. It was the body of John Young of Memphis. This was the first day of October, 1862. The next day was spent in getting the proper dispositions made for the assault. On the 3rd, the earth seemed to tremble with the thunder of artillery and the roar of small arms. It was a struggle to the death in which both sides lost heavily. The position had been rendered strong by heavy earthworks and much of the front had been covered by fallen timber, which made the approach to the main works difficult. All that day it went well with the Confederates, though the killed and wounded were numerous. As the cavalry took no part in the main battle, we could see pretty well what was going on in the rear. There it was a bloody spectacle as the killed and wounded were borne back for treatment and burial. That was the first time for me to see our poor fellows wrapped in their blankets and buried in shallow trenches. The horror of it! Even on the morning of the fourth, those of us in the rear thought that all was well in front, for we had heard that Price, who was fighting on the north of the railroad, had gone over the heavy works and into the town. And so he had, but the brave men under Lovell on the right under the terrible fire of the Federals had failed to make a successful assault. Suddenly there was a calm, which we could not understand. But it soon flashed upon us that we were beaten, and our army was in full retreat. During the previous night McPherson's division from Jackson had re-enforced Rosecrans and was ready to press the retreating Confederates. Hurlburt's division, too, was marching from Bolivar to intercept the retreating column. There was now likely to be some lively work for the cavalry. When we reached Davis' bridge, the scene of the affair heretofore related, Hurlburt was there to dispute our passage. With McPherson in our rear we were apparently "in a box." Shrewd generalship on the part of the Federals would have captured our whole army. Van Dorn boldly attacked Hurlburt at the bridge, while his trains were ordered to take the only road of escape — that up Hatchie river.

The cavalry preceded the trains, and, crossing the river, attacked Hurlburt in his rear. For several hours there were two Federal and two Confederate forces engaged and one of each fronting two ways. Van Dorn drew off at the proper time and followed his trains. The Federals were not disposed to follow, as good generalship would have dictated, for our troops, wornout and hungry, could have made but a feeble resistance. The streams had no water in them and our soldiers drank the wells dry. When a beef was killed the hungry men were cutting the flesh from the carcass before the hide was off. In the midst of this distress, I had my only sight of Sterling Price. He was riding at the head of a small escort and apparently in deepest thought. He had left many of the brave men whom he loved dead on the field of Corinth. He was the idol of his men, a great Missourian and a good man. But the result at Corinth had made him sad. The disaster brought other troubles in its train. The morale of the army was not good, the citizens were discouraged and many a soldier gave up the fight and went to his home within the Federal lines. We retired to the vicinity of Holly Springs. . . .

. . . We spent a few weeks at old Pharsalia, on the Yokona river, where we constructed rude winter quarters, or "shanties," for timber was abundant. We had a great snowstorm, and had to keep fires glowing. We had much pleasure here in receiving and entertaining for a part of a day Mrs. R. P. Neely, of Bolivar, and her daughter, Miss Kate, the latter of whom had been banished from her home by Gen. Brayman, the Federal commander of the post. Mrs. Neely was a splendid type of the true Southern woman, who, like all her children, stood always ready to make sacrifices for the Southern soldiers. She was a woman of most charming personality and gentle refinement, that could have filled almost any station to which ladies are called. Mrs. Elizabeth Lea Neely lived to a great age, and retained to the end the profound respect of all the good people of Bolivar. As for Miss Kate—now Mrs. Collins, of Memphis—she was, or rather is, a woman of the Grace Darling or Mollie Pitcher type, who would go to the rescue of those in peril, or take her place at the guns, if it were to repel the enemies of her country. May her days be long and happy. . . .

The rest of the month of July, 1864, was spent by the Confederates in the rich prairie country below Okolona. About Gunn's church we found the fields full of green corn, some in the roasting ear and much of it in that state of maturity when it is best to make jaded horses thrifty. Watermelons were cheap and abundant. There was no talk of scant rations. The farmers had been raising corn and hogs for war times. These conditions wonderfully revived the spirits of the men. Cornbread now and no biscuit. Plenty of greasy bacon and some with a streak of lean and a streak of fat. This held on a sharp stick and over the fire, and with the gravy dripping on the bread, was something good to look at. Some managed to always have a little sugar and coffee which they had secured with other captured spoils.

As a rule, Confederate soldiers did not tolerate rye or other substitutes for coffee. They wanted the "pure stuff" or nothing. The weather was warm, and sleeping in the open air was refreshing. Company E had not stretched a tent for more than a year. Occasionally quartered in unoccupied houses, the men were generally protected against the elements by rude structures of such material as was at hand, but mostly by captured rubber cloths, stretched over a pole resting in two forks stuck in the ground. If only one was to be accommodated, a convenient sapling was bent down till it assumed the shape of a bow and its top secured to the ground. Then the rubber cloth was stretched over this so that a soldier could crawl under. In both cases, the shelter was called a "shebang." A good rest and full stomachs went far towards getting those of us who had been spared ready for the next campaign. We left the goodly land where "if you will tickle the soil with a hoe, it will laugh with a harvest." We went to Oxford to meet our late antagonist, General A. J. Smith, who was moving south with another fine army. Forrest with a greatly reduced force was compelled to meet him. It might be remembered as the wet August, for it rained almost incessantly. It would require every available man now. We stretched out our thin line along Hurricane creek, six miles north of Oxford. The Federals were crossing the Tallahatchie at Abbeville a few miles north of our position. Skirmishing began at once with the advance of the superior force of the Federals. By the 10th of August, 1864, Forrest had all his forces in line except Buford's division, which was posted at Pontotoc to watch any movement east by the Federals. Before the main body of the Confederates arrived Smith had driven Chalmers' division to the south side of the Yokona, several miles below Oxford. On the approach of reinforcements the Federals fell back across Hurricane creek to their former position. The heavy rains continued to fall and added greatly to the discomforts of our men. It was impossible to keep even moderately dry under the best *"shebangs"* that could be constructed, because the ground was saturated. We continued to strengthen our works with such poor material as we could get. At best, they would have given us poor protection in case of attack.

Rucker's Brigade was now a thing of the past and the Seventh Tennessee was attached to Richardson's Brigade, commanded by Colonel J. J. Neely. At his instance I had been temporarily detailed to attend to some clerical and other work in the ordnance department. For the time being I stopped at the quarters of Lieutenant-Colonel White, commanding the Fourteenth Tennessee, where we spent most of the time in trying to keep dry. Rations were in plenty, but we could scarcely get dry wood enough to cook them. Much of our ammunition was ruined and in our skirmishes many of the cartridges would not explode. All efforts to induce the Federals to cross to our side of the shallow creek failed, though our men frequently crossed to their side and, having engaged their advance, fell back hurriedly with the design of drawing them into a disadvantageous place. Colonel Neely one day, between showers, concluded to make an effort to lead the Federal cavalry into a well planned ambuscade by offering them superior inducements. The Fourteenth Regiment under White was ordered to cross the creek, dismount and get in a well-chosen place in the thick bushes and parallel with the road. A detachment of Neely's escort, with which I crossed over, was to ride forward, engage the Federal advance briskly, and retreat in some confusion. The enemy took the bait and came on at a canter. Luckily for them, their flankers struck the right of the dismounted regiment and gave the alarm. However, part of their pursuing force came up to where the escort was posted. The dense growth of timber on this spot so obscured the view that the Federal cavalry soon found themselves face to face with, and in short range of, our reserve and those who had rallied. It was a most exciting contest for only a minute or two, and chiefly with pistols, on our side, but both parties seemed to have lost the knack of hitting anything, for I saw no dead or wounded, though we quickly drove the enemy upon their reserve and kept up a spirited gunplay until it was our time to fall back. Everybody realized the inability of the Confederates to cope with the greatly superior force of the Federals, and we were liable to be driven from our position by a heavy flank movement at any time. A knowledge of this, of course, was possessed by the rank and file, and the suspense concerning coming results was great. In the midst of our anxiety, Colonel White received orders to prepare rations for an expedition. That something radical was on the tapis was evident. Only picked men and horses were wanted. It got abroad in camp that we were going to Memphis. That looked radical, but pleased us. There was a weeding out of sick men, sore back and lame horses. The camp took on new life. As the duties of my special assignment were about discharged, I could have asked to be relieved and to be returned to my own company, which was not under orders, but I preferred to take part in whatever excitement was in store for us, so I said nothing and went to Memphis with Colonel White. . . .

We retired at our leisure to Mississippi, where news soon reached us that the Federals had driven Chalmers, with his inferior force, to the south side of the Yokona, and were committing depredations in and around Oxford. They had burnt the courthouse and many other buildings, including the fine residence of Jacob Thompson, with its hundred thousand dollars worth of furnishings. It was said, and it turned out to be true, that Mrs. Thompson was robbed of such valuable articles as she could hastily carry out. In giving his men such license, General Edward Hatch had revealed his true character as a man. He had won renown on the battle-field, and shown himself to be an able commander and skillful tactician, but had disgraced himself in the eyes of all advocates of civilized warfare.

Just as Forrest had anticipated, the Federals began to fall back from Oxford, as soon as their commander heard the news from Memphis.

General James R. Chalmers was entitled to great praise for the skillful manner in which he had handled his troops and concealed from the enemy the absence of Forrest. He held a position that required tact, discretion and courage, and met the expectations of his chief. I remember him well, and can recall his character as that of a man who, as occasion required, could move an audience by his eloquence, charm the fastidious with his felicity of diction, and gallantly lead his men in battle. Personally, "Little Bun" was popular with the rank and file, as he was one of the most approachable of men. Scrupulously uniformed and finely mounted, he presented an attractive figure on review. A man of literary taste, he sometimes courted the muses. He was the reputed author of some words I heard sung in war times to the air of Bonnie Doone. These words might well be brought to light again and take their place in popular esteem by the side of "Dixie" and "The Bonnie Blue Flag." Perhaps some one of those who used to be called "the pretty girls of Bolivar," but who, alas, are now wearing frosted crowns, could find in their old portfolios the words which might serve to keep green the memory of a gallant Confederate.

To rest in shady groves, to sleep by lulling waters, to hear the song of birds, the hum of bees, the tinkling bells of lowing kine, bring more pleasing thoughts to mind than those of war and deadly strife. To things like these we turned after the Memphis raid, but not for long. The people praised the deeds of Forrest's Cavalry, the marvel of horseback fighting, and the worthy rival of trained infantry, but the soldiers' paeans of victory always had a minor note of sorrow for our desolate land, the tears of our widows and orphans, and our increasing casualties in battle. Our poor fellows were falling, and our line becoming shorter, as the living pressed their shoulders together.

We camped on the Yokona, at Oakland and Grenada, and I returned to Company E. . . . My desire to see my child must have touched a tender chord in his heart, as he said that the General would return by a certain hour, and that, if I would call again, I would likely get the pass. . . .

I stopped at the Smith cottage, a well-known landmark, just across from the Methodist Church. I gazed up at the old steeple in respectful silence, and felt glad to stand in its shadow once more. But I am now at the door of the cottage, which was closed. I step along the veranda to an open window. Unobserved, I gaze for some moments on the picture within. To me, at least, "the prettiest and loveliest boy" in all the land, engaged in childish pranks with his colored nurse. I hesitated to break the spell, for it seemed to me that happiness had reached its full fruition. Ernest was a happy little boy in a happy home, for war times, as his aunt, the late Mrs. Henry W. Sample, was devoted to him as she had been devoted to his mother. I never could repay her for all her kindness to me and mine, but I place here in print a sincere tribute to her memory as that of a noble woman, who was altogether unselfish, whose religion was a daily affair, who cultivated a charitable spirit, who reached out her hand to those in trouble, and who went to her grave with the love and respect of the people among whom she had lived seventy-two years. . . .

Four miles north of Athens, a blockhouse, with thirty-two men was surrendered. We bivouacked for the night, thinking that we had made a fine beginning. Eleven miles from Athens, there was a strong fort, which protected what was known as Sulphur Branch trestle, a structure three hundred feet long and seventy-two feet high. In order to destroy this, it was necessary to capture the fort and two large blockhouses. On the morning of the 25th of September, the Confederate artillery was concentrated on the fort, in which were several rude cabins covered with oak boards. At the same time, Forrest ordered a heavy force to advance on foot against the position. There was severe fighting for only a little while, as our artillery quickly scattered the lighter timbers and roofs of the cabins in every direction, and killed many of the garrison. The Federals ceased firing, but did not display the white flag. Their commander had already been killed, and there seemed to be great consternation in the fort. They surrendered as soon as a demand was made on them. This surrender included the two blockhouses. I saw no more horrid spectacle during the war than the one which the interior of that fort presented. If a cyclone had struck the place, the damage could hardly have been much worse. Here, again, the spoils were great, including three hundred cavalry horses and their equipments, a large number of wagons and ambulances, two pieces of artillery, all kinds of army stores, with nearly a thousand prisoners. Forrest was compelled now to send south a second installment of prisoners and captured property under a strong guard, the first having been sent from Athens. Sulphur Branch trestle being demolished, we moved towards Pulaski. The lame and disabled horses were now replaced by captured ones, and all the dismounted men, who had been crowded to the limit to keep up on the march, were furnished with horses. Some of our men were engaged in tearing up railroad track, while others were driving the enemy back towards Pulaski. Within six miles of the town we had heavy fighting, and again within three miles. At the former place, I saw the dead body of Stratton Jones, another schoolboy of mine, and the eldest son of Judge Henry C. Jones of Florence, now, perhaps, the oldest citizen of his city, and one of less than half a dozen of the surviving members of the Confederate Congress.

At the Brown farm, still nearer to Pulaski, we captured a corral containing about 2,000 negroes, who were being supported by the Federal commissary. They were a dirty and ragged lot, who were content to grasp at the mere shadow of freedom. Forrest ordered them to remove their filthy belongings from the miserable hovels, and set about two hundred of the latter on fire. Here was the richest depot of supplies I had seen since the capture of Holly Springs by Van Dorn. A bountiful supply of sugar and coffee was distributed to the men. Our horses were put in fine condition here by many hours of rest and good feed. Our loss for the day was about

100 in killed and wounded. That of the Federals was very much greater. . . .

. . . I have concluded to conclude this book with the following conclusions:

1. That it is an everlasting pity the war was not averted because of the great mortality of good citizens on both sides, the backset given to the morals of the whole country, the sectional feeling engendered and likely to endure for a season, and the loss of wealth and prestige by the Southern people.

2. That the victors in a civil war pay dearly for their success in the demoralization of the people at large by having so numerous an element supported by the government; in the rascally transactions connected with army contracts; and in the enlargement of that class of pestiferous statesmen (?) who have been aptly described as being "invisible in war and invincible in peace."

3. That the most peaceful of Southern men can be readily converted into the most war-like soldiers when convinced that they have a proper grievance; can march further on starvation rations and in all kinds of weather, and will take less note of disparity of numbers in battle than will any other soldiers on earth.

4. That the South, in the war period, was essentially a country of horseback riders, and her young men furnished the material out of which was formed, when properly handled, regiments of cavalry that were practically invincible, even when confronting an adversary of twice or thrice their own strength.

5. That Forrest's men demonstrated the fact that Southern cavalrymen, fighting on foot, can meet, with good chances of victory, a superior number of veteran infantry in the open field.

6. That in cavalry operations, the most essential thing is a bold and dashing leader, who will strike furiously before the enemy has time to consider what is coming, and with every available man in action.

7. That Nathan Bedford Forrest, by his deeds in war, became an exemplar of horseback fighting, whose shining qualities might well become the measure of other deeds on other fields when war is flagrant.

8. That there is not an instance recorded where so large a body of defeated soldiers returned so contentedly to their former pursuits, "beating their swords into ploughshares and their spears into pruning hooks;" yes, thousands of them going into the fields to plough and plant with the same horses they rode in battle.

9. That the unpreparedness of both sides at the beginning of the war emphasizes the necessity for a thorough preparedness of our united country for any emergency, that is to say, that while Uncle Sam needs not to be strutting around "with a chip on his shoulder," and his hat cocked up on the side of his head, he should be able to say to "the other fellow" that he is rich in men and munitions and, moreover, has the finest navy that floats.

William C. Falkner, Novelist[1]   Alexander L. Bondurant[*]

Summer with its teeming life, sunshine and warmth; with its ripening fruits and fragrant flowers is followed by Indian summer. Now the fruits have mellowed, and the fields are golden with grain. A languorous haze fills the air, and the sun seems to halt in his course as he approaches the nadir.

It is in this Indian summer period of man's life, when activity is followed by contemplation before senility has set in, that many, who have done yeoman service in their day, record their impressions of the events that they have witnessed and the parts they have played. From the earliest times youth has sat at the feet of age, and learned valuable lessons to be utilized when it assumes fully life's burdens. But no such guerdon awaits us in connection with the life of the subject of this sketch, for he was cut off in the flower of his age, his step still elastic, his eye undimmed. He was living in the fullest sense, and had not stopped to reduce his life-history to writing; and so his chronicler has to collect these scattered leaves wherever he can, and as best he may, arrange them into a connected whole.

It is the purpose of this paper to recall to the minds of those who knew him, and to place before those who knew him not the main facts pertaining to the life of William C. Falkner, lawyer, soldier, financier, student and author. The title, therefore, is rather suggestive of one phase of his life, a phase that culminated late, than inclusive of the whole.

William C. Falkner was born in Knox County, East Tennessee, July 6, 1826. His family was of Welsh descent and his forefathers had been pioneers in this region. He was very reserved in speaking or writing of himself, so little can be gathered directly with reference to the early years of his life; but he always manifested a deep affection for his mother, and its seems certain her character and influence over him were powerful factors in the determination of his later career. The careful reader detects in his writings a love for and comprehension of Nature in her many moods that doubtless came to him amidst the romantic surroundings of his boyhood home. From Tennessee his family removed to Missouri, and there his father died. The lad was now cast upon his own resources, and, further, felt the responsibility of providing for his widowed mother and orphaned brothers and sisters. The future seemed to hold little of promise for him in Missouri, and so he decided to seek fortune elsewhere.

*From *Publications of the Mississippi Historical Society*, 3 (1912), 113–25. Dr. Bondurant, a leader at the University of Mississippi, wrote this when he was professor of Latin there. He was a close friend of the Falkner family as well as young William Faulkner. This is the "official" biography of Colonel Falkner that canonized him; doubtless young Faulkner knew it well.

Mississippi was, at this time, a virgin land, and thither he determined to go; a bold undertaking for a lad of seventeen with no money, and no friends along the road. Foot-sore and weary he arrived at Ripley, Mississippi, then a pioneer inland town. Here he had relatives, and naturally looked for sympathy and encouragement; but in this, at first, he was disappointed. He now went to work with his hands doing anything that offered, but the days seemed long, and the nights weary. It is said that he went finally to a neighboring town, Pontotoc, to find work, but met with discouragement, and seeking a secluded spot gave vent to his grief. While here a little maid, Holland Pearce, came along, and seeing his sadness gave him sympathy and words of cheer. The lad was helped, and treasured in memory the sweet girl face, and the heartening words; later a young lawyer, the self-same lad now grown to man's estate, came back and claimed and won her heart and hand. But let us follow his early struggles with fate. A college education seemed beyond his reach, but he was an insatiable reader, and was filled with an earnest desire to obtain the best education possible under the circumstances. There was a teacher in the village of Ripley at this time, James Kernan, a native of Ireland, and to him young Falkner repaired. He studied in the winter and worked in summer in order to defray his expenses for the coming school term. In addition to this he taught elementary classes called "little A. B. C's." It seems to be certain that he was largely indebted to this teacher for proper direction in reading. Later he went to a relative, who at that time was a prominent lawyer, and requested to be allowed to read law in his office; but the lawyer refused, giving as his reason his insufficient preparation for the study. But one of Falkner's beliefs was that a man could be whatever he desired to be, and so, nothing daunted, he turned to his former teacher, who had hung out his shingle in a rough log office; and there the tyro conned Blackstone, and fitted himself for the examination which he successfully passed. He had, to an unusual degree, the power of application and forged rapidly to the front in his chosen profession.

The young man did not forget the mother he had left behind him, and constantly sent her means from his slender earnings. Fortune at last began to smile upon him, and determined in his wooing as in all his undertakings, he obtained the hand of Miss Holland Pearce, who made him a faithful and devoted wife. He was married in 1847, but she survived only a few years leaving one child, J. W. T. Falkner, who has lived to reflect credit upon an honored name, and at this writing is a member of the Senate in this State.

The news of Texas' struggles for independence fired the heart of one who was always alive to the sorrows of the oppressed, and when the United States espoused this cause he volunteered as a private. He saw much service, and was wounded several times; but his gains were greater than his losses, for by his gallantry, courtesy and uniform kindliness he won for himself the esteem of his comrades, and the respect of the commanding officers, and was chosen an officer by his companions in arms.

Upon his return home he began anew the practice of his profession, and, in addition, engaged largely in planting. Naturally he was a slave owner, but was always a humane master. He was married a second time to Miss Elizabeth Houston Vance, of Alabama, the marriage occurring in 1851. To them were born the following children: William Henry, who died in early manhood; Willie M., now Mrs. N. G. Carter, of Ripley; Bama L., now Mrs. Walter McLean, of Memphis; Effie, now Mrs. A. E. Davis, of Ripley; besides several children, who died in infancy or early youth. During this period he was a close student of the Bible and Shakespeare, and though he had never had the opportunity for the study of Latin and Greek, he made a careful study of the master pieces of these great literatures in translation, gaining in this way a fair knowledge and appreciation of Homer and Virgil, and other classical authors. He was keenly alive to the advantages of a college education, and sent his brother and son to the University of Mississippi. He did not care for office, but ever took an active interest in the upbuilding of his adopted State, and had great influence in all political gatherings. He did not use this influence to advance himself, but ever strove to see that the best men filled the offices, both State and country. He was an old line Whig, and later allied himself with that branch of the Whig party that at first was ridiculed by those of a different political creed. But it is a significant fact that many times a name applied first by enemies in derision has been worn later as a badge of honor and this is true of *The Know Nothing* party, which held that America should be for Americans, and that in order to have a homogeneous Anglo-Saxon community the waves of foreign immigration that threatened to engulf the State, must be arrested. And now, after half a century, we find a multitude of earnest men accepting the tenets of this party irrespective of political creed.

Colonel Falkner was intensely southern, and held strongly to the sovereign right of a sovereign State to secede, and when the North each year grew more exacting in her demands, and those who opposed slavery in the nation's counsels grew daily more bitter in their attacks upon the slave power, he preached boldly this doctrine as a remedy for existing evils. When the die was cast, he at once responded to the call to arms, and went to work with enthusiasm to enlist men for the conflict, which he fully realized was to be no "thirty days matter." He was chosen Col. of the second Mississippi regiment, and led his command to Virginia. His former adjutant writes that he was an excellent disciplinarian, but ruled more by kindness than by force.

In the first battle of Manassas, the second Mississippi played a prominent part. Under the command of Col. Falkner they were in the thickest of the fight. Col. M. C. Galloway, formerly of the *Memphis Appeal* wrote that as he was pressing forward to charge the enemy General Beauregard asked, "who is the knight with the black plume? Men you may follow where he leads," and that thus Col. Falkner earned this honorable soubriquet. A battery was working havoc amongst the Confederate forces, and General Johnson said that it must be taken. Col. Falkner offered his command for the undertaking, and was completely successful, though his loss was heavy. General Bee said that he hoped to live to tell of Falkner's daring on that eventful day. The following dispatch was sent to a Mississippi paper at the close of the battle by a spectator: "A Mississippi Regiment covered itself with glory. Editor of *Mississippian*: The victory is ours. Col. Falkner of 2nd Mississippi Regiment, charged and took four pieces of Sherman's battery. His loss was a hundred killed and wounded." At the end of the day Col. Falkner was in command of the brigade, succeeding for the time the gallant General B. E. Bee, who had been mortally wounded in the engagement. He lost from his regiment four captains killed and two wounded. He was wounded slightly, Major Blair severely, and Lieut-Col. B. B. Boone was reported missing.

When apprised soon after the battle of the birth of a little daughter in his home, he wrote to his wife to name her Elizabeth after the one who had been so faithful a helpmeet to him, and to add Manassas to commemorate the victory of southern arms. The army went into winter quarters near Harper's Ferry, and having engaged board at a farm house for his wife and children whom he had not seen since the beginning of the campaign, he sent his adjutant, Captain Guyton, to bring them to him. The mails were very irregular and he had received no news from his family for some time prior to their arrival. Meanwhile his little son, Vance, and his baby girl whose name commemorated his country's victory and his own honor, had sickened and died. When the mother and the surviving children came to him, after embracing her and them, he looked around for the boy and his baby girl. The mother then told him of their bereavement. One of the children writes that the impression made upon her by her father's grief as he ordered the cot and the crib to be removed, will never be forgotten. His family spent most of the winter with him. After serving for about a year with the Virginian army, he withdrew from this branch of the service and returned to Mississippi. Colonel Falkner had won the esteem of all with whom he was associated, and his retirement was greatly deplored as will be seen from the following letter:

"Lee's Farm"
"April 23d, 1862

"Sir:
"I take the liberty of offering my testimony in behalf of Col. Falkner, late of the 2d Mississippi regiment. This gentleman has served with me in command of that admirable regiment for the last eleven months. Its discipline and instruction during all that time prove his zeal

and capacity—as his courage was proved on the field of Manassas. I regret very much to lose him. If he can be replaced in the army in a position adequate to his merit, be assured that it will be fortunate for the service as well as the efficiency of the troops he may command.

"Most respectfully,
"Your obt. sert.
"J. E. Johnston,
"General."[2]

"The Hon. J. W. Randolph,
      Sec. of War."

I quote from a letter of the same date from Brigadier General Whiting to Mr. Randolph:

Colonel Falkner is one of the best officers in this army. His entire devotion to his regiment, its condition, efficiency and discipline due to him, his extraordinary exertions to recruit it, the skillful manner in which he has commanded it all entitle him to the gratitude of the men, and especially the consideration of the Government. But he has been defeated by demagogues and affords another illustration of the crying evils that the election system in our army has wrought, and is producing. . . .

I forward an order published in the withdrawal of Col. Falkner who will in the impending engagement give me the advantage of his services on my staff. I most earnestly recommend Colonel Falkner to the consideration of the President, once more expressing my regret that he who led the 2nd so well on the day of Manassas, should be so untowardly debarred from its command at present.

In special order No. 96, dated April 22, General W. H. Whiting says:

To the great regret of the Brig. General commanding, a regret expressed also by his superiors Maj. Gen. (E. Kirby) Smith and Gen. Johnston, Colonel Falkner in consequence of the vote of his regiment in the election just held, retires from the command.

The services of this distinguished officer of Mississippi, from Harper's Ferry to Winchester, Manassas, the 21st of July, Evansport to Yorktown, merit the approval of his countrymen and the reward of his government. Faithful, careful, diligent and strict, he has combined and displayed in his career all the qualities which make a colonel of first class. The Brig. General is happy to be able to say, that while he has commanded the brigade, Col. Falkner's regiment has been brought by the constant care of that officer, to a high state of discipline and efficiency.

His adjutant, Captain Guyton writes of him: "A more gallant and brave officer was not found in the service. He stood high in the estimation of his superior officers. In his judgment and foresight they seemed to have the utmost confidence, frequently consulting him in regard to grave matters pertaining to the army." General Whiting had a communication read to all the regiments in his command, in which he complimented the retiring officer not only upon his gallantry in the war then in progress, but on his distinguished services on the battle fields of Mexico.

Colonel Falkner remained at home only a short while, and then under a commission from President Davis he raised a partisan regiment of cavalry and returned to the service. He was in the commands of General Forrest and Chalmers, and took part in the battles of Corinth, Rienzi, Brice's Cross Roads, Harrisburg and Collierville. During this period his characteristic courtesy to woman was illustrated by the following incident: On one occasion having captured the wife of a Federal officer, he sent her to his own home, where she was received as a guest by his wife, and later restored to her own people under a flag of truce. It is interesting to recall that this act of kindness was not forgotten, for, from time to time, the Falkners heard from their former guest.

When the great questions over which the conflict was waged, had been settled by the arbitrament of arms, he accepted the issue in good faith, and began life anew. At the beginning of the war he had accumulated by his industry, energy and sound judgment a considerable fortune, but nearly all this was lost. He began again the practice of law in partnership with Judge J. W. Thompson, and the firm prospered. He identified himself with the Democratic party, and worked to repair the ravages that war had wrought in his State. He writes thus of reconstruction: "Let the past bury the past—let us cultivate a feeling of friendship between North and South. Both parties committed errors—let both parties get back on the right track. Let us try to profit by our sad experience—let us teach forgiveness and patriotism, and look forward to the time when the cruel war shall be forgotten. We have a great and glorious nation of which we are very proud, and we shall make it greater by our love and support. It was a family quarrel, and the family have settled it, and woe to the outsider who shall dare to interfere.

"The Union shall live forever, and those unpatriotic politicians who have maimed it shall be driven into obscurity. Let peace and good will, brotherly love and good faith, exist between the North and South, and let Satan take those who wave the bloody shirt."

He finally retired from the practice of the law in favor of his son, Hon. J. W. T. Falkner, and gave his time to writing and business. A friend writes of him: "As a business man he was industrious, and persevering; quick to see the opportunity and prompt to act, and was very successful in most of his enterprises, the greatest of which was building the Ripley Railroad."

This project originated with Col. Falkner. He was sitting on the square with some merchants, when a number of wagons from Saulsbury, Tennessee, drove up, well loaded with merchandise of various kinds. This served to remind them that trade properly belonging to them was being diverted into other channels. Col. Falkner proposed that they build a railroad to Middleton, Tennessee. At first the suggestion was not approved, but he succeeded in rousing interest in the project, the people of the town subscribed liberally, and he went tirelessly to work. At this time there was a law on the statute books of the State which gave a subsidy of four thousand dollars a mile for the construction of standard gage roads. He set to work to have this statute changed so as to include narrow gage roads and succeeded, though opposed by two railroads then in existence. But there were not sufficient funds to complete the project. Col. Falkner appealed to President Moses Wicks, of the Memphis and Charleston Railroad, and he agreed to furnish the iron and rolling stock, if the company would grade the road and place the ties. The subsidy act expired by limitation August 31, 1872, and so a race against time began. The work was rapidly pushed to completion, and on August 30, a train passed over the whole length of the road containing the commissioners, who passed upon it; and it was agreed that this was a pretty big undertaking for a neighborhood. This is said to have been the first narrow gage railroad built in the United States.

Col. Falkner was the president of the road and succeeded in putting it on a paying basis. It was his purpose to extend the road until he made of it a trunk line to the gulf. He writes in *The Ripley Advertiser*, June, 1886.

> Every one who desires the welfare of the State, should rejoice to see this grand enterprise prosper. I am putting forth all my energy, have laid aside all other business — am investing largely of my private fortune to put the enterprise on its feet. . . .
>
> An idea prevails that we expect to stop at Pontotoc; but we hope and believe we will not stop short of the gulf. We will (if possible) build on an air line from Jackson or Bolivar, Tennessee, to Ship Island. . . . A corps of engineers is now surveying a line from Middleton to Hickman, Kentucky on the Mississippi side who propose to unite with us and make a continuous line from the gulf to some point near Cairo.

But though so busily engaged in this enterprise, he still found time to take an active interest in the political well being of his State. In 1876 he was one of the Tilden electors. At this time the South was still in part under the domination of the "carpet-bag" régime, and Col. Falkner earnestly desired to see his section restored to its rightful place in the national government. He made an active canvass for Mr. Tilden, paying his expenses out of his private purse, and refused to be reimbursed.

No view of the character of Col. Falkner would be complete that did not emphasize his charity. He was the friend of the widow and the father of the fatherless in his community. He kept in mind always his early struggles to gain an education, and to make for himself a place in the world, and was ever ready to help deserving young men with his counsel and with his purse. He did not much encourage the giving of Christmas presents between the various members of his family, but at this time would fill boxes with provisions and clothing to be given to the poor, and would encourage his children to take part in this charity; but in his giving he observed due care to withhold the name of the giver, for he held that true charity brings its own reward.

He was a loving and faithful husband and father, and offered to all his children those educational advantages that had been denied him. One of his many enterprises that redounded to the good of the community was the founding of Stonewall College.

His close reading and study of the masters of English prose, his wide and varied experience as lawyer, soldier, and man of affairs, coupled with close powers of observation, fitted him for readily wielding the pen. His first publication, which came out when he was just grown up, was entitled "The Life of MacCannon" and gave the history of a man who had gained a bad notoriety in the community. He contributed later to a *Know Nothing* paper, entitled *Uncle Sam*. But not until some years after the close of the war did he address himself seriously to writing. He first wrote a drama called "The Lost Diamond." It is a play of war times and abounds in thrilling situations and tragic interest, comparing favorably with "Shenandoah," which has had very marked success on the boards. The play was presented several times in Ripley and always to crowded houses. The actors were young people from the town, and the piece was carefully rehearsed and staged under the direction of the writer. The proceeds were devoted to charitable purposes.

His first novel, "The White Rose of Memphis," appeared first as a serial in *The Ripley Advertiser*. The story attracted favorable attention while it was coming out; later it was published in book form. The book is dedicated to Col. M. C. Gallaway, of the *Memphis Appeal*. "In days long since past, when angry clouds lowered above me and dangers clustered thick around me, a time when friends of mine were few, though greatly to be desired — it was my good fortune to find in your generous heart those noble sentiments of true friendship that have proved of inestimable value to me. . . . I have the honor to inscribe this work to you, only regretting it is not more worthy of the honorable name of the generous friend to whom it is dedicated." The author is one of the first to utilize the Great River for literary purposes. We have a merry party starting from Memphis for a trip to New Orleans. Captain, crew and passengers have decided to make a fête of the maiden trip of *The White Rose of Memphis*. On the night before the party starts a masked ball is given aboard. Then comes the embarcation, and we have a vivid picture in a few words of all engaged from captain to "roust about." The city gathers on the bluff to witness the fine boat as she looses her moorings and glides smoothly from the wharf, first up stream and into the current, then graceful as a sea gull she sweeps by the city and salutes the watching crowd as she passes. The party on board decides to remain in masque; and the Queen of Scotts is appointed mistress of the revel. The Queen of Sheba first decides to hold a rival court, but finally peace is declared between the contending majesties, and the Queen of Sheba with her gentlemen and ladies in waiting join the cortége of the Queen of Scotts. The day is then apportioned by the Queens. In the morning they are to meet upon the deck and have stories; in the afternoon this is to be repeated; and in the evening they are to have, for awhile, recitations and songs, and then to woo Terpsichore until Morpheus summons them.

The plan is approved by all and a constitution under which they are to live adopted. The knight Ingomar is called upon for a story and he so interests the party that his narrative is kept up throughout the voyage. It is a personal sketch and brings in many interesting characters. The book gives a spirited view of the beginnings of the city of Memphis. We have depicted with ability and faithfulness, the brave young man, the loving and acute young woman, the steamboat captain, then a picturesque figure, the detective, the tattling woman, the unjust judge, the faithful negro servant, and last, but by no means least, the devoted dog. The book is melodramatic, but shows a vivid imagination and very considerable talent. The trip of the children afoot from Nashville to Memphis is ably depicted; we bless the world for such characters as Dr. Dodson and Lottie. A reviewer says of the book, "We know of nothing in modern literature more beautiful than the tramp life of the three heroic and innocent children. It is an idyl sweet as any poet sung. The incidents of the story though unusual and startling are introduced with such an artistic hand as to seem natural and inevitable. It is a delightful tribute to woman glowing throughout with the spirit of true chivalry."

He wrote two other books, "The Little Brick Church," a novel, an interesting story of New York of the long ago, and "Rapid Ramblings in Europe," a book of travel.

Col. Falkner was elected to the Legislature of the State from the County of Tippah, November 5, 1889, and on the same day was shot upon the streets of Ripley. He survived only twenty-four hours, thus closed suddenly and tragically the career of a man who had done much for the people of his section and the State at large. His death was mourned by multitudes who knew him throughout the State, and many who knew him not bitterly lamented his untimely taking off. I give below an extract from the masonic tribute paid him by the members of his home lodge. "He was a public spirited citizen, being a promoter of all public works. . . . and to him the people of Tippah, Union and Pontotoc Counties are largely indebted for the railroad facilities which they now enjoy. Of him as an interesting author, a successful lawyer, a faithful citizen, we need not speak as these are things known to all men; but of him as a true and tried Mason we wish to bear testimony."

The closing extract is taken from a resolution passed by the Legislature. "Whereas, We feel that in his death this house has lost a wise counsellor and able debater, the State a true and noble citizen, his county its best friend, his family a devoted head and brave protector; therefore, be it resolved, That in recognition of his preëminent services to his country in war and peace — as soldier, statesman writer and citizen in every walk of life; this preamble and resolution be spread upon the minutes of the House as a weak testimonial of the high esteem in which he is held by this body and the people of the State, and as a feeble tribute to his undying memory."

Notes

1. The writer wishes to express his appreciation of the valuable information given him by Hon. J. W. T. Falkner, and Mrs. N. G. Carter, children of Col. Falkner, and Mrs. M. H. Crockett, his lifelong friend [Bondurant's note].

2. Falkner's modern biographer, Donald Philip Duclos, tells me that Falkner requested this and the following letters in an attempt to be reinstated in the C. S. A. as a general (editor's note).

Flexible Strutless Biplane Travels at Enormous Speed
                                                         Anonymous*

From the standpoint of the spectacular, there is nothing in the aeronautical world that can approach a new American biplane known as the Christmas "Bullet." It is the fastest thing with wings, and in many ways the most astonishing. In flight it has attained the tremendous speed of 195 miles an hour — which is about 50 miles an hour swifter than the record-breaking Loening monoplane.

In design, the "Bullet" is as daring as its performance is remarkable. It is absolutely strutless and does not even employ bracing wires. Its wings have almost birdlike flexibility. They are supple, resilient, and self-adjusting. They are able to bend in three separate planes, which supposedly allows the craft to maintain its equilibrium automatically in any kind of weather and makes it less subject to the racking effect which results in rigid machines when shocks are encountered in the air. When at rest, the wings droop in a negative dihedral, while in flight they can assume positive and negative amounting to 18 in. from horizontal in either direction. Obviously this gives the wing tips a 3-ft. range of flexibility, so that it is not departing from fact to describe their motions as birdlike.

Some of the "Bullet's" specifications are interesting. The span of the top plane is 28 ft., and that of the bottom one, 12 ft. The chords are 5 ft. and 2½ ft., respectively. The angle of incidence amounts to three degrees, the gap, 4 ft., and the length of the fuselage 17¼ ft. A six-cylinder Liberty

*From *Popular Mechanics*, 31, No. 4 (April 1919), 551. For an illustration of the Christmas "Bullet," see the introduction.

motor of 185 hp. is used. The landing speed is 60 miles; three-quarter throttle speed, 175 miles, and extreme normal speed, 197 miles an hour. Contrary to what one might expect from performance, the machine is not light. It weighs, when loaded, 2,100 lb., which means a wing load of 12 lb. to the square foot.

An accident, which is reported to have killed the pilot and badly injured the plane some weeks ago during a test flight, would seem to indicate that the craft has a low factor of safety. The designer, however, makes claims to the contrary. Several machines of the type are being manufactured for foreign shipment, and the construction of a giant model, with wing spread of 180 ft., and four motors aggregating 3,000 hp., is planned for a nonstop transatlantic flight. It is to be a land machine, unequipped for making a descent at sea.

[The Siege of Oxford]   Maud Morrow Brown*

[Isaac A.] Duncan was right in his surmise [when writing his son William, serving with the Lamar Rifles in Virginia] that if the army continued to fall back the enemy would be in possession of Holly Springs, Oxford, and the rest of the county. During the summer [of 1862] the enemy cut the lines of communication so that little could be brought in from the outside. Medicine for the soldiers became scarce; salt was fifty cents a pound and could hardly be got even at that. The County Board of Police (now Board of Supervisors) arranged to get salt for soldiers' families and distributed it, 5 lbs. for adults, 2½ pounds for children. By November Grant's army was advancing on Oxford and the soldiers left in the hospital [which had been temporarily set up in the University buildings] were rushed to Granada. Knowing something of what to expect from what had happened to neighboring towns citizens hastened to try to hide their possessions. Many and ingenious were their hiding places. One woman threw her silver into the cistern. Many buried their valuables. The food supply in the county was getting low. So many men had gone to war that most of the crops had been raised by women, the old men, the young boys and what slave labor they could control. Mr. J. W. Anderson remembers that in the North Eastern part of the county the women had even split rails to fence in their previous crops. The food supplies were hard to hide and usually found by the Yankees. One remarkable hiding place for valuables

*Transcribed by Arthur F. Kinney from "Lafayette County, 1860–1865: A Narrative," a typescript by Mrs. Calvin Brown as chapter historian of the Albert Sidney Johnson Chapter of the United Daughters of the Confederacy, 1935 (pp. 28–33, 36, 47), now housed in the Mississippi Collection, University of Mississippi. Published here for the first time with permission of the curator and the author's estate. Incidents related here may be compared with those in *The Unvanquished* and "My Grandmother Millard."

was the attic of Mr. B. P. Howell's home on what was then called Pontotoc Street. An unceiled [sic] closet in one room gave access to an attic that extended over another large room. Into this attic Mrs. Howell put many of the belongings of her friends. Mr. T. D. Witherspoon, pastor of the Presbyterian Church, had sent her the suit he had bought to be married in, his wedding being postponed when he had gone with the Lamar Rifles. Mrs. Howell also saved the church silver—the baptismal font and the communion service. Mrs. Roscoe sent her imported blankets, her carpets, and her lace curtains, as did Mrs. Isom and many others. A large wardrobe was placed in such a way that its door, when opened, hid the closet door and Mrs. Howell supposed that that saved the closet and the attic for the Yankees always ran for the wardrobe and never once looked into the closet.

Grant reached Oxford December 2, 1862. There is so much information about the devastation of his army that one can hardly choose abstracts. The soldiers overran the county helping themselves as they went. Mrs. W. S. Neilson wrote in her diary:

> The 7th Kansas Jayhawkers camped in our yard and garden and occupied part of the house. Killed nearly all our fowl, took all my meat, potatoes, nearly a barrel of molasses, all the meal, destroyed nearly 300 bushels of corn, burned the plank off the crib, the palings off the garden and yard fences, took all the fodder we had, took jars of butter, milk jars, pans, cups, coffee-pots, sheets, towels, hoes, two carving knives, cooking vessels and a great many little things . . . a fine mule, saddle, bridle, blanket, also a good mule from one of the servants . . . nearly all the Negroes from town. We lost two that went off with them and one boy twelve years old that they shot. He was looking at them on the fence when one of the 31st Illinois shot him. Our town will never look like itself again.

Their taking the servant's mule agrees with "Aunt" Jane Wilbourn's account of the suffering of the Negroes. She says the Yankees robbed them thoroughly, professing not to believe that their masters would allow them to own their belongings but insisting that what was in their cabins really belonged to the white folks. Her master had brought her some gold half moon ear-bobs once when he came home from a trip and they took them—"And I'm mad at those Yankees yet about my ear-bobs," she says. Aunt Jane says the scene in the Yankee camp on the lawn of the Presbyterian church was very laughable. The Yankees had taken many handsome silk frocks from the wardrobes of the white ladies and given them to the Negroes. Then they had these Negro women to cook for them in the camp. Aunt Jane says a big black woman in a silk evening dress with the train tucked up over her arm stirring a stew in a big black pot over a camp-fire looked very funny. And well it might!

Mrs. E. H. Pegues wrote to her son much the same details as Mrs. Neilson wrote in her diary: "Nothing but devastation left [she adds].

Wherever the Yankees went they proclaimed freedom to the Negroes, told them everything left belonged to them to use and sell and do whatever they pleased with. When the Yankees first entered Oxford they broke into Thomas' cellar and destroyed every thing."

There were faithful Negroes and disloyal ones just as there were two kinds of Yankee soldiers. At Liberty Hill the Yankees raided Mrs. Hasting's smokehouse. She asked them to leave her enough to feed her children which they did. At Woodson's Ridge they emptied every smokehouse and raided the residences except that they left in haste when they dashed into the house of Mr. H. H. Kimmons and found his family of eight in bed with the measles. Miss Patty Frierson recalls the happenings at College Hill. The troops that camped there were Sherman's men, getting in practice perhaps for the later march to the sea. They devastated the community pretty completely but their commanding officer protected the church. His chaplain held services there but he put away all the song books for fear his men would abuse them. . . .

Grant's army stayed three weeks in Oxford. Then Van Dorn took Holly Springs and Grant's forces, warned by a message, retreated to Memphis in great haste. One of their camps on the hill side across from the former home of Mr. Huldric Price came up to the cottage where Mrs. Wohlleben lived. She was much surprised to see the camp suddenly thrown into confusion. The bugle sounded "Boots and Saddles," and the troops departed in such haste that they left much equipment behind. Then she missed her baby, Belle, a toddling child. Frantically she and the older children hunted and called. Then they got an answer from beyond the fence. Belle had crawled under. They found her hanging by her left arm over the side of a big black and fairly hot pot of peas, her face besmeared with peas and pot-liquor and her right hand doing valiant service in getting peas into her mouth. The whole neighborhood had peas for supper. It was Christmas day and they had never had a better Christmas meal. . . .

Even after Van Dorn's successful attack at Holly Springs in December, 1862, the Confederate army was not able to regain control of North Mississippi. Van Dorn soon took his troops for the fighting in Tennessee and this section was practically abandoned to the enemy. The army which had been encamped at Abbeville but had been forced to fall back in November to Granada, had been transferred to Tennessee early in February (in diary of Mr. J. A. Bigger). Lafayette County suffered many hardships during this year. Raid after raid swept through destroying what little stores they had been able to get together. Not only did they suffer from northern armies but, especially in the country districts, from Moss Backs — men who were hiding out to escape conscription who would come to the homes pretending to be southern soldiers and demand food. In the Cambridge community there was an outlaw band headed by Raz Boyd. He called himself a Tory, went about stealing horses or any thing else he could find and terrorizing women and children until he was finally hanged. The freed negroes also presented a problem. Near Cambridge the old men and the boys organized the Tallahatchie Home Guards to protect their community, the boys going on into the army as they became old enough or as the age limit was lowered. The young women of the community presented them a flag.

[The Battles of Corinth and Vicksburg]
Fletcher Pratt*

South of the Memphis-Corinth panel were two Confederate forces; Earl Van Dorn, a tall, stately man, noted as a lady-killer, with 16,000 protecting Vicksburg, and Sterling Price, "Old Pop Price" with the same number at Tupelo on the vertical railroad. The latter gave Grant headaches by shifting about rapidly; Washburne of the staff woke at three one morning to find the general chewing the butt of a pencil and muttering over what Price would be up to next. On the 15th September he found out; a cavalry scout from Corinth found Price's whole army in Iuka and at the same time came word that Van Dorn was moving toward Holly Springs. One of two things—either the rebel commanders were preparing a concentric move on Corinth, or they were assembling to cross the Tennessee and go north to wipe out Buell from the rear while Bragg pinned him with a front attack.

Whichever way it was, Grant saw that the Confederates should have joined before moving. He could assassinate Price; Van Dorn was long distant on bad roads. Rosecrans' Corps, 9,000 strong, was ordered south and east from Corinth in a circuit to cut off Price's retreat. Ord's division from Bolivar, 8,000 more, came down from north and west to strike Price in rear when he faced Rosecrans; the reserve was hurried forward to hold Rienzi and keep Van Dorn from sticking his nose into the operation.

Ord arrived first, on the night of the 18th, and the trap was set. He was to fall on when he heard the sound of Rosecrans' cannon. Rosecrans, a majestic-looking man with the face and mind of an old Greek orator, pushed in lustily at dawn, striking the Confederate outposts across a bare knoll just south of the town. Price, dumbfounded and frightened at finding a Union army south of him, put in three-quarters of his force in a

---

*Reprinted, with permission, from *Ordeal by Fire: An Informal History of the Civil War* (New York: Harrison Smith and Robert Haas, 1935), pp. 136–42, 250–57. Faulkner autographed his copy of this book put out by his publishers as he was working on *The Unvanquished*. It contains maps and illustrations by Merritt Cutler and has this epigraph from Ecclesiasticus 44: "Their seed standeth fast, and their children for their sakes. Their bodies are buried in peace; but their name liveth forevermore."

smashing counterstroke that brought Rosecrans to a standstill, and the battle stabilized into a parallel-order rifle fight with little advantage on either side. There was a strong north wind; Ord never heard the guns and did not move till he became impatient, along toward evening. By that time it was too late; Price had found a road leading southeast that Rosecrans, in his excitement, had forgotten to close, and pulled out. There was still a chance to cut up his retreat but Rosecrans went to bed without giving the necessary orders, so that was lost, too. Price lost his trains and some prisoners and it began to dawn on him, as it had on Johnston before, that U. S. Grant was a poor man to take chances with.

Also like Johnston before him, he retreated into Mississippi, where he joined Van Dorn; the two cooked up a plan to stun Grant with a blow. They felt cautiously forward to Grand Junction, at the center of the big triangle of roads, with their united armies, but found Grant had abandoned the effort to keep the Memphis-Corinth railroad operating, so that blow landed in air. However, the point was propitious; they could turn on Memphis, Bolivar or Corinth and whichever one they hit it would hurt. Memphis was hopeless; the river was full of Union warships with large, ugly cannon; a move on Bolivar would bring both the Memphis and Corinth forces onto their rear. Therefore, it had to be Corinth. Fortunately Van Dorn had a map of the forts there, sent through by the star of the rebel spy service, Aurelia Burton. Rosecrans' dispositions were faulty (he was in charge of the place); he had his troops strung out around the weak line of outer redouts, and Battery Robinett, the keystone of the inner defenses, was as yet without guns. The outer works could easily be rolled up by a flank attack, and while the Union forces were in disorder, a heavy column driven through the soft spot at Robinett, splitting their army in two. Van Dorn's superior numbers made the task easy; he circled to the north to gain the added advantage of a surprise attack.

There was nobody to tell him that Aurelia Burton had been in a Federal prison for the last three weeks, or that Rosecrans knew all about her map and his plan. Battery Robinett bristled with masked artillery; Grant had anticipated Van Dorn's deduction. General McPherson, a new man, was coming down with 5,000 to take the Confederates in the rear as soon as they were committed to the attack on Rosecrans, Ord with 7,000 more was moving to cut their line of retreat at Holly Springs.

The Union line was just behind the outer redoubts, divisions McArthur, Davies and Hamilton from west to east, division Stanley in reserve, south of the town. At dawn the drums beat; the rebels came swarming through the woods on McArthur's left in an attack that, for all preparation, was half a surprise. McArthur held around a hill where forts and railroad meet; Van Dorn's other divisions came on against Davies. His defense was too good; a rebel regiment broke, and Davies' men went shouting forward in pursuit. It drew them in an eccentric from McArthur, and a split opened between. Maury of Van Dorn perceived the gap and threw a brigade into it, then another; McArthur's right, Davies' left, were taken in rear and went to pieces. Hamilton tried to save things by turning in from his side, but Price struck him so hard he was held pinned. The Union front began to break up; McArthur lost his hill and the whole line reeled back.

The country was wooded and difficult, the rebel advance slow. Rosecrans brought Stanley up and halted things with a fierce bayonet charge beneath the westering sun, and as night came down drew within his inner lines.

The cannon hammered all night long; all night long the generals rode through their lines, shifting regiments. When morning came, Stanley's fresh division was in Battery Robinett, the Union center; McArthur to his left, Davies and Hamilton on his right, north of the town. Van Dorn ordered Hébert's division to attack McArthur and attract Rosecrans' reserves thither; with the action on that side well begun Price's whole army was to slam straight through Battery Robinett. Everything went wrong with the Confederate arrangements; Hébert had a stomach-ache, and instead of beginning the attack at daybreak sent his surgeon at nine o'clock to report illness. Van Dorn galloped off in a rage to lead the movement in person, and being in a rage, flung his men on in reckless, heavy masses that were riddled by McArthur's cool fire.

Price heard the crash of guns to the south and deeming it meant Hébert's success, headed his columns for Battery Robinett. They ran into the masked artillery and such a storm of shot as no man in that army had seen and lived; two regiments were practically wiped out in less than twenty minutes. The supports broke; Price rallied them and came on again, at the same time swinging his left against Davies. Battery Robinett was too strong; again there was a repulse with ghastly losses, but Davies' outnumbered wing gave way and Price's column got into the town. For half an hour there was a savage street-fight, while the wild black eagle of the Eighth Wisconsin screamed with delight from his perch on their standard. The rebels penetrated to the very yard of Rosecrans' headquarters and the general snapped pistols at them from an upper window, but Hamilton threw a brigade in from his wing, Stanley brought some artillery from the other, and the Confederate advance was driven out with gun and bayonet, utterly broken and disorganized. Van Dorn's last reserve was gone. Just then MacPherson's skirmishers showed up in Price's rear and terrified what was left of his men. Van Dorn's army shambled hastily off into the forests south, with only one sound brigade to cover its retreat.

Rosecrans had his victorious soldiers paraded and rode through the lines congratulating them to the sweet music of their cheers; then treated them to a good meal and twenty-four hours' rest before taking up the pursuit. By that time it was too late; Ord, who had gotten into position with his 7,000, held up the rebels for six hours at the passage of a stream near Holly Springs, but Van Dorn, with no pursuit on his rear, easily flowed round the obstacle and back to safety in the jungles of central Mississippi. The defeat finished him as an army commander; when he arrived at Vicksburg he found an order to turn the command over to General J. C. Pemberton, a relative of Jefferson Davis' wife, who talked so profoundly about military matters in the Richmond drawing-rooms that he was believed to have considerable talent.

History repeats itself. Twice now the Confederates had surprised one of Grant's armies, twice it had meant the end of a commander and the ruin of his army—and twice the army had escaped because there was no pursuit.

Two days later Grant's army was around [Jackson in preparation to lay siege on Vicksburg]. Johnston had begun to fortify, but he was caught half-prepared. He posted his men in the trenches, wiring frantically for reënforcements. Too late; before the key stopped clicking Sherman had stormed his lines at one spot, McPherson had cut through another. Grant came into town so fast that when he stepped into the mill, he found the looms still spinning army cloth with "C. S. A." woven in each bolt. Lesson—never kick a man when he's down—the year before some of these same Union soldiers had been led through Jackson, footsore, hungry prisoners from Shiloh; when they asked for food the generous Mississippians threw clods at them for dam-yankees. Now they burned the place out, enjoying themselves very much.

The country was bad for scouting and Pemberton had few horse; it was the 11th May before he learned that Grant was pointed on Jackson. By this time he was 42,000 strong, enough to fight; he had a touch of inspiration—strike south, sever the umbilical cord of communications that must bind Grant to the river at Grand Gulf, then round up the starving Union army. On the morning of the 14th his advance elements crossed the Big Black toward Cayuga and Pemberton learned to his horror that Grant's movement was already full born, with no communications at all. That same night came a despairing telegram from Johnston—"Turn at once . . . too late—" and then the wire went dead as Sherman's bluecoats dashed into the Jackson streets.

Pemberton turned round and hurried back toward Jackson as fast as his bandy legs would carry him but that last broken message had the right of it—too late. Just outside Edwards' Station, his cavalry points were taken and he realized that the Army of the Tennessee was upon him. He tried to retreat and slip away around a Union flank. Too late; the roads were full of Federal troops, they would eat up a retreat. There is a high hill just south of the main road, Champion's Hill. Pemberton ordered up his artillery here and formed for a stand, with division Stevenson holding the hill, divisions Bowen and Loring across the southward roads.

The Union army was coming west on parallel roads. McClernand had the advance out of Raymond with four divisions, Grant himself found division Hovey on the north road and rode with it toward Champion's Hill, speed, speed. The rebels' guns there opened just as a messenger arrived from McClernand to say he had found more Confederates in line across the fields on his front. Grant made a plan out of hand, the old plan of Iuka and Corinth, sound, simple and brilliant — send Hovey against Champion's Hill with drive enough to attract Pemberton's reserves thither; then let McClernand with his four big divisions break through the weak Confederate line before him, fall on their rear as they faced Hovey and bag them all. The time for delivery of the message would be just enough to let Hovey's attack draw Pemberton's eye. He wrote the order, then rode in with Hovey's van.

They rushed the hill through a hot fire, and carried along by Grant's energy, gained the southern peak, piercing the Confederate center. Pemberton, alarmed at the prospect this opened, drew reënforcements from Loring and Bowen. Laggard McClernand ruined the plan by failing to press home; Pemberton's reserves collected round Hovey and drove him out. But Grant was not done yet; divisions Logan and Crocker of McPherson's had come up while the fight was going on. In a moment Grant changed plans from breaking one rebel flank to breaking the other, and sent the two new divisions round the head of the hill to attack it from the north.

The eminence was slotted with ravines and swept by artillery fire, but Logan and Crocker lapped clear round the Confederate left, went up the crest with irresistible dash and hurled the defenders down the other side into rout, their organization completely broken. The pursuit was so hot that Grant's men got the only crossings of Baker's Creek before division Loring, retiring under McClernand's languid pressure. Loring found the passes held and wandered south along the stream, leaving wagons, cannon, finally muskets and cooking utensils, and weeks later filtered through to Mobile with a few worn-out men.

That night a spy reached Grant's camp; he had been long among the rebels, they had made him official courier and he bore a dispatch from Johnston to Pemberton — Come north with all haste, leave Vicksburg to its fate, but save your army. Too late. Grant sent Sherman and McPherson to drive the flying enemy with speed and double speed behind the Big Black to spoil any such movement. The next morning they were before the bridge there; the rebels had a *tête-de-pont*, with trenches and artillery, to hold the crossing. As Grant rode along, surveying it, a colonel he did not know accosted him with a message. When Halleck in Washington had heard of the campaign, the mere thought of such audacity nearly drove him out of his mind; the rash leader was unreachable by telegraph (no communications!) but this officer had ridden day and night with peremptory orders that the army should be returned to the west bank of the Mississippi. "That will be difficult under the present circumstances," remarked Grant.

"Shall I report, sir, that you refuse to obey?" demanded the colonel, angrily. At that moment there was an outburst of cheering; both men turned round to see General Lawler go past in his shirt-sleeves, leading a charge for the *tête-de-pont*. The Confederate line burst like a rotten melon; Grant filed the peremptory order among the other forgotten correspondence in his pocket and a day and a half later the Army of the Tennessee laid Vicksburg under siege.

As Sherman stood looking down from the Chickasaw Bluffs he had striven in vain to win the year before, he said to Grant: "Until this moment I never believed in your success. But this *is* a campaign; this is a success, if we never take the town." It was — one of the most flashing strokes on record; in seventeen days Grant had marched 130 miles, split the Confederate forces in two, won five battles and besieged their greatest stronghold. Pemberton had lost 14,000 men, Grant barely 2,000 — Julius Caesar could have done no more.

Now the siege. The works were very strong; on the first day Grant tried an assault. It broke down with loss, like Lee's at Malvern Hill; just as the general ordered withdrawal there came a note from McClernand that he had partial possession of two forts and wanted pressure elsewhere to help him win them. Sherman was sent in again; there was another repulse with more loss, and then Grant discovered that McClernand had been drawing the long bow; he had gained nothing but the ditches before his two forts. To round the matter out the politician-general issued a vainglo-rious order of the day saying that if Sherman and McPherson had done their parts as bravely as he, the place had been taken. Grant learned of the order first through the newspapers; within the hour McClernand's expla-nation was demanded; within twenty-four he had been sent home to do his growling in Illinois and Ord had been appointed to his corps.

The siege. Heavy guns came down river; day and night they threw shells into the place, while the parallels crept close. Every house was shot through, the inhabitants lived in holes in the clay. "Mother didn't want to have a cave. She was afraid the roof would come down and said she would rather be killed outright than buried alive. A shell passed through the room just as we left the breakfast table, and one side of the house looked like a pepper-shaker, it was so full of Minie balls. Mrs. Lovatt and her baby were killed by a cannon-ball that day." Provisions ran desperately short, flour cost $1,000 a barrel, meat $250 a pound.

Bill of Fare, Vicksburg Hotel

SOUP
Mule Tail

BOILED
Mule bacon and poke greens. Mule ham, canvassed.

ROAST
Mule sirloin

DESSERT
White oak acorns
Beech-nuts

Blackberry-leaf tea

All through May and June this went on, while Johnston strove to gather an army of relief in the background. He got it up to 30,000, but Stanton was rushing more men to Grant on every boat down river. On the 28th June Sherman turned to face Johnston with 40,000 men and blood in his eye; the army of relief retreated hurriedly. Curious symbolical note — as Sherman rode through a plantation yard he noticed a book lying in the mud and dismounted to rescue it. It was a copy of "The Constitution of the United States" and on the flyleaf was written — "My property — Jefferson Davis."

All through May and June. On the first day of July there was only one moldy biscuit apiece for the garrison and somebody left a note on General Pemberton's doorstep — "I tell you plainly men are not going to lie here and perish. Hunger will compel a man to do almost anything. — One of your soldiers." He called a council of war; the generals agreed that further resistance was futile and too late; and on the fourth of July, the glorious fourth, the greatest fourth since '76, the flag came down, the Confederate army stacked arms, and Grant's men marched into "the Gibraltar of the West" singing "The Battle-Cry of Freedom." Six days later the steamer *Imperial* ran through unarmed from St. Louis to New Orleans and Lincoln proclaimed exultantly "The Father of Waters once more flows unvexed to the sea."

[War Comes to Holly Springs]   Olga Reed Pruitt*

The first raid made by Federal soldiers on Holly Springs occurred early in 1862. The raiding party came from the south and stopped to ask some questions of an old Negro before entering the town.

"Who is the richest man in town?" they asked.

"Mr. William Mason," the old man answered promptly and innocently.

That was the information they wanted so they sought out this house, the home of William Mason and his family.

*"War Comes to Holly Springs," "How Music Saved Holly Springs," and "High Brass on the Move" from *It Happened Here: True Stories of Holly Springs* (Holly Springs, Miss.: privately printed, 1950), pp. 48–49, 52–55, 58–59. Pruitt relies on memoirs, scrapbooks, newspaper clippings, and interviews for the details of well-known stories. Holly Springs is about twenty miles north of Oxford, and about sixteen miles from the location of the Sartoris plantation. Reprinted with permission of Olga Reed Pruitt.

Pushing their way inside, they ransacked the place, the completeness of their destruction being exceeded only by their fiendish ruthlessness.

With their bayonets, they gleefully punched out the eyes in portraits done in oils. They tore the keys out of the piano. They piled the china on the walk and with their guns, shattered the fragile pieces. They made raucous sport out of dashing priceless cups and saucers against the walls. As a parting indignity, a bayonet was thrust through the front door.

A few months later, in mid-December, the Mason family watched as Grant's army jauntily began the march on Vicksburg from its Holly Springs base. For three days and nights the Federals passed the house, marching four abreast, and the Masons prayed that they'd never reach Vicksburg.

To the east, Confederate General Van Dorn knew that Grant was on the march, leaving his base of operations with supplies valued at $8,000,000 stored here almost unprotected. On Dec. 20, with a handful of men, Van Dorn raided the town, totally destroying or capturing all Federal stores. Loss of his supplies made it necessary for Grant to turn back to Memphis and plan the Vicksburg attack via the Mississippi River.

Holly Springs was again on the line of march. Angry, hatred-filled Federal soldiers began returning on December 21 and the rear guard in the backward movement left the city on Jan. 13, 1863. During that time the country from Oxford to the Tennessee line was laid waste. Holly Springs presented a scene of terror and horror.

William Mason's home escaped complete destruction only because it had already been denuded of everything but its imperishable pride.

The Yankees themselves gave Maria Bodie Mason the credit for saving Holly Springs from destruction in 1863. Her Steinway piano was her weapon of defense.

Maria went with her husband, Carrington Mason, to live in Memphis following their marriage in 1860. Soon, however, war seemed inevitable between the states and his father, William Mason, advised the young couple to come out to Holly Springs.

"Memphis is sure to have trouble," he told them, "and Holly Springs will be quieter. It will be off the path of either army."

Little did he dream that Holly Springs would be shuttled back and forth in the possession of the armies of the North and South until it had changed hands 59 times.

This house was then a two-story mansion, and Maria and Carrington moved in and settled down.

Maria's prized possession was her Steinway piano. When young Mason married the Tennessee heiress, they spent their honeymoon in New York where she had been educated. As a surprise wedding gift, William Mason ordered the piano and Henry E. Steinway, founder of Steinway and Sons, selected and presented the rosewood instrument to Maria on her honeymoon. It was the only Steinway and by far the most expensive piano in North Mississippi when General Grant made Holly Springs his head-quarters and base of supplies in 1862.

With Vicksburg as his objective, Grant had moved his family, the whole array of general staff, women, hangers-on, traders and what-not, to Holly Springs and began massing an enormous store of ammunition and supplies for the Vicksburg offensive. For two weeks the Federal Army rested here then began the march south, leaving a brigade of infantry and a portion of the 7th. Illinois Cavalry here.

Colonel Murphy had been left in charge of the garrison when, on December 20, General Earl Van Dorn surprised his army at dawn and so completely destroyed Federal supplies that the attack on Vicksburg was delayed until early in 1863.

In the pale light of morning, Van Dorn's men stormed into Holly Springs down the Ripley road. As the 1st Mississippi Cavalry, the advance regiment of McCullough's brigade, galloped in from the northeast and pressed on toward the Fair Grounds in search of the Federal cavalry, many of Grant's men ran from their tents firing as they came.

The 2nd Missouri dismounted at the edge of town and charged on foot dispersing any infantry that was encountered. The Texas brigade approached from the east, coming in by the railroad depot. A detachment of Texans was posted so as to prevent surprise from the south.

The Tennessee brigade approached from a northerly direction, preventing possible reinforcements from Bolivar as well as watching the dirt roads coming from Memphis on the west.

A long train of boxcars loaded with rations and clothing just ready to be sent to the Federal front, was standing in the railroad yard and a torch was applied and the train consumed. The depot buildings, the Court House and many houses were filled with supplies of all kinds. The public square contained hundreds of bales of cotton. A large brick livery stable and the adjacent Masonic temple were packed with unopened cases of carbines and Colt's army six-shooters. From 7: am to 4: pm.; army depots were first plundered and then burned; sutler's shops shared a like fate. Cotton speculators were required to share their money with the victors but were allowed to witness the burning of their stolen cotton without personal restraint. The torch was applied to all that could not be carried away.

The women of Holly Springs, many of them still in their night gowns and with their dishevelled hair floating in the winter wind, clapped their hands with joy and shouted encouragement to the raiders. The scene was indescribable, with Federals running, Confederates, yelling and pushing, tents and buildings burning, torches flaming, guns popping, sabres clanking, negroes and abolitionists begging for mercy. More than 2,500 prisoners were taken, Col. Murphy's infantry surrendering even as 4,000 men, sent back by Grant for his relief, pressed on to Holly Springs from the south. Van Dorn's Texans and Tennesseans held them off until the Confederate victory was complete.

By a little after 4: pm all the Federal property, save what could be appropriated, had been destroyed, the prisoners had been parolled and Van Dorn resumed his march northward.

The raid so incensed Federal authorities that troops under Gen. Benjamin Henry Grierson were sent to take revenge on Holly Springs. These troops became known locally as "Grierson's Thieves."

Maria Mason was leisurely dressing one morning after the raid when her negro maid, Adelaide, dashed wildly upstairs.

"Lawd, Miss Maria, look" she gasped.

From behind the window curtains, they counted 30 handsomely uniformed Federal officers hitching their horses to the picket fence.

"What we gon' do, Miss Maria, what we gon' do?" Adelaide panted, wringing her hands.

"Now, now, Adelaide," her mistress comforted, patting her shoulder, "don't be frightened. Remember we are Southern women." She drew herself up proudly and her eyes flashed. "Go down and invite them in. Tell them your mistress will be down when she has finished dressing."

"Please, Miss Maria, I can't," Adelaide pleaded bleakly but tottered away never the less, to do as she was told.

Mrs. Mason took her time and carefully added extra dainty touches to her dress.

Suddenly, someone downstairs began running tentative fingers along the keys of the piano. Softly at first then skillfully and happily as though savoring to the fullest the perfect tones as they rippled from his fingers. Maria could hardly believe her ears. A Yankee, playing like that.

Then the music swung exultantly into her own song, "Whispering Wind," dedicated to her by Wollenhaupt, the composer. Curiosity filled her as she descended the stairs and, with the conscious dignity of a well-born, proud Southern lady, swept into the parlor. Only then did she realize that it was Gen. Grierson and his staff who were her visitors.

With the ease of one born to the graceful conventions, Maria Mason welcomed the Federal officers to her home.

"But who was the lovly musician?" she asked.

"The General," they told her, proudly.

She complimented Gen. Grierson on his playing and asked him to play again.

"Where did you get this handsome piano, Mrs. Mason?" he asked her. She told him and then asked, "Under whom did you study, General?"

"I studied under Wollenhaupt in New York."

"What a happy coincidence," she cried. "I, too, studied under Wollenhaupt."

"Then possibly you can help me, Mrs. Mason," he said quickly. "Wollenhaupt told me that his finest pupil was a Miss Maria Bodie from

Nashville. He asked me to inquire about her while I was in the South. Did you ever hear of her?"

"Why, yes," she laughed, flushing, and then watched him gasp in amazement as she said, "I was Maria Bodie."

She opened a bound volume and showed him the copy of "Whispering Wind" dedicated to Maria Bodie in Wollenhaupt's own handwriting. Gen. Grierson could hardly believe it.

Twice each day, after that, at ten and four the General came with members of his staff and they had a concert. He played and Maria Mason played then they played duets together. He ordered a cordon of soldiers placed around the house to protect it and sent baskets of food. Maria Mason, wise with the wisdom of Confederate women, invited her friends to meet him.

Gen. Grierson finally told her what his mission was in Holly Springs. He had been sent to destroy the town as revenge for the Van Dorn raid. Instead, he had reported that he found a group of intelligent, cultivated people and that many of them were nursing wounded Federals in their homes.

"And you and your piano can take credit for saving Holly Springs," he said.

One Colonel Everett, with the Federal army under Gen. Grant, was quartered upstairs [at Butler's Drug Store] at the time. Being awakened by the thunder of cavalry charging along the plank street below, he rushed downstairs.

Peering around the corner of the building in the dim light of early morning, Col. Everett saw the Texas brigade approaching down Van Dorn Avenue, firing as they came. And the Texans saw him peeking fearfully at them. They joyously took a shot at him which clipped the building above his head.

Falling fragments of brick and mortar were just the incentive needed by the Colonel for hasty action. He turned and began running south down Market Street, the dignity of high brass being forgotten in the urgency of his need. He came to Sims stage coach stand and galloped briskly across the lot; he traversed the cemetery, darting around some graves, jumping others, until he finally cleared the rear fence where he lost himself in the woods beyond. There he stayed in trembling "retirement" until the raid was over and he joined returning Federal forces coming up from the south.

A few local citizens witnessed the officer's wild flight and Col. Everett returned to Holly Springs in 1916 and himself related his experiences of the day.

During Van Dorn's raid, a Federal pay car at the depot was blown up and the paymaster's office near Palmer's Grocery Store on the square destroyed. Federal currency cluttered the sidewalks and streets uptown but the proud citizens refused to touch the vile stuff. At the depot, however, a local resident was passing on a mule. He dismounted, laid great sheafs of uncut bills across his mule for a blanket then rode home to start a fortune with the currency he had picked up.

The Battle of Hurricane Creek   Howard L. Bahr and William K. Duke*

The cavalry engagement known as the Battle of Hurricane Creek was fought on 13 August 1864 between elements of Federal General Edward Hatch's brigade and the understrength Confederate division of General James R. Chalmers. In a strategic context, the engagement was one result of General William T. Sherman's determination to occupy Bedford Forrest in north Mississippi, thereby distracting that capable raider from the vulnerable Federal communications behind the Atlanta campaign. In the spring and summer of 1864, four successive Federal expeditions were launched from Memphis, specifically charged to "follow Forrest to the death." The fourth and most ambitious of these incursions set out from Grand Junction, Tennessee, on 2 August 1864, comprising 18,000 men of all arms under the command of General A. J. Smith. A veteran force, Smith's column would see a number of clashes in the month ahead. Not least among these would be the fight at Hurricane Creek.

For the first ten days of August, the Confederate force in opposition was commanded by General Chalmers and comprised a 1,000-man cavalry brigade and Captain J. C. Thrall's battery of artillery. This force skirmished with the head of the Federal column and fought a major action at the Tallahatchie River, followed by a fourteen-mile running battle to Oxford and beyond. On the evening of 10 August Forrest, with the balance of Chalmers' division, joined Chalmers in Oxford, and on the afternoon of the eleventh this reconstituted command moved into position on the south bank of Hurricane Creek, some five miles north of the Oxford courthouse.

The topography of the creek bottom favored the Confederates, as the high ground rose on their side. On these heights, with the aid of impressed Negroes, Forrest constructed a line of rail and log breastworks in the very face of the Yankees at Abbeville. Throughout the long afternoon and night the Confederates worked unmolested, and by the afternoon of the twelfth

*This essay was written for this volume and is published here for the first time by the permission of the authors. A longer version of this study, "The Wet August: Andrew J. Smith's Mississippi Campaign," appeared in *Civil War Times, Illustrated* 16 (November 1977), 10–19. Faulkner situates Sartoris near Hurricane Creek, where he often took Boy Scout troops, to examine the battlegrounds during the time of writing *Flags in the Dust*.

their line was established. A party of Federals made a show in front of the works and were driven away; beyond that the twelfth saw no action.

Why did Smith, aggressive fighter that he was, allow these rebels to concentrate and entrench? Why, with the weight of 18,000 men, did he not bring a constant and overwhelming pressure to bear on Forrest's understrength command? Part of the answer lies in the old axiom that no foot of ground in north Mississippi could be held for the Union unless a Union soldier was standing on it. Harassed by guerillas, burdened by vast stores and his responsibility to keep the Mississippi Central Railroad open, Smith kept his force strung out along the line of the railroad from Holly Springs to Abbeville and could only bring the point to bear on the enemy. More conjectural — but reasonable in the light of previous Federal experience — is the presumption that the mere weight of Forrest's name was enough to make Smith cautious. Whatever the reason, Smith made no real move until 13 August, when he launched the advance that would result in the Battle of Hurricane Creek.

This Federal column, made up of five regiments of infantry, a battery of horse artillery, and a brigade of cavalry, left Abbeville about noon. Almost immediately the two cavalry companies in the van (B and I of the 2nd Iowa) met Confederate skirmishers, whom they drove for some three miles before encountering a body of Confederate cavalry. This new opposition was stiff enough to throw the advance into confusion, but at last the balance of the 2nd Iowa was brought up in support and after a brief skirmish the Confederates were driven away. The Federal column resumed its advance and drew up at last on the north bank of Hurricane Creek.

The ensuing engagement, which would last until dusk, was remembered by several participants as being the sharpest of the campaign. Certainly the casualty figures available reveal that, at least for the Federals, it was the most expensive; Smith lost six killed and nineteen wounded that day. These figures are ludicrous when compared with the carnage of even a secondary battle in this war, and the military advantage won and lost was small. Yet Hurricane Creek is significant to the campaign, and we can be sure it was of sublime significance to the six Federals and the unknown number of Confederates who died there.

The engagement began and ended a cavalry fight. No Confederate infantry was on the field — indeed, there was none involved in the campaign at all — and the Federal infantry spent the afternoon lying in the woods under Confederate artillery fire. They would not cross the creek until the Confederates had left the field.

But if the infantry did not move forward, at least it did not retreat, so that the center of the Federal line was secure. Hatch was therefore free to use his left and right wings of cavalry against the Confederate flanks. Colonel M. H. Starr, with the 6th and 9th Illinois regiments, went downstream to strike the Confederate left. His main attack was directed against Colonel Hinchie P. Mabry's brigade, with only the left of Tyree Bell's being engaged. Colonel Starr was engaged some three hours, but finally executed a crossing of the creek and drove the Confederates from their works.

Meanwhile, Colonel Thomas P. Herrick, moving against the Confederate right, encountered stiff resistance from the entrenched rebels. The 7th Kansas Cavalry (Jayhawkers) held the right of Herrick's brigade, and Sergeant Morris Davidson of Company A was sent with four men to scout a gap between the Federal left wing and center. Realizing that a similar gap existed in the Confederate line, Davidson and his companions dismounted, crossed the creek, and came up behind the left of Colonel Robert McCulloch's Confederate brigade. The Kansans opened fire at once and McCulloch, thinking he was outflanked, fell back. At the same time Starr was driving the Confederate left and with the collapse of both wings Forrest was obliged to fall back on Oxford.

The Battle of Hurricane Creek was over. Forrest was in Oxford again and Hatch, with darkness coming on, was reluctant to pursue. After some countermarching by the infantry the Federal force retired to their bivouac at Abbeville.

The Battle of Hurricane Creek was typical of thousands of small-unit actions during the Civil War. Fought without any hope of decisive victory by either side, such engagements were little more than gambits on the part of commanders whose primary concern was the strategic situation. In this light Hurricane Creek may be considered a Confederate victory, since Smith's failure to follow up his advantage was contrary to the nature of his mission. On the other hand, the campaign as a whole was a Federal success as it accomplished the goal set out for it by General Sherman: to distract Forrest from the Federal lines of communication in Georgia and Tennessee.

Smith would remain in north Mississippi until 23 August. The last days of the campaign would see the burning of Oxford and Forrest's memorable — but ultimately futile — raid on Memphis. Chalmers, with the gallant remnant of his command, would continue to harass the Federal column, fighting his last action with the Federal rearguard at Abbeville on the twenty-third. Though overshadowed by subsequent events — particularly the Memphis raid — the Battle of Hurricane Creek remains a significant footnote in the checkered fortunes of Federal and Confederate arms in north Mississippi.

II BEGINNINGS

Landing in Luck

The machine levelled off and settled on the aerodrome. It turned and taxied back and stopped, headed into the wind again, its engine running idle. The instructor in the forward cockpit faced about and raised his goggles.

"Fairish," he said, "not so bad. How many hours have you had?"

Cadet Thompson, a "barrack's ace," who had just made a fairly creditable landing, assumed an expression of assured confidence.

"Seven hours and nine minutes, sir."

"Think you can — hold that stick back, will you? — think you can take her round alone?"

"Yes, sir," he answered as he had answered at least four times a day for the last three days, with the small remaining part of his unconquered optimism in his voice. The instructor clim[b]ed slowly out onto the lower wing, then to the ground, stretching his legs. He got a cigarette from his clothes after a fashion resembling sleight-of-hand.

"You've got to solo some day. The C.O. gave us all a raggin' last night. It's chaps like you that give this stage such a name for inefficiency. Here you have had seven hours, and yet you never know if you are goin' to land on this aerodrome or down at Borden. And then you always pick a house or another machine to land on. What ever brought you to think you could fly? Swear I don't know what to do with you. Let you try it and break your neck, or recommend you for discharge. Get rid of you either way, and a devil[i]sh good thing, too."

A silence that hung heavily about Thompson's unhappy head. The instructor, sucking his cigarette, stared off across the aerodrome, where

*From "Weekly Short Story," ed. Professor Erwin, *Mississippian*, 9, No. 10 (26 Nov. 1919), 2, 7; transcribed by Arthur F. Kinney. Certain peculiarities of spelling and punctuation, which may be Faulkner's own experimentation, are left unchanged; only obvious typographical errors are emended as noted. Reprinted by permission of Jill Faulkner Summers, executrix of the Faulkner Estate. This is Faulkner's first published fiction; Cadet Thompson may be an early sketch of what eventually becomes Young John Sartoris.

other wild and hardy amateurs took off, landed and crashed. A machine descended tail high, levelled off too soon and landed in a series of bumps like an inferior tennis ball.

"See that chap there? He's probably had half your time but he makes landings alone. But you, you cut your gun and sit up there like a blind idiot and when you condescend to dive the bus, you try your best to break our necks, yours and mine too; and I'll say right now, that's somethin' none of you rockin' chair aviators is goin' to do. Well, its your neck or my reputation, now. Take her off, and what ever you do, keep your nose down."

Thompson pulled down his goggles. He had been angry enough to kill his officer for the better part of a week, so added indignities rested but lightly upon him. He was a strange mixture of fear and pride as he opened the throttle wide and pushed the stick forward—fear that he would wreck the machine landing, and pride that he was on his own at last. He was no physical coward, his fear was that he would show himself up before his less fortunate friends to whom he had talked largely of spins and side slips and gliding angles.

All-in-all, he was in no particularly safe frame of mind for his solo flight. He gained spe[e]d down the field. The tail was off the ground now and Thompson, more or less nervous, [though] he had taken the machine off like a veteran with the instructor aboard, pulled the stick back before the machine had gained speed sufficient to rise. It lurched forward and the tail sank heavily, losing more speed. He knew that he had gone too far down the field and should turn back and take off again, so he closed the throttle. When the noise ceased he heard the instructor shouting at him, and the splutter of a motor cycle. Sending after him, were they? Cadet Thompson was once more cleanly angry. He jerked the throttle open.

His subconscious mind had registered a cable across the end of the field, and he had flown enough to know that it was touch and go as to whether he would clear it. He was afraid of rising too soon again and he knew that he would not stop in time were he to close the throttle now. So, his eyes on the speed indicator, he pulled the stick back. The motion at once became easier and he climbed as much as he dared.

A shock; he closed his eyes, expecting to go over and down on his back in the road below. When nothing happened he ventured a frightened hurried glance. Below him was the yellow of a wheat field and the aerodrome far to the rear.

So the cable had broken! Must have, for here he was still going forward. His altimeter showed two hundred feet. Thompson felt like shouting. Now he'd show 'em what flying was. Rotten, was he? He'd pull a perfect landing and walk up to that officer and tell him just what kind of a poor fish he was.

"Blasted Englishman," he said, ["]thinks he's the only man in this wing who can really fly. Bet if he'd a' hit that cable he'd a' been on his back in that road, right now. Wish t'hell he was."

He made his turn carefully. Below at the e[d]ge of the aerodrome stood the ambulance, its crew gaping foolishly at him. "Like fish," he thought, "like poor fish." He leaned out of his cockpit and gestured pleasantly at them, a popular gesture known to all peoples of the civilized world.

Eight hundred feet. "High enough," he decided, and made another circle, losing height. He picked his spot on the field. "Now," he thought, cut the throttle and pushed the stick forward. He found a good gliding angle, wires singing, engine idle and long flames wrapping back from the exhausts. The field was filled with people running about and flapping their arms. Another machine rose to meet him. He opened the throttle and closed it again, a warning. "Why'n the hell don't they get off and lemme land?" he wondered.

The other machine passed him in a long bank, its occupants shouting at him; one of them carried something to which he gestured and pointed frantically. Thompson came out of his dive. They circled again and he saw that the object was about the size and shape of a wheel? A wheel from the landing gear of a machine. What kind of a joke was this? Why had they brought up a wheel up to show him? He'd seen lots of wheels. Had two on his machine — on his machine — wheels? Then Thompson remembered the cable. He had stripped a wheel on that cable, then. There was nothing else it could mean. His brain assimilated this fact calmly. Having lost a wheel, he had nothing to land on. Therefore it were quite pointless to bother about landing, immediately, anyway. So he circled off and climbed, following cautiously by the other machine, like two strange dogs meetin[g].

"Sir," said an orderly, entering the mess where the C.O[.] and three lesser lights were playing bridge, "sir, the Flight Commander, B Flight, reports that a cadet is abaht to crash."

" 'Crash?' " repeated the C.O.

"Out 'ere sir. Yes, sir, 'e 'assn't got no landing gear."

" 'No landing gear?' What's this? What's this?"

["]Yes, sir. 'E wiped it orf a-taking orf, sir. 'E's abaht out of petrol and the Flight Commander says 'e'll be a-coming down soon, sir."

"My word," said the C.O., going to the door and closely followed by the others.

"There 'e is, sir, that's 'im in front."

"My word," said the C.O. again and went off toward the hangars at a very good gait.

"What's this? What's this?" Approaching the group of officers.

"Cadet Thompson, sir," volunteered one, ["]Mr. Bessing's cadet. Oh, Bessing!"

Bessing came over, lifting his feet nervously.

"What's all this, Mr. Bessing?" The C.O. watched him narrowly. An instructor gets a bad name when his cadet crashes, he is responsible for the cadet's life as well as the machine.

"Rotten take off, sir. He tried to rise too soon, and when he failed, instead of comin' back and tryin' again, he carried right on. Struck that cable and lost his right wheel and he's been sittin' up there ever since. We sent another chap to pull him up a bit. He's almost out of petrol and he'll have to come down soon."

"H-m. Didn't send him up too soon, did you, Mr. Bessing?"

"Chap's had seven hours, sir,["] he protested, and produced Thompson's card.

The C.O. studied it a moment, then returned it.

"Wharton, sir["] He helped the C.O. to a light and lit a cigarette for himself.

"Good lad, good lad," said the C.O., shading his eyes as he [stared] into the sky. "Something in you people at this wing, though. Cadets and officers both. N.C.O.'s got it, too. G.O.C. gave me a jolly raggin' not a fortnight ago. Do something. Do something, swear I will."

The drone from the engines above suddenly ceased. Thompson was out of petrol at last. The two machines descended in a wide spiral, and they on the earth stood watching him as he descended, as utterly beyond any human aid as though he were on another planet.

"Here they come," Bessing muttered half aloud. "If he only remembers to land on his left wing—the fool, oh, the blind, bounding fool!"

For Thompson's nerve was going as he neared the earth. The temptation was strong to kick his rudder over and close his eyes. The machine descended, barely retaining headway. He watched the approaching ground utterly unable to make any pretence of levelling off, paralyzed; his brain had ceased to function, he was [all] staring eyes watching the remorseless earth. He did not know his height, the ground rushed past too swiftly to judge, but he expected to crash any second. Thompson's fate was on the laps of the Gods.

The tail touched, bounded, scraped again. The left wing was low and the wing tip crumpled like paper. A tearing of fabric, a strut snapped, and he regained dominion over his limbs, but too late to do anything—were there anything to be done. The machine struck again, solidly, slewed around and stood on its nose.

Bessing was the first to reach him.

"Lord, Lord!" he was near weeping from nervous tension. ["]Are you all right? Never expected you'd come through, never expected it! Didn't think to see you alive! Don't ever let anyone else say you can't fly. Comin' out of that was a trick many an old flyer couldn't do! I say, are you all right?"

Hanging face downward from the cockpit, Cadet Thompson looked at Bessing, surprised at the words of this cold, short tempered officer. He forgot the days of tribulation and insult in this man's company, and his recent experience, and his eyes filled with utter adoration. Then he became violently ill.

That night Thompson sat gracefully on a table in the writing room of a down town hotel, tapping a boot with his stick and talking to sundry companions.

" — and so, when my petrol gave out, I knew it was up to me. I had already thought of a plan — I thought of several, but this one seemed the best — which was to put my tail down first and then drop my left wing, so the old bus wouldn't turn over and lie down on me. Well, it worked just as I had doped it out, only a ditch those fool A.M.'s had dug right across the field, mind you, tripped her up and she stood on her nose. I had thought of that, too, and pulled my belt up. Bessing said — he's a pretty good scout — "

"Ah-h-h — " they jeered him down profanely.

"Look at the nerve he's got, will you?"

"He' — "

"Ah, we know you! Why, the poor bum crashed on his solo, and listen at the line he's giving us!"

["]Well, Bessing said — "

"Bessing said! Bessing said! Go tell the G.O.C. what Bessing said!"

"Dammit, don't I know what Bessing said? Ask him! That's all. [You're] a bunch of poor hams that think you can fly! Why I got an hour and a half solo time. You poor fish. Ask Bessing! there's a guy that knows what's what."

He flung out of the room. They watched him with varying expressions.

"Say,["] spoke one, a cadet but recently enlisted and still in ground school: "D' you think he really did all that? He must be pretty good."

"That guy? That guy fly? He's so rotten they can't discharge him. Every time he goes up they have to get a gun and shoot him down. He's the "f" out of flying. Biggest liar in the R.A.F."

Thompson passed through again, with Bessing, and his arm was through the officer's. He was deep in discussion evidently, but he looked up in time to give them a cheerfully condescending:

"Hello, you chaps."

The Hill

William Faulkner*

Before him and slightly above his head, the hill crest was clearly laid on the sky. Over it slid a sibilant invis[i]bility of wind like a sheet of water, and it seemed to him that he might lift his feet from the road and swim upward and over the hill on this wind which filled his clothing, tightening his shirt across his chest, flapping his loose jacket and trousers about him, and which stirred the thick uncombed hair above his stubby quiet face. His long shadow legs rose perpendicularly and fell, ludicrously, as though without power of progression, as though his body had been mesmerized by a whimsical God to a futile puppet-like activity upon one spot, while time and life terrifically passed him and left him behind. At last his shadow reached the crest and fell headlong over it.

The opposite valley rim came first into sight, azure and aloof, in the level afternoon sun. Against it, like figures rising in a dream, a white church spire rose, then house-tops, red and faded green and olive half hidden in budded oaks and elms. Three poplars twinkled their leaves against a gray sunned wall over which leaned peach and apple trees in an extravagance of fragile pink and white; and though there was no wind in the valley, bent narrowly to the quiet resistless compulsion of April in their branches, then were still and straight again except for the silver mist of their never ceasing, never escaping leaves. The entire valley stretched beneath him, and his shadow, springing far out, lay across it, quiet and enormous. Here and there a thread of smoke balanced precariously upon a chimney. The hamlet slept, wrapped in peace and quiet beneath the evening sun, as it had slept for a century; waiting, invisibly honey-combed with joys and sorrows, hopes and despairs, for the end of time[.]

From the hilltop the valley was a motionless mosaic of tree and house; from the hilltop were to be seen no cluttered barren lots sodden with spring rain and churned and torn by hoof of horse and cattle, no piles of winter ashes and rusting tin cans, no dingy hoardings covered with the tattered insanities of posted salacities and advertisements. There was no suggestion of striving, of whipped vanities, of ambition and lusts, of the drying spittle of religious controversy; he could not see that the sonorous simplicity of the court house columns [was] discolored and stained with casual tobacco. In the valley there was no movement save the thin spiraling of smoke and the heart-tightening grace of the poplars, no sound save the measured faint reverberation of an anvil.

The slow featureless mediocrity of his face twisted to an internal

*From the *Mississippian*, 12, No. 20 (10 March 1922), 1, 2; transcribed by Arthur F. Kinney; certain emendations have been made where noted for obvious typographical errors. Reprinted by permission of Jill Faulkner Summers, executrix of the Faulkner Estate. "The Hill," Faulkner's second published story, is his first portrait of the solitary, even "futile" figure who will eventually become Young Bayard Sartoris.

impulse: the terrific groping of his mind. His monstrous shadow lay like a portent upon the church, and for a moment he had almost grasped something alien to him, but it eluded him; and being unaware that there was anything which had tried to break down the barriers of his mind and communicate with him, he was unaware that he had been eluded. Behind him was a day of harsh labor with his hands, a strife against the forces of nature to gain bread and clothing and a place to sleep, a victory gotten at the price of bodily tissues and the numbered days of his existence; before him lay the hamlet which was home to him, the Tieless casual; and beyond it lay waiting another day of toil to gain bread and clothing and a place to sleep. In this way he worked out the devastating unimportance of his destiny, with a mind heretofore untroubled by moral quibbles and principles, shaken at last by the faint resistless force of spring in a valley at sunset.

The sun plunged silently into the liquid green of the west and the valley was abruptly in shadow. And as the sun released him, who lived and labored in the sun, his mind that troubled him for the first time, became quieted. Here, in the dusk, nymphs and fauns might riot to a shrilling of thin pipes, to a shivering and hissing of cymbals in a sharp volcanic abasement beneath a tall icy star. . . . Behind him was the motionless conflagration of sunset, before him was the opposite valley rim upon the changing sky. For a while he stood on one horizon and stared across at the other, far above a world of endless toil and troubled slumber; untouched, untouchable; forgetting, for a space, that he must return. . . . He slowly descended the hill.

The Lilacs   **William Faulkner***

We sit drinking tea
Beneath the lilacs on a summer afternoon
Comfortably, at our ease
With fresh linen on our knees,
And we sit, we three
In diffident contentedness
Lest we let each other guess
How happy we are

*Privately hand-printed by Faulkner in January 1920; initially published as the opening poem in *A Golden Bough* (New York: Harrison Smith and Robert Haas, 1933), pp. 7–11. Copyright 1933 and renewed 1961 by William Faulkner. Reprinted from *The Marble Faun And A Green Bough*, by William Faulkner, by permission of Random House, Inc. Here the desolate mood of "The Hill" is applied to war and to soldiers.

Together here, watching the young moon
Lying shyly on her back, and the first star.

There are women here:
Smooth-shouldered creatures in sheer scarves, that pass
And eye us strangely as they pass.
One of them, our hostess, pauses near:
—Are you quite all right, sir? she stops to ask.
—You are a bit lonely, I fear.
Will you have more tea? cigarettes? No?—
I thank her, waiting for her to go:
To us they are like figures on a masque.
—Who?—shot down
Last spring—Poor chap, his mind
. . . . doctors say . . . hoping rest will bring—
Busy with their tea and cigarettes and books
Their voices come to us like tangled rooks.
We sit in silent amity.

—It was a morning in late May:
A white woman, a white wanton near a brake,
A rising whiteness mirrored in a lake;
And I, old chap, was out before the day
In my little pointed-eared machine,
Stalking her through the shimmering reaches of the sky.
I knew that I could catch her when I liked
For no nymph ever ran as swiftly as she could.
We mounted, up and up
And found her at the border of a wood:
A cloud forest, and pausing at its brink
I felt her arms and her cool breath.
The bullet struck me here, I think
In the left breast
And killed my little pointed-eared machine. I saw it fall
The last wine in the cup. . . .
I thought that I could find her when I liked,
But now I wonder if I found her, after all.

One should not die like this
On such a day,
From angry bullet or other modern way.
Ah, science is a dangerous mouth to kiss.
One should fall, I think, to some Etruscan dart
In meadows where the Oceanides
Flower the wanton grass with dancing,
And, on such a day as this
Become a tall wreathed column: I should like to be
An ilex on an isle in purple seas.
Instead, I had a bullet through my heart—

—Yes, you are right:
One should not die like this,
And for no cause nor reason in the world.

'Tis well enough for one like you to talk
Of going in the far thin sky to stalk
The mouth of death: you did not know the bliss
Of home and children; the serene
Of living and of work and joy that was our heritage.
And, best of all, of age.
We were too young.
Still — he draws his hand across his eyes
— Still, it could not be otherwise.

We had been
Raiding over Mannheim. You've seen
The place? Then you know
How one hangs just beneath the stars and sees
The quiet darkness burst and shatter against them
And, rent by spears of light, rise in shuddering waves
Crested with restless futile flickerings.
The black earth drew us down, that night
Out of the bullet-tortured air:
A great black bowl of fireflies. . . .
There is an end to this, somewhere:
One should not die like this —

One should not die like this.
His voice has dropped and the wind is mouthing his words
While the lilacs nod their heads on slender stalks,
Agreeing while he talks,
Caring not if he is heard or is not heard.
One should not die like this.
Half audible, half silent words
That hover like gray birds
About our heads.

We sit in silent amity.
I am cold, for now the sun is gone
And the air is cooler where we three
Are sitting. The light has followed the sun
And I no longer see
The pale lilacs stirring against the lilac-pale sky.
They bend their heads toward me as one head.
— Old man — they say — How did you die?

I — I am not dead.

I hear their voices as from a great distance — Not dead
He's not dead, poor chap; he didn't die —

[The original opening of *Flags in the Dust*]

William Faulkner[*]

In the following transcription all cancelled material has been enclosed in angled brackets; words and phrases deleted within cancelled sections have been enclosed in double and triple angled brackets. A few deleted words are unreadable; these are recorded as "illegible word" within square brackets.

The only editorial change made in this transcription is the introduction of paragraph indention. It was Faulkner's practice, in his manuscripts, to indicate paragraph breaks by extra space between lines; here I have followed instead his practice of indenting when he typed his manuscripts for the printer.   George F. Hayhoe

Flags In The Dust[1]

1.

One < late > < February > June dusk, < one > in 191 < 7 > 8) — < one of those treacherous apocryphal days neither spring nor winter > — a tender drove up to an aerodrome up toward Arras and stopped before the squadron office. It contained a single < occupant in a > passenger < in a fur-collared trench-coat, who dismounted a little unsteadily with the driver's assistance talking to the driver in a loud steady voice > who was talking to the driver in a loud steady voice, < and whom the driver > The driver descended first and assisted him < out — > to dismount unsteadily — a huge young giant with a bleak ruddy face < and a fur-collared > beneath the casual slant of his cap, < and a fur-collared trench-coat, > who bade the driver a florid farewell and crossed the supply 'drome toward the < officers' mess > sheet-iron ediface < He pulled himself together and > which housed the officers' mess.

< Here he encountered among others a slight lean > The room was lighted by kerosene lamps with tin reflectors and < cozy with a light glowing stove > and it was occupied by several lounging men. The newcomer slammed the door behind him and raised his voice in a shout and tugged his trench-coat off and flung it < onto a chair > to the floor. An orderly appeared at another door.

"Yes, Sir."

"Whiskey," the newcomer said. "Whisky for < everybody > everyone. My chit. < Damed > I am Comyn, of the Irish nation, and its bloody < cold > dry driving up from Wing," he stated, < Damn cold, driving

---

[*]First published as "The Rejected Manuscript Opening of *Flags in the Dust*," *Mississippi Quarterly*, 33, No. 3 (Summer 1980), 371–83; reprinted with permission of the editor of *Mississippi Quarterly*, George F. Hayhoe, and Mrs. Jill Faulkner Summers, executrix of the Faulkner Estate. Mr. Hayhoe has made additional corrections especially for this volume.

down from Wing," 65." he added. >looking about. "Oh, I say, Sartoris," he said to a <slight lean> tall lean youth with reckless <merry ey> blue eyes and tawny hair, "One of those new Camel squadrons came through Wing today, replacing 65. There's a Sartoris in it. Any of your people?"

"It's Bayard," Evelyn Sartoris said, springing to his feet. "Hell, I'm going up there." He too raised his voice, but at that moment the orderly returned with <bottles a> a tray of bottles and glasses. "Nip over and tell the Flight Sergeant of B to <have the> get Mr Sartoris' machine out," he directed.

"Dont be a pukka fool," his <squadron comma> flight-commander said from his chair, without raising his head from the French pictorial magazine he perused. "You cant fly up there at this hour."

"Why not? It aint dark yet, is it?" Sartoris demanded of the newcomer, who with his cap thrust to the back of his head and the light full on his flushed face was unsteadily building himself a dynamic drink.

"Not yet," the other answered. "Let him go, Mac," he added to the <oblivious> flight-commander, "plenty of light if he bounces."

"And <hav> let him wash out a perfectly good machine?" the flight-commander said. "Plenty more pilots at Pool, but it takes 4 days to replace a machine. Sit down, Sartoris."

The newcomer blundered into a chair and took a long swallow from his glass. "Damn <cold> dry, driving up from Wing," he repeated "I tell you what: there's a night-flying squadron up there some where: you might get on up there, and if it's too dark to get down, you might just sort of hang around until they <light their flares.> turn on their searchlights."

"Or you might ask the major to 'phone up and have them put out flares for you," another suggested.

"Oh, go to hell," Sartoris snapped. "Let me have the tender, will you, Mac?"

"Sit down, Sartoris," the flight-commander <sa> repeated, "and you other chaps <to> shut up. Oh, Steward." The orderly appeared again and the flight-commander added: "Take that whisky out. Mr Comyn's had enough." He turned to Evelyn Sartoris <again.> "Why not telephone up there, if you cant wait until tomorrow? <I wouldn't go up there tonight.> It'll take you all night to drive up there," and he <turned to> raised his magazine again.

"Well," Evelyn Sartoris agreed, "I reckon that's what I'll have to do."

Bayard and Evelyn Sartoris were twins, and between them was the nearest thing to affection there had ever been between Sartoris men. They passed inseparably and to the scholastic detriment of both, through preparatory school; whereupon it was deemed best to separate them in college. So Bayard, the older, went to Virginia and Evelyn to Princeton in the same year. Their holidays and vacations they spent together; and New York policemen came to know them during week-ends and to wish them dead.

At the end of their junior year they were 23, and in June of 1916 they got themselves shipped as deck-hands on a cattle boat and reached Bristol in time. "I reckon we better cable grandfather where we are," Evelyn suggested belatedly. Which they did, and a week later, as cadets in the Royal Flying Corps, they wrote fuller details.

Ground school in the gray and ancient benignance of Oxford quadrangles, then flying school. They wrote <dutiful and> dull and dutiful letters home at monthly intervals; Evelyn presently from a hospital where he lay with a broken leg as the result of <a crash.> an accident he had suffered while trying to loop a <Sopwith Pup> Bristol scout off the ground Bayard visited him from time to time, appearing one day with a shoulder strap to his Sam Browne and a pip on either shoulder. "You'll get yours as soon as they let you out of here," he assured his brother. "Then we'll celebrate."

"You damn right," Evelyn sitting in a chair with his leg propped before him, agreed. "We'll raise hell."

But before Evelyn's leg was healed Bayard had gone out to Flanders to a Spad squadron. They wrote to one another very occasionally, and Evelyn was well again and celebrated America's entry into the war by himself, and in May, '16 he crossed the Channel with wings on his breast also, and he and his brother were in Boulogne the same day without knowing it—Evelyn going to Pilots' Pool and Bayard returning to England; without knowing it, on his way home. He had been loaned to the infant United States Air Service, and while Evelyn was up toward Arras in a Cleigel Camel squadron, Bayard in his foreign martial harness and a thin English veneer that <became> sat well upon him, after a fashion, was swanking his wings and his pale Bedford cords and shiny boots and a small dull-gold moustache and that <fatal,> bleak, hooded falcon expression flying had given him, about Memphis where he taught American would-be aces to fly and troubled the dreams of many a maiden heart.

There he met and married Carolyn White, < <and left her in his grandfather's house and returned to war [illegible partial word] meanwhile> > and brought her to his grandfather's house in north Mississippi, < <and in April, '18 he was < < <ordered b> > > recalled to England hurriedl> > He was able to fly home every week-end, and presently they had settled down into an idyllic routine which lasted through the winter and into the next spring, when it was interrupted by the German general staff. < <and> > He was recalled hurriedly by his adopted government, and in June, '18 Bayard went out again in a < <Dolphin> > squadron of S.E.5's. >

< < <Yesterday had been treacherous. > > Yesterday had been a day of balmy langours, but when his batman waked him with a cup of bitter scalding tea the dawn was like a portent. It lay somewhere to the east, a sluggish chalky rumor, and the air was damp and raw with channel winds. Yet he stood and smoked his cigarette with actual impatience while

his machine was being rolled out and mechanics moved like intent ghosts about it. The dawn patrol was just getting away and he had to wait until the reluctant engines choked and coughed to a steady high crescendo, sank idling, then soared again as the flight rushed singly across the 'drome and rose and assumed formation and faded diminishing into the gray east. >

Here his small dull-gold moustache and that bleak, hooded-falcon expression which flying had given him captured the fancy of Carolyn White. She was a slight girl with a small supple body, and there was about her always a latent epicene unrepose. Or rather, hers was that dynamic fixation of carven sexless figures caught in moments of action, strife. Her body was like a mechanism all parts of which must move in performing the most trivial action. She was the only woman among a family of men — a father and four brothers — and her energy <flashed> gleamed fluidly among their identical hereditary inertias like mercury among dull pebbles. Bayard Sartoris was rather like mercury too, and they flashed together through the brief affinity of glitter for glitter and, because of the circumstance that they both happened to be going in the same direction, they merged. But again as mercury, without any actual surrendering of their individualities as distinct atoms capable, nay eager, to resume each its intact and lonely course <at> on an instant's impulse.

So in a rosy glow of alcohol they were married, Bayard in blue dress uniform and Carolyn in white veils like a bright small flame smothered in tulle and the more dangerous because of it, with the wild bronze flame of her hair curled momentarily with orange blossoms. From the church door they passed arm in arm beneath an arcade of borrowed and rented swords while a flight of aeroplanes from the field 18 miles away dropped roses on the roofs of the surrounding buildings and sometimes into the street near them, and so to a new and expensive apartment in the proper part of town.

They slept here occasionally, and sometimes, accompanied by a few of Bayard's military associates and a <number of> corresponding number of casual maidens and wives, they stopped in at a nearby delicatessen and bought prepared foods in cardboard containers and brought it home, and sitting about on the floor or upon expensive instalment-plan furniture, they ate from the greasy paper vessels with engraved and costly new silver and monogrammed napkins. But neither of them were here very often alone, nor very much at all. Carolyn spent the days in her car or at the aerodrome, her car surrounded by a ring of officers and cadets, telling them presently about her child with humorous and annoyed consternation; inculcating it, she explained, while it was young with the smell of castoral oil which bade fair to constitute its sole heritage. She even named it almost as soon as she was certain, and she and <the> all of their hectic and rootless associates were soon speaking of it as though it were a mature and accomplished actuality; a despotic factor <in their lives> of uncertain temper whose vagaries could neither be anticipated nor ignored.

This manner of living would have continued indefinitely had it not been for the German High Command. Cambrai fell; the echo of it came faintly across <[illegible partial word]> seas to them; then Baupaume, and the echo was a little louder; and then Amiens was a peremptory sound not to be ignored, and in May '18 Bayard was recalled by his adopted government. He took his wife to his grandfather's home in northern Mississippi, where dogwood still bloomed among the accomplished new green of the hills, and crabapple in the sheltered ravines, and apple trees in the orchard below the barn, <The orchard could be seen from the windows of the room> and they lay one night together in the room Bayard and John had always shared. But John was somewhere back of Amiens, working out the blind destiny of his race, while Bayard and his wife lay in the room where <John's> <ghosts of John's violence lay like impalpable dust on all the furniture> ghosts of his and John's violent complementing days <lay like> was like an impalpable dust on all the furniture, watching through the window the snow-blanched and windless apple trees below the barn, talking quietly and soberly at last. War had been just a glamorous sound, as wind afar off is a sound; but now it was become an imminence of individual words and the bloody price of those words. Cambrai. Amiens. Facts. Boulogne, Calais, Paris. More than possibilities: probabilities; and a red flame beyond which that which was to be fitted its blind puzzle picture together, invisible and unguessable. Beside him on the pillow the wild bronze flame of her hair, hushed now in the darkness, and she lay holding his arm in both of her hands and they talked quietly, sober at last, watching through the windowless curtains the still, bloom-frosted apple trees in the orchard below the barn.

In June Bayard went out again with a squadron of S.E.5's, into and beyond that red flame from which letters emerged so sparsely. The long sad days of summer accumulated, placid lonely days remote among the blue hills from disastrous things. Her <life's supple flame was changing> body's supple <unrepose> flame was changing, centering, losing its suppleness and its <flame> line.

[There is a gap at this point between pages 003 and 03.]

<helmet and settled his goggles. At a motion of>

He approached his own machine as it rested with its propeller idling in the east wind, but before he reached it the engine ceased its racket and his flight-sergeant's head <rose> appeared above the cock-pit rim. "All right, Sir," the sergeant said, swinging his legs out and dropping to the ground.

Evelyn Sartoris <climbed> in his shapeless garment mounted stiffly and fastened his belt. A mechanic stood at each wing-tip, a third approached the nose of the machine and laid his hands on the rigid lateral bar of the propellor.

"Off, Sir," he said. Evelyn Sartoris touched the switch.

"Off," he repeated. The mechanic revolved the propellor twice, then stood back.

"Contact, Sir." Evelyn drew the stick back to his stomach and snapped the switch on.

"Contact."

The mechanic caught the propellor and brought it downward with a great <backward swing of his body> sideways swing of his body. The engine caught and the mechanic moved aside, and Evelyn Sartoris pushed the throttle slowly forward. The machine trembled and shivered and the mechanics at the wing-tips braced their backs against its tugging, and against the paling <da> east the propellor was not even a blur. He closed the throttle and fastened the chin-strap of his helmet and settled his goggles. At a motion of his hand a mechanic withdrew the chocks from the wheels, at another motion those at the wing-tips released them, and he pushed the throttle forward and trundled out across the 'drome, gaining speed. Then he let the stick go forward a little and the jolting became a long bounding rush, <that ceased too presently.> and drew the stick back a fraction, and this too ceased.

Over Arras where he and Bayard rendezvoused, he had not long to wait before the other machine came up, and in an isolation of thin mist filled with the racket of their <own> two engines they saw each other again after 18 months. <and> Evelyn watched the other machine.

The light increased—a substance with texture and without visibility, like mist, and presently Arras lay vaguely in it beneath him and he fired a short burst to warm the oil in his guns against any necessity. He had not been there long before his brother arrived, and in an isolation of thin mist filled with the racket of their two engines, <and high above that earth they were born to walk upon.> they saw one another again after 18 months—Evelyn in his tiny death-trap of a Cleigel Camel (the British had perforce to throw everything in, <then) and Bayard in his long-nosed S.E. with its long nose, and undercarriage set well beneath the wings> then, and Evelyn had not got his new machine) and Bayard in his S.E. with its long nose and its undercarriage set far back beneath the wings, high above that earth they were born to walk upon, and <Evelyn thumbed his nose at his brother and waggled his wings> as Bayard came up on and shot around him in a steep bank, Evelyn thumbed his nose at his brother and waggled his wings, and for a time they whirled about each other like playful dolphins in the pale isolation of the mist.

Then Evelyn began to mount and Bayard followed him. But though the mist thinned a little it still was about them when Evelyn's Camel was almost to its maximum altitude, whereupon Evelyn put his nose down a little and <turned> pointed it eastward. <Bayard came> Presently Bayard drew opposite him and shook his head violently, <waving his arm> gesturing with his arm to the southward. But Evelyn thumbed his nose at his brother and held to his course until Bayard dashed < ahead of him and with short rushes forced him to> directly < ahead> in front of him, still waving him back. Evelyn dived beneath the other and put his engine full out, but Bayard in his faster machine overtook him and shot past and whirled and with short threatening rushes < forced Evelyn to bear away give way> was forcing Evelyn to give way until Evelyn pointed his machine carefully and fired a burst from his Vickers guns across his brothers nose. Then Bayard fell behind and a little above him and came doggedly on. Evelyn turned and thumbed his nose at the blur of the other propellor.

What's come over old Bayard? he wondered. Aint any Huns back that way. Wonder what he thought I wanted with him — just to look at his mug? Being in America again did it, I reckon. The land of the kike and the home of the wop, where all men are brave and the women are all virgins through the last reel. It was going to be clear after all; the mist was swirling slowly into < denser> distinct shapes. Pretty soon the sun would break out and among the cloud battlements like < castles on fire> silvery castles on fire he and Bayard would rush, trailing wisps of rainbow vapor from sheets and bracing-wires; and like knights they would < rush> dart from out a pearly port-cullis and bag enough Huns for breakfast. That's what old Bayard needed: just let him smell a Hun, and he'd be all right; he'd forget about < his so> having wasted damn near a year with a woman in the land of the eager and rich, and remember what his Uncle George Windsor gave him those wings and that shiny new machine for.

"Oh, my, I dont want to fly,

I want to go < home> huo-o-ome" Evelyn sang in an unmusical barytone, and then it happened.

He avoided a collision by inches, stalling, and other blunt things fell through slowly swirling vapor shapes and he fired at their short viscid bellies from the center of a web of streaked fading smoke while invisible mice gnawed at his center-section and he was hit without knowing it. As he whipped out of his stall he looked for Bayard, but the S.E. was gone and as he rolled still firing he searched the mist beneath him. It too was breaking and through slow interstices he saw earth and a long sheet of sunlight in sharp relief across it. Then he was hit again, and again, and holding his machine in a tight bank he flashed between two huns < rushing> whipping over to fire at him again and above the cold < ch> garrulity of his own guns he could hear thin bullets nailing upon his < [illegible words]> engine cowling and through the delicate blur of his propeler he saw Bayard again, falling upon one of the enemy with the other 3 huns on his tail.

But the machine on his own tail Evelyn could not shake off. He held in his tight bank and prayed and cursed. Bayard < [illegible word]> with his four huns < he> was gone; the fifth sat off and poked at Evelyn as the sixth one chased him in a circle. He was bleeding into his seat and his legs were cold, but he held on, firing a burst at the second enemy whenever he saw a chance, trying < manoever after> trick after trick to dislodge the other. It'll have to end soon, he found himself thinking quietly, Bayard already. . . . Then he saw Bayard again, and his legs were quite cold, and then he < found without surprise that the German's tracer was no longer following him> noticed that the German's tracer, lacing about him, had become a thin chill of vapor about the nose of his machine, and he looked back. < The < < German > > hun and Bayard hovered < < above him > > The swirling mist shapes were breaking into < < cloud shapes> > cumulae tinged with gold, and above him the hun and Bayard hovered, watching him; and at that moment a single puffing explosion < < came> > came from beneath his engine cowling and a < < burst > > bubble of hot < < sickening> > air < < [illegible word] leaving a sickening castor-oil odor> > burst against his face, leaving him surrounded by a sickening odor of castor oil and a tongue of orange flame blistered along the fuselage fabric, swirling into black smoke. He unfastened his belt and stood upright in the cockpit and < < chaffed his dead legs> > released the stick and dragged his dead legs outside, and just as he leaped the sun broke in long golden lanes far < < [illegible word]> > away the silver parapets of clouds, and in its beam he thumbed his nose at his brother and to the peering pink face of the hun he tended a sweeping, magniloquent salute. >

The mist wraiths were piling shape upon shape into slow cumulae tinged with gold, and above him the hun and Bayard banked and he could see their downward-staring faces; and at that moment a single puffing explosion came from beneath his engine cowling and a bubble of heat burst against his face, leaving him surrounded by a sickening odor of boiling castor oil, and a long orange tongue blistered along the fuselage fabric and swirled on in the propellor blast to black smoke. Without hesitation He released the stick and unfastened his belt and stood upright in the cockpit and dragged his dead legs overside, and sat on the < edge> cockpit edge with his feet dangling and pushed the stick sharply forward. Just before he jumped the sun broke in a long golden lance through the silver parapet of the clouds, and in its beam he thumbed his nose at his brother, and to the peering pink face of the German he made a sweeping and magniloquent salute

Note

1. The first seven pages of the manuscript of *Flags in the Dust* at the University of Virginia Library are numbered 01–02, 002–003, 03–05, and contain material much of which does not appear in the surviving typescript of the novel, although a number of details from these pages were incorporated into other parts of the book when Faulkner revised *Flags* as he typed it. The text of these seven pages is continuous except for a gap between pages 003 and 03 (nor are pages 02 and 03 consecutive); the system of numbering and the gap in the text indicate that at least one page of an even earlier draft must have existed and been discarded.

Presumably these pages were added to the manuscript after the author had begun the pages bearing a regular numbering sequence; however, page 01 contains the title "Flags In The Dust" at its top, and page 1 has only the section or chapter number "1." It seems likely, then, that the present page 1 (a revision of an earlier page 1 with the title?) was written after page 01; the manuscripts of *The Sound and the Fury*, *Sanctuary*, and *As I Lay Dying* all bear their titles at the head of the first page. The appearance of "Evelyn" as an early first name for John Sartoris — he appears as "John" on page 003 — indicates the priority of the rejected opening, since that name is not used later in the manuscript. The heavy revisions within these seven pages also suggest that they were written before the pages which are regularly numbered. These revisions, involving not only words but whole blocks of material and shifts in narrative focus and setting, show Faulkner's difficulties in finding the right beginning for his novel.

The rejected opening may well be the donnée of *Flags in the Dust*, despite Faulkner's difficulties with it, and his eventual abandonment of it. I do not agree with the theory advanced by Max Putzel that this section is an early attempt at a short story about the Sartoris twins which predates Faulkner's conception of the novel. (See "Evolution of Two Characters in Faulkner's Early and Unpublished Fiction," *Southern Literary Journal*, 5 [Spring 1973], 47–63.) This manuscript episode, with its lack of any sense of completeness, is clearly related to a much larger work. Moreover, the major incident which it relates, the death of John Sartoris, is the basic motivation for many of Bayard's actions in *Flags*, and Bayard's three waking and dreaming nightmares in the novel all concern his twin's death and his own helplessness and inability to prevent it. [George F. Hayhoe].

[On the Composition of *Sartoris*][1]   William Faulkner*

[*It was*] One day about 2 years ago I was speculating idly upon time and death when the thought occurred to me that doubtless [*with years*] as my flesh acquiesced more and more to the standardized compulsions of breath, there would come a day on which the palate of my soul (?)[2] would no longer reach to the simple bread-and-salt of the world as I had found it in the finding years, just as (after a while)[3] the [*gourmet's*] physical palate remains apathetic until teased by truffles. And so I began casting about.

All that I really desired was a touchstone simply; a simple word or gesture, but having been these 2 years previously under the curse of words, having known twice before the agony of ink, nothing served but that I try [*to evoke*] by main strength to recreate between the covers of a book the world as I was already preparing to lose and regret, feeling, with the morbidity of [*youth*] the young, that (that I was not only on the verge of decrepitude, but that) [*I was already 9 years older than God*] growing old

*Transcribed by Donald Gallup, James B. Meriwether, and Michael Millgate, with emendations by Joseph Blotner, and published as "William Faulkner's Essay on the Composition of *Sartoris*" by Joseph Blotner, *Yale University Library Gazette*, 47, No. 3 (January 1973), 121–24. Reprinted with permission of Stephen Parks for the *Gazette* and Jill Faulkner Summers, executrix of the Faulkner Estate. A variant transcription by Max Putzel is in *Publications of the Bibliographical Society of America*, 74 (1980), 361–78. This is Faulkner's fullest statement on the abridgment for publication of *Flags in the Dust*.

was to be an experience peculiar to myself alone out of all the teeming world, and desiring, if not the capture of that world and the feeling of it as you'd preserve a kernel on a leaf, (to indicate the lost forest) at least to keep the evocative skeleton of the dessicated leaf.

So I began to write, without much purpose, until I realised (that to make it [*personal and*] truely evocative it must be personal, in order to) [*that I should need people, characters*], to not only preserve my own interest in the writing, [*to*] but to preserve my belief in the savor of the bread-and-salt. (So I put people in it, since what can be more personal than reproduction, in its true way, the aesthetic and the mammalian. In its own sense, really, since the aesthetic is still the female principle, the desire to feel over the bones spreading and parting with something alive begotten of the ego and conceived by the protesting unleashing of flesh.) So I [*put*] got some people, some I invented, others I [*took*] created out of tales I learned of nigger cooks and stable boys (of all ages between one-armed Joby, [*who*] 18, who taught me to write my name in red ink on the linen duster he wore for some reason we have both forgotten, to [*Aunt*] old Louvinia who remarked when the stars "fell" and who called my grandfather and my father by their Christian names until she died) in the long drowsy afternoons. Created I say, because they are composed partly from what they were in actual life and partly from what they should have been and were not: thus I improved on [*nature*] God, who, dramatic though He be, has no sense, no feeling for, theatre.

And neither had I, for the first publisher to whom I submitted [*the book refused it*] 600 odd pages of mss. refused it on the ground that it was chaotic, without head or tail. [*It*] I was shocked: my first emotion was blind protest, then I became objective for an instant, like a parent who is told that its child is a thief or an idiot or a leper; for a dreadful moment I contemplated it with consternation and despair, then like the parent I [*veiled my own eyes in the shut my own eyes*] hid my own eyes in the fury of denial. I clung stubbornly to my illusion; I showed the mss to a number of friends, [*I even went the length of refusing to let another publisher even see it*] who told me the same [*thing*] general thing — that the book lacked any form whatever; at last one of them took it to another publisher, who proposed to edit it enough to see [*what was there*] just what was there.

In the meantime I had refused to have anything to do with it. I prefaced this by arguing hotly with the person designated to edit the mss on all occasions that he was clumsy enough [*not*] to be sure to − − −. I said, "A cabbage has grown, matured. You look at that cabbage; it is not symmetrical; you say, I will trim this cabbage off and make it art; I will make it [*look*] resemble a peacock or a [*book or 3*] pagoda or 3 doughnuts. Very good, I say; you do that, then the cabbage will be dead."

"Then we'll make some kraut of it," he said. "The same amount of sour kraut will feed twice as many people as cabbage. [*"The trouble is,"* he said, *"Is that you have about 6 books in here. You were trying to write*] *them all at once.*] A day or so later he came to me and showed me the mss. "The trouble is," he said, "Is that you have about 6 books in here. You were trying to write them all at once." He showed me what he meant, what he had done, and I realised for the first time that I had done better than I knew and the long work I had had to create opened before me and I [*contemplated*] felt myself surrounded by the limbo in which the shady visions, the host which stretched half formed, waiting each with it's portion of that verisimilitude which is to bind into a whole the world which for some reason I believe should not pass utterly out of the memory of man, and I contemplated those shady but ingenious shapes by reason of whose labor I might reaffirm the impulses of my own ego in this actual world without stability, with a lot of humbleness, and I speculated on time and death and wondered if I had invented the [*teeming*] world to which I should give life or if it had invented me, giving me an illusion of greatness

Notes

1. It was probably in the latter part of 1926 that William Faulkner began a novel which he would call "Flags in the Dust." By mid-October of 1927, he had completed it and submitted it to Boni and Liveright, the publisher of his two previous novels. Five weeks later Horace Liveright rejected it. "Flags in the Dust" was subsequently rejected by several other publishers. After a time, Ben Wasson, a college friend of Faulkner's employed in New York by the American Play Company, took over the typescript for Faulkner and submitted it finally to Harcourt, Brace and Company. There it was read by Harrison Smith, who recommended it to Alfred Harcourt. Harcourt offered to take the book if it was revised with substantial deletions. Faulkner accepted the proposal, and he and Wasson both made revisions. The novel was published on 31 January 1929, under the title *Sartoris*.

About two years later Faulkner composed one and one-fifth pages, untitled — probably for the use of Morton Goldman, the literary agent who succeeded Wasson — in which he described the composition of the novel and his reaction to the events that followed its submission to Boni and Liveright. The version of the essay printed here (from the original manuscript in the Collection of American Literature of the Beinecke Rare Book and Manuscript Library) was written in ink in Faulkner's small and often difficult hand, with many cancellations and five marginal interpolations. The account looks forward as well as backward, not only to "Flags in the Dust" but also to later stories and to novels such as those in the Snopes trilogy in which he would use material first adumbrated in "Flags in the Dust."

This previously unpublished essay which follows was transcribed by Donald Gallup, James B. Meriwether, and Michael Millgate, with a few emendations by the present writer, who was kindly given access to this material by the Yale Library for use in his forthcoming biography of William Faulkner.

The italicized material in brackets was canceled by Faulkner, and the passages within parentheses were (with one exception) interpolated into the text from the 2½-inch left-hand margin kept by Faulkner on his 8½-by-11-inch pages for such additions. The underlined blank indicates a word not yet deciphered [Joseph Blotner].

2. This question mark and parentheses were written thus in the text proper and not interpolated from the margin.

3. This phrase was written above the line and marked by Faulkner for insertion.

III EARLIEST REACTIONS

Romance Has Its Gall

Herschel Brickell*

Despite certain structural defects, and despite a style that at times is overmannered and overdecorated, Mr. Faulkner's third novel is a notable advance over *Soldier's Pay* and *Mosquitoes*, in both of which a fine talent made itself distinctly felt. The second book, *Mosquitoes*, was a good deal of a tour de force, and of no particular significance, but there was good writing in it, and occasional sardonic bits of portraiture that linger in the memory. The first was a post-war novel, by no means perfect, but with some unforgettable passages.

In *Sartoris* Mr. Faulkner has told the story of a Southern family of the romantic type. The family name Bayard gives the suggestion of chivalry, and the Sartorises were all of the hidalgo strain, haughty, wicked, more than a little vain, and courageous to the last degree. Most of all, the novel concerns itself with the fragment of life that is left young Bayard Sartoris, back from the war where he and his brother John were aviators and where John met his death. The reckless daring of an elder Bayard who, fighting under that beau sabreur of the Southern armies, Jeb Stuart, once rode his horse into the midst of General Pope's headquarters to seize a supply of coffee, is inherited by the younger, and added to it is a desperate hatred of life without the adored brother.

Bayard the younger comes home to the ancestral mansion in the hills of Northern Mississippi, where his grandfather, still another Bayard, and his "Aunt Jenny," born a Du Pre and the widow of a Sartoris, keep their state. He sets out at once with a fast automobile to try to kill himself, and very nearly succeeds; once he rides a stallion bareback and comes off unscathed except for a cracked head. The slow life of the country flows around him as he pursues his vertiginous way. Eventually he marries the quiet, self-possessed Narcissa, who knows him for a Sartoris, but who cannot resist him. And eventually he gets his wish to be quit of life, leaving behind him a son, to carry on the Sartoris tradition. It is "Miss Jenny," the most completely realized and vivid character in the book, and making it

*Reprinted, with permission, from the *New York Herald Tribune*, 24 February 1929, Sec. ix, p. 5.

worth reading for herself alone, who says to Narcissa, when Narcissa has decided to call the baby Benbow after her own family, in the hope of staving off the Sartoris curse: "Do you think that because his name is Benbow he'll be any less a Sartoris and a scoundrel and a fool?"

There is something undeniably anachronistic about Mr. Faulkner's wild Southern family and its colored retainers, something that belonged to the South of an earlier day. Bayard's swift automobile seems as out of place as his talk of airplane fighting in France; one feels that he should be trying to break his neck from the back of a good horse, and talking of cavalry charges. . . . The element of time is not fixed firmly anywhere in the book, and it shifts even to the point of confusion in the early chapters. But it is more the spirit of the book than its incidents that seems to belong to another period. As excellently and delightfully done as some of Mr. Faulkner's Negro characters are — for example, Old Simon, the family coachman — they wear the air of having stepped directly from the pages of Thomas Nelson Page.

However, life moves slowly back in the Mississippi hill country, and it is hard to question the authenticity of Mr. Faulkner's story when one comes upon an occasional picture, such as young Bayard's drinking party after his adventure with the stallion, or the same gentleman's visit to a family that specializes in sons and fox-hunting, or the office of an old-fashioned country doctor. These bits are inimitably done; Mr. Faulkner has a trick that is to be found in some of Ernest Hemingway's short stories, and occasionally, in *The Sun Also Rises*, of building up by minute detail a scene of uncanny lifelikeness, and of imparting the perfect "feeling" of the scene to the reader. The prose of the two men is wholly unlike, to be sure, as Mr. Faulkner writes long and complicated sentences, and uses as many "ands" to the page as the King James Version, but they both have the power of making the rest of the world stand still while they show their readers something. There are dramatic, real and beautiful passages in *Sartoris* that call for cheering and hat-tossing.

It is only when the novel stands forth to be examined as an entity that its faults are revealed. The worst of these is Mr. Faulkner's habit of leaving loose threads in his fabric; there are at least half a dozen in *Sartoris* that should have been made fast in the pattern. A character will be carefully drawn and incidents related, and the wary reader knows a trail is being laid, but when the book is finished the trail has led nowhere. It would have taken at least two large volumes for Mr. Faulkner really to have finished off the stories he has sketched in his book.

It appears to me that whatever faults the novel may have it is worth reading, even worth plowing through the opening pages, where the style is annoying in its complexity, for the downright excitement of many of its passages. If it does not depict the South of the present day as some of us know it and as most of us think of it, it does depict a glamorous country, where romance still lives, even though the romance be tinctured with wormwood, and bitter to the taste. And it discloses a novelist of real imaginative power, who is more than half a poet.

A Southern Family   Anonymous*

We have had so many novels recently with the decaying South as background, and so many with the destinies of a single family as subject, that Mr. Faulkner's book risks all sorts of comparisons. But this author's self-confidence is considerable and best expressed in his dedicatory note to Sherwood Anderson, in which he thanks that totally dissimilar writer for his kindness "with the belief [sic] that this book will give him no reason to regret that fact." Unfortunately, the assurance with which Mr. Faulkner apparently undertook his labor of gratitude to a fellow-writer was not enough to prevent it from being a work of uneven texture, confused sentiment and loose articulation.

This story of a Southern family whose members one and all belong to a dying order of society has little persuasiveness and less unity. In his solicitude to present the Sartoris family as it exists today, its chronicler finds it necessary to supply a genealogical scheme of its progress from earlier times, and to do this makes frequent use of "flash-backs" into the past, in the form of long and often unprofitable anecdotes which seriously interrupt the direct realization of the present. Also, he has obfuscated his canvas by peopling it with more characters than the dimensions of his book can sustain. By the time the several representatives of the Sartoris clan proper have begun to take on a few recognizable lineaments they are crowded from the scene by the constant ingress of wives, neighbors and other citizens of the community. Nor are the features of the three or four main figures sharply enough established to make them stand out with due proportion. Old Bayard Sartoris never becomes much more than a Southern version of the cranky old Tory that we have encountered so often in the plays and novels of John Galsworthy. Around young Bayard, who comes nearest to affording the centre of the drama, the author has built up a legend of reckless gallantry and romantic disillusion which is never quite realized. Perhaps the most clearly defined is Aunt Jenny, the garrulous and indefatigable spokesman of the female Sartorises, who is nevertheless thoroughly monotonous and one-sided.

By such superficial treatment of his major characters, Mr. Faulkner has of course weakened and obscured his theme. It is only by implication that one deduces the theme is the struggle of the old masculine hierarchy of the South to survive in a modern industrial society. But one cannot be

*From the New York Times, 3 March 1929, Book Review, Sec. 8, p. 9, col. 1. Copyright 1929 by the New York Times Company. Reprinted by permission.

too certain, for Mr. Faulkner appears as little interested in the working out of a theme as in the consistent creation of character. His principal interest, it would seem, lies in quantitative variety, in assembling within a single book the widest possible range of characters, situations, moods, effects and styles. Perhaps this indicates a spirit of enterprise not unhealthy in a new writer, and that in some future work Mr. Faulkner will be able to exercise more rigorous selection and concentration.

The Whole and the Parts   Anonymous*

Mr. Faulkner's characters are so alive that they leave us, on first reading, almost dizzy, while, like his hero Bayard, his "young voice goes on and on, recounting violence and speed and death." But in the end we have that strange quickening of our sympathies towards all life, toward men and animals, natural beauty and the great mysteries of love, birth and death that is the gift of great poetry. As in the novels of Dostoevsky, to whose work Mr. Faulkner's is most akin, the accidents, indignities and heroisms of his characters become more than themselves, become symbols of "the blind tragedy of human events," the garments and the adventures of the soul. We know of no one now writing fiction in English who shows the potential power of Mr. Faulkner; his style reminds one of his descrip- tion of an unbroken stallion. "The stallion stood against the yawning cavern of the livery stable door like a motionless bronze flame, and along its burnished coat ran at intervals little tremors of paler flame, little tongues of nervousness and pride. But its eye was quiet and arrogant."

If some greater faith than he has yet found can master him, there is no telling to what far country Mr. Faulkner may not take us safely, as well as to that nearer country to which he often journeys, the country called hell. And even there, even now, he can give us wonder and beauty.

In *Sartoris* we see in flashes; and in the wild acts, thoughts and memories of the family, its friends and retainers during less than two years we are given a picture of the South, of four generations and two wars, tossed at us apparently haphazard, yet more complete, because more stimulating to our imaginations, than many volumes of detailed family chronicles. We move "among ancient phantoms of the soul's and body's fortitudes, in those regions of glamorous and useless striving where such ghosts abide." The men of the Sartoris family are born out of their time, they belong to the days when in playing with death and in the love of a comrade-in-arms consisted all the real life of men. They are "pawns shaped too late and to an old dead pattern, and of which the Player

*Reprinted, with permission, from the *New Statesman and Nation*, 3, No. 58 N.S. (2 April 1932), 428–30.

Himself is a little wearied. For there is death in the sound of it, and a glamorous fatality, like silver pennons downrushing at sunset, or a dying fall of horns along the road to Roncevaux." What this way of life means to the women Mr. Faulkner well knows, and he has given us two unforgettable pictures of the calm courage of Bayard's wife, and the angry courage of his great aunt, "that indomitable spirit that, born with a woman's body into a heritage of rash and heedless men and seemingly for the sole purpose of cherishing those men to their early and violent ends. . . . How much finer that gallantry which never lowered blade to foes no sword could find; that uncomplaining steadfastness of those unsung (ay, unwept too) women than the fustian and useless glamour of the men that obscured it."

Mr Faulkner's style can be described in his own epithets; it can be as "brutal as sabre blows," it can be "richly desolate" or filled with "grave obscurity like a still pool of evening water." His humour can be as startling as the geranium which he calls a "merry wound," or rich with sympathy and observation, as when he says of the old darkey coachman that he was so proud that he "contrived to strut sitting down."

Four Times and Out? Willard Thorp*

Mr. Faulkner's *Sartoris* will make him a popular novelist. It may, in fact, bring the Faulkner Club to an ignominious end by making him a book-society choice. Mr. Gerald Gould, whose proud immaculateness prevented his reading *The Sound and the Fury*, can venture inside its covers without any fear of meeting a Freudian bugaboo. It may even please him.

If one were feeling that way, one could suggest that the story of the Sartoris family, and in particular of young Bayard's tragedy, was evolved by crossing *Beau Geste* with *Death of a Hero*. There is, aside from certain impressive episodes which were bound to be sharply told since Faulkner is telling them, a noticeable effort to derive some meaning from the tale of a family whose men fling their lives recklessly away while their women-folk with a resigned impatience watch them die. But the comment does not go beyond interjected notes on Bayard's inescapable doom and the "blind fate" which controlled the family fortune. Clearly Faulkner never decided what this doom was.

In two earlier novels Faulkner invented a new style and wisely or unconsciously limited himself to the kind of story which demanded no other skills than those he possessed. Again here he has augmented the technical resources of the novelist by showing how unnecessary it is to tell

*Reprinted, with permission, from *Scrutiny*, 1, No. 1 (September 1932), 172–73.

a story covering several generations by the linear method. *Sartoris* has an extraordinary depth because events widely separated in time, but spiritually akin, are made to seem simultaneous. In this respect it is an achievement, for it puts to new uses the discoveries of Proust, Joyce and Virginia Woolf.

But Faulkner proposed to do more than write a saga in a new way. He not only attempts irony and the sinister, in which modes he is accomplished, but true tragedy as well. We are, that is, asked to believe that young Bayard is a tragic hero though he has not as much right to the dignity as Hotspur. The author of his being was rebuffed by the cold despair which kept everyone except his twin and idol from knowing his heart. It is impossible to have much sympathy for a skyrocket.

The novel was put to press too soon. There are bad repetitions, dissonances and absurd echoes, *e.g.* that sour reminiscence of Keats which closes the book, particularly unfortunate because of its association with (of all people) Horace Benbow. Faulkner, if he goes on at this rate, can easily lead the pack that help the *Saturday Evening Post* sell mouthwash to 50,000,000 Americans. He probably will. That way passed Robert W. Chambers — he, too, wrote a first novel — and Hergesheimer and others. Only the propagandists among American novelists, Dreiser, Sinclair, Dos Passos, are sufficiently self-willed not to succumb to the disease of mediocrity.

[Our People]   Dale Mullen*

The Unvanquished is a book of a wider and more immediate appeal than any other that Mr. Faulkner has written. Those Oxonians who — though very proud of, and wishing to pay just tribute to, their friend and neighbor — have found his writing too involved and difficult for their minds to follow or his subjects too revolting for them to stomach, will find here a book that they can understand, can enjoy, can leave lying on their living room tables, a book that they can proudly recommend to their friends among those less fortunate people who must live in other places, saying: "Here is a book about the Oxford country, about our people and the war they fought, a book by an Oxford man." (The simple fact that the greater part of this book appeared originally in the *Saturday Evening Post* should be sufficient evidence of the intelligibility and morality.)

This is the story of Old Bayard Sartoris as a boy and young man. He and his grandmother (Granny) and his negro playmate (Ringo) are living

*Reprinted, with permission, from the *Oxford Eagle*, 10 February 1938), 1, 5; transcribed from the files in the Lafayette County Courthouse, Oxford, by Arthur F. Kinney for this volume and reprinted here for the first time.

on the Sartoris plantation, near Jefferson, Miss., while his father (the legendary John Sartoris) is away at war. Vicksburg has fallen and the Yankees are occupying North Mississippi. The meetings between the Yankees and these three (Bayard and Granny and Ringo) form episodes of courage, heroism, and high good humor.

Mr. Faulkner has always been concerned with the revolt of men against their environment and against themselves. His most persistent subject has been the attempt of Southerners to free themselves from all the things that have made them into the beings called Southern, or rather, perhaps, the attempt of Southerners to establish themselves as individuals both apart from and within the pattern of their southern heritage. In "An Odor of Verbena" Bayard (now a young man and a student at the University) learns that his father had been killed by one Redmond. He knows that when he reaches home his father's wife will have two pistols waiting for him and he knows that every man in Jefferson will expect him to kill Redmond. And everything within him and without that is Southern demands that he do so. "Already I was beginning to realize, to become aware of that which I still had no yardstick to measure save that one consisting of what, despite myself, despite my raising and my background (or maybe because of them) I had for some time known I was becoming and feared the test of it; I remember how I thought. . . . At least this will be my chance to find out if I am what I thought I am or if I just hope; if I am going to do what I taught myself is right or if I am just going to wish I were." Bayard knows that he does not want to kill Redmond; moreover, he knows that he can not kill him. As with all of Faulkner's characters and as with, perhaps, everybody, Bayard does not reduce his problem into so many words, but we might say that his problem is this: He must prove himself to the satisfaction both of Jefferson and of himself. Jefferson would be satisfied if he killed Redmond, but this action would not satisfy himself even if he were able to do it. And as, again, with all of Faulkner's characters he does not effect a conscious solution. He moves forward with events and circumstances seemingly beyond his control to what may be termed a happy ending.

On the same general theme is the phase of this book that deals with Drusilla Hawk (Bayard's third cousin who becomes his step-mother) and with the triumph of the white southerners over the carpetbaggers. Early in the book she says: "Living used to be dull, you see. Stupid. You lived in the same house your father was born in, and your father's sons and daughters had the same sons and daughters of the same negro slaves to nurse and coddle; and then you grew up and fell in love with your acceptable young man, and in time you would marry, in your mother's wedding gown, perhaps, and with the same silver for presents she had received; and then you settled down forevermore until you got children to feed and bathe and dress until they grew up, too." Drusilla's acceptable young man was killed at Shiloh before she had had time to marry him and Drusilla had refused "the highest destiny of a Southern woman — to be the bride-widow of a lost cause." So Drusilla tried to escape from the pattern of the Southern Lady by cutting her hair short, by dressing like a man and riding in John Sartoris's troops, by coming after the war to Jefferson to assist in the rebuilding of the Sartoris plantation and to take a part in the struggle against the carpetbaggers. But she was yet Southern; her attempt to escape was made by fighting like a man for the very ideas that made her what she did not want to be. She assists in the defeat of the carpetbaggers: but their defeat is also hers.

But for the most part this is the book of Granny and the two children, Bayard and Ringo, in their teens. This is the story of the part they take in the war when all hope for victory or preservation is gone, their part in the prolongation (because of the South's "indomitable undefeat") of the war two years after it has been lost. These are not stories that can be summarized and retold in a paragraph. And to say that they are at once tragic, heroic, and prepostrously comic is not adequately to describe them. But that is all that can be said in this short space.

It may be interesting to note here that Mr. Faulkner has changed his story somewhat since he wrote *Sartoris*, which was published in 1929. Many of the incidents in this book were sketched briefly in the earlier one (which dealt with the old age of Bayard and his son, Young Bayard.) But details have been changed; some characters have been added, and others dropped (Bayard's two sisters, for instance).

Faulkner's Dismal Swamp   Louis Kronenberger*

The twisted heritage which the Confederate South bestowed upon its descendants is something few of them have renounced. It has got into their blood, and all that their weakened minds can do is resort to a rather vague, rueful, and inadequate irony. The truer irony is that they are its victims, forever driven on to commemorate their loss of Eden till one greater man (and where will he come from?) restore them and regain the blissful seat. The South languishes in race infantilism. The South is a fetishist because of something that disrupted its childhood; it goes on fondling a faded gray uniform with epaulets, a sword put up in its worn tired scabbard.

The South, to be sure, knows it moments of awareness and revulsion, as who would not, seeing impoverished brains and bodies in crazed retreat, seeing backward children lost in benighted folkways. But frequently these are moments of fascination also, for the process of decay can

*Reprinted, with permission, from the *Nation*, 146, No. 8 (19 February 1938), p. 212, col. 2 and p. 214, col. 1.

take on rich and gorgeous colors. We have evidence of this powerful revulsion and fascination in the works of Mr. Faulkner, who is a poet of disintegration, a necromancer of half-lights, but as yet no true visionary. Mr. Faulkner's saga of Jefferson, Mississippi, and its environs — spread out through half a dozen books — is, if not the only end, at least one end to a story that begins with drums and bugles, high-bred horses and gallant women. The decline and derationalization of the South can go no farther than Mr. Faulkner has taken them; it is now only possible for him to carry the story back to its source.

So here are tales of the Sartoris family during the War Between the States — a series of vivid exploits seen through the eyes of Bayard Sartoris as a boy, and set down by him long afterward. His father John, a reckless soldier and skirmisher, is away from home, where Bayard is living with his grandmother and the slaves. Always at his side is the Negro boy Ringo, presumably his half-brother. The status of Ringo in the family circle is one of the most interesting things in the book, as to my mind Ringo is by far the most interesting character. But for those who read *The Unvanquished* in the spirit that millions have read *Gone with the Wind*, it will be the grandmother who holds the stage — that indomitable ramrod, fierce as only sheltered and ladylike women can be. Lies, theft, murder itself count less with her than the twirling of a fan when it comes to saving the South, and her courage is quite equal to her criminality. I suppose that a great many women like Rosa Millard lived and behaved as she did during those desperate years. I am not so cynical as to refuse them homage. But they will never remind me of anything but the theater.

What Faulkner thinks of such women, and of such exploits as they achieved, and of all the disorder and valor and Marquis of Queensberry bloodshed that went on, is never altogether clear. The point of the book seems to be made when Bayard returns from law school after his father has been shot by an enemy, and defies the Southern code with a gesture that surpasses it. He will not kill his father's murderer; but neither will he ignore the insult. He goes unarmed to Redmond's office and lets Redmond shoot at him. This substitution of moral for physical bravura leaves the whole series of incidents uncomfortably question-marked. Certainly the tone and proportions of *The Unvanquished* are heroic rather than satiric. Certainly the merits of "the Cause" and the fortitude with which the Cause was defended — though I don't doubt that Mr. Faulkner has separated them in his own mind — are never clearly separated in the story. The very title of the book bespeaks an irony purely literary; it has the same double meaning as a pun. The book, at any rate, is pretty high-romantic stuff, cinema stuff, though where *Gone with the Wind* is pure Hollywood, *The Unvanquished* is coated with the expressionism of the foreign studio.

As writing, this is much the simplest book that Faulkner has written in a long time. To be sure, one keeps stumbling over nonsense like "Then he flung the door violently inward against the doorstop with one of those gestures with or by which an almost painfully unflagging preceptory of youth ultimately aberrates," but for the most part *The Unvanquished* gains from having been partly published in the *Saturday Evening Post*. As thinking, however, it seems to me as wilful, cluttered, sunless as ever. Faulkner is a master of sensation, the more lurid the sensation the better, and can throw marvelously strange lights over any scene he selects. But if he is fitted by neither temperament nor training to be a rational novelist, then, if he is to survive, he must move on from the company of the spellbinders to that of the seers; he must acquire and articulate a profounder moral sense, a capacity to enlarge life after the manner—to name the greatest—of a Dostoevski or an Emily Brontë. I do not see where, in this book, he has done more than brightly varnish rotten timber. I do not see where this book does more than repopulate a scene that Faulkner would do better to forget about. We are told, quite sensibly, that novelists should deal with the material they know best. But not forever, surely; and not if that material is a swamp, slowly, voraciously sucking the novelist in.

In the Shadow of the South's
Last Stand

Alfred Kazin*

Every elegist is in his own way a historian; and though I should hate to accept William Faulkner as the historian of the South, even his South, he has already proclaimed himself, through his hot, twisted novels, one of its most stubborn apostles. You may believe that he is a "Southern realist," that silly tag applicable to Thomas Wolfe and Erskine Caldwell alike, or you may believe that his spectres and lurking mists are all manufactured in Oxford, Mississippi; but what these Sartoris stories (really a loosely episodic novel) tell me again is that Faulkner's love and hatred for his region are so inextricably meshed that his passion in the struggle of the will against itself, the anguish and joy with which a man may tremble on the bleeding earth he knows and yet hate himself for his enmity.

Sometimes this can be maddening. There are pages in this book that mean nothing, for he can write like a willful, sullen child in some gaseous world of his own, pouting in polysyllabics, stringing truncated paragraphs together like dirty wash, howling, stumbling, losing himself in a verbal murk. But what counts is the terror that encloses it, the steady beat of a heart almost enraptured by the sense of doom and the revolt against it, the continuous descent through fear and custom until one is pierced by that

*Reprinted, with permission, from the *New York Herald Tribune*, (20 February 1938), Sec. IX, p. 5. The editor's subtitle reads, "A Brilliant Story Wherein Mr. Faulkner Speaks as a Stubborn Apostle of the Defeated."

terrible insistence on the dignity of loneliness and the joy in the compromises made with it. Not the South's doom, necessarily; not even the doom of its most degraded people. But the doom sensed by a tiring understanding, the fear that the ubiquitous "I" of Faulkner's stories will fail before death overcomes him.

It is out of this welter that the beauty of many of these pages springs, a sick, tattered beauty, if you will, but we must not be surprised that for Faulkner, as for so many American writers, excellence is bred by an overwhelming if single and broken intensity. But there is humor here that may be misleading because it is so grave (all Faulkner characters cough like mules when they want to laugh), and there is the warmth and good robust coloring of his sullen attachment to cruel and silly folkways. Faulkner takes prejudices for gospel because they are the facts of life to him, but he hammers them down and rings them with known consequences, so that the people who might offend us most in real life here burst through the page with a hoarse wit that is almost charming because it is so true, and with a vigor that is irresistible.

The Sartoris family in these stories embodies the philosophy of the Confederacy, but their adventures suggest much more. Colonel John Sartoris goes off into the woods with a band of partisans; and at home, Granny waits and sulks, preserving her prim ante-bellum notions of decorum, while the fifteen-year-old Bayard Sartoris and his slave playmate, Ringo, worry and plot, take random shots at Union soldiers, and try to pass the mysterious barrier between their childish invincible faith in the South and the evident squalor and defeatism growing upon their elders. The Negroes become restless; vague rumors of emancipation leak through; and then suddenly the hard, noble lines of the Southern system break up around their heads. Caste and family, manners and creed shrivel and fall apart. While the Southern troops starve and groan at the front, the people behind are caught in a compulsion to move and escape.

It is at this point that the book surges ahead with astounding inventiveness. As the Sartorises move on in their wagon the roads are choked by an army of slaves, squealing and pleading a new messianic faith. A Negro woman falls abandoned in the road and refuses Granny's offer of help. "Hit's Jordan we are coming to. Jesus gonter see me that far." Bayard and Granny look for their mules, confusedly tracing Union movements and hoping for a glimpse of Colonel Sartoris. The river is blocked by the troops, and becomes Jordan to the slaves trying to pass against their artillery. The bridge, unfinished, fails them; the Negroes, singing and chanting, are beaten back with scabbards. Without food, dismayed by their own recklessness and feverish with expectancy, the army of slaves, some looking for their masters and some hiding from them, move in a steady, tortured procession over the countryside. And over them all falls the shadow of the South's last stand.

Buoyed up by their success in retrieving mules from the Yankees,

Granny and her two young charges forge order after order on the proper letterheads, and find themselves wealthy, for a brief period, in mules. Finally Ringo, having signed General Grant's name to one order, decides that no one else will do. "Granny found out that Ringo objected to having the Yankees think that Father's folks would have any dealings with anybody under the General-in-Chief." They are caught and let off; but then their troubles begin. The Negroes are beaten but return ambitiously, the great mansions tumble to earth and the broken soldiers return wearily to bewail their defeat and humiliation.

It is characteristic of Faulkner that here the end of the war and the moldy period of carpetbag rule follow each other so neatly and so inevitably that the pervading sense of frenzied retribution always following upon defeat is sharpened as the book goes along. For Bayard Sartoris, who tells the story and carries most of the wounds, the war has never ended and never will end. There is no freedom from hatred, for war continues within war, war against the snickering element, conscience, and against the Reconstruction politicians on top, against the disintegration of hallowed mores and the very fear of disintegration. The unvanquished must play out the drama required of them: their lands may be ruined, their women lost, their former slaves victorious, but they must continue to seem unvanquished, to act like the masters they have ceased to be.

Thus, when at twenty-four Bayard is called from the university to avenge his father, shot in a political quarrel, he accepts the challenge as a matter of course, though he is tortured by his love for his young stepmother. He may have nothing against the man, but Bayard knows that he will be waiting, that the people in the neighboring houses will be listening. He must kill because it is expected of him, but as he walks along with the revolver in his pocket, eagerly watched by the town audience, yet dizzy with the recollection of a sprig of verbena his stepmother wore the night she declared her love for him, he is acting the appointed role, for the murder will be the last possible affirmation, the revenge against Appomattox.

Faulkner's description of this scene is so brilliant that the brief flurry of action suggests everything in a spatter of tense details. Bayard may be the walking, breathing symbol; but he is the savior of the Sartoris world and its destroyer, for in the very act of revenge and redemption he knows that nothing can be done. A murder will be a prolongation, and the sick and the dying will breed the same living failure. The land is dead forever, and though the unvanquished hammer and shout, they have insured their defeat by their fear and violence. It is this understanding, set forth now cumbersomely, now magnificently, but always with a hard, swift insistence that makes so many other American writers seem pallid and sleepy. That is William Faulkner's achievement.

Tattered Banners   Kay Boyle*

There are two Faulkners—at least to me there are two: the one who
stayed down South and the one who went to war in France and mixed
with foreigners and aviators; that is, the Faulkner of the Sartoris saga (and
the countless other savagely and tenderly chronicled documents of the
South) and the Faulkner who wrote "Turn About," for instance, and "All
the Dead Pilots" and *Pylon* with no perceptible cooling of that hot
devotion to man's courage although the speech, the history, the conflict
were no longer his strict heritage. I believe these two separate Faulkners
(separated more by a native shyness of the foreigner than any variance in
ideology or technique) possess between them the strength and the vulnerability which belong only to the greatest artists: the incalculable emotional
wealth, the racy comic sense, the fury to reproduce exactly not the
recognizable picture but the unmistakable experience, the thirst for
articulation as well as the curiosity and the vocabulary—that rarity—to
quench it. The weaknesses there are, the errors, the occasionally strained
effects, are accomplished by the same fearless, gifted hand.

It is not difficult to reconcile the two Faulkners; perhaps as simple as
recognizing that a man is a good host or a good guest, but rarely both. On
his own ground Faulkner is explicit, easy, sure; on someone else's he is a
little awed, a little awkward, provincially aware of the chances he is
taking. But I believe it is in the willingness to take these risks that
Faulkner's whole future lies. That *The Unvanquished* happens to be one
more chapter in the Sartoris saga is no valid description of it, nor that it is
a book about the Civil War—a Civil War in which the issue of black and
white is lost in the wider issue not of justice and tyranny, subjection and
freedom, or even sin and virtue, but merely of life and death. For one who
loves Faulkner's work and has followed it closely and impatiently, the
difficulty lies in isolating this book or any book from the others and trying
to say this or that of it: his genius is not this book or perhaps any given
book but resides in that entire determined collection of volumes which
reveal him to be the most absorbing writer of our time.

On the face of it, this book is the story of an old lady whose home has
been razed by Yankees and who sets out across the country, first driving
two mules and then, when these are confiscated, two horses, wearing a
borrowed hat on her head and holding over it a borrowed parasol. It is
told in her grandson's words, at the outset a boy of twelve who goes with
her on that imperiously reckless adventure which leads toward Jordan,
toward her career of racketeering and, like any Chicago gangster's, toward
atrocious death; a boy who in the twelve years covered by the story
matures first in emotion, then in conviction, and finally in act. "Ringo and

*Reprinted, with permission, from the *New Republic*, 94, No. 1214 (9 March 1938),
136–37.

I had been born in the same month," he says of the Negro boy who is their sole companion on the drive toward retribution, "and had both been fed at the same breast and had slept together and eaten together for so long that Ringo called Granny 'Granny' just like I did until maybe he wasn't a nigger any more or maybe I wasn't a white boy any more, the two of us neither, not even people any longer. . . ." And toward the end of the book when they are both twenty-four, he says of Ringo in a man's language then: "He was sitting quietly in a chair beside the cold stove, spent-looking too who had ridden forty miles (at one time, either in Jefferson or when he was alone at last on the road somewhere, he had cried; dust was now caked and dried in the tear-channels on his face) and would ride forty more yet would not eat, looking up at me a little red-eyed with weariness (or maybe it was more than just weariness and so I would never catch up with him). . . ." This process of development, subtly, heedfully, skillfully accomplished through the seemingly inevitable metamorphosis of speech makes the book a record not only of an individual's but a nation's, possibly a civilization's progression from violence to a passive and still undefinable bewilderment.

Elsewhere, the movement of that other group, the march of the liberated Negroes toward Jordan, starts like a whisper in the book, becomes "a kind of panting murmur" as they pass in the night, and swells to "women and children singing and chanting and trying to get to that unfinished bridge or even down into the water itself, and the cavalry beating them back with sword scabbards. . . . They just pass here without food or anything, exactly as they rose up from whatever they were doing when the spirit or the voice . . . told them to go. . . . Going to cross Jordan. . . ."

It is, then, the sentimental and glamorous story of one old lady who set out to find and ask a Yankee Colonel to return to her a chest of family silver tied with hemp rope, two darkies, Loosh and Philadelphy, and the two confiscated mules, "Old Hundred" and "Tinney"; and like a single and undaunted fife still playing, it is as well the essence of that war, a thing as intrinsically and nationally and gallantly the South's as the revolution is France's and the rebellion Ireland's: become now a legend, almost a fable of tattered banners, makeshift uniforms, incredible courage and inhuman ferocity. It has those weaknesses which can be found throughout Faulkner's work: the full-length portraits which abruptly become caricatures not likenesses of the living, the "ladies" without face or substance, the repetitions, the maudlin lapses, the shameless voice of the evangelist declaiming in solemn, flowery passages. But it has that fabulous, that wondrous, fluxing power which nothing Faulkner touches is ever without. The word for it may be glamor or may be sentiment, but both these words are mutable and I have used them here without contempt, applying them in their best sense as attributes to fact. They can confuse, they can disguise, but they can as well bring to the familiar a heightened, an isolated and a therefore truer legibility. They were elements in that electric atmosphere and mystic climate in which Poe's men and women lived and have survived and they are a vital part of Faulkner's quicker, more comprehensive world. Faulkner and Poe, set far enough apart in time, are strangely kin: unique in our history in their immunity to literary fashion, alike in their fanatical obsession with the unutterable depths of mankind's vice and even more with his divinity.

If writing remain one of the Arts— with a capital A and be damned to the current mode of splitting it two ways in a poem or a fresco on a wall — if its sensitive execution still demand the heart and the endurance which have kept artists lying prone on scaffoldings painting year in, year out, and if its success depend on its acceptance as convincing tragedy or comedy, then it can quite simply be said of Faulkner that he is the rare, the curious, the almost ludicrously authentic thing. In this book, as in his others, he writes with that "fierce desire of perfection" which contemporaries said Michelangelo evidenced when "flinging himself on the material of marble," vehemently seeking expression for "the human elements of fervor and tenderness."

IV SUBSEQUENT COMMENTARY

[An Early Recognition]

Donald Davidson*

In *Sartoris* as in [William Faulkner's] two previous books we discover a hero who is a bit cracked, and, as in *Soldiers' Pay*, it is the nervous strain of war that causes the sickness of mind and the feverish thirst for activity that is finally destructive. But in this novel the mad hero, a "doomed" or "fey" person if there ever was one, is surrounded by a group of rather normal persons — the persons, major and minor, of a good Southern family in a good Southern community.

Bayard, the last of the Sartorises, comes of a "doomed" line. The Sartorises, like the men of the Irish song, always went forth to battle and always fell — fell unluckily, unnecessarily, and foolishly, but always with the utmost abandon and gallantry. The Sartoris women, when the men threw their lives away, were left with the braver and harder tasks of continuing the establishment and coddling the bruised warriors. The latest scion of the Sartoris line, that gloomy and inexpressive Bayard, was an aviator in the World War and came home to find himself dislocated from all reasonable relation with human affairs.

He had been lucky enough to get through the war alive, but his melancholy is not bettered by the loss of his brother, also an aviator, whose death he has possibly caused. With no battles left to fight, Bayard dulls his misery with a series of meaningless anodynes: he speeds insanely along the country roads in a racing car, scaring negroes and keeping his family on edge; he rides wild stallions; he drinks fiery liquor. Literally he drives himself to death, for after he has tried all manner of machines which only wound and do not kill, he at last gets a full answer to his suicidal frenzy. He rides to his fate in a newly invented, untried aeroplane. And again the women are left to carry on the traditions; the indomitable Miss Jenny, scolding and realistic, says to Narcissa, the wife of Bayard who has named the new born child "Benbow" in order to escape or avert the fatality of family names: "Do you think that because his name is Benbow, he'll be any less a Sartoris and a scoundrel and fool?"

*Reprinted, with permission, from the *Georgia Review*, 20, No. 4 (Winter 1966), 460–62. Originally published in the *Nashville Tennessean*, 14 April 1929, Magazine Sec., p. 7.

141

In this novel, though there are occasional touches of humor and though a diverse gallery of characters gives the narrative complexity, there is really nothing but tragedy. Tragedy is inherent in every syllable of Mr. Faulkner's careful sentences. There is fatality, there is inescapable despair, on every page. I cannot help suspecting some allegorical meaning is in "Sartoris." The gloomy, unspeaking Bayard is a type of the man of this age whose only mortal satisfaction is in doing himself to death with machines. There is no end to his masculine foolishness; he is incurably romantic and childish. But the women are different; they are true realists. It is with more than a hint of a feminine world that the strong-minded Miss Jenny says: "It always does me good to see all those fool pompous men lying there with their marble mottoes and things . . . I reckon the Lord knows his business, but I declare, sometimes. . . ."

William Faulkner's *Sartoris*   Jean-Paul Sartre*

With the necessary perspective, good novels come to resemble completely natural phenomena; one tends to forget that they have authors, one accepts them as one does stones or trees, because they are present, because they exist. *Light in August* is one of these hermetic, mineral-like works. One does not accept *Sartoris* in just this way, and that is what makes this book so precious. Faulkner reveals himself in it; his hand and his craft are easily discernable throughout. I have come to realize the great resource of his art: disloyalty. I know that all art is disloyal. A painting distorts its perspective. There are, however, "true" paintings, and there are those which consciously deceive.

This "man" we discover in *Light in August* — I think of the "man" of Faulkner in the same way that one thinks of the "man" of Dostoevsky or of Meredith — this divine animal who lives without God, lost from the moment of his birth, and intent on destroying himself; cruel, moral even in murder; then miraculously saved, neither by death nor in death, but in the final moments which precede death; heroic in torment, in the most abject humiliations of the flesh: I had accepted him without reservations. I had never forgotten his proud and threatening face, his blinded eyes. I found him again in *Sartoris*. I recognized the "somber arrogance" of Bayard. Yet I can no longer accept the "man" of Faulkner: he is an illusion. Just a matter of lighting. There is a certain formula: it consists in not telling, remaining hidden, dishonestly secretive, — telling *a little*. We are furtively informed that old Bayard is shocked by the unexpected return

*Reprinted, with permission, from *Yale French Studies*, 10 (1952), 95–99; translated by Melvin Freidman. The essay first appeared (in French) in *Nouvelle Revue Française*, February 1938.

of his grandson; almost imperceptibly, in a truncated sentence, which risks passing unnoticed, and which, it is hoped, will pass nearly unnoticed. Following this, when we expect thunderbolts, we are shown gestures, prolonged indefinitely. Faulkner is not unaware of our impatience. He plays upon its effect, by talking loquaciously about gestures. There are others who employ similar devices: the realists, Dreiser. But Dreiser's descriptions attempt to teach, they are documentary. The gestures here (putting on boots, mounting a staircase, jumping on a horse) do not attempt to describe, but rather to conceal. We watch for the one which will betray Bayard's anguish; but the Sartorises are never intoxicated, they never betray themselves through gestures. Yet these idols, whose gestures have the appearance of threatening rituals, also possess consciousness. They speak, they reflect upon themselves, they stir. Faulkner knows this. On occasions he carelessly unveils to us a consciousness. But this is like the charlatan who shows us the box when it is empty. What do we see? Nothing more than what one can see from the outside: gestures. Then again we startle the unsuspecting consciousness on the verge of sleep. Once again gestures: tennis, piano, whiskey, conversations. And this is what I refuse to accept; everything conspires to make us believe that the consciousness is always empty, always thus fleeting. Why? Because consciousness is too human a thing. The Aztec gods do not have these delicate conversations with themselves. But Faulkner knows very well that consciousness is not and cannot be empty. He realizes this well enough to write: "She forced herself once more to think of nothing, to keep her consciousness immersed, as a little dog that one keeps under water until he has stopped struggling."

Yet he fails to tell us what there is inside this consciousness that one would like to drown. It is not that he wishes exactly to conceal it from us; he wishes rather that we guess what it is, because divination renders magical whatever it touches. And the gestures begin again. We should like to say, "too many gestures," as one said to Mozart, "too many notes"; too many words also. Faulkner's volubility, his abstract style, superb, anthropomorphic in the manner of a preacher: still more illusions. The style congeals everyday gestures, weights them, overwhelms them with epic splendor, and makes them sink like leaden dogs — a contrived effect. This is the loathsome and overbearing monotony, this ritual of the everyday, Faulkner aims at; gestures, this is the world of ennui. These wealthy people, without either work or leisure, proper yet uncultivated, prisoners on their own soil, at once master and slave of their negroes, are victims of their own tedium, and try to fill time with their gestures. But this boredom (has Faulkner always been able to distinguish the tedium of his heroes from that of his readers?) is only an appearance, a defense Faulkner assumes against us, that the Sartorises assume against themselves. Ennui is in the social order, it is the unvarying languor of everything that can be observed, heard, touched. Faulkner's landscapes suffer from the same tedium as his characters. The real drama is *behind*, behind the lethargy, behind the gestures, behind the consciousness. Suddenly, from the depth of this drama, surges the Act, like an aerolite: an Act — finally something happens, a message. But Faulkner continues to deceive us; he rarely describes these Acts. What he is doing is meeting and resolving an old problem in the technique of the novel: Acts are the essential element of the novel. One prepares them with care and then, when they happen, they are bare and glossy as bronze; infinitely simple, they slip between our fingers. One can say no more about them; it should merely suffice to designate them. But Faulkner does not name them, does not ever speak of them and, consequently, suggests that they are ineffable, beyond language. He will only show their results: an old man dead in his chair, an auto overturned in the river and two feet which appear above the water. Motionless and brutal, as solid and compact as the Act is fleeting, these results appear and unfold definitive, inexplicable, in the midst of the fine, dense outpour of everyday gestures. Later, these indecipherable bits of violence are transformed into "stories": they will be designated, explained, and recounted. All these men, all these families have their stories. The Sartorises carry the weighty burden of two wars, of two series of exploits: the Civil War, in which Grandfather Bayard died, the war of 1914, in which John Sartoris died. Stories appear and disappear, pass from mouth to mouth, are drawn out in the company of everyday gestures. They are not entirely from the past; they represent rather a "super-present": "As usual, old man Falls had brought John Sartoris into the room with him. . . . Freed as he was of time and flesh, he was a far more palpable presence than either of the two old men who sat shouting periodically into one another's deafness." They create a poetry of the present and of its fatality: "fatal immortality and immortal fatality." It is with stories that Faulkner's heroes forge their destinies: across these carefully constructed narratives, embellished sometimes by several generations, an unmentionable Act, buried for years, motions to other Acts, charms them, entices them as a rod attracts the thunderbolt. The artful power of words, of stories — Faulkner, however, does not believe in these incantations: ". . . what had only been a wild escapade of two youngsters, thoughtless and unheeding, inebriated by their own youth, developed into the highest form of gallantry and of tragic beauty, to the point where two angels, distraught and fallen, had, in modifying the course of events . . . ennobled the history of the race. . . ." He never allows himself to be entirely taken in, he knows what they are worth, since it is he who tells about them, since he is, as is Sherwood Anderson, "a storyteller, a fabricator." He, however, dreams of a world in which stories should be believed, where they would truly act upon men; and his novels depict this world of which he dreams. The "technique of disorder" of *The Sound and the Fury* and of *Light in August*, these inextricable mixtures of the past and the present, are well known. I believe that I have found the double origin of this in *Sartoris*: it is, on the one hand, the irresistable need of telling a story, of halting the most pressing action to interject a narrative—a characteristic trait, it appears to me, of many lyrical novelists—and, on the other hand, this faith, half sincere, half conjured up, in the magical power of the story. But when he wrote *Sartoris*, he had not yet put his technique to the test; he manipulated passages from the present to the past, from gestures to stories, with considerable awkwardness.

Here is, then, the man he presents to us, and whom he wishes us to accept. This man eludes us. One cannot grasp him through his gestures, which are only a façade, nor through his stories, which are fabrications, nor through his acts, lightning flashes which defy description. Yet beyond the acts and the words, beyond the empty consciousness, the man exists. We have a presentiment of a true drama, a kind of intelligible symbol which explains everything. What is this exactly? The decline of race or of family, an Adlerian inferiority complex, a repressed sexual urge? Sometimes the one, at other times another: it depends upon the narratives and the characters; often Faulkner fails to inform us about it. And, furthermore, he really does not care much. What concerns him is rather the "nature" of this new being he suggests to us: a nature preëminently poetical and magical, whose contradictions are numerous but veiled. Caught up in the midst of psychological manifestations, this "nature" (what other name can we give it?) participates in psychical existence. This is not even completely the workings of the unconscious, for it appears frequently that the men controlled by it, turn round towards it and contemplate it. But, on the other hand, it is as immutable and stable as an evil destiny. Faulkner's heroes carry it inside them from the moment of their birth. It has the persistency of stone or rock, it is a "thing"—a "chose-esprit," a solidified spirit, opaque, following in the wake of consciousness, shadowy, yet limpid in essence. This is the magical object, *par excellence*. Faulkner's creatures are victims of sympathetic magic: a stifling atmosphere of sorcery surrounds them. And this is what I meant by "disloyalty." These magic spells are not possible, not even realizable. So Faulkner is careful not to make us conceive of them. All his methods conspire merely to suggest them.

Is he wholly disloyal? I do not think so. If he lies, it is generally to himself. A curious passage from *Sartoris* gives us the key to his falsehoods and to his sincerity:

> "Your Arlens and Sabatinis talk a lot, and nobody ever had more to say and more trouble saying it than old Dreiser."
>
> "But they have secrets," she explained. "Shakespeare doesn't have any secrets. He tells everything."
>
> "I see. Shakespeare had no sense of discrimination and no instinct for reticence. In other words, he wasn't a gentleman," he suggested.

"Yes . . . that's what I mean."
"And so, to be a gentleman, you must have secrets."
"Oh, you make me tired."

Ambiguous dialogue, doubtless ironical; for Narcissa is not especially intelligent, and Michael Arlen and Sabatini are inferior writers. And yet it seems to me that Faulkner reveals a great deal of himself. If Narcissa, perhaps, is a bit deficient in literary taste, her instinct, on the contrary, is sure, when it causes her to choose Bayard, a man who has secrets. Horace Benbow is perhaps right in liking Shakespeare; but he is weak and loquacious, he tells everything: he is not a man. The men whom Faulkner admires — the mulatto in *Light in August*, Bayard Sartoris, the father in *Absalom, Absalom!* — have their secrets. They do not tell them themselves. Faulkner's humanism is doubtless the only acceptable one: he despises our well-adjusted conscience, our conscience with its engineer-like garrulousness. But does he not realize that his imposingly somber figures have only an exterior dimension? Is he deceived by his own art? He doubtless would not be satisfied with our secrets being forced back into the unconscious. He dreams of an absolute obscurity in the very depth of the "conscious," of a complete obscurity that we should ourselves create within ourselves. Silence: silence outside of us, silence inside us; this is the impossible dream of an ultra-puritanical stoicism. Does he lie to us? What does he do when he is alone? Does he get along with the inexhaustible small-talk of his too-human consciousness? To answer these questions we would have to know him.

Introduction [to *Sartoris*]   Robert Cantwell*

I

William Faulkner's third novel, *Sartoris*, first published in 1929, is in many respects a key volume in his works, the one that sets the pattern for them all. *Sartoris* introduces the two great families who figure directly or indirectly throughout his cycle of novels — the Sartoris family and the Snopes family. In *Sartoris* Faulkner first outlined the town of Jefferson that is the center of his fiction. And, finally, *Sartoris* marked a decisive change in his attitude toward his own work. His first two books, *Soldiers' Pay* and *Mosquitoes*, were bright and sardonic, and sometimes brilliant,

*Reprinted, with permission, from *Sartoris*, Signet edition (New York: New American Library of World Literature, Inc., 1953) pp. vii–xxv. Cantwell's essay appeared through several editions for more than a decade, and first framed *Sartoris* for countless readers; copies of this edition are now relatively rare.

novels, but they were characterized by a casual and indifferent air, while with *Sartoris* his purpose became serious and has remained so ever since.

The change, which can almost be felt in the prose as the novel proceeds, is one of the most dramatic and unusual developments in literary history. Faulkner has told how he began to write fiction under the influence of Sherwood Anderson, to whom *Sartoris* is dedicated: he noticed that Anderson had a pretty good life, only working in the morning, and he thought that he would like to be a writer himself. Mrs. Anderson told him that if he wrote a novel she would get Sherwood to read it, and if Sherwood liked it he would get his publisher, Liveright, to publish it.

Faulkner wrote *Soldiers' Pay* in six weeks, and took the manuscript to Mrs. Anderson. She returned it the next day, saying, "Sherwood says if he isn't required to read this he'll get Liveright to publish it." And so Faulkner became a novelist, Liveright giving him advances of $200 apiece on his next two novels. "And then," he said, "I liked that money. It seemed to me a mighty easy way to earn money."

In his recent book *William Faulkner*, the critic Irving Howe has suggested that Faulkner was pulling the public's leg with his story. But he has so concluded by leaving out the most important part of it. What Faulkner was saying was that the same attitude toward his writing lasted until he wrote *Sartoris*. He was halfway through *Sartoris* when suddenly "I discovered that writing was a mighty fine thing," he said. "You could make people stand on their hind legs and cast a shadow. I felt that I had all these people, and as soon as I discovered it I wanted to bring them all back."

His story is confirmed by the lift in the quality of his writing in *Sartoris*. And after *Sartoris* Faulkner turned out in a few months, in an unbroken surge of creative activity, the great books on which his standing as a novelist depends: *The Sound and the Fury, As I Lay Dying, Sanctuary* (though it is not generally listed with them, and he has written disparagingly of it), *Light in August*. When he turned away from the Sartoris theme and the locale of Jefferson, as in *Pylon* and *The Wild Palms*, the result was a sense of strain in the books: he seems to be trying to recapure his earlier inspiration in them, rather than to actually possess it. When he returned to the Sartoris story and setting with *The Hamlet* in 1940 he wrote one of his best novels.

The dividing line in his work between its arty and frivolous earlier phase, and the power of its great period, is in *Sartoris*. More specifically, it is in something in *Sartoris* that reached beyond the novel itself and gave Faulkner the vision of his work as a whole. His first two novels were satires, but the basis of their satire is uneven, so that they often seem an expression of personal irritation and nervous rejection. Turning from them to *Sartoris* we find ourself at once in the concrete reality of the town of Jefferson, seventy-five miles from Memphis, a town in upland country, lying in tilted slopes against the unbroken blue of the hills, in the midst of good broad fields richly somnolent. As the novel proceeds we become aware of a mysterious sense of excitement and intensity, communicated by the sensuous images of the town, the country and the woods, rather than (as is customary in Faulkner's books) the violent action or the violent imagery.

There are the landmarks so often found in Faulkner's novels, the brick courthouse with stone arches rising among the elms, the monument of the Confederate soldier under the trees, shading his carven eyes with his stone hand, and the courthouse square, with its unbroken low skyline of old weathered brick. Four miles from the square, beyond the streets arched with trees, is the Sartoris house, white and simple, with a curving drive and iron gates, set among oaks and locust trees, with wisteria and roses at one end of the veranda, and inside a curving stairway of white spindles and red carpet, an expanse of shuttered sunlight broken by the crystal chandelier and the tall mirror.

From the veranda Colonel Sartoris could watch the two trains a day that ran over the railroad he had built, seeing them "emerge from the hills and cross the valley into the hills, with lights and smoke and a noisy simulation of speed." Below the Sartoris house is the bed of salvia where the Yankee patrol searching for Colonel Sartoris stopped their horses. At one side is the barn around which he ducked, expecting a bullet between his shoulder blades. In the cool and shadowy recesses off the Sartoris house are the mementoes of the Colonel—his sword in a velvet sheath, his cavalry saber, his army forage cap of the 1840s, a silver oil can presented to him on the completion of his railroad, a frogged and braided Confederate coat, two silver-mounted dueling pistols and a three-barreled derringer. The parlor in which Colonel Sartoris lay after he was murdered is now seldom used, the shrouded furniture looming in the solemn obscurity "with a sort of ghostly benignance." At the end of *Sartoris*, and at the beginning of the Sartoris legend, nothing is left of the family, and the house is lifeless except for the murmur of the Negroes and the music of the young widow of the last Sartoris, playing the piano in the twilight "peopled with the ghost of glamorous and old disastrous things."

II

All the major themes of Faulkner's later novels, and many of the characters, have their origin in *Sartoris*. His best stories, and sometimes whole novels, are developments and expansions and continuations of incidents in this book. A single sentence in Part III—"Flem, the first Snopes, had appeared unheralded one day behind the counter of a small restaurant on a side street, patronized by country folk"—is developed into the 421-page tragicomedy of *The Hamlet*, eleven years after *Sartoris* was published. The short stories—*There was a Queen, Centaur in Brass, Mule in the Yard, Ad Astra, The Unvanquished, All the Dead Pilots, My Grandmother Millard, A Rose for Emily, Shall Not Perish* — continue stories begun in *Sartoris*, or deal with the same characters. The sinister town of Frenchman's Bend first appears in the novel. A few weeks after finishing *As I Lay Dying* Faulkner made Frenchman's Bend the setting for the terrific opening scene of *Sanctuary*. It is now a gangster hideout, and when Horace Benbow (who appears in *Sartoris*) stops for a drink of water he sees in the underbrush across the spring the beady eyes and the pistol of Popeye, the sadist and killer. Still later Faulkner devoted the whole of *The Hamlet* to telling how the monstrous Snopes family took over the village of Frenchman's Bend, with its life as dense and clogged as the canebrakes around it, contaminating the region like the flow from a poisoned stream.

More importantly the theme of Faulkner's works as a whole appeared in *Sartoris*. According to George O'Donnell, who first worked out its implications, it is the conflict of the Snopes and the Sartoris world: the Sartorises being recognizeable human beings who act traditionally, according to a vital social code, and the Snopeses being people who act only from self-interest, and without regard for the legitimacy of their means. At the time *Sartoris* opens, the Snopeses have already gotten a foothold in the town of Jefferson, one of them becoming a vice-president of the Sartoris bank. On the one side are the people who in varying degrees accept or represent the Sartoris standard — the De Spains, the Sutpens, the Compsons, the Benbows, the Griersons, plantations owners and Civil War heroes. On the other side are Ab Snopes, the patriarch of the clan, the barn burner, who breaks the way for the family invasion by threatening to burn the barn of any landowner who opposes him; Flem Snopes, who becomes the banker; Montgomery Ward Snopes, the draft dodger; I. O. Snopes, of *Mule in the Yard*, who drives his mules on the railroad track so he can collect damages from the railroad; Mink Snopes, the killer of *The Hamlet* — clowns, pimps, blackmailers, horsethieves, perverts, sadists, murderers, operating through "that technically unassailable opportunism which passes among country folks — and city folks too — for honest shrewdness." The Snopeses wheedle their way into jobs, they graft, lie, cheat and steal, they set one Negro workman against another by telling each that the other is after his job, they trade their wives for minor political posts or junior partnerships in business, and they climb, climb and climb, devoting to their tireless self-seeking their considerable brains, their cold hearts, and their sacred honor.

Sartoris opens with a scene in which two old men have been talking about Colonel Sartoris, and his ghost lingers in the room after they have grown silent. The town is at the point of coming under the control of the Snopeses. The descendants of Colonel Sartoris — the members of the Sartoris world — are unable to deal with them. Horace Benbow in *Sartoris* and in *Sanctuary* is ineffectual; Quentin Compson in *The Sound and the Fury* kills himself; Jason Compson in the same novel survives and holds his own against the Snopeses, but only by becoming a kind of super-Snopes himself. One wild Sartoris grandson has been killed in the war and the other, Bayard, drives his car wildly over the country roads, insults the townspeople and throws away his life, half-contemptuously. Old Bayard Sartoris, the banker, maintains the outward forms of the old way of life, symbolized by his riding to his bank in his carriage. Aunt Jenny Sartoris Du Pré, the sister of Colonel Sartoris, alone survives from the days of the Colonel, and she is principally engaged in arranging the marriage of Bayard Sartoris and Narcissa Benbow to provide a Sartoris heir. But Narcissa is being blackmailed by one of the Snopeses. (In a story published several years later, *There Was a Queen*, we learn that when Narcissa confesses to Aunt Jenny the old lady dies in her chair, the final indignity to the Sartoris standard destroying her will to live. "Born Sartoris or born quality of any kind ain't *is*, it's *does*," says the Negro cook. "Because Miss Jenny quality. That's why. And that's something you don't know nothing about, because you born too late to see any of it except her.")

Colonel Sartoris is a ghost at the beginning of *Sartoris*, but he is a singularly benign ghost: "Freed as he was of time and flesh, he was a far more palpable presence than either of the two old men. . . ." He is a living reality to the people who have known him, and the recollections of him are kindly and affectionate, though they often seem to deal with his violent deeds, and an intense significance somehow clings to them though the actual relics — the few heirlooms, the legends, the puzzled interpretations of his life — are few and inadequate for the feeling aroused. He seems to throw over life the sort of spectral benignance that clung to the shrouded parlor where he lay after he was murdered.

He dominates the novel. In actual fact, we are not told a great deal about him, either in this book or in the whole cycle of novels that he inspired.[1] In the Civil War episodes of *The Unvanquished* Colonel Sartoris behaves with courage and ingenuity and with a patrician dignity that makes him, like Lee, an embodiment of the gallantry of the Lost Cause. The heroic recklessness of other branches of the Sartoris family has been checked in the case by his sense of social responsibility. Their failure to live up to his standard, and the difference between the raw new South and the mellow plantation landscapes of his day and the courtly nobility of his generation, contribute to the torment of inadequacy of the generation of Quentin Compson and Bayard Sartoris. In the same way, the purity of Aunt Jenny Sartoris' embodiment of old Southern womanhood — her delicate features and white hair, her heroic past, including her dance with Jeb Stuart and the times she dominated carpetbaggers and Confederate skulkers by her commanding presence — contrasts with the sexual crises of the women in the later novels: Candace Compson and Dalton Ames in *The Sound and the Fury*, the brothel scenes of Temple Drake and Red in *Sanctuary*. Their conflict is not one of conscience, as in Hawthorne's New England, but stems from a violation of their sense of quality; Temple and

Candace, and indeed all the girls in Faulkner's novels, encounter in sex a social struggle, either the outrage of something for which Aunt Jenny stands as a symbol, as in *Sanctuary*, or the acceptance of a role which means a subjective sense of exclusion from her world, as in *The Sound and the Fury* and *Requiem for a Nun*.

And in the same way, the young men are unable to live up to Colonel Sartoris' legend. The wild desperation of young Bayard Sartoris' life causes the heart attack that kills Old Bayard. His death provides a momentary intermission in the spiraling descent of the Sartorises traced in the novel, a sudden, though temporary, return to reality, the heightened awareness found in the description of Bayard's flight to the cabin in the hills and in the fox hunt—the frost in the motionless air, the dry, wild and good-natured dignity of the country people, the firelit interiors, the thin blue haze pungent with cooking odors, the ringing, bell-like sound of the dogs echoing among the hills where the hunters sit motionless on their horses in the frosty moonlight. Something has happened to the writing between these passages and the first part of the book, and something still greater between them and the sardonic humor of Faulkner's first books, a sudden acceptance of the world around Bayard Sartoris and a pervading sense of enjoyment and participation in it.

The wonderful scene of Bayard's Christmas with the Negro family, moving in its timid eventlessness, and tragic in its revelation of the numbing of Bayard's faculties—the sharpness of his eyesight on the littered hearth, and his blindness to the Negro children—is music, a passage of pure lyricism despite its surface roughness, an interlude of peace whose loveliness is achieved, not by the quality of the writing, certainly not by any prose poetry of the sort Faulkner sometimes attempts, but by an acceptance of the ordinary on its own terms. The effect is to reveal the angular unrealities of Bayard's life that have preceded it. It is as if society had always known only Picasso-like glares and angles in its social relations and suddenly became aware of quiet Flemish interiors all around it. Still more, the flight to the woods and the scene in the Negro cabin (which Howe compares with some justice to the wolf hunt in Tolstoy's *War and Peace*) throws its light on the wildness of Bayard's wanderings that follow: his vague trip to Mexico and Brazil, and his death trying to fly some crack-pot inventor's newly-designed plane, in which the distortions are perhaps too accentuated and the cryptic passions merely give an impression of carelessness and haste in the writing.

So in the end there is only young Bayard's widow playing the piano in the twilight of the old Sartoris house. By some intensity of telling, rather than by their actions or their words, we are made to feel that the Sartoris destiny is truly tragic. Some quality of mystery and high purpose really appears, even though what they do often seems melodramatic, their courage only foolish recklessness, and their devotion to their code only a narrow family pride. There are few passages in Faulkner's writing where his writing in detail equals the over-all scope of his work, and even in the scenes in the hills there are oddly inappropriate images—"The sun that spread like a crimson egg broken on the ultimate hills" or the frost compared to "a scintillant rosy icing like that of a festive cake"—while we are often reminded in the course of the story of how many other people have written cycles of novels about a family, and of how often even the best of them, the Buddenbrooks and the Forsythes, grow wearisome with their own internal importances. But *Sartoris* is saved from the fate by the deadly seriousness that clings mysteriously to the Sartoris destiny. The Sartoris failure has something to do with the separation of Bayard from his own hills, and perhaps with the separation of all of us from our own; with the social numbing whose result is to make moments of awareness of the physical world and of simple relations rare and infrequent or forced; and perhaps with the torment of *The Sound and the Fury*, and the brutal triumph of Popeye in *Sanctuary* and Flem Snopes in *The Hamlet*.

III

The quality that adds intensity to *Sartoris* is inspiration, and the sources of inspiration are always beyond the reach of critical analysis. About all we can say is that continued effort along probably fruitful lines insures a greater likelihood of inspiration finding an outlet when, if ever, it occurs. Faulkner had been writing for a considerble period on *Soldiers' Pay* and *Mosquitoes* when he was inspired with the concept of Colonel Sartoris that came with this book. The vision of the still-to-be-written Jefferson novels has charged each part of it with an intensity beyond its immediate content. Sometimes, in the incident of Colonel Sartoris and the carpetbaggers, for example, the lesson seems to be only that had Colonel Sartoris' side won the Civil War, the world would be different. But more often there appears to be something practically useful in his life, though we are not altogether clear as to what its meaning is, as if he had invented something in society that has been lost. There are other obvious sources of Faulkner's inspiration—he had returned to his own countryside emotionally as well as physically, and to his own family's legend, for Colonel Sartoris is modeled on Colonel William C. Falkner, his great-grandfather. But I believe that the principal source is in the inward tension set up by the attempt to reconcile the historical figure of Colonel Falkner with the fictional creation of Colonel Sartoris as an embodiment of the old Southern virtues.

Colonel Falkner was born in Knox County in Eastern Tennessee in 1825 (though the authorities differ as to the exact time and place) and was taken to Ste. Genevieve, Missouri, where his father died, as a child. As an orphan he walked from Middleton, Tennessee, to Ripley, Mississippi, to make his home with an uncle, some time between the ages of ten and fourteen—an epic journey of which he wrote a brilliant, if romanticized, account in his novel *The White Rose of Memphis*. For four years, while he went to school, he worked in the Ripley jail, employed by the sheriff — another experience of which he made good use in *The White Rose*.

In 1845 an emigrant family named Adcock, moving from Tennessee to the West, stopped for the night at the camping grounds north of Ripley. A man named McCannon killed all the members of the family with an ax, stole the slaves and started back to Tennessee. McCannon was caught near the Tennessee line and a mob prepared to lynch him. Young Falkner started out at midnight with the posse after McCannon, rode twenty miles, and helped rescue the murderer from the mob, despite guns drawn against him. McCannon was taken back to Ripley to stand trial. There, however, another mob got him away from the authorities. Again at the point of being hanged, McCannon gained some time by promising to tell the full story of the crime. He confessed, and in the period before his execution told the story of his life to young Falkner, who wrote it up and had it printed as a pamphlet, on credit, at the press of the Ripley *Advertiser*.

He offered the pamphlet for sale on the day of McCannon's execution. It was a terrific success, and after paying the newspaper, Falkner cleared $1,250, the first money he had ever earned. His enemies later pictured him hawking the pamphlet to the crowd while McCannon's body was still spinning from the limb of a tree in the yard before the Ripley courthouse — they still do, in fact. But there is no contemporary evidence for such a grisly scene, nor any indication in Falkner's character of a tendency to work in that fashion.

There is abundant contemporary evidence, however, that Falkner's pamphlet aroused intense hostility from prominent people in nearby communities — Tuscumbia, Alabama, and Holly Springs, Mississippi, among others — who were mentioned in McCannon's narrative as his friends and the companions of his drinking bouts. These threatened to horsewhip Falkner, or worse. The Ripley *Advertiser* came to Falkner's defense. It stated that there was no young man in the community who stood higher in terms of moral integrity and courage. These comments were exchanged early in 1846. In May of that year, when the Mexican War began, Falkner was elected first lieutenant of the Tippah Volunteers, his commission being dated June 1, 1846. The company was attached to the Second Regiment, Second Mississippi Infantry, and saw service in Mexico, where Falkner was wounded on April 14, 1847.

The second lieutenant of the company was Robert Hindman, whose brother, Thomas Hindman, was a private in the ranks.[2] These were the sons of a prominent and long-established family, the father a hero of the War of 1812, who lived in a new mansion two-and-a-half miles from Ripley. Young Falkner and the Hindmans were friends. After the war, they returned to Ripley, where Falkner married Miss Holland Pearce, of Knoxville, Tennessee, and began to practice law in his uncle's law office.

On May 8, 1849, Falkner met Robert Hindman, apparently beside the Hindman house. To his astonishment, Hindman violently attacked him. He stated that he knew of no reason for Hindman's fury, and his account is altogether convincing. Hindman drew a pistol. Falkner grabbed his arm. Hindman, who was stronger, threw Falkner back against the wall of the house. (Both Hindman brothers were large, powerful men, locally remembered as "brave, fearless, high-strung," or even aggressive in the extreme, inclined to be reckless, but "no braver men ever lived than those two brothers.") Hindman placed his pistol at Falkner's breast and pulled the trigger.

The gun failed to fire. Falkner drew his knife. Hindman cocked the gun again and fired again. The pistol again failed to fire. Subsequent examination revealed that the bullets did not exactly fit; the hammer did not quite strike the cap. As Hindman tried to fire the third time, Falkner stabbed and killed him.

Falkner was arrested, charged with murder. The case split the town. The trial was not held until February, 1851, the next regular term of the court. In the meantime, Falkner's wife died, after bearing him a son, William Faulkner's grandfather. Thomas Hindman, who had just been admitted to the bar, made his first speech as the prosecuting attorney, "pregnant with bitter denunciation." But the evidence made out a clear case of self-defense, and Falkner was acquitted.

As he stepped from the courtroom into the Ripley street, Thomas Hindman attacked him. In the struggle, Falkner killed a man named Morris, a Hindman partisan in the feud that was dividing the town.

Falkner was immediately re-arrested and tried for the murder of Morris and again acquitted.

On this occasion, as he stepped forth free, he met Thomas Hindman in the dining room of the Ripley hotel. Hindman drew his pistol, but dropped it, and it fired as it hit the floor, the bullet striking the ceiling above Falkner's head.

Hindman challenged Falkner to a duel. Falkner did not believe in dueling as a matter of principle, but he accepted the challenge, and prepared to meet Hindman at 6 A.M. April 1, 1851, at the dueling ground 400 feet from the Arkansas bank of the Mississippi River, opposite the foot of Jefferson Street in Memphis. There were to be no seconds or surgeons present, and only one witness, who was to do nothing but keep out of the way. Both men were to be armed with two pistols at fifty paces, and at the word were to advance on each other, firing as often as they wished or were able.

Before the duel, Falkner and a friend, Dr. De Soto, met Hindman. De Soto drew his pistol and started to shoot Hindman, but Falkner grabbed the gun, and the hammer struck his hand.

The witness chosen was Colonel Galloway, an editor of the Memphis *Appeal*, who had a reputation as a peacemaker. He learned that Falkner knew of no reason for the Hindmans' animosity and succeeded in preventing the duel, Hindman subsequently moving to Arkansas.

Falkner remained in Ripley, where he became a leader of the Know-Nothing Party, and the editor of its paper, *Uncle Sam*, which held it together.[3] When the Civil War began, Falkner raised his own company, The Magnolia Rifles of Tippah County, and was elected Captain February 23, 1861. The Magnolia Rifles became part of the Second Infantry of the Confederate States Army, of which Falkner was elected Colonel. He had in the meantime, in 1850, married a second time, his second wife bearing him four children, three daughters and a son. The Second Infantry under his command played an important part at the Battle of Bull Run, after which it went into winter quarters at Harper's Ferry. There Mrs. Falkner and the children joined the Colonel, one son and a new-born daughter, christened Elizabeth Manassas, having died in Ripley in Colonel Falkner's absence. In the elections in the spring of 1862, John M. Stone, a former station agent at Iuka on the Memphis and Charleston Railroad, was elected Colonel of the Second Mississippi, and Colonel Falkner returned to Ripley. He bore a commission from Jefferson Davis to raise a cavalry regiment.

Some local sources in Ripley imply that Colonel Falkner's Civil War record was "nothing to be proud of." Actually, no such interpretation need be made of his return. The time was after the Confederate disaster in Grant's capture of Fort Donelson and Island Number 10, and the need for cavalry in the vast country, now wide-open for invasion, was evident even before Shiloh, only forty-odd miles away. Also, the strange local situation in Northern Mississippi, always exceptional in the course of American history, warranted the presence of an experienced officer who knew the country. Falkner organized the Seventh Mississippi Calvary, sometimes called the First Partisan Rangers. He had his regiment up to full strength in the spring, but in the fall of that year it was completely disorganized. In March, 1863, we find him reporting to the head of the Confederate Secret Service in the Middle West that the men were leaving the regular army to enroll in the irregular state units, where they were not subject to discipline and were able to live at home. He reported that they were foraging off the people, stealing all the horses (a forecast of Ab Snopes), terrorizing the women, and confiscating the property of those they called Tories. He reported that robberies and the murders of unarmed citizens were a daily occurrence, that the independent squads were growing rich by speculation and trading with the enemy, and that the people would not be able to make a crop unless some protection was afforded them. He added a note that "the Genl" — meaning Forrest — "need have no fears of my being surprised or overpowered, because I know every creek, road and path in these northern counties."

A Northern expedition that set out for Ripley in May, 1864, from Memphis, reported that for forty miles the country was completely devastated. In July of that year, Ripley itself was destroyed. The circumstances were strange. When Sherman started for Atlanta, he ordered a movement of 8,000 troops from Memphis to distract Forrest and to prevent Forrest striking his lines of communication. When this force reached Ripley, a Northern officer, Colonel De Witt Thomas, asked Colonel Falkner's wife (who he said was a very intelligent woman) where General Forrest was and how many men he had. Mrs. Falkner laughed and said that Forrest had left the region to go after Sherman, but had now returned and would attack in a few days. She said that Forrest had 28,000 men.

The Northern commander stopped in Ripley and held a council of his senior officers. He said that he wanted to turn back, since Forrest had probably concentrated an overwhelming force with him. His officers were inclined to agree with him, but since a previous expedition had turned back only a short time before, they felt the blow to morale would be disastrous.

The decision was therefore reached to continue. On the morning of June 10, 1864, the two armies met at Guntown, or Brice's Cross Roads, on Tishmingo Creek. From its physical description, the town is probably the original of Faulkner's legendary town of Frenchman's Bend. The result was a Northern debacle. The Northern losses were 2,240 men killed, wounded or missing, 22 guns, 250 six-horse wagons, a thousand rounds of artillery ammunition and 300,000 rounds of small-arms ammunition, and great stores of medical and quartermaster supplies. Forrest, who had about 8,000 rather than 28,000 men, lost 96 men killed. At dawn the next day, the fleeing Northern officers reached Ripley. Mrs. Falkner had breakfast prepared and invited Colonel Thomas to eat with her. "She wanted to know," he said, "if I did not find her words very nearly correct."[4]

After the Civil War, as is told in *Sartoris*, Colonel Falkner built the Ripley, Ship Island and Kentucky Railroad. At the height of his prosperity he operated a plantation of 1,200 acres, managed a hundred tenants, and ran a grist mill, cotton mill and sawmill. He started a college, Stonewall College, and wrote and produced a play about the Civil War, *The Lost Diamond*. In 1880 the plant of the Ripley *Advertiser* burned and Colonel Falkner advanced the money to get the paper started again, also writing *The White Rose of Memphis* as a serial to help the paper along. With its background as the inside story of something comparable to the Falkner-Hindman feud, *The White Rose* was a sensation, and doubled the circulation of the paper before it was reprinted as a book. (It went into thirty-five editions, and sold 160,000 copies before it went out of print in 1909.)[5] He then wrote an historical novel, *The Little Brick Church*, and a book about his travels in Europe.

In *Sartoris* Colonel Sartoris is described as having been elected to the legislature after a hard fight. In life, Colonel Falkner was nominated to the Mississippi legislature while he was absent in New York. At five o'clock on the day of his election he walked into the public square at Ripley.

According to contemporary newspaper accounts, he stopped to talk with an old friend, Thomas Rucker, about sawing some timber.

The two men were approached by a Ripley businessman, J. H. Thurmond, Falkner's partner in the building of the railroad and now his business rival and personal enemy. Acording to the Memphis *Appeal* Thurmond drew a pistol without speaking and pointed it at the Colonel.

"What do you mean, Dick?" Falkner said. "Don't shoot!"

Thurmond fired, and the bullet, a .44-calibre, entered Falkner's mouth, passed under his tongue, breaking the jawbone, and lodged in the right side of his neck under his ear. The shot was at such close range that Thomas Rucker's face was powder-burned. Colonel Falkner fell to the pavement. His son-in-law, Dr. Carter, wiped the blood from his face. Sitting on the pavement, Falkner turned to Thurmond, who remained standing nearby, and said, "Dick, what did you do it for?"

He died at eleven o'clock that night, November 5, 1889. Thurmond was tried and acquitted in one of the most sensational trials in the history of northern Mississippi. He moved to North Carolina, where he established another fortune in the textile industry, and the Falkners, after selling the railroad, began the moves that resulted in their settling in Oxford, Mississippi, where William Faulkner now lives across the street from the old home of Jacob Thompson.

"Great God," says one of Faulkner's Negro characters, after a comparable tragedy. "White folks." It is an appropriate comment for so strange and violent a career. The legend of Colonel Falkner was alive throughout the years of Faulkner's youth. The manner of Colonel Falkner's death was not a topic of casual conversation. It is still a delicate subject in the region. When Wiliam Faulkner was writing his great novels Colonel Falkner was still a living reality to people who lived around Ripley. They spoke of him as if he were still alive, up in the hills somewhere, and might come in at any time. As late as 1938, when I asked about Colonel Falkner there, I encountered the sensation described in the opening sentences of *Sartoris*, that of a living presence in the room, summoned up by the intensity of feeling that the Colonel's life and death had aroused.

Ordinarily I do not take much stock in supernatural visitations, but I must admit that I felt uneasy at the response when I inquired about Colonel Falkner, and I felt that the people of whom I inquired were even more uneasy than I was. Last year, in gathering some additional facts from Ripley, I encountered an even deeper sense of disquiet, as if the people who supplied the information feared that by doing so they ran the risk of arousing the spirits of Colonel Falkner and those of his former opponents to resume their quarrels. In retrospect, the opening sentences of *Sartoris* are an extremely unusual beginning for a novel. What is that specific description again? the banker and the pauper sitting silently in the presence of the dead man that is more real than they are? A strange beginning for *Sartoris*, but an even stranger beginning for the cycle of novels that it inspired. The discovery that William Faulkner made when he was halfway through *Sartoris*, that writing was a mighty fine thing, was a potent revelation. It led to the creation of a picture of a whole society, a whole area, though three generations, the visualization of a kind of life previously unsuspected. It formed a vision of the South and of Southern small town life that has profoundly modified American thought, and influenced American literature so deeply that much comtemporary writing scarcely reflects anything else. It led to the thirty years of labor to which Faulkner referred in his speech accepting the Nobel Prize.

A powerful visitation. In my own case, in asking about Colonel Falkner, I did not get quite the same impression of benignity in the spectral invocation that is ascribed to Colonel Sartoris' return in *Sartoris*. Fear would be a better word. But it is true that the ghost itself seemed benign, the fear being associated with something other than the recollection of Colonel Falkner personally. In any event, the legend of Colonel Falkner is so real that the opening scene of *Sartoris* is simply an acute description of a social fact in the region around Ripley. And this leads to an observation which must strike every reader who tries to relate Faulkner's fiction to the Mississippi countryside.

It is commonly asserted that the strength of Faulkner's novels comes from the depth of his absorption with the life of his own region. Most critics would agree that a prevailing weakness in modern American literature is the lack of a comparable sense of identification in most writers. Faulkner has consequently always been a central figure to the regionalists. He has been their proof of the advantage to the author of remaining in his own home town, close to his origins, among people he knows, with traditions he understands, and away from the vast anonymous crowds of the cities with whom he can have at best only a formal kinship. I am in agreement with their argument in general, but *Sartoris*, and still more the legend of Colonel Falkner, seem to me to prove that the writer must choose most carefully the small town he is to remain in. Faulkner's achievement was not that he chose to live in a provincial community, but that he selected this particular one. The life of northern Mississippi on which he focused his imagination needed an interpreter in the way that desert regions need irrigation. The immense influence of his work stands as a renewed affirmation of what one man can do.

In the same way, the importance of *Sartoris* is not that Faulkner celebrated a provincial hero who represented the spirit of the Old South, but that he focused his imagination on the extraordinary complexities of the life of Colonel Falkner. The paradox of Colonel Falkner was that, depsite the violence of his legend, he was known as a man of peace. It was remembered of him, when *The White Rose* was published, that he had lived for forty-four years in the community and had never been involved in any difficulty after the Hindman feud. It was also recollected that for years he had moved through the town at the height of the tension, refusing to be provoked into violence and yet avoiding the fate that came to him on the late November afternoon of his old age. It was recognized that he was an unusual character, a businessman who combined with business the imagination shown in *The White Rose*, a plantation-owner who combined with Southern courtliness a practical and enterprising spirit, a railroad builder who brought to industry something of the code of the planter aristocracy, an army officer who combined his military exploits with concern for the civilian population, and finally a man of peaceful inclinations who displayed an effective resistance to violence. Hence the curious quality of the passages in *Sartoris* in which Colonel Sartoris' violent deeds are recollected wih connotations of peace and benignity. Hence also the strange impression that the book communicates, that though Colonel Sartoris is merely an old Southern gentleman, his story nevertheless has some obscure practical significance to the modern world — something to justify retelling it, to branch out to the stories of the Snopeses and Frenchman's Bend, to account for thirty years of labor. And this, perhaps, is the reason why the Sartoris novels make us feel that, had his side won, the world really would have been different, just as our picture of northern Mississippi would have been different if William Faulkner had never written his novels. The victory of a Colonel Falkner, or of Colonel Sartoris, would not have been that of the Old South in the Civil War, but an emerging part of the Old South that combined its best qualities with something better.

Notes

1. Colonel Sartoris, who dies in 1876 in *Sartoris*, was still alive in 1894 in *A Rose for Emily*. His importance in the short story was slight; he told Miss Emily that she owed no taxes, since the town owed her father money.

2. According to *Biographical Sketches of Gen. Pat Cleburne and Gen. T. C. Hindman*, by Charles Edward Nash, a kinsman of Hindman by marriage, Hindman who had "a wonderful talent for getting into fusses" and was "ambitious and overbearing," was promoted to first lieutenant in Mexico for valorous conduct.

3. The Know-Nothing Party was an attempt to substitute anti-Catholic and anti-foreign agitation for the issue of slavery that was dividing the country. At the height of its influence in 1855 the Know-Nothings elected governors and legislatures in New Hampshire, Massachusetts, Rhode Island, Connecticut, New York, Kentucky, and California, and nearly carried Texas, Virginia, Georgia, Alabama, Mississippi and Lousiana. It was a secret, fraternal order, organized in lodges like the Masons, and only members who reached the higher degrees knew its full name ("The Sons of '76, or Order of the Star-Spangled Banner") or its precise objectives. They answered questions about it by saying "I don't know," which resulted in its popular name.

After leaving Mississippi, Hindman as a young lawyer and politician conducted a whirlwind campaign against the Know-Nothings, which were at the point of dissolution nationally, and became famous for having destroyed the Know-Nothings forever in Arkansas. He fought, or barely avoided by the action of peacemakers, a number of duels. At a political rally, Colonel Falkner strangely spoke in his favor.

In 1858, Hindman accused a politician named Rice of selling out to the Know-

Nothings. Rice left town, Helena, Arkansas, and returned with his brother. Saying that he feared he would not have a fair chance, Hindman asked the help of Pat Cleburne, a young drug clerk, formerly a British Army officer, and later one of the finest officers in the Confederate Army. As the two men walked past Moore's Dry Goods store on the streets of Helena, a shot from behind the door, at a distance of three feet, missed Hindman. A second shot struck Cleburne in the back. A physician, a cousin of the Rice brothers, standing across the street, shot Hindman in the breast, and was killed, as both Cleburne and Hindman, before falling, shot him in the bowels. Cleburne hovered between life and death for ten days. Hindman was not seriously wounded.

Dr. Nash, in whose drugstore Cleburne worked, and who wrote his recollections by both men, feared to remove the bullet from Cleburne's back. It was later removed by Hindman's brother-in-law.

Hindman became a power in Arkansas politics, built a mansion in Helena (later a Catholic school), and resigned his seat in Congress as secession got under way. He enlisted as a private in Yell's Rifles, was elected captain, became a Confederate Major-General, and fled to Mexico, where he operated a coffee plantation, after the Civil War. His wife's parents had objected to his courtship of her. They sent her to a Catholic school, St. Agnes, in Memphis, to get her away from him. Posing as her uncle, Hindman managed to see her at the school, and they were subsequently married. In Mexico Hindman seems to have prospered, but Mrs. Hindman objected to the children being brought up under Catholic influence, and they returned to Helena during Reconstruction. At a political meeting, Hindman objected to statements made by Clayton Powell at a Negro meeting and was killed.

4. Colonel Thomas' report of his conversations with Mrs. Falkner are included in *The official Records of the War of the Rebellion*, volume 77.

5. Now again available, in a new edition published in 1953 by Coley Taylor and The Bond Wheelwright Co.

Foreword [to *The Unvanquished*]   Carvel Collins*

The Unvanquished is the story of Bayard's victory. William Faulkner's most romantic novel, it is clear and fast-moving. But when it first appeared, in 1938, its critical reception demonstrated the prevailing confusion about Faulkner's fiction. The range of opinions in the book reviews of the time proved the truth of the statement Robert Penn Warren later made: "The study of Faulkner is the most challenging single task in contemporary American literature for criticism to undertake."

Kay Boyle, always perceptive, was ahead of her time in her review of the novel when she credited Faulkner with "the strength and the vulnerability which belong only to the greatest artists: the incalculable emotional wealth, the racy comic sense, the fury to reproduce exactly not the recognizable picture but the unmistakable experience." She accorded *The Unvanquished* "that fabulous, that wondrous, fluxing power which nothing Faulkner touches is ever without." She went on to express an opinion

*Foreword by Carvel Collins from *The Unvanquished*. © 1959 by New American Library. Reprinted by permission.

less widely held then than today: that Faulkner is "the most absorbing writer of our time."

But some of the other reviewers of this novel, just over twenty years ago, demonstrated the misunderstanding and hostility which dogged Faulkner until after the Second World War and his winning of the Nobel Prize, when his reputation rose to a level with that of the foremost writers America has produced. On rereading those reviewers one puzzles why they applied to *The Unvanquished* their standard charges against Faulkner; for the central idea of the novel is explicit, its style relatively simple, and its demonstration of Faulkner's phenomenal storytelling power quite obvious.

One problem worrying some of the reviewers was whether *The Unvanquished* is actually a novel. Because six of the seven chapters appeared originally as stories in *The Saturday Evening Post* and *Scribner's Magazine* between 1934 and 1936, some critics said that Faulkner had not made a novel by revising and assembling those six parts and adding the previously unpublished final chapter. A similar charge has since appeared against Faulkner's *The Hamlet*, and is equally false. Just as *The Hamlet* is unified by the steady, monstrous rise of Ab Snopes's son to corrupt power, so *The Unvanquished*, in much happier vein, is unified by Bayard Sartoris' rise to maturity and true courage.

Skillfully interwoven with Bayard's development are other themes which enrich the novel, among them the baleful influence of the "poor white" Ab Snopes, as well as slavery with its aftereffects, the evil of which Faulkner clearly presents, and which he finally points up by showing Ringo's ultimate lack of opportunity. *The Unvanquished* relates to other Faulkner works by its themes and by many of its people, chiefly the Sartoris family, Ab Snopes, and the McCaslin twins. But we need no longer follow the critical opinion that Faulkner's major contribution to our literature is the fact that most of his books form a loosely interlocked series about his imaginary Yoknapatawpha County. Readers increasingly see that Faulkner has created several works of art, each having a unity of its own and giving readers pleasure apart from its presumed position in his "saga."

Though a number of Faulkner's other novels have more scope and depth, *The Unvanquished* is attractive for its moving presentation of Bayard's growth. In Chapter I, "Ambuscade," we see him, twelve, childishly committing the violence of firing at the Union soldier and hiding from punishment behind Granny Millard's skirts. Succeeding chapters show him growing older surrounded still by the violence and chaos of war. In "Vendée," only fifteen, he follows the code in full revenge. In "Skirmish at Sartoris" he experiences one more episode in his family's record of violence. It is in the final chapter of the book that Bayard, at the age of twenty-four, comes to a greater test than his pursuit of Grumby nine years before. After Redmond shoots Colonel Sartoris, who purposely went unarmed in repudiation of violence, when Drusilla, Ringo, and the people of the town expect Bayard to perpetuate the code of revenge, he grows up completely: facing Redmond he breaks the chain of violence. This hopefulness at the conclusion of the novel increases when not only the town recognizes the maturity of Bayard's action but Drusilla, herself grown up, awards him the sprig of verbena.

Bayard accomplishes his triumph of character in part because Granny Millard, even when involved in what she considered sin, set him an ethical example from his earliest days. But the triumph is not alone Bayard's aided by Granny's teaching; Colonel John Sartoris shares it too. That this is so is well stated by James Meriwether in an excellent, unpublished dissertation to which I am indebted: "Father and son both faced Redmond unarmed; had it not been for the example of his father, perhaps Bayard could not have so faced Redmond; had it not been for the memory of the father, perhaps Redmond would have aimed at the son."

In writing a novel about this hopeful development, Faulkner drew much from the history of his own family, chiefly of his great-grandfather, Colonel William C. Falkner, who closely resembled Bayard's father. Both the real Colonel Falkner and the fictional Colonel Sartoris formed their own troops for the Civil War and won colonelcy by election. After both lost re-election for leadership of their regiments, they returned home and formed partisan cavalry units.

Colonel Falkner was almost as dashing as his fictional counterpart, for in the words of Andrew Brown, who is a fine student of Mississippi history, Colonel Falkner, shortly after he organized his regiment, "decided on a move that illustrates his self-confidence and his rashness." At the head of his one regiment of raw recruits, who were "armed mostly with shotguns," he assaulted Rienzi "which was garrisoned by three veteran regiments under the command of hard-bitten Sheridan," and led his men "in a thundering charge down the main road into the town."

Like Colonel Sartoris in the novel, Colonel Falkner went on to become locally well known in combat. Mrs. Virgina Bardsley's excellent, unpublished biography of Colonel Falkner, which she has kindly lent me, reproduces an official letter praising his courage at First Manassas. According to local legend, Colonel Falkner, wearing a large feather in his hat, so distinguished himself in the battle that General Beauregard reputedly told nearby soldiers to follow "the knight with the black plume." Later Jeb Stuart — and who could better judge? — complimented Falkner's regiment for its gallantry in that action.

Early in the War, Colonel Falkner, in an episode on which his great-grandson may have drawn for Colonel Sartoris' dramatic escape in Chapter II of *The Unvanquished*, barely got away when Union troops surrounded his home town of Ripley, Mississippi. After the war, still the model for Sartoris, Colonel Falkner became a community leader and devoted himself to building a railroad.

Both the fictional and real men were involved in violence more personal than war. Colonel Falkner killed two men in Ripley, for which the courts acquitted him on grounds of self-defense. Finally he modeled for the fictional Sartoris even in the manner and violence of his own death. His former partner in the railroad, a man named Thurmond, fell out with him as Redmond did with Colonel Sartoris in *The Unvanquished*. Though Colonel Falkner knew Thurmond was threatening to kill him, like Sartoris in the novel he went unarmed. According to two Ripley residents interviewed by Mrs. Bardsley some years ago, he was as conscious of what he was doing as Colonel Sartoris, for he said "that he had killed his share of men and hoped never to shed another drop of blood, so that if anyone shot, it would be Thurmond and not he." And it was Thurmond—who shot him dead in the public square.

In *The Unvanquished* William Faulkner drew on his family's history for more than events. That it gave him real understanding of how Bayard felt when he became "the" Sartoris at the death of his father is suggested by a statement Faulkner made in 1955 while visiting Japan. To a question about family responsibility in Mississippi he replied, "We have to be clannish just like the people in the Scottish highlands, each springing to defend his own blood whether it be right or wrong." He went on to say that a family usually has an hereditary head, "the oldest son of the oldest son and each looked upon as chief by his own particular clan." He concluded that this is "because only a comparatively short time ago we were invaded by our own people—speaking in our own language, which is always a pretty savage sort of warfare."

Having chosen that warfare as the exciting backdrop for *The Unvanquished*, Faulkner writes of it well. By the time of the fall of Vicksburg, when the novel begins, the Confederate defeats at Shiloh and Corinth had opened northern Mississippi to the Federal armies. The confusion which permitted Granny Millard, Ringo, Bayard, and Ab Snopes to carry on their fantastic "mule business" was real enough; for the border region of north Mississippi, as Brown puts it, was "overrun by both the Union and Confederate armies but controlled by neither."

For artistic purposes Faulkner somewhat alters the timing of the events of the War, and in Chapter VI he places Reconstruction much closer to the surrender at Appomattox than it was in reality. But he catches the essence of the confused conflict over north Mississippi in addition to presenting the collapse of the Confederate hope for victory. As Meriwether has pointed out while noting its historical discrepancies, *The Unvanquished* is not primarily about the Civil War; so objection to the spacing of the military events in the novel serves little purpose, especially when the spacing gives shape and force to the drama of Bayard's growth to real manhood.

The day is past when readers considered it Faulkner's chief function to explain his section of the South and the detail of its history. They now recognize him to be artist instead of sociologist or regional historian. By setting not only *The Unvanquished* but many of his other works in the part of our country which he knows best, he is not so much recording the life of that particular region as making it a base from which he examines, in book after book, significant aspects of man's life in general.

Faulkner's feeling about man's endurance and courage, virtues he implicitly gave to the young Southerner Bayard Sartoris in *The Unvanquished*, appears explicitly in the address he made "To the Youth of Japan," when they — half a world away from Yoknapatawpha — were suffering the aftermath of another war, another defeat. Having spoken of the people of the South in the Civil War and their particular troubles during Reconstruction, William Faulkner went on to speak of man in general and to add that in his opinion art has one high purpose — which surely we may conclude that *The Unvanquished* serves:

> I believe our country is even stronger because of that old anguish since that very anguish taught us compassion for other peoples whom war has injured. I mention it only to explain and show that Americans from my part of America at least can understand the feeling of the Japanese young people of today that the future offers . . . nothing but hopelessness, with nothing . . . to hold to or believe in. Because the young people of my country during those ten years must have said in their turn: "What shall we do now? . . ."
>
> I would like to think that there was someone there at that time too . . . to reassure them that man is tough, that nothing, nothing — war, grief, hopelessness, despair — can last as long as man himself can last; that man himself will prevail over all his anguishes, provided he will make the effort to . . . to seek not for a mere crutch to lean on, but to stand erect on his own feet by believing in hope and in his own toughness and endurance.
>
> I believe that is the only reason for art. . . . That art is the strongest and most durable force man has invented or discovered with which to record the history of his invincible durability and courage beneath disaster, and to postulate the validity of his hope.

A Reading of Faulkner's *Sartoris* and "There Was a Queen"

Haney H. Bell, Jr.*

Though he had written at an earlier date both *Mosquitoes*, a satirical novel with a New Orleans setting, and *Soldiers' Pay*, a book which treats the homecoming of a dying soldier, it was not until he wrote *Sartoris* in 1929 that Faulkner succeeded in publishing his first serious novel. As Robert Cantwell has astutely observed, Faulkner began his writing career

*Reprinted, with permission, from *Forum* (University of Houston), 4, No. 8 (Fall–Winter 1965), 23–26.

with a rather cavalier attitude toward the profession. He liked the money it promised; he didn't think it would prove too laborious, and he didn't think it would take up too much of his time. He apparently maintained this attitude through the writing of his first two books and half-way through his third, and then suddenly he discarded it and became a writer with serious intentions and a serious purpose. It is almost as if he had suddenly discovered where he was going and how he was going to get there. *Sartoris* then stands as an important work because it represents not only the proper direction but also the point of no return for Faulkner in his labors. So long as he wrote on the theme that he began to develop in earnest in the latter half of *Sartoris* — the theme of the Southern chivalric tradition and its struggles — just so long did he write successfully. Whenever he departed from this theme, he wrote unsuccessfully.

Since *Sartoris* forms such a line of demarcation between the old and the new Faulkner, it behooves the careful and conscientious reader to pay close attention to its genealogy, chronology, and interpretation. It is the purpose of this article to treat some of the problems that appear in these areas, especially the areas of genealogy and chronology.

The action of *Sartoris* covers slightly more than a year — from the early spring of 1919 to the latter part of June of 1920; but through the memories and the reminiscences of the various characters, particularly Virginia Sartoris Du Pré (Jenny), it covers a much greater period of time. Through these recollections the reader is permitted to see the entire Sartoris family from Colonel John Sartoris, who, while still a young man, came from Carolina to build the Mississippi homestead before 1850, to Captain Bayard Sartoris, his great-grandson, who was killed while testing an airplane in 1920. We even get a glimpse of Colonel John's great-great-grandson, Benbow Sartoris (Bory), who is born just before the book ends.

The oldest Sartorises, the parents of Colonel John Sartoris, resided in Carolina in a house that was burned by the Yankees during the Civil War, and there is no indication that they ever left the state. They had four children — John Sartoris, Bayard Sartoris, Virginia Sartoris, and another daughter whose name is never given. Of these four children, John is the only one who had any offspring. He married a girl whose family name was Millard — her first name is not given — and prior to her death, which occurred presumably before she was thirty years old, she gave him three children — Bayard Sartoris and two daughters whose names are never given. Of these three, Bayard is the only one who married, but by this marriage he managed to perpetuate the Sartoris name by fathering an only child, a son whom he named after the boy's grandfather John. This last John married Lucy Cranston and by her he had twin sons, Bayard Sartoris and John Sartoris. John never married, but Bayard had two wives. The first was Caroline White, who died giving birth to their only child, a son named Bayard Sartoris, who in turn died at birth. Bayard's second wife was Narcissa Benbow, and they had one child, a son named Benbow

Sartoris, and he becomes the only hope for continuing the Sartoris line. However, he is too young at the conclusion of the book to give any indication as to whether or not the name of Sartoris will end with him. These are all of the people who figure prominently on the white side of the Sartoris family.

While he was establishing the beginnings of the white Sartoris line in Mississippi, Colonel John Sartoris had not been totally negligent toward the Negro side! By a Negro woman, he had a daughter named Elnora, who thus became the half-sister of Colonel Bayard Sartoris, for whom she cooked. Elnora's mother's name is never revealed, but the reader is informed that she was the wife of Simon Strother, Colonel Bayard Sartoris's Negro coachman. Whether or not she was married at the time that she found favor in the eyes of Colonel John Sartoris is not known, but it is probably of no importance, for it is not likely that it would have made much difference one way or the other.

Elnora, probably in 1902, had relations with Simon Strother, her mother's husband, and by this union her son Isom was born to become the half-brother of Saddie and Joby, who were Elnora's children by her husband Caspey, who was also her half-brother since they both had the same mother but different fathers—Caspey having been sired by Simon Strother. These are all of the people who figure prominently on the Negro side of the Sartoris family, and if it all seems a little confusing, the attached genealogical chart will serve as a guide through these complex relationships.

Despite the fact that *Sartoris* was published in 1929, the Sartoris family saga must not have been complete in Faulkner's mind because three years later he wrote the short story entitled "There Was a Queen," which carries the story line of *Sartoris* nine years forward in time to the summer of 1929, and rounds out the book. It is in the story that we learn of the miscegenation in the Sartoris family. It is never mentioned, indeed never hinted at, in the book.

Perhaps Faulkner had not thought of making the Sartoris family guilty of miscegenation when he wrote the book. It is possible that he introduced it into his story as an afterthought. It could have come about as the result of a number of considerations, and it is unlikely now that we will ever know exactly how it happened. In any event, we know that it did happen for this is made abundantly clear in "There Was a Queen."

Doubtless there are many people who can find it in their hearts to wish that Faulkner had never written "There Was a Queen" because it complicates and confuses the dates mentioned and alluded to in *Sartoris* as well as the Sartoris genealogy as it is outlined in the book. However, whether or not it meets with general approval, Faulkner did write the story; and furthermore it forms in actuality the final chapter of the book. Without the story we would not be permitted to witness the death of the last old time Sartoris—Miss Jenny—when she is told the complete story of

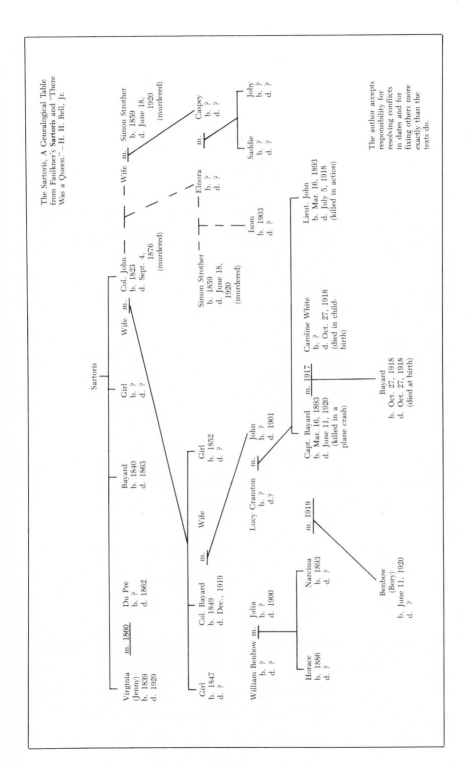

The Sartoris, A Genealogical Table from Faulkner's **Sartoris** and "There Was a Queen."—H. H. Bell, Jr.

Sartoris

Virginia
(Jenny)
b. 1839
d. 1929

m. 1860

Du Pre
b. ?
d. 1862

Bayard
b. 1840
d. 1863

Girl
b. ?
d. ?

Wife   m.   Col. John
b. 1823
d. Sept. 4,
1876
(murdered)

Wife   m.   Simon Strother
b. 1859
d. June 18,
1920
(murdered)

Simon Strother
b. 1859
d. June 18,
1920
(murdered)

Caspey
b. ?
d. ?

m.

Saddie
b. ?
d. ?

Joby
b. ?
d. ?

Girl
b. 1847
d. ?

Col. Bayard
b. 1849
d. Dec., 1919

m.   Wife

Girl
b. 1852
d. ?

John
b. ?
d. 1901

m.   Lucy Cranston
b. ?
d. ?

Capt. Bayard
b. Mar. 16, 1893
d. June 11, 1920
(killed in a
plane crash)

m. 1917   Caroline White
b. ?
d. Oct. 27, 1918
(died in child-
birth)

Elnora
b. ?
d. ?

Isom
b. 1903
d. ?

Lieut. John
b. Mar. 16, 1893
d. July 5, 1918
(killed in action)

William Benbow m. Julia
b. ?   b. ?
d. ?   d. 1900

Narcissa
b. 1893
d. ?

m. 1919

Bayard
b. Oct. 27, 1918
d. Oct. 27, 1918
(died at birth)

Horace
b. 1886
d. ?

Benbow
(Bory)
b. June 11, 1920
d. ?

The author accepts responsibility for resolving conflicts in dates and for fixing others more exactly than the texts do.

the obscene letters which the peeping Tom, Byron Snopes, had written to Narcissa, the widow of the now deceased Captain Bayard Sartoris. The heart of this genteel old warrior cannot bear the stress of this last and greatest indignity to the Sartoris name, and she dies quietly sitting in her chair staring through the colored glass window panes which she had brought with her in a hamper from Carolina in 1869, when she had come to live with her brother, Colonel John.

Moreover, the fact that the story reveals that Elnora is half Sartoris helps to explain her fierce loyalty to the family which at times goes far beyond the loyalty that one would expect a servant to show a master, however close they may have been. It also helps to explain why Elnora when speaking of Narcissa says, "I got nothing against her, I nigger and she white. But my black children got more blood than she got. More behavior."

Her "black children," as Elnora referred to them, were a mongrel lot. It will be remembered that Isom, who was born in 1903, had been fathered by Simon Strother, the husband of her mother. Saddie and Joby, her other two children, had been sired by her husband Caspey, who was also her half-brother. Hence, even though they had some Sartoris blood in them, they had a lot of other blood too.

The usual chronological inconsistencies that one finds in many of Faulkner's works begin to appear when one compares *Sartoris* with "There Was a Queen." For example, Narcissa received her first letter from Byron Snopes in 1919, yet in 1929, she says to Miss Jenny in "There Was a Queen," "It was those letters. Thirteen years ago: don't you remember?" This would mean that she received her letters in 1916. A careful reading of both works will indicate that Faulkner intends the reader to settle upon 1919 as the correct date here.

Again speaking in June of 1929 in "There Was a Queen" Narcissa tells Miss Jenny, "Then it was almost twelve years ago, and I had Bory, and I supposed I had got over it [her fear that the obscene letters would be made public]." This would yield 1917 as Bory's birth year, but the reader has been told unequivocally in *Sartoris* that Bory was born on June 11, 1920 — the same day that his father, Captain Bayard Sartoris, was killed testing an untried airplane in Dayton, Ohio. Here Faulkner obviously intends June 11, 1920 to be the accepted date.

And again Miss Jenny, thinking to herself, in 1929 in "There Was a Queen" muses that "it was in the garden that she and the younger woman (Narcissa) who was to marry her nephew and bear a son, had become acquainted. That was back in 1918, and young Bayard and his brother John were still in France. It was before John was killed [July 5, 1918], and two or three times a week Narcissa would come out from town to visit her while she worked among the flowers. 'And she engaged to Bayard all the time and not telling me.' "

Faulkner apparently just forgot here what he had written earlier. As has been noted above, Bayard was married to Caroline White in 1917, and they had a son (Bayard) on October 27, 1918. Both mother and son died when the son was born. Bayard didn't attend the funerals because he was still in France. He did not return home between the time of his leave in 1917 when he married Caroline White and the termination of his military service in the latter part of 1918. Hence, it can be seen that Bayard could not possibly have been engaged to Narcissa while he was still married to Caroline. The truth of the matter is that he began seeing her after he returned from France in the latter part of 1918.

And still again in "There Was a Queen" we are told that the Federal Agent had had Narcissa's letters for twelve years. This would mean that she had lost them in 1917. However, the reader is informed clearly in *Sartoris* that Narcissa discovered their loss the day before she was married in 1919. They had disappeared the same night that Byron Snopes had robbed Colonel Bayard Sartoris's bank and had left town. It turns out also that he had stolen the letters and that he had dropped them in his attempt to escape.

There is little or no symbolism in *Sartoris* and primarily for this reason its interpretation offers few if any problems. The main theme, of course, is that of the degeneration of a once genteel family through three successive generations — from Colonel John Sartoris to young Captain Bayard Sartoris. In tracing the course of this degeneration, the reader can hardly overlook the prevalent role that violence plays in the demises of the various Sartoris men. Most of them seem to have a love of and a distinct penchant for violent action. It is almost as if it were an integral part of their natures, and it sometimes overflows the limits of the Sartoris family itself and engulfs the husbands of Sartoris women.

Colonel John Sartoris murdered four men, and when he grew tired of bloodshed, he was himself murdered by Redlaw. His brother Bayard, an aide to General J. E. B. Stuart, was shot from his horse during the Civil War when he singlehandedly raided a Yankee field kitchen in search of anchovies, of all things. His brother-in-law whose name was Du Pré, the husband of Virginia Sartoris, was likewise killed in action in the Civil War. His grandson John Sartoris died of wounds he received in the Spanish War. His great-grandson John Sartoris was shot down in a dog fight by a German ace named Ploeckner, a pupil of Richthofen himself, in the first World War. His great-grandson Bayard Sartoris, the twin brother of John, was killed while testing an airplane that nobody else would fly. In fact, the only Sartoris man who did not die a violent death, and the only one to reach sixty years of age, was Colonel Bayard Sartoris, and the only reason that he managed to accomplish this is probably that as he himself said he had been born too late for one war and too soon for the next. He died from a heart attack brought on by the auto wreck he was involved in while riding with his grandson Bayard, and Miss Jenny "thought what a joke they had played on him — forbidding him opportunities for swashbuckling and then denying him the privilege of being buried by men, who would have invented vainglory for him."

The tradition of violence also engulfs Simon Strother, who is to be regarded as a Sartoris man by virtue of his being married to the Negro woman whom Colonel John Sartoris had violated and by the way he is treated in death by Miss Jenny. At sixty years of age, he was murdered by an unknown assailant when he was discovered in the house of Meloney Harris, the young "mulatto girl whose smart cap and apron and lean, shining shanks had lent such an air to Belle's [Belle Mitchell's] parties."

Speaking in general, the degeneration of the Sartorises takes place in three stages, and these stages are represented by Colonel John Sartoris, Colonel Bayard Sartoris, and Captain Bayard Sartoris. Colonel John was the "getter." It was he who moved to Mississippi and erected the Sartoris homestead, and it was he who sat on the veranda that he had constructed and watched the two trains a day that he owned run on the railroad that he had built across the valley land that he had acquired. He had fought with commendable valor in the Civil War, and he had made the name Sartoris legendary in and around Jefferson. He had accumulated large land holdings and he served as a second father to his two sisters, both of whom left Carolina to come and reside with him in Mississippi.

Colonel Bayard was the "holder." He inherited the money, the land, and the other holdings of his father, but he added nothing to them during his rather uneventful life. He was the president of the Sartoris Bank, but in reality he did nothing more than live off what he had inherited. The Sartoris name begins to decline with his generation, for it added nothing to the glamor or the wealth of the family.

Captain Bayard was the "destroyer." He virtually threw away his own life, and he, in effect, killed his grandfather, Colonel Bayard. He was never gainfully employed, and lastly, he married a girl who got a vicarious thrill out of receiving obscene letters from an unknown correspondent. She is far removed from the Sartoris women of old even as Bayard is far removed from the Sartoris men of old — in more than years.

When one has finished reading *Sartoris* and "There Was a Queen," he has read the entire story of the Sartorises. They are gone forever, but their legend lives on; and the thoughts which Faulkner's mind was forced to ponder as he wrote about them greatly enrich many of his subsequent works. This is perhaps the greatest tribute that can be paid these two works.

Escape into Myth: The Long Dying of Bayard Sartoris

John William Corrington*

I

Sartoris, William Faulkner's first novel dealing with Yoknapatawpha County and its people, represents one of his most lucid studies of the problem of order and its symbolizations in the post-war South. Faulkner traces, in the saga of the Sartoris family and its decline, a paradigmatic account of the South's alienation from the values of post-war U.S. society. The novel deals with politics and finance, social mores and folk-attitudes only in the most off-hand way because Faulkner understood that there is only one place where the manifold tensions of life in pragmatic existence are rendered articulate, that place being "the human heart in conflict with itself."

The titanic struggle of Faulkner's people in the years following their abortive war for independence is concerned, on the psychic level, with the necessity of re-establishing some viable order to replace that which has been annihilated, to forge new symbolizations, new formulations which can replace those lost with the blasted ante-bellum regime. In this struggle to find symbols around which some meaningful order can coalesce, which will elicit consent both personal and public and form a basis for action in the new reality, history becomes myth. Olga Vickery has discussed the process: "The 'truth' of these legends is not in question since cold, unadorned facts, measurements and statistics are no substitute for the vision of the enthralled imagination and the passionate heart making out of the brutality and confusion an enduring spectacle of human courage and faith and self-sacrifice."[1]

In the confusion and disillusionment of the reconstruction years, followed by decades of general privation, isolation, ignorance, bitterness and boredom, it was the myth of "the South" which became the organizing and valuating symbol structure for such people as the Sartorises, already withdrawn too far from the land to lose themselves again in its simple and total demands as the MacCallums did, yet too sensible of human values generally to fall into the pattern of the voracious Snopeses. As we will see, the Sartorises are both creators of and subscribers to this fabric of myth, this tenuous but vital mode of thought and conduct which, to Faulkner's mind, is clearly the private paradigm of an order which, between the Confederate War and the 1914–18 War, serves to sustain the Southern psyche, to preserve what self-respect and feeling as a people remains after the trauma of the War.

The overriding public myth, founded upon the exploits of Robert E.

*Reprinted, with permission, from *Recherches Anglaises et Américaines*, 4 (1971), 31–47.

Lee, Jackson, Stuart, Forrest, and the Confederate soldier generally, is recapitulated and reinforced by private but no less compelling structures common to individual communities and families. In this sense, if Lee is the Olympian figure about whom the whole complex of "Southern myth" organizes itself, Colonel John Sartoris is the *genius loci*, the local representative of the same myth. The idea of "Sartoris" is thus not simply a family possession: it is shared by a whole raft of near kin and kin-by-marriage, of townsmen and country people, of Negro servants. The tensions of existence in history are sustained time after time by reference to this legend and its meaning to the people of Jefferson.

II

In order to establish the context in which the action of *Sartoris* takes place, it is necessary to examine first the final section of *The Unvanquished* in order to see, as it were, the pragmatic "history," the factual genesis of the Sartoris myth.[2] While most of the constituents are given at least briefly in *Sartoris*, the sketchy details leave us far short of a satisfactory picture of that critical time when Colonel John Sartoris laid the foundations of the myth in war and in the uneasy peace which followed.

One of the most significant aspects of the Sartoris myth as it is manifested in *The Unvanquished* is its deep influence on those not directly connected with it; on that body of people who stand near the Sartoris men expecting certain conduct from the Sartorises by which to orient their own attitudes. These figures are essentially choric; they comment on the action of the Sartorises and are themselves in some measure responsible for it, though they are not part of the immediate family.

In "An Odor of Verbena," George Wyatt, a local businessman and longtime friend of Colonel John Sartoris, plays this role. He offers, along with "five or six others" of the Colonel's old troop, to take care of Redmond (the name in *Sartoris* is Redlaw) who has killed the Colonel. He discovers that Bayard has no pistol, and says, " . . . staring at [Bayard] with his pale outraged eyes and speaking in a whisper thin with fury: 'Who are you? Is your name Sartoris?' " (U/309). But after Bayard's unarmed confrontation with his father's killer, Wyatt meets him again: "You ain't done anything to be ashamed of. I wouldn't have done it that way, myself. I'd a shot at him once anyway. But that's your way or you wouldn't have done it" (U/314). Later Wyatt sees the meaning of Bayard's act: " 'Well, by God,' he said again. 'Maybe you're right, maybe there has been enough killing in your family without — Come on' " (U/314). George Wyatt speaks for the town. The demands of the myth have been met: Bayard has satisfied the form of family conduct, already a property of the town, an essential part of its self-articulation, and he has done so on his own terms. Myth and personal integrity have meshed perfectly. As Colonel

John Sartoris, "tired of killing men, no matter what the necessity or the end," walks to his death unarmed, so Bayard follows. Not in imitation, but as countersignature of his father's act. "I have accomplished my aim," Colonel John Sartoris tells Bayard as he announces his intention to meet Redmond unarmed. As Wyatt sees, Bayard has done the same, and by so doing has balanced, sustained and even enlarged the legend which the later ruthless years of Colonel John Sartoris' life had nearly tainted.[3] Bayard is not bound to accept the pistols and the demonic destructive vision proffered by Drusilla Hawk in order to fulfill his duty, but if he rejects the chaotic nightmare of her lust for blood and death, he must steer between that chaos and the profound shame of inaction, of failing to confront his father's killer.

Every human being, every society moves within the tensions of existence and the spiritual darkness of unstructured experience in terms of one formulation of meaning or another. In the post-bellum South, in what Donald Davidson has called a "tradition society," an enclave of symbols — and values springing from those symbols — was created against the threatening horror of public and private annihilation, of values, of the end of existence as a people. Such symbolizations obviously draw upon the most available and meaningful material, and once the order is established and firm in the people's assent, existence outside the modes of conduct prescribed by these symbols becomes unthinkable. Bayard wants to be "thought well of" (U/304), he tells Miss Jenny, and as he plans to meet Redmond the next day he says, "I must live with myself, you see" (U/300). It is not "public opinion" or personal pride which presses Bayard into his confrontation. It is both, simultaneously and equally, and these demands are absolute, mixed and merged so totally that no real separation of one motive from the other is possible.

We may conclude our discussion of the genesis of the Sartoris legend by noting that neither Colonel John Sartoris nor Bayard is guilty of empty gesture: John Sartoris walks to his death to square certain accounts, to complete a "little moral house-cleaning." Bayard meets his father's killer unarmed as an act both of inheritance and renunciation; he takes upon himself the identification of "the Sartoris," but sets aside the murderous habits of his father. The balance between duties within existential reality and the Sartorises' transcendent valuation of themselves, each other, their society and their moral responsibilities is struck and established in perfect equipoise. The legend is founded; family and community stand in interrelation to one another, mutual legatees of a *mythos* which has become basic to the psychic order of both.[4]

III

We move now from 1876 to 1919. Forty-three years have passed, and Bayard is now Colonel Sartoris. The courtesy title represents the town's respect for him, engendered from that moment of his meeting with Redmond, and based on his Sartoris heritage as well as his own accomplishments as a banker and leading citizen. Bayard (we shall call him "Old Bayard" now, in order to distinguish him from his grandson) is sixty-seven, a grandfather whose son John is dead of wounds and fever contracted in the Spanish-American War, and who has lost one grandson, the third John Sartoris, in an air battle of the 1914–18 War.

Superficially the situation which called the Sartoris myth into being and has continued to nourish it has changed little in the intervening time. The South remains in tranced meditation of its calamitous past. But even as *Sartoris* opens, Faulkner adumbrates the beginning of change, that first thread-thin crack in the monolithic surface of the myth which has its local and living articulation in the Sartorises. Caspey, a servant of the family and Simon Strother's son, has just returned from Europe and the War, and his assent to the old order has been withdrawn: "I don't take nothin offen no white man no mo', lootenant ner captain ner M.P. War showed de white folks dey can't git along widout de cullid man. Tromple him in de dus', but when de trouble bust loose, hit's 'Please, suh, Mr. Cullud Man . . . You is de savior of de country.' And now de cullud race gwine reap de benefits of de war, and dat soon" (S/66). Caspey speaks of the "benefits" of war. Disorder seems to him useful, and he believes the existing order will be overturned by the demonic ramifications of overwhelming and chaotic events which have taken place half-way across the world. But Caspey anticipates. A week later, he encounters Old Bayard. In an exchange of words, Old Bayard knocks him down a flight of stairs with a piece of stovewood. His father Simon helps him up: "I kep' tellin' you dem new-fangled war notions of yo'n wa'n't gwine ter work on dis place. . . . And you better thank de good Lawd fer makin' ye' haid hard ez hit is. You go'n git dat mare, and save dat nigger freedom talk fer townfolks: dey mought stomach it" (S/83). The old order remains, for the time being at least, intact, with the increasingly uncertain consent of those, Negro and white, who live within it.

At the same time, that order and its external symbolizations are being subjected to new stresses of various kinds, some as obvious as Caspey's prophetic but abortive gesture of independence, others less explicit but nonetheless corrosive of established values: Old Bayard's heart condition, the fact that his son and one of his grandsons are dead, and, as we will see, young Bayard's new automobile. Byron Snopes' presence as a bookkeeper in the bank together with his daring to write anonymous loveletters to Narcissa Benbow further suggests undermining of the old order represented in pragmatic existence by Old Bayard and transcendentally by the statue of Colonel John Sartoris which stands above the graveyard and stares out over the valley. Old Bayard senses the onset of this decline. He tells Dr. Peabody: "I have already outlived my time. . . . I am the first of my name to see sixty years that I know of. I reckon Old Marster is keeping me for a reliable witness to the extinction of it" (S/104). Old Bayard, of course, is speaking of the Sartoris family's extinction. But he is speaking as well of that time he claims to have outlived, and of the symbols and values created and projected by it. If the order symbolized by the Sartoris family is to survive, it must have continuity in the person of young Bayard. He must follow in the established line, step into the breach left by Old Bayard even as Old Bayard had established himself as "the Sartoris" at the time of his father's death.

The drama of *Sartoris*, while it focusses primarily on young Bayard's long and terrible search for a place within the complex structure composed of a society in pragmatic existence and a transcendent myth shared by all the male members of the family, is also concerned with the surrounding figures who are still within the myth's grip, and who therefore tend to exert pressures of one kind or another upon young Bayard.

The spokesman for the myth, those who constantly allude to it, who strengthen it and are strengthened in turn by it, are Will Falls, Simon Strother, and Miss Jenny chiefly. But the myth is no longer of pragmatic importance for the rest of the community. The semibarbaric virtues and vices of the Sartorises once essential to survival in history are now, for the most part, a portion of the treasured past of Jefferson and its people. New challenges, new demands, new ideas have begun to filter into the community. There has been a new war; natives of Jefferson have fought in the "yankee army." The myth is now not the source of new action but of old pieties. Still, within the family circle and its close adherents the Sartoris myth remains something more than a memory: it is a demanding pattern for conduct telling of old things done, of things yet expected, things remaining to be done.

Will Falls recollects the past, indeed, lives in it. His conversations with Old Bayard are interminable detailed recreations of a past dim even to Old Bayard. Still, Will Falls' salve heals Bayard's wen, suggesting not only the residual value of the past, but the questionable superiority of "progress" as represented by Dr. Alford, the new physician who insists that the wen should be removed by surgery.

Simon Strother, the elderly Negro who has been a servant of the family since John Sartoris' time, is as attached to the past and to the myth which is its paradigmatic representation as is Will Falls. But, while Will Falls talks of the past, Simon brings it into the present. The past is not really past; on the contrary, Simon speaks to Colonel John as he works in the yard: "Yo' own son, yo' own twin grandson, ridin' right up in yo' face in a contraption like dat . . . and you lettin' 'um do it. You bad ez dey is. You jes' got ter lay down de law ter'um, Marse John. . . . You jes' got to resert yo'-self, Marse John. Ain't Sartorises sot de quality in dis country since befo' de war? And now jes' look at 'um" (S/113–114). To Simon, the myth is not simply ritual recitation of past courage and the order flowing out of war's chaos by imposition of the Sartoris charisma; it remains a pattern of action, and the long-dead Colonel John must, like another Arthur, return to reinforce, to "resert," his order, to prevent the derailment of that formulation which once guided community action and feeling. Again, like Will Falls', Simon's attitude represents, simultaneously, a repudiation of the present, and yet a valuable and honest loyalty in no way merely sentimental.

Finally there is Miss Jenny Du Pre, whose position in the family and role in the novel are both ambiguous. Mrs. Vickery has attempted to clarify Miss Jenny's contrarities:

> The Civil War Sartorises have . . . taught her to accept and even anticipate a certain form of behavior in their heirs. Eventually this expectation becomes so strong that she is outraged by the manner of Old Bayard's death. But coupled with her conviction that a violent death is *noblesse oblige* for any Sartoris is her woman's practicality and common sense which picks up the pieces and re-establishes order. . . . Yet always she is waiting for the news that one or both of them have fulfilled their obligation to their name and ancestors by departing life in fittingly dramatic fashion. Actually, by her semi-humorous carping on the inevitable end of each Sartoris, she contributes to that end by admitting the closed nature of the pattern of life they have embraced.[5]

The flaw in Mrs. Vickery's analysis is evident: she takes Miss Jenny's estimation of Sartoris conduct, of the meaning and use of the myth, at face value. She reduces a theoretical discussion of literature to the level of cliche: "woman's practicality and common sense." At the same time she acknowledges that Miss Jenny sets up the "violent death" motif as an expected mode of conduct — something less than a "practical and common sense" attitude. Miss Jenny insists on the inherent "foolishness" of the Sartoris men; but no one else in the novel describes their conduct similarly, and with the possible exception of Narcissa Benbow, no one else seems to see it in such light. If there is a pathological attitude expressed in the novel, it would seem to be Miss Jenny's.

Miss Jenny is a kind of Cassandra issuing self-fulfilling prophecies. Her attitude can be explained only by attributing to her three simultaneously held feelings: 1. Incomprehension of the motives of the Sartoris men from Colonel John through young Bayard, it being easier to account for them with a "formulated phrase" than to fathom the fugitive forces that move them. 2. A continuous and understandable dread of their conduct and its implications, and 3. A certain perverse pride in this behavior; a less dramatic but no less obvious variety of the pathological fascination with death exhibited in "An Odor of Verbena" by Drusilla Hawk.

The product of these attitudes combined in Miss Jenny tends to depreciate and cheapen motives she cannot really grasp, causes her to feign disgust or even unconcern for the fatal outcome of these motives, and finally creates a compulsive need to re-tell the dramatic circumstances of each immolation after it has occurred.

Thus we complete our examination of the Sartoris myth and those who partake of it; of its place in Jefferson when young Bayard Sartoris returns from France. We note that neither Old Bayard, Will Falls, Simon, Narcissa nor the MacCallums discuss the past with him, or even bring up the death of his brother Johnny. If there is, in the myth, some element of compulsion, the articulation of it is clearly and completely in the hands of Miss Jenny Du Pre.

IV

Now, what of young Bayard Sartoris? What kind of man is he? He is, first of all, at least superficially arrogant and self-contained. If we are to believe Miss Jenny, his love for his first wife and child was only perfunctory: "Bayard love anybody, that cold devil. . . . He never cared a snap of his fingers for anybody in his life except John" (S/56). He is, moreover, capable of unmotivated viciousness, illustrated by his frightening Simon into near-hysteria with his new car: "When Bayard glanced the cruel derision of his teeth at him presently, Simon knelt on the floor, his old disreputable hat under his arm and his hand clutching a fold of his shirt on his breast" (S/116). Beyond this, Bayard is irresponsible: he risks the lives of Simon and Narcissa in his car, and he finally claims his grandfather's life in a final automobile accident. His own inner chaos tends to spread until it touches those around him. Narcissa is fascinated by the very recklessness that she claims to hate in the Sartoris "beasts"; thus she reflects the confusion or ambivalence we have seen in Miss Jenny.

But Bayard's character is yet more deeply flawed. He has not the moral courage to return home after the accident in which his grandfather is killed, and he flatly lies to the MacCallums, pretending by his lies and evasions that his grandfather is still alive, fearing all the time that Rafe or one of the others will discover that Old Bayard is dead, and the manner of his death. Moreover, it seems at least possible that Bayard has misrepresented the manner of Johnny's death in France. He repeats the story of that morning flight three times in the novel: once to his grandfather, once in part to Rafe MacCallum, and, finally, in detail again to Narcissa. In the first and third telling, Bayard uses almost identical phrases to describe how Johnny jumped from his plane. In the first and second tellings, Bayard blames his brother's recklessness. He claims that Johnny was "drunk, or a fool." "I tried to keep him from going up there, on that damn Camel . . . any fool could 'a' known that on their side it'd be full of Fokkers that could reach twenty-five thousand and him on a damn Camel. . . . He was already high as he could get, but they must have been five thousand feet above us . . ." (S/45). Later, when he is at the MacCallum's place, Bayard faces, at least in thought, the consequences of his past recklessness:

. . . for an instant he saw the recent months of his life coldly in all their headlong and heedless wastefulness; saw its entirety like the swift unrolling of a film, culminating in that which he had been warned against and that any fool might have foreseen. Well, damn it, suppose it had: was he to blame? Had he insisted that his grandfather ride with him? Had he given the old fellow a bum heart? And then, coldly: *You were afraid to go home. You made a nigger sneak your horse out to you. You, who deliberately do things your judgement tells you may not be successful, even possible, are afraid to face the consequences of your own acts.* Then again something bitter and deep and sleepless in him blazed out in vindication and justification and accusation; what, he knew not, blazing out at what, whom, he did not know: *You did it! You caused it all; you killed Johnny* (S/311).

It is not possible either to accept or reject outright the notion that Bayard has played some part in Johnny's death. It *is* possible that he has frozen, found it impossible to act swiftly enough, when his brother needed him. But this is not given either in *Sartoris* or in "All The Dead Pilots," and can be surmised only from what we know of Bayard's character. Still, whether Bayard's feeling of guilt is justified or not, he is clearly guilty of his grandfather's death, and of the deceit and failure of nerve which follow. Still, we must probe deeper to find the source of his self-destructive urge. Mrs. Vickery has given a useful hint toward that source: "There is a tenseness each time he takes a chance and risks his life that is foreign to Johnny's casualness."[6] This "tenseness," this incapacity to set aside all, as Johnny did, in seeking "a desire so fine that its escape was a purification, not a loss" (S/73), is Bayard's primary flaw. Bayard is described as "cold," as "rigid." Miss Jenny thinks of him, ". . . he has no soul" (S/200). Narcissa echoes this sentiment when she says, "He doesn't love anybody. He won't even love the baby. He doesn't seem to be glad, or sorry, or anything" (S/298). The root of Bayard's anguish is a fear and an uncertainty of his own courage so profound that he finds himself driven by it to prove over and over again that he in fact is what he fears he is not: a Sartoris. This fear explains his coldness and cruelty, his lies and evasions and compulsive irresponsibility — even his repetitive nightmares and the need to retell over and over the last moments of Johnny's life and the fearless manner of his death. It is that hour in the sky near Amiens that has crippled Bayard. He has witnessed the meeting between his twin, his own image, the only person he has ever loved, and that death he fears so much. He cannot believe that he too is brave, can as easily and gracefully fulfill the demands of the Sartoris myth as did Johnny.

It is the essence of this myth, re-told endlessly by Miss Jenny and acted out in pragmatic reality by Johnny, that haunts Bayard. At the same time, it would be absurd to think, as Mrs. Vickery would have us do, that Bayard is maladroitly attempting suicide in his various accidents. On the contrary, he is trying *not* to destroy himself, is trying to find some act, some mode of experience in reality through which he can come to terms simultaneously with the burden of life in existence, with the laughing ghost of his dead brother, and with that myth which stands above them all and is given concrete presence in the statue of Colonel John Sartoris which stands in the cemetery overlooking the valley.[7]

If Johnny's death can be compared to that of Colonel John Sartoris in its casual acceptance of what each considers inevitable, then young Bayard can be said to be searching for the same kind of compromise between death and life without meaning that his grandfather, Old Bayard, had found in his confrontation with Redmond. But in young Bayard's world the possibilities for heroic action are strictly limited, and he is left with such empty gestures as fast driving or riding a dangerous horse. Still, those around him, especially Rafe MacCallum, seem in some measure to understand. When the horse trader shouts that the horse will kill Bayard, MacCallum draws out a roll of money: "Let him be," he says, "That's what he wants" (S/132). Not to be killed, but to come close to it — close enough to gain some measure of that certainty which always escapes him, something to hold his brother's ghost at bay, to satisfy the tacit terms of living as a Sartoris. Later, when he drives at the bridge off which he had crashed before, and terrifies Narcissa who is with him, he tries to explain: " 'I didn't mean — ' he began awkwardly. 'I just wanted to see if I could do it' " (S/263). If the significance of Bayard's risk-taking is still not plain, Will Falls explains the idea as he recalls Colonel John Sartoris to Old Bayard:

> Ever' now and then a feller has to walk up and spit in deestruction's face, sort of, for his own good. He has to kind of put a aidge on hisself, like he'd hold his axe to the grindstone. . . . Ef a feller'll show his face to deestruction ever' now and then, deestruction'll leave 'im be twell his time comes. Deestruction likes to take a feller in the back. . . . Deestruction's like airy other coward. . . . Hit won't strike a feller that's a-lookin' hit in the eye lessen he pushes hit too clost[8] (S/234–35).

". . . lessen he pushes hit too clost," Will Falls says, finishing his unconscious prediction of the meaning and direction of young Bayard's doom. Bayard has not the capacity to hone himself to that healing, renewing edge, and when he approaches it, he is always tense. Not so with Johnny, who, after a dangerous ride and parachute jump from a balloon, looked "merry and bold and wild." Aunt Sally, recalling the event, thinks Bayard had made the jump. But Narcissa corrects her: "Bayard wasn't even there. It was John did it. He did it because the man that came with the balloon got sick. John went up in it so the country people wouldn't be disappointed. I was there" (S/72). Johnny, like his great-grandfather, risks himself for the benefit of the people, no matter how trivial the occasion may be. He is naturally a Sartoris, and up to the last moment of his life, he does not seem to know the debilitating terror that haunts his twin, Bayard:

. . . he [Bayard] still waked at times in the peaceful darkness of his room and without previous warning, tense and sweating with old terror. Then, momentarily, the world was laid away and he was a trapped beast in the high blue, mad for life, trapped in the very cunning fabric that had betrayed him who had dared chance too much, and he thought again if, when the bullet found you, you could only crash upward, burst; anything but earth. Not death, no: it was the crash you had to live through so many times before you struck that filled your throat with vomit (S/203–04).

The corrosive fear of falling, a fear Johnny is specifically noted not to have had, torments Bayard's dreams. Over and over he remembers or dreams of Johnny's death and his own fear. At one point, after his grandfather's death, while he is at the MacCallum's place, he considers suicide: ". . . he stood for a moment in the icy pitch darkness with the shotgun in his hands, and as he did so, his numb fingers fumbling at the breech, he remembered the box of shells on the wooden box on which the lamp sat. A moment longer he stood so, his head bent a little and the gun in his numb hands . . ." (S/322). But the moment passes, and he puts the gun down, opens the door and stares outside:

In the sky no star showed, and the sky was the sagging corpse of itself. It lay on the earth like a deflated balloon; into it the dark shape of the kitchen rose without depth, and the trees beyond, and homely shapes like sad ghosts in the chill corpse-light. . . . He was shaking slowly and steadily with cold; beneath his hands his flesh was rough and without sensation; yet still it jerked and jerked as though something within the dead envelope of him strove to free itself . . . (S/323).

A manifold of symbolization is gathered here: the sky without a star which recalls the "meteoric violence like that of fallen angels" of Bayard's earlier discussion with Rafe MacCallum in the back of the grocery-restaurant (S/126), as well as adumbrating Narcissa's later thought regarding Miss Jenny's endless talk of the Sartoris doom: "And now she is trying to make me one of them; to make my child just another rocket to glare for a moment in the sky, then die away" (S/358). The absence of stars, the corpse-like sky, the image of a "deflated balloon," "sad ghosts" and "corpse-light" all form a cluster of images pointing to Johnny, and to the "glamorous old disastrous" myth which Johnny has entered leaving Bayard to endure existence among "dark shapes" and "homely shapes" "without depth." But Bayard's flesh jerks as if something within the "dead envelope" of his body "strove to free itself," to join Johnny, to turn from existential meaninglessness to the eternal and transcendent being of the Sartoris myth. Earlier, Bayard had thought of the emptiness of life: "Nothing to be seen, and the long span of a man's natural life. Three score and ten years to drag a stubborn body about the world and cozen its insistent demands. Three score and ten, the Bible said. Seventy years. And he was only twenty-six. Not much more than a third through it. Hell"[9] (S/160). Hell indeed, and no way to find meaning, no release since suicide would be degrading, to fall away from the demands of the myth and from Johnny's example. Again, while he is at the MacCallum's place, he thinks of the impasse in which he exists: ". . . he too was dead, and this was hell, through which he moved with an illusion of quickness, seeking his brother who in turn was somewhere seeking him, never the two to meet" (S/322).[10] Bayard is trapped in existence, tortured simultaneously by the memory of his brother's easy courage, his own strangling fear, and the banality of his life. Nothing matters beyond these tensions, and there seems to be no way to escape them. He has not the resources to resolve these tensions as Old Bayard did his.

V

It would be easy enough to draw all these divergent threads together carelessly, concluding that Bayard finally manages to bring off the suicide which he has attempted at least three times before his last flight in an experimental plane. But if we so conclude, we fall into Miss Jenny's error; we tend to confuse appearance with reality by refusing to weigh subtleties, as when Narcissa detects "Miss Jenny still talking of Johnny, confusing the unborn with the dead" (S/358). By so doing, we devalue the novel and its meaning. In fact we accept Miss Jenny's simplistic valuation and assume that four generations of Sartoris men have been marked not by fatality, but by mere "fustian and useless glamor." Such a reading is shallow, and fails to take into account the profound experience of men in war, in a wilderness preceding that war, chaotic social ruin afterward, and of the kind of "recklessness" which has tended to run parallel to the "heroic" in every age. Miss Jenny's view of the Sartoris men is valid enough — insofar as it represents the view of women toward the exploits of men at all times. But we must remember that Miss Jenny is given an outsize role in *Sartoris*; it is her opinion which we constantly hear, which is the quantitatively major voice offset only by the relatively minor voices of Will Falls, Simon and the MacCallums. We misread *Sartoris* if we fail to see that, beyond Miss Jenny's opinion, young Bayard's agony and displacement are real. Miss Jenny's interminable commentary serves well as a technical counter-balance to Bayard's alternately absurd and tragic action and introspec-tion. But Miss Jenny must be considered no more than one of several observers. Her view of things is not to be accepted without circumspec-tion. If, after all, anyone in *Sartoris* is obsessed with fatality and doom, it is Miss Jenny herself — not Old Bayard, Johnny, or young Bayard.

Keeping these various discussions and reservations in mind, we can, I think, now formulate a substantial explanation for young Bayard's risktak-ing and his death, and establish at the same time the meaning of *Sartoris* and the myth which animates it.

To begin, Bayard feels, with considerable reason, that he is not the equal of his dead twin. Bayard's sense of guilt, whether baseless or not, and his realization of fear are coupled so as to force him to acts, which, he feels, may re-establish his own worth, his equality with Johnny as a bearer of the Sartoris name. Bayard's tragic failure does not consist in his attempting to establish a place for himself in the pattern of the family myth; it is precisely his incapacity to hold in balance the tensions between that myth and pragmatic reality which destroys him. He cannot find an honorable compromise between the traditions of his family and existence in reality. His grandfather had accomplished exactly such a compromise. By refusing to kill, Old Bayard had asserted his own character, his own version of the myth. On the other hand, young Bayard is trapped in a psychic impasse; his fear makes Johnny's natural courage, and the self-certainty that springs from it, impossible. His incapacity to find meaning in the love of Narcissa and the approaching birth of his child makes ordinary life a burden. Unable to find in himself the resources he knows were present in Johnny, as well as in Old Bayard and Colonel John Sartoris, his final alternative is to seek some banal approach to death like the one he manages at last to find. But this is the cheap way to resolve the tensions of the myth: one enters into its eternality by the back door.

Kenneth Burke has made an interesting observation on the idea of suicide in literature and one which is particularly relevant to the case of young Bayard: "Look closer at poetic examples of the 'death wish' and you will see that the symbolic slaying of an old self is complemented by the emergence of a new self. In fact, though every action and person in the plot led downwards, we should find an assertion of identity in the constructive act of the poem itself."[11] However many quarrels we may have with Burke's idea in other contexts, it would appear to satisfy the equation we are presently attempting to solve. We have said on the one hand that young Bayard is not seeking death and on the other that he can find no other resolution of his psychic impasse. Both statements are true, and it is through Burke's formula that we can force the paradox to provide an explanation without violating its integrity and that of the novel.

Young Bayard's "death wish" is not the result of a taste for cheap theatrics but of desperation: he has been left alone by the twin upon whose love and courage he has always depended; he is constantly badgered by Miss Jenny and her prophecies of violence and death. He has found nothing to value as highly as that which, through Johnny's death, he has lost. It is not difficult for Bayard to repudiate the "two-bit war" in which the Sartoris myth arose, but that myth as it is manifested in his dead twin exerts compelling force on him. At last, failing to find any compromise between the implicit claims of the myth and pragmatic existence, Bayard commits himself to rebirth in the myth itself. He chooses, without realizing it, to join Johnny, his father, his grandfather, his great-grandfather and great-granduncle. Unable to live as they did, he manages at least to die in similar fashion; that much of the myth's demands he fulfills. At last, he takes the myth at Miss Jenny's simplistic valuation of it. By his manner of joining the other Sartorises who have died violently for various reasons incomprehensible to Miss Jenny, Bayard resolves his own dilemma and lends some color of truth to her claim that the myth is nothing but "fustian vainglory."

Still he does manage in his own confused way to become part of the Sartoris pantheon. In the penultimate scene of the novel, his grave and tombstone are set alongside the others; he is at last a Sartoris. Over Bayard and his kinsmen stands the statue of Colonel John Sartoris:

> He stood on a stone pedestal, in his frock coat and bareheaded, one leg slightly advanced and one hand resting lightly on the stone pylon beside him. His head was lifted a little in that gesture of haughty pride which repeated itself generation after generation with a fateful fidelity, his back to the world and his carven eyes gazing out across the valley where his railroad ran, and the blue changeless hills beyond, and beyond that, the ramparts of infinity itself (S/375).

This brooding and arrogant statue of Colonel John Sartoris is symbolic of the myth which sustained the Southern psyche for the better part of a century. As the Colonel's back is turned to the world, as his eyes pass over the mere material accomplishment of his railroad toward first the land, and then on to "the ramparts of infinity itself," he mirrors the mind and heart of the South. Integrity, for such men as young Bayard, was bound up with their capacity to stand within the bounds of the type exemplified by John Sartoris. The question posed by Mrs. Vickery of young Bayard's "doing violence to his humanity" by his service to the myth[12] is essentially bogus. The notion that one should or can live in "history" — by which one assumes Mrs. Vickery means life in existence — as opposed to the *mythos* resulting from whichever symbolization of reality one accepts, is itself an illusion. Speaking of the Sartoris myth, Mrs. Vickery says, ". . . as this legend developed, it replaced history and itself assumed the validity of an historical pattern.[13] I do not know what "validity" adheres to an "historical pattern." Every human being has, in one sense, a history, and it is finally that personal symbolization of the meaning of existence to which a man commits himself, to which he offers fidelity. The Sartoris myth provides a construct of order and of valuation for those who choose to accept it. Critique of a paradigmatic symbol such as that embodied in the statue of Colonel John Sartoris, and in the myth attached to him, must be conducted within the limits of theoretical terms as carefully chosen as those used in examining the Israelite or Christian *mythos*. The meaning of *Sartoris*, for all the ambiguities introduced by Miss Jenny and Narcissa, is more than a mere study in *weltschmerz*: "Perhaps Sartoris is the game itself — a game outmoded and played with pawns shaped too late and to an old dead pattern, and of which the Player Himself is a little wearied. For there is death in the sound of it, and a glamorous fatality, like silver pennons downrushing at sunset, or a dying fall of horns along the road to Ronceavaux" (S/380).

The game finally is life in existence, and the pattern, symbolized by the Sartoris myth, may be obsolete. But no meaningful symbolic order has replaced it. Opposed to that "glamorous fatality" in *Sartoris* is only the "windless lilac dream, foster dam of quietude and peace," exemplified by Narcissa, the delicate glass vases, vague reveries and gentle adultery of her brother Horace. For young Bayard these are not enough. It is finally the old myth that claims his assent, and into which at last he enters, reborn in the stone apotheosis of the Sartoris graveyard.

Notes

1. Olga M. Vickery, *The Novels of William Faulkner*, Louisiana State University Press, 1963, 17.

2. I am aware that, since *The Unvanquished* was published almost a decade after *Sartoris*, it is possible to question in theory the use of the latter work to illuminate the earlier. But the question is relevant only if we are attempting to establish some point of style, artistic development, or ideational change on Faulkner's part. On the contrary, we are tracing the configuration of a symbol which is constant in Faulkner's writing concerning the Sartoris family. So far as can be determined, "An Odor of Verbena," as it touches upon the problem we are discussing, is primarily a widening, a filling in of detail left unspecified in the earlier novel. Colonel John Sartoris is the same in both works; his last words are the same, the nature of his posthumous influence is the same. The change of tone between *Sartoris* and *The Unvanquished*, while it deserves a study of its own, can be generally summarized by noting that *The Unvanquished* is told by Old Bayard in the first person; *Sartoris*, while third-person in narrative form, is essentially under the *aegis* of Miss Jenny. It is a woman's view of the Sartoris family history, and the blind spots in understanding the meaning of that history are, insofar as they are reflected by the omniscient narrator, precisely those we find in Miss Jenny's running commentary. In order to establish the myth in its integrity, free of any single point of view, it is necessary to ignore or at least recognize the subjectivity of Miss Jenny in *Sartoris*, and that of Old Bayard in *The Unvanquished*. It would not be irrelevant to note that a monograph is needed to illuminate the question of "dependability of the narrator" in Faulkner's fiction.

3. Bayard sees his father change from a genuinely heroic soldier whose ironic fearlessness is a natural characteristic into an intolerant and proud man who cannot bear any form of challenge to his authority. In those last days the Colonel comes to have "the intolerant eyes which . . . had acquired that transparent film which the eyes of carnivorous animals have and from behind which they look at a world which no ruminant ever sees, perhaps dares to see, which I have seen before on the eyes of men who have killed too much, who have killed so much that never again as long as they live will they ever be alone" (U/288).

4. Readers of *The Unvanquished* will recognize that the entire book is concerned with the genesis of the Sartoris myth, and that our concentration on "An Odor of Verbena" is a matter of condensation. The moment of coherence, the instant in which the myth becomes organized, seems to be when Bayard walks into Redmond's office. The earlier material dealing with Bayard and Ringo and their vengeance upon Grumby, that of the escape of Colonel John Sartoris from the Northern army and of his post-war business and political career — all of it amounts to a series of anecdotes until, with his death and Bayard's response, all the past seems to acquire focus and meaning. For our purposes, the difference between folk-tale and myth comes when ultimate issues and actions force past occasions into a

structural or thematic relationship retroactively. The folk-tale is always discrete; the myth is a gathering of events around a central act or idea.

5. Vickery, 25.

6. Vickery, 20.

7. On several occasions, as Bayard drives at high speed, he passes the cemetery: ". . . the cemetery with his great-grandfather in pompous effigy flashed past . . ." (S/119). Most significantly, in the fatal ride which concludes in his grandfather's death: "Now they were facing the bluff on which the cemetery lay; directly above them John Sartoris' effigy lifted its florid stone gesture and from admidst motionless cedars gazed out on the valley where for two miles the railroad he had built ran beneath his carven eyes" (S/305). In the final pages of the book, when Miss Jenny goes to see Bayard's grave, she looks at the statue of her long-dead brother: "He stood on a stone pedestal, in his frock coat and bareheaded, one leg slightly advanced and one hand resting lightly on the stone pylon behind him . . ." (S/375). The statue thus serves as a motif, a recurring reminder of the legend's beginning, its founder, and its end.

8. This need to test oneself against death is hardly unique in Bayard. Close literary parallels can be found in Hemingway's conception of courage as "grace under pressure", in his notion that courage is a muscle which must be exercised. Norman Mailer explicates Hemingway's suicide by reference to this idea: "How likely that he had a death of the most awful proportions within him. He was exactly the one to know that cure for such a disease is to risk dying many a time. Somewhere in the deep coma of mortal illness or the transfixed womb of danger, death speaks to us. If we make our way back to life, we are armed with a new secret" (*The Presidential Papers*. p. 104).

Mailer continues this line, suggesting that Hemingway did not intend suicide, but the renewal of risk. The same concept informs the balcony-walk of Stephen Rojack in *An American Dream*, though Mailer moves from psychic renewal to ritual magic in the scene, and extends its field of effectiveness beyond the risk-taker to those for whom he offers his risk.

9. The idea that all those who had taken part in the 1914–1918 War were, in a sense, dead runs through a number of Faulkner's books and stories. It is cited with direct reference to Bayard in "Ad Astra." The Indian subadar says: "What will you do? . . . What will any of us do? All this generation which fought in the war are dead tonight. But we do not yet know it." And again: "You will see. . . . Those who have been four years rotting out yonder . . . are not more dead than we." The post-war *malaise*, the meaningless gnitpicking of civilian life, as typified in the glass-blowing and covert adultery of Horace Benbow, is set against the Sartoris myth and its incarnation in Johnny and explains Bayard's discontent with the unheroic possibilities of life.

10. The death-and-damnation-in-life symbolism implied here, familiar enough from Marlowe to Coleridge has been discusses with considerable effectiveness by Eric Voegelin in a recent article "Immortality: Experience and Symbol" (*Harvard Theological Review*, Vol. 60, n° 3, July 1967), q.v. See particularly pp. 244–248 and p. 261.

11. *The Philosophy of Literary Form*, New York (Anchor Books), 34.

12. Vickery, 26.

13. Vickery, 27.

The Evolution of Two Characters in Faulkner's Early and Published Fiction

Max Putzel*

At thirty-six, Faulkner mailed to New York a brief account of how he came to write *Sartoris*, how in effect he became a novelist. "So I began to write, without much purpose, until I realized that to make [that lost world] truly evocative it must be personal. . . . So I put people in it, since what can be more personal than reproduction, in its two senses, the aesthetic and the mammalian?"[1]

Like all his recollections this one must be received with some reservations. He had, in fact, been creating persons for seven years, his first being a character modeled on himself when young. That was a product of daydreams, an indulgent self-caricature. He saw himself in heroic postures, triumphing in the face of death, thumbing his nose at disaster. And he mocked his fantasies before anyone else could.

His first person was Cadet Thompson of the Royal Air Force, in which Faulkner had served at Toronto the year before publishing in a college periodical his first short story, "Landing in Luck." When it appeared in 1919 Faulkner was still sporting his British uniform in Oxford, Mississippi. While he had not yet learned to fly, his sense of theatre took him into the cockpit of every airplane he ever heard or read about. He became obsessed with the nightmare of death in a plane crash.[2]

The short story tells of a callow pilot's first, all but disastrous solo flight, after a few hours of instruction. Unaware that he has sheared off a landing wheel during his clumsy take-off, Cadet Thompson circles the flying field and gestures jovially at the shocked crowd gathering below — "a popular gesture known to all peoples of the civilized world." An ambulance crew stands by helplessly but by some fluke of chance the cadet manages to land, "the wing tip crumpled like paper," without being hurt. He hangs absurdly by the seat belt of his uptilted plane, is violently sick, yet walks off to brag of his prowess.[3]

Thompson reappears as Cadet Lowe on the first page of Faulkner's first novel, *Soldiers' Pay*, still callow and now disgruntled because "they had stopped the war on him." Nicknamed "One Wing," doubtless an unexplained allusion to the accident recounted in the short story, he fancies he recalls the war he had missed; it swims to him "through the adenoidal reminiscences of Captain Bleyth, an R.A.F. pilot," presumably his flight instructor from England.[4]

This cadet is bitterly envious of Donald Mahon, the scarred veteran he meets on the Pullman car with the other demobilized soldiers. "To have

*Reprinted, with permission, from the *Southern Literary Journal*, 5, No. 2 (Spring 1975), 53–58. This is Section II of the original essay, slightly abridged.

been him! he moaned. Just to be him. . . . To have got wings on my breast. . . . I would take death tomorrow."[5] For all his prominence in the opening pages of the novel, Cadet Lowe soon disappears from its action and is heard from thereafter only in sophomoric letters he writes the war widow Margaret Powers, who has sent him home to his mother. "I have done a little flying," he tells her, "but mostly dancing and running around." Like his author in 1919, he is thinking of attending the university.[6]

The cadet's frustrated yearning for wings and combat scars provides a clue to Faulkner's self-identification with Lieutenant Mahon and a motive for Mahon's next incarnation as Evelyn Sartoris, hero of the unfinished short story "Flags in the Dust." . . . Faulkner filed this five-page manuscript and a two-page insertion in with the manuscript of the same name, but later retitled *Sartoris*. The first fragment tells how Evelyn and his twin brother Bayard meet by appointment in two airplanes flying low over France. They have not seen one another for eighteen months, and their brief, wordless rendezvous is interrupted by the sight of a more powerful German fighter plane, which Evelyn flies off to attack. He is hit by a bullet. His plane takes fire and explodes. But before jumping to his death he thumbs his nose at his brother "and to the peering pink face of the German he [makes] a sweeping magniloquent salute."[7]

That "popular gesture," the nose thumbing, is what links the dying veteran to his prototype, Cadet Lowe. It is as if Faulkner wanted first to impersonate himself as he was, then as he might have been. Even without the benefit of the *Sartoris* manuscripts, Harold E. Richardson sees that in *Soldiers' Pay* both Cadet Lowe and Lieutenant Mahon "pose a double and conflicting identification for the artist." In his University of Southern California dissertation Richardson speculates on the motives that led Faulkner to formulate this double impersonation, seeing himself both as the warlike and dying ancestor and the absurdly imitative surviving descendant. The fantasy of double identity seems to him to be the product of "unavoidable, inherent frustration," Faulkner's peculiar problem of identity, "the struggle to discover his individuation and the part that the past, especially that symbolized by his ancestry, plays in that struggle. This problem," he concludes, "runs like a steady current through his early work."[8] In *Sartoris* the process is compounded by further splits, so that we have identical twins, the old colonel and the young—a confusion of identities reminiscent of Plautus and *Comedy of Errors*.

The manuscripts provide detailed evidence of the stages Faulkner went through. In the earliest draft, presumably five pages of a short story, Evelyn Sartoris has a twin brother on his way back to Memphis and a grandfather in Mississippi. Two pages are added, filling in Bayard's earlier history. Here it becomes clear that the twins are also from Mississippi, but Evelyn's name has become John, and Bayard is married to a Carolyn White, a modern girl who had used to buy their supper in a delicatessen and live in an apartment. That Faulkner identifies with both brothers is further borne out by the appearance, especially John's "bleak, hooded falcon expression."[9]

Despite superficial resemblances, John is no self-portrait, however. In another version, "All the Dead Pilots," he has also lived with his grandfather and great-aunt on a Mississippi plantation, but he has a "working vocabulary of perhaps two hundred words." There too he is shot down by a superior enemy aircraft, but Faulkner tried out other versions of his violent end.[10]

In the unpublished story "With Caution and Dispatch," there is no mention of a twin brother. Here Sartoris becomes a type of warrior whose courage verges on stupidity and invites extinction—all implied in the name *Bayard*. He has much in common with the British general who arrives at his training camp to give the newly commissioned fliers their first battle orders: to "proceed under arms and with caution and dispatch" for active duty in France. The general has a "rich port-winey voice in actual retrograde in a long limbo filled with horses: Fontenoy and Agincourt and Crecy and the Black Prince." Sartoris is another survival of the Hundred Years War, and unregenerate Prince Hal. Insolently inattentive during the briefing, determined regardless of orders to see his girl in London that night before the company's departure, he lies in bed fully dressed "like the stone effigy on a fifteenth-century sarcophagus."[11]

In a fine paper on Faulkner's military training in Toronto, Michael Millgate calls attention to his amazing ability to capitalize on "the most incidental experiences, the briefest encounters, the merest hints of character, behaviour, emotion." Remarking on his custom of flaunting his Canadian uniform after his return to Oxford, Millgate quotes from a Toronto *Star* news item. Cadets who had ordered uniforms just before the Armistice were finding themselves "unable to meet obligations due Toronto tailors." One jarring, implausible passage in "With Caution" introduces a dunning Scottish tailor who hounds the young officer as he is seeking his girl in a London restaurant later the same night. "Damn it, Cohen . . . I mean McKensie," he exclaims, shaking off the tailor. It will be recalled that in "All the Dead Pilots" Sartoris has an unpaid tailor's bill in his pocket just before he dies.

This small, inexplicable detail seems to involve a private irony. Like the Faulkner family the Sartorises have pretensions to a chivalric pedigree but may be of humble origin. The name *Sartoris* has a noble ring but is Latin for "the tailor's." Is the overbearing, snobbish young American, rudely refusing to pay his tailor for the British officer's uniform he wears, simply another cruel stroke of self-caricature? Is the name *Sartoris* perhaps a covert allusion to *Sartor Resartus*, required reading for freshmen in the twenties? Both are possibilities.[12]

Another unanswered question is why "With Caution" was abandoned. As indicated by a passage or two I have quoted, it has about as much style as "Dead Pilots" or "Ad Astra." My hypothesis is that Faullkner disliked its ending because it was sharply at variance with that version of John's death around which *Sartoris* developed. In the novel he had been shot down, while in "With Caution"—frustrated and enraged to find his girl basking in the attentions of a decorated staff officer—he flies off in a fog and crashes on the deck of a warship in mid-channel. He dies on 6 July 1918, and in a much revised passage we learn that "a Canadian bugler would blow Last Post for Sartoris" in a little cemetery behind Rozieres.[13] That ending is incompatible with the "brutal tale" Bayard tells Narcissa in the third part of *Sartoris*. While the death scene and John himself are subordinated in the novel Faulkner began in 1926, there can be no doubt that they disclose the germ from which it evolved.

The manuscript of *Sartoris* begins nevertheless with an elaborate portrait like the ones mentioned earlier: old Bayard is found rummaging among family relics in the attic of his big house near Jefferson. In the course of revision the portrait is omitted, as are the opening lines: "Sartoris. Bayard Sartoris: a fatal name. There is death in it, yet they clung to it stubbornly and died young, the males did, leaving behind them . . . a single arrogant gesture against oblivion—a gesture puny and foredoomed and arrogantly unaware or disregardful of it; and being so, greeklike and rather fine."[14] The novel may be about the deaths of the two Bayards, but the name is still "the tailor's," and the gesture no more than a thumbed nose.

Notes

1. Norman Holmes Pearson quoted briefly from this fascinating two-page MS. in "Faulkner's Three Evening Suns," *Yale Univ. Library Gazette*, 29 (October 1954), 61–70.

2. Faulkner's military training is described by Gordon Price-Stephens, "F and the Royal Air Force," *Mississippi Quarterly*, 18 (Summer 1965), 119–200; and Michael Millgate, "WF, Cadet," *Univ. of Toronto Quarterly*, 55 (January 1966), 117–32.

3. *William Faulkner: Early Prose and Poetry*, ed. Carvel Collins (Boston and Toronto, 1962), pp. 42–50. The name *Thompson* could derive from that of Faulkner's grandfather, John Wesley Thompson Falkner.

4. *Soldiers' Pay* (New York, repr. 1954), pp. 7, 9. Bleyth recurs in "Elmer," later evolving into Horace Benbow in *Sartoris*. See Dennis diss., "The Making of *Sartoris*," pp. 82–90.

5. *Soldiers' Pay*, pp. 45–46.

6. *Ibid.*, p. 187.

7. Alderman MS. "Flags in the Dust," box 2, ser. I A, it. 3-a, p. 05. And compare Dennis diss., "The Making of *Sartoris*," p. 56.

8. Harold E. Richardson, "WF: From Past to Self-Discovery," Diss. Univ. Southern Calif, 1963, pp. 245, 247n. (University Microfilms No. 64-2602).

9. Alderman MS. "Flags in the Dust," p. 002.

10. *Collected Stories*, p. 514.

11. Alderman TS. "With Caution and Dispatch," box 25, ser. II B.

12. Millgate, "William Faulkner: Cadet," p. 127. For other speculations on the origin of the name see Elizabeth M. Kerr, *Yoknapatawpha: Faulkner's "Little Postage Stamp of Native Soil"* (New York, 1969), p. 88n,; and Cleanth Brooks, *The Yoknapatawpha Country* (New Haven and London, 1963), p. 381.

13. Alderman TS. "With Caution," p. 31. The date of composition is uncertain but probably much earlier than the revisions Faulkner made while working on *The Hamlet* about 1939.

14. Alderman MS. "Flags in the Dust," p. 1.

"With Caution and Dispatch": "Deliberate speed, majestic instancy"

Nancy Belcher Sederberg*

In some respects "With Caution and Dispatch" resembles a cross between "All the Dead Pilots" and "Turnabout." Like the former story, "With Caution and Dispatch" contains more of John Sartoris' skirmishes with his commanding officer and the war bureaucracy, as well as his antic shenanigans in Camels; and, like the latter tale, it features a series of near-fatal crashes, one into the afterdeck of an apparently Brazilian merchant ship off of the British coast. Yet, the similarities between "With Caution and Dispatch"[1] and the earlier stories are less significant than the differences. "With Caution and Dispatch" lacks both the saving comedy of "All the Dead Pilots" and the controlled counterpoint of "Turnabout." Further, although it contains some semisuspenseful scenes, the story as a whole is confusing because it lacks cohesion, plausible motivations for characters' actions, and, most of all, consistency of tone. Nonetheless, "With Caution and Dispatch" is a fascinating culmination to Faulkner's World War I and flying short fiction for at least two reasons: it recapitulates almost all of the central symbolic motifs, characters types, and themes of the previous stories, and it reveals a duality at the very core of Faulkner's vision of war, which is latent in most of the other works.

According to Joseph Blotner, "With Caution and Dispatch" dates from about the time of "Turnabout," which was published in the *Saturday Evening Post* in March 1932. In 1939 when "With Caution and Dispatch" remained unsold, Faulkner rewrote parts of it on the backs of the setting copy of *The Hamlet*. The subsequent extant versions of the story include a 47-page typescript, two nonconsecutive typescript pages, both in the Alderman Library, University of Virginia, and a 38-page revised typescript from Jill Faulkner Summers' private archive, which is the version published in *The Uncollected Stories*.[2] The published version contains

---

*Revised by the author from a dissertation (University of South Carolina, 1977) and published for the first time with the author's permission.

three sections, the first of which is a much condensed form of the 47-page typescript.

The plot of "With Caution and Dispatch" is perhaps best described as episodic. In all of the versions, we pick up the protagonist, John Sartoris, as his squadron has just been ordered to proceed "with caution and dispatch" to join the March 1918 resistance on the Somme.[3] Sartoris, though, proceeds with temerarious inefficiency toward this destination, first by deviating from the flight pattern — both inadvertently and deliberately — making a forced landing in a field, and then by detouring to London before reporting to the aerodrome at Brooklands. The following morning, without proper authorization for his second Camel or common sense, he takes off for France in a driving rain storm during which, somewhere over the English channel, he crashes into the afterdeck of what anomalously appears to be a Brazilian merchant vessel.[4] At this point the 47-page typescript breaks off. Part II of the published rendition places Sartoris without explanation aboard a British destroyer which escorts him, under arrest, back to England and then to Edinburgh, where his commanding officer, Captain Britt, bails him out. Part III concludes as Sartoris crashes a third Camel, finally rejoining his squadron near Amiens.

The earlier long typescript version, which corresponds to part of section I of the published one, is both more dramatic and digressive, more sentimental and sardonic. It contains an elaboration of the plot in which Sartoris is placed "in pawn"[5] to Britt for having previously forayed into the off-limits Leicester Lounge in London to drink and meet his girl friend, Kit. To keep Sartoris from breaking orders the night before they depart for France, Britt takes Sartoris in tow for an evening with some stuffy friends of his father's in Kent. This version also contains a complicated "conspiracy" through which Britt again thwarts Sartoris' attempts to see Kit in London while he is on unauthorized leave, a comic confrontation with Kit's senior staff officer escort, a conversation with Sartoris' first flight instructor, Major Fritz Goar, and his final bedding down for the night at a Y.M.C.A. canteen — all before the crash scene which culminates Section I.

One of the more perplexing aspects of this earlier typescript is the inconsistent and often confusing characterization of Britt. Although Sartoris sees Britt's actions as persecutory, the reader probably perceives them as predominantly protective and disciplinary. However, like Spoomer in "All the Dead Pilots," Britt may have a personal motive for keeping Sartoris away from Kit as well. Although Britt allows all of the other aviators to spend their last evening in town, as long as they are back in bed by midnight,[6] he adamantly refuses to permit Sartoris to go. He also knows too well Kit's projected appearance at Murray's.[7] Sartoris at one point ambiguously muses: "He believed now that he had begun to smell the mouse when Britt dived at him that last time in the grain field. I got back here [to London] too quick, he thought. Too easy. But why? And Murray's. Britt didn't care where Kit was going to be. Then he understood. Yes. But why for that too?"[8] Yet, as the story progresses, the sexual rivalry between Sartoris and Britt — if any — suddenly transfers to Kit's current escort, a beautiful, patrician senior-staff captain named Swanny Ewing. After a brief comic interlude in which Sartoris is frustrated in his attempt to avenge his honor because such suave officers do not engage in fist fights, Sartoris apparently forgets about both Britt and Swanny for more mundane matters of getting to bed and to France. An equally plausible motive for Britt's strategems to keep Sartoris out of London might be to thwart his heavy drinking, which is much emphasized in the earlier typescript.[9]

Another confusing element of Britt's characterization, particularly in the 47-page typescript, concerns tone. In the earlier version the narrator explicitly contrasts Britt's "hard cold disbelieving" gray eyes with Sartoris' pale but merely "baffled and outraged" ones.[10] Britt's voice is described in both typescripts as "cold and precise as a surgeon's knife."[11] (The name Britt may suggest brittleness, as well as the fact that he is a Briton.) Further, like both the flight sergeant and the C.O. in "Landing in Luck" and Spoomer in "All the Dead Pilots," Britt is concerned with formal rules and appearance, as illustrated by his wry admonition to his men to keep in formation on the way to France, or "At least try to look like something to the tax-payers while we're over England."[12]

Yet Britt also has a number of positive qualities lacking in these earlier prototypes — in particular, concern for his men's welfare, humanizing feelings, and, most of all, a sense of humor. He specifically coaches his men in methods for survival should they crash. Further, when Sartoris complains about spending his last night in Kent, Britt retorts, " 'Do you think I like it either? . . . This is my last night in England too' " and asserts that he also may be killed in action.[13] Britt additionally shows some élan in the means by which he curbs Sartoris' movements in London. (He first telephones Kit, but failing to reach her, he turns Sartoris' overdrawn tailor, MacKensie, upon him by stating that Sartoris has received a check from home and wishes to take the opportunity of being in London to pay the bill, though he has been in a crash and may not recall his intent. The tailor is to take Sartoris to some quiet place, thus removing him from proximity to Kit at Murray's.) Lastly, Britt sometimes breaks regulations himself, as when he "plays horse" by leading the squadron in a farewell salute to England and then zooms behind Sartoris' tail.[14]

The published typescript, by eliminating the ambiguous "persecution" subplot, portrays Britt's motivations for his quasi-paternal protection of Sartoris as more professional than personal. Further, although he becomes increasingly irritated by Sartoris' deviance from military regulations "for no reason"[15] and his penchant for crashing Camels, he remains ironically indulgent, as shown by the exasperated reverse psychology of his final injunction to Sartoris: "Get back and crash this one before tea if you can."[16]

Sartoris' characterization is also fraught with confusing incompatibil-
ities. Clearly, he is meant to be a sympathetic character. Throughout the
story, the tone of the descriptions of Sartoris' plight is heavily weighted in
his favor. For example, as Sartoris barely escapes collision with a compatri-
ot's plane which falls out of formation during the departure for France, we
are told that he feels "frightened and raging."[17] In the longer typescript as
Sartoris becomes progressively pent in by Britt's devious stratagems in
London, he is described as "baffled and outraged" and then "near to
bursting with rage and frustration."[18] Faulkner also insures the reader's
sympathy for Sartoris by references to his doom by other characters, the
narrator, and Sartoris himself. In the earlier rendition, for instance,
Sartoris' unpaid tailor, MacKensie, mournfully explains to Sartoris' first
flight commander, Major Fritz Goar, why he cannot accept payment from
the army for overdue bills: "It's just how things are now. They wish to look
smart while they are in town and I like to see them looking smart. And
then after a week or so they go out and they dont come back. . . . I dont
want that money. If they can go out there, I can make them clothes to go
in."[19] Sartoris leaves a parcel of old clothes at a pub because "I'll be dead
by that time [eleven o'clock the following morning when the establishment
opens], he thought, walking on among the spare light of the /city/ waiting
city within its invisible ring of squatting Archie batteries and searchlights.
I wont live long enough to wear out the one's I'm standing in."[20] The
fragility of Sartoris' existence is also emphasized by his nostalgic reminiscence that he and Fritz Goar "had existed, breathed breath and been
aware of the hot and living blood, within the same intricate frail web of
wire and wood and linen supported coherent and intact in the high
velocity of air . . . now they would part (it was England, it was 1918)
perhaps forever."[21] At this point in the 47-page typescript the narrator
factually foreshadows that "Actually it was to be forever, because on the
sixth the following July /Sartoris would be dead in a cemetery back of
Neuville St. Baast/ a Canadian bugler would blow Last Post for Sartoris in
a little cemetery behind Rozieres."[22] The equivalent scene in the revised
typescript is more understated and even humorous because of the ambiguity regarding whether Sartoris is going to get shot by Britt or rewarded for
his heroism. Musing about Britt's M.C., which you have to be British-born
to receive, Sartoris thinks, *"But I'm going to get something,"* at which
point the narrator deftly interjects, "He was. He was going to get it on the
coming fifth of July. But he would only have to have been born at all to get
what he was going to get."[23]

Both versions of the story, then, dramatize Sartoris' frustration and
fear, but the earlier one tilts more toward either a sentimental or satirical
treatment of the former, whereas the latter presents a more realistic
acceptance of his well-founded fear. For example, in scenes added to the
later rendition, Sartoris is at first infuriated that Britt followed him
because he thought he was afraid. He attempts to retaliate by inverting his

own role in the initial scene by chivvying with the careful Scotsman Atkinson, who waves him off with "frantic rage."[24] But just prior to the Amiens crash, Sartoris confusedly admits to himself that "Only he was afraid; he couldn't seem either to keep on remembering that or forgetting that or something."[25] There is real pathos in Sartoris' persistent impotence in finding the front in France. As his symbolically handless watch ticks on, he laments that "He would become a legend in all the allied armed forces; he saw himself an old man, wild-faced and with a long white beard, scrabbling up the cliff somewhere between Brest and Ostend fifty or sixty years from now, piping the number of a disbanded and forgotten squadron, crying, 'Where's the war? Where is it? Where is it?' "[26] Yet this scene and the equivalent one in the earlier typescript also undercut Sartoris for his self-indulgent daydreams of grandeur:

> They had all gone in to town, to spend that last evening which it now seemed to him had been the very moment he had enlisted for—the young lion martial and /magnificent/ splendid among the lights and the glitter and the music, and the woman smells and the woman-laughter and, at the last and within reason, the woman-tears. As the son of glory began to rise; and he opening his eyes and for a moment unable to move because of the fiery pains in his cramped muscles, blinking at Britt standing in the door in the fading light.[27]

Indeed, the reader's introduction to Sartoris ironically juxtaposes his ignorance with the great battles and warriors of British history, as he sits listening to the general's voice "telling again the old stale tale: Waterloo and the playing fields of Eton and here a spot which is forever England. Then the voice was in actual retrograde in a long limbo filled with horses—Fontenoy and Agincourt and Crécy and the Black Prince—and Sartoris whispering to his neighbor from the side of his rigid mouth: 'What nigger is that? He's talking about Jack Johnson.' "[28] Likewise as he later stands "alien and unattached and almost obfuscate" on a curb-edge in London, the narrative voice describes Sartoris as "the foreigner come out of curiosity to chance his life in the old-men's wars, not even aware that he was watching the laboring heart of a nation in one of its blackest hours."[29]

This dichotomy in the treatment of Sartoris mirrors a similar duality within his characterization between romantic and sardonic attitudes toward the war. From one perspective, the story as a whole can be seen to document Sartoris' growing recognition as a result of his personal plight of the dehumanization and ineptitude of those who run the war—the senior staff and the war bureaucracy. At one point in the 47-page typescript, for example, Fritz Goar asks Sartoris if he has not learned anything at all in the last six months, and Sartoris bitterly replies that "I've learned a good deal since noon today."[30] He even more cynically retorts to a sergeant at the Y.M.C.A. that "If I ever get out of this one, I would join the German army now."[31] Yet, from the very beginning of the story, Sartoris confusingly combines commitment with cavalier disregard for the war effort. As they loop in a farewell salute to old England, for instance, he satirically notes, "Naturally it would have occured to someone to play horse for awhile since there was nothing urgent in France: only a Hun break-through over the collapsed Fifth Army and General Haig with our backs to the wall and believing in the justice and sanctity of our cause" (the earlier rendition adds him thinking "Salute to old mud. . . . Salute to old nothing").[32] Further, although the initial near-collision is certainly not Sartoris' fault, he proceeds to fool around with Britt, and, after he has been ordered back into formation, Sartoris deliberately dives at maximum velocity until his pressure gauge blows and he is forced to crash land in a grain field.

Likewise, later in the story, Sartoris evinces a similar conflict between disdain and envy for his superiors. As he explains by telephone to someone at headquarters the cause of his first crash, he "decided at once that it [the voice] knew too much what it was talking about to be a general's."[33] Yet, in the 47-page typescript he observes Major Bishop at Murray's with apparent veneration, returned from France with "his Victoria Cross and his bag of fifty-odd victories," but then he "stalk[s] rigidly on." Similarly, upon seeing Swanny Ewing's chest covered with medals, he wonders "how any man in just three years and eight months could have been that brave."[34] Yet, when actually confronted with his rival for Kit, Sartoris irreverently remarks, "With our backs to the wall. . . . Have the staff got its back to the wall too? Because we cant see you, we're in front of it." He then proceeds to flick his fingers through Swanny's medals, sarcastically asks for a diaper pin, and states, "Give him another. D.S.T. Distinguished Sheries of Thighs," and offers, in impotent recognition of its uselessness, to fight.[35] This ambivalence even permeates Sartoris' feelings for Goar. Although Sartoris clearly admires Goar greatly because he was the one who taught him how to fly and shares with him a sense of professional camaraderie, he laments that if they ever meet again Goar will "be a blasted colonel or something."[36] Only the unprofessional soldiers receive Sartoris' unqualified respect — "either actual flying people or people who, despite the last four years, were still by inclination and thought and behavior civilians and so were interested only in getting on with the war."[37] Conversely, the regimentation and inhumanity of the war bureaucracy receive Sartoris' unqualified condemnation in both versions.

The war bureaucracy, for example, is characterized as exasperated or coldly enraged "by his patient and passive need," which merely disrupts the busy peaceful flow of forms.[38] Sartoris both recognizes and regrets the fact that once he steps outside the bureaucratic treadmill, he is doomed. At one point, for example, the narrator notes that Sartoris becomes a nonperson, even before his actual demise: "officially in France and corporeally in England, he therefore did not exist at all." (Interestingly, in the published version Sartoris deliberately "decided to preserve his anonymity,"[39] whereas in the earlier one his presence in London is more plausibly motivated by his desire to see Kit, and he laments having left the progression of official orders—"Lympne to London to Brooklands to France—which he should never have got out of.")[40] Like many Faulkner protagonists, Sartoris becomes progressively committed to a dubious course of action through a combination of stubbornness and the escalating costs of reversing his direction. Near the conclusion of Part I, Sartoris knows there are sea-defense aerodromes where he could land safely and stay out of the storm, but to do so would mean that he would "relinquish without recourse and succumb without hope to the rigid brazen oakleaves and the iron scarlet tabs the instant his wheels touched the ground."[41]

Although no final reconciliation between Sartoris' polar perspectives of respect and revulsion for the war and those who run it perhaps is possible, a partial one does exist. Sartoris apparently believes in the Allied cause and sincerely attempts to adapt to military life; however, by nationality, training, and temperament, he cannot. He is alienated first through being an American in a British unit. Additionally, he is a casual and thus, by definition, outside of the normal bureaucracy. As he tells the Y.M.C.A. sergeant, Hoffmeyer, "I'm a casual, you see. That means you dont belong to anything, and every time you try to pass anybody behind a desk, they wish you still didn't belong to the human race too."[42] Regimentation, in particular, is antithetical to Sartoris. He does not even comprehend the young Y.M.C.A. woman's shocked query, "You mean that in the English army you can just walk around anywhere you want at night and stop at any hotel you want to when you get tired like a — drummer?" The narrator explains for Sartoris that "He didn't know. He had never thought about it; he had never been in any other army."[43]

Sometimes Sartoris' failures to conform result from his lack of knowledge or misinformation about how the system functions.[44] At others, Sartoris' miscalculations stem from his inability to adjust to the unexpected, as when he makes a perfect gravity landing in a grain field, only to hit an unforeseen depression which unceremoniously upends his craft, causing him a bloody nose.[45] The war itself is the ultimate representation of a situation in which it is necessary but impossible to make rational projections. As he falls off to sleep in the Y.M.C.A. canteen, Sartoris pathetically attempts to plan for his future, thinking that all he wants is to get away,

> out of England, not forever of course, because after six or seven or at the most, eight months at the front he would return on Home Establishment, whereupon if he had had luck, if he managed to last out the first two or three months / and had / until he had learned enough about it to keep from being shot down by anyone less than a Richthofen or a Voss or an Almenroeder, and from then on manage to pull his own weight, perhaps to acquire the three Huns which were the equivalent of the cost of training a pilot,[46] or at least keep from utterly disgracing himself through fear, he might be even a captain, considered capable by the

powers of commanding a flight, keeping the younger ones whom he would conduct over the lines for their first time from being killed before they had had time to discover what it was about.[47]

Finally, the oxymoron of the title "With Caution and Dispatch" captures the central dilemma of being dependent for succor upon an inhumane and sometimes even contradictory system which is attempting to impose order upon the chaos of war.[48] The paradoxical directive demands too much of Sartoris, for he lacks both the circumspection to deal rationally with contingencies and the discipline to fulfill his orders with dispatch. Thus, as Sartoris imprudently proceeds toward his intended destination in France, he only hastens his own imminent dispatch.[49]

"With Caution and Dispatch" combines symbols, character types, and themes from all of the previous war stories. Sartoris, like Cadet Thompson in "Landing in Luck," is a fairly green recruit undergoing the first real tests of his flying skill,[50] which he likewise fails through taking unnecessarily dangerous risks. Yet, to a greater extent than Thompson, Sartoris is exonerated through sympathy for his plight against the combined "conspiracy" of Britt (in the earlier typescript), the bureaucracy, and the weather, as well as by his own and others' recognition of his doom. Sartoris also is both a better flier than Thompson and has more respect for the intricacies of the machine he operates.

Sartoris also in some respects resembles Corporal Jeyfus in "Love," who likewise is romantically attached to an unfaithful female who deserts him for a high-ranking officer with ribbons.[51] "With Caution and Dispatch" further recalls "Love" in its labyrinthine implausibilities of plotting, inclusion of gratuitous comic anecdotes, and scenes of social satire.[52] In particular, the description of the ex-country-club barman in "Love" as a "thin, horse-faced man who looked like a Methodist Sunday School superintendent" contributes to the portrayal of four minor characters in the earlier rendition of "With Caution and Dispatch."[53]

"With Caution and Dispatch" is reminiscent of both "The Leg" and "Crevasse," too, in its juxtaposition of a symbolic pastoral landscape against a progressively sinister atmosphere of paranoia and death. Specifically, the description of the green English countryside into which Sartoris first crashes — "an oblong of sprouting grain bounded on both sides by hedgerows, at one end a copse, at the other a low stone wall" — recalls the locale of Corinthia's cottage in "The Leg."[54]

The sterility and spiritual death associated with the machine age also unites "With Caution and Dispatch" with both "Crevasse" and "Victory." The 47-page typescript of "With Caution and Dispatch" reuses specific images from the later story of cheaply constructed buildings and a protagonist falling asleep like a corpse on a cot in a cubicle.[55] "With Caution and Dispatch" is also closely linked to "Victory" through the themes of the conflict between individualism and the implacable regimentation of military systems (symbolized by the motif of shaving) and of foreigners alienated in London (symbolized by the motif of standing on street corners while the masses throng by).[56] The stereotype of the penny-pinching Scot also unites "With Caution and Dispatch" with both "Victory" and "Thrift," for at one point in the earlier typescript Sartoris returns to his tent to retrieve a pound note hidden in a mattress by the Scot Atkinson and ironically finds only ten shillings.[57]

Perhaps the closest resemblance to "With Caution and Dispatch" is the story "All the Dead Pilots" in which Sartoris undergoes similar sexual rivalries over Kit and a bar-maid in Amiens, as well as near-crashes in his Camel, before he is fatally shot down. Both stories also stress the common theme of the undercutting of myths about the romanticism of war with sobering realities. Yet, the comic revenge motif in "All the Dead Pilots" is replaced in "With Caution and Dispatch" by a quest simply to survive *to* the Front. The overall tone of the latter story is also more darkly sardonic, at least in the earlier typescript version.

"Ad Astra" also presages "With Caution and Dispatch" in its tone, techniques, and characters. The first long typescript shares a remarkably similar atmosphere of heavy drinking and deracination. Further, both tales (as well as "Landing in Luck," "Honor," "Death Drag," and "Turnabout") use the technique of symbolic stasis outside of time to represent a sort of psychic death-in-life.[58] Monaghan's illusions and disillusions, likewise, bear some resemblance to Sartoris'; they both begin by believing in the war but come to see it as a grotesque and meaningless charade.

"With Caution and Dispatch" also shares common character types and themes with "Honor," "Death Drag," and "Turnabout." Such seasoned older officers as Rogers in "Honor," Jock and Captain Warren in "Death Drag," and Captain Bogard in "Turnabout" presage the understated majors Hough and Fritz Goar in the first typescript of "With Caution and Dispatch." The dual treatment of machines as both a means to earn money and as entertainment for the masses in "Honor" and "Death Drag" suggests the simultaneously serious and antic aspects of war in "With Caution and Dispatch." "Turnabout" is also closely linked to "With Caution and Dispatch" through the themes of innocent youths confronted by situations beyond their comprehension or control and of war as a vicious, dehumanizing game. Further, both Hope and Sartoris show considerable courage and flamboyance in their futile flights against death. Sartoris' feelings of frustration and impotent rage in the last story likewise mirror Bogard's analogous emotions at the conclusion of "Turnabout."

In a final analysis, though, "Turnabout" is a much better story than "With Caution and Dispatch," for two interrelated reasons: distance and proportion. Whereas in "Turnabout" the reader is sympathetic yet detached from both Bogard and Hope because of the continual counterpointing of their polar positions, in "With Caution and Dispatch" Britt and Sartoris are inconsistently portrayed, and the tone is too tenderly indulgent toward Sartoris, particularly in the earlier rendition. "Turnabout" is also controlled through the taut symmetry of its scenes, as well as the quick reversals of plot and fortune. In contrast, the loose, episodic structure of "With Caution and Dispatch" disperses both conflict and interest. The reader finally feels that Faulkner made a wise decision in 1959 to defer publication of "With Caution and Dispatch" — at least until someone offered him $50,000 for it tax-free, or he actually had in hand a good, sound $500 hunting hound that he wished to purchase.[59]

Notes

1. Francis Thompson, "The Hound of Heaven," quoted in *A Treasury of Great Poems, English and American*, ed. Louis Untermeyer, rev. ed. (New York: Simon and Schuster, 1955), p. 1002. See n. 48 below.

2. Jospeh Blotner, ed., *Uncollected Stories of William Faulkner* (New York: Random House, 1979), p. 711, n. For a description of the nine pages on the versos of the setting copy of *The Hamlet*, which I have not seen, refer to James B. Meriwether, *The Literary Career of William Faulkner: A Bibliographical Study* (Columbia: Univ. of South Carolina Press, 1971), pp. 33, 87. The 47-page typescript (numbered 1–47, with typed material also on the versos of pp. 36 and 40) has holograph corrections in a hand that Blotner characterizes as late 1940s. See Blotner, *Faulkner: A Biography* (New York: Random House, 1974), I, 291n. The two nonconsecutively paged typescript (numbered 1, 10) seems to be slightly closer to the published version. Blotner also notes in *Uncollected Stories* the possible parallels of the 47-page typescript to the 100-page unproduced film script *A Ghost Story* which Faulkner wrote for Howard Hawkes. *Uncollected Stories* is hereafter cited as *US*.

3. The 47-page typescript states the destination as France, whereas both the 2-page typescript, p. 1, and the *Uncollected Stories* version, p. 642, state "to destination known henceforth as zero." The date also changes from 26 March 1918 in the 47-page typescript, p. 1, to − th March 1918 in the 2-page typescript to "blank March 1918" (*US*, 642).

4. The situation in "Turnabout" is slightly different in that the crashes dramatized within the story are avoided, though barely, and it is an Argentine rather than a Brazilian vessel. The function of the Brazilian ship in "With Caution and Dispatch" remains somewhat enigmatic. Faulkner apparently intended the reader to assume that it actually was a British ship traveling under false disguise — perhaps a spy ship, which would explain the enraged response of the crew and his quick escort off it on one of his Majesty's destroyers. Neither the officer with a Victoria cross and scar nor Britt can offer him any explanation better than the latter's "There's a lot goes on in this war, and the others too I suppose, that subalterns and captains too are not supposed to see" (*US*, 660). The use of Brazil as a neutral ship is also curious: Brazil declared war on the Axis powers in October 1917, well before this story takes place. It is possible that Faulkner erroneously thought Brazil still to be neutral.

5. 47-page typescript, pp. 2–3. Later Sartoris explains the situation in much the same terms to Major Fritz Goar, p. 29.

6. In the 47-page typescript, p. 2, Britt tells the men to be back in bed by midnight; in the 2-page one, p. 1, he tells them to be back in bed by nine in the morning and gives a reason — they will take off at ten — suggesting a more flexible and sympathetic attitude.

7. 47-page typescript, p. 6. The Murray's atmosphere also occurs prominently in *A Fable* and Elliott White Springs' part-fictional, part-autobiographical novel *War Birds: Diary of an Unknown Aviator*, first published anonymously in *Liberty: A Weekly for Everybody* as "War Birds: The Uncensored Diary of an American Aviator in France, His Loves and Hates — Gay Parties and Air Flights" (3, 14 August–30 November, 1926), and in book form published by George H. Doran (1926). The 1927 Grosset & Dunlap edition added a foreword which

made the book appear to be the diary of John McGavock Grider, who was killed in action, edited by his comrade, Springs.

8. 47-page typescript, p. 22.

9. For discussions of Sartoris' drinking in the 47-page typescript, see especially pp. 3–4, where Britt admonishes Sartoris to "try to stay sober. At least what you call sober," and Sartoris sarcastically notes that "Thank God whiskey was one thing at least there was enough of even in wartime" and proceeds to tell a wonderful anecdote about how he keeps from having to drink alone (which one wishes Faulkner had found a more suitable location for): "he would take the whiskey-glass in his left hand; he would remove his hat /and hand it to/ with his right /hand/ and hand it to his companion (or opponent); he would drink the whiskey then the water and set the glasses down and take his hat back and put it on his head." Sartoris also notes with disdain that they are served at Kent "a glass of soda slightly discolored with whiskey (I bet it's at least a fountain pen full, he told himself) and so not enough of either to keep him awake" (p. 7). He both drinks at a pub in London and asks the sergeant at the Y.M.C.A. canteen if he has a drink.

10. See 47-page typescript, pp. 2, 25. This version also makes Britt's reaction to Sartoris' crash stronger: "Britt came at him again, diving quite low; there was something coldly furious and grimly unbelieving in the very shape of Britt's Camel and in the very snarl of the engine /es/ as Britt zoomed on, looking back and shaking his fist again."

11. *US*, 643; 47-page typescript, p. 8. The latter contains a type "surfeon's."

12. *US*, 643; 47-page typescript, p. 9.

13. 47-page typescript, p. 3.

14. In the first scene in the 47-page typescript (p. 2), Britt is bareheaded and does not return the salute of the general. He also leans against the wall casually with his hands in his pockets, his M.C. and D.F.C. ribbons and wings "smudged," as he tells Sartoris adamantly that he cannot go to London, thus confusingly contrasting his cavalier attitude toward the war with a seemingly callous and rigid treatment of Sartoris.

15. *US*, 660.

16. *US*, 664.

17. 47-page typescript, p. 10; *US*, 644.

18. 47-page typescript, pp. 25, 28. See also p. 22 on which Sartoris is described as feeling "grim and sardonic outrage."

19. 47-page typescript, pp. 29–30.

20. 47-page typescript, p. 31. It seems significant that for someone as sartorial as Sartoris clothing should symbolize stability. For example, after the crash on the ship, he muses that "The watch inside his right wrist still ticked, but the guard and crystal and all three of the hands were gone, vanished into the bizarre limbo of crashes where shoes and socks and luck tokens and goggles and sometimes even ties and braces disappeared." At the end of the story Britt gives him a new pair of goggles. (*US*, 653, 664).

21. 47-page typescript, p. 30. The quotation contains a typo "beeen." The phrasing of this passage bears resemblance to the descriptions of airplanes in "All the Dead Pilots" and "Death Drag."

22. 47-page typescript, p. 31. The deleted material is crossed through on the typewriter. For a detailed discussion of the slight changes in dates and places among the various versions of John Sartoris' saga, including the manuscripts of "All the Dead Pilots" and "Ad Astra," the published versions, and *Flags in the Dust* and *Sartoris*, see Chapter IV, p. 262, n. 44, in my dissertation, "William Faulkner's World War I and Flying Short Fiction: An Imaginative Appropriation of History," Diss. Univ. of South Carolina 1977.

23. *US*, 657.

24. *US*, 662.

25. *US*, 663. This scene reverberates off the earlier one in which "even in just two days he had forgotten the land, forgotten the old stale smell of the base-colonel's hat," and the more seasoned aviators Britt and Tate and Sibleigh remark that "when you got really close to the war, you were free of it" (p. 658), with the ambiguous referent for it being both the brass and fear. This same pronoun ambiguity is used in the references to what Sartoris was going to get; see n. 23 above.

26. *US*, 659.

27. 47-page typescript, pp. 4–5. Faulkner's method of undercutting Sartoris here is similar to Joyce's treatment of Stephen Daedalus' composition of his villanelle in *A Portrait of the Artist as a Young Man*, which ends in a kind of ecstatic wetdream (New York: Viking Press, 1968), pp. 217–24. Interestingly, this passage, on p. 219, also contains a reference to "the victory chant at Agincourt." See n. 28 below.

28. *US*, 642; the version in the 47-page typescript, p. 1, ends with Sartoris asking a question " 'What nigger? Is he talking about Jack Johnson?' " The 2-page typescript version, on p. 1, omits Sartoris' irreverent remarks. The words "the old stale tale" are added to the published version (reechoed on p. 658), as is the reference to the aeroplanes unromantically described as "dull and ungleaming in the intermittent sun."

29. *US*, 648. The version in the 47-page typescript, p. 22, is slightly different and does not contain the reference to the old men's wars, showing a more cynical treatment of the upper echelons in the published version.

30. 47-page typescript, p. 28.

31. *US*, 644.

32. 47-page typescript, p. 10.

33. 47-page typescript, p. 16; *US*, 647.

34. 47-page typescript, p. 26.

35. 47-page typescript, p. 27. The phrase "Distinguish Sheries of Thighs" is used satirically by Sartoris to characterize Captain Spoomer in "All the Dead Pilots." See *These 13* (New York: Jonathan Cape & Harrison Smith, 1931), p. 86; *Collected Stories of William Faulkner* (New York: Random House, 1950), p. 514.

36. 47-page typescript, p. 31.

37. *US*, 648; 47-page typescript, p. 43.

38. *US*, 648; the wording is slightly different in the 47-page typescript, p. 42.

39. *US*, 647.

40. 47-page typescript, p. 45. Cal in Springs' *War Birds*, pp. 151–52, undergoes similar mishaps and follows an almost identical route to Sartoris'; however, Cal simply gets a new machine and proceeds uneventfully for France.

41. 47-page typescript, p. 45; *US*, 650.

42. 47-page typescript, p. 41.

43. 47-page typescript, p. 34.

44. For example, he tells a man at the Y.M.C.A. canteen a humorous anecdote about how when he came over on the boat he was told by one of the sailors that if he put down Church of England on his enlistment forms that he would have to attend services every Sunday, so he chose instead to state Roman Catholic, and all during his cadethood at five o'clock every Sunday, and sometimes during the week, he was paraded to matins (47-page typescript, p. 34). This incident is typical of Sartoris' confrontations with military regulations, for every time he tries to avoid one bureaucratic pitfall, he catapults himself into a worse situation.

45. The recurrent motif of Sartoris' bloodied nose serves as a humorous reminder of his vulnerability. After his second crash, he gingerly bathes his noses and bemusedly remarks that

"if he crashed another one, he would need a periscope merely to walk around with" (*US*, 653; see also 646, 663).

46. In Springs' *War Birds*, pp. 187–88, the diarist somewhat differently states the cost of training a pilot as equivalent to getting one Hun. In the version in *US* (663–64), Britt pointedly tells Sartoris that his shenanigans have already wiped out the cost of his training, so he will have to shoot down six huns before he can even start counting.

47. 47-page typescript, p. 40.

48. The title may be an allusion to Thompson's "The Hound of Heaven," n. 1 above, as well as to such conflicting admonitionary aphorisms as "Look before you leap," and "He who hesitates is lost" by which we attempt to accommodate the complexity of the world. It also may echo a marvelous list of contradictory orders in James Warner Bellah's "The Captain's Cordon Rouge," *Saturday Evening Post*, 200 (12 November, 1927), 22, which Faulkner probably was familiar with: the men are instructed "1) If you see a submarine, open fire at once." However, "2) No shots are to be fired at anything without orders from the fire control on the bridge." Similarly, "4) [Assume] Battle stations on the first ring of the alarm bell." Yet, "5) When the alarm bells, rings, do not assume battle stations until an officer arrives."

49. The title "With Caution and Dispatch" also contains numerous piquant puns, such as the obsolete meanings of dispatch as dismissal or an act of killing or gaining quick riddance of someone; the last meaning of caution as a noun is one who arouses astonishment or commands attention, as Sartoris certainly does. See *Webster's New Collegiate Dictionary* (Springfield, Mass.: G. & C. Merriam, 1979), pp. 326, 175.

50. Sartoris ironically notes prior to his first crash that "The field was all right; anyone who had had as much as forty hours on Camels could land one in it" (*US*, 645). In contrast, Cadet Thompson in "Landing in Luck" solos after only slightly more than seven hours. See text of "Love" chapter and nn. 16–17.

51. The love attachments in both stories are also treated with similar humorous symbolism. For example, in the 47-page typescript of "Love" (p. 44), the Major greets Corporal Jeyfus by stating, "I see you are still having trouble with that heart." Likewise in "With Caution and Dispatch," 47-page typescript, p. 26, Sartoris enviously notes that his Roman-counsellike rival, Swanny Ewing, was "in full dress and plated over the left breast with medals until he would have been bullet-proof, even at point-blank range anywhere on that side between collarbone and waistline."

52. See, for example, the scene in Kent, 47-page typescript, pp. 5–7.

53. Typescript of "Love," pp. 36–37. In "With Caution and Dispatch," the punctillious Corporal Botts who confiscates Sartoris' machine in the 47-page typescript, p. 14, is caricatured as "a thin, gray-haired . . . man who looked exactly like a volunteer dissenting preacher"; Sartoris' tailor, MacKensie, is described as a "once plump man with a sensitive ministerial face," p. 23; and the two Y.M.C.A. men, the ineffectual elderly one who is apparently the canteen's nominal director, and Sergeant Hoffmeyer, who loans Sartoris his bed for the night, are respectively described as "a plump, rosy, baby-skinned man of forty or so, who looked like a Sunday School superintendent dressed in a uniform hired that afternoon from a costumer for a military charade to raise money for a civic fund" and as "a tall ruddy / ~~faced man~~/ [written in pencil above the line] man with a horse's face/" (pp. 33, 35). The elderly matrons who run the canteen are also characterized by Hoffmeyer as still thinking "this war is just a great big Sunday School" and for the sake of their religion refusing to believe that he could be anywhere after eleven o'clock except in bed (pp. 36, 38). *War Birds* undercuts the Americans for thinking "they are on the way to a Sunday School picnic" (p. 205).

54. *US*, 645; 47-page typescript, p. 12. See also the earlier description of "greening England slid[ing] slowly beneath them, neat and quilted," *US*, 643; 47-page typescript, pp. 9–10. Similar imagery occurs in "The Leg."

55. This image, in slightly varied forms, occurs at three points in the 47-page typescript of "With Caution and Dispatch." First, Sartoris lies down for a nap in his tent on

"the naked springs without even unfastening his belt, cold, rigid, and composed, like the stone effigy of a knight on a fifteenth century sarcophagus" (p. 4). Later Sergeant Hoffmeyer is described as "On the cot and covered to the chin . . . lying there beneath the unshaded light with the decorous immobility of a corpse" (pp. 35–36). Finally, Sartoris lies down in the same cot "with folded arms, so that he lay in somewhat the same attitude in which the horse-faced sergeant had been lying, quiet, composed on his back in that new, still paint-reeking, /intact/ cubicle not /of American set/ lifted intact out of America and carried three thousand miles and set down, still intact, in the alien dark" (pp. 39–40); deleted passages are crossed out in pencil. Similar imagery occurs in "Victory."

56. In a particularly important passage in "With Caution and Dispatch," Sartoris emerges into Picadilly and stands "at the curb-edge of London, that England in that spring of 1918" as women and soldiers bustle by" (p. 648); the versions in the 47-page typescript, p. 22, and the two-page typescript, p. 10, are slightly different. Alexander Gray in "Victory" stands on a curb in Picadilly and begs.

57. 47-page typescript, pp. 18–19. The first page is crossed through in pencil and by typewriter; the second repeats it, with revisions and the addition that "No wonder it's taking them four years to win the war."

58. Faulkner creates a sense of symbolic stasis outside time first during the rainstorm over the channel when Sartoris suddenly becomes surrounded: "the air, the rain, roared with a tremendous bellowing. It was not in front of him, it was everywhere: above, beneath, inside of him; he was breathing it, he was flying in it as he had been breathing and flying in the air." Then suddenly the Brazilian flag looms before him (US, 650; 47-page typescript, p. 46). Time also is slowed almost to stoppage during the crash scene: "The Camel went up the side of the ship like a hawk, a gull up a cliff-face. *Why dont I crash?* he thought. He opened his eyes. The Camel was hanging on its propeller, no longer moving," and the faces in the crow's nest "hung as solitary and peaceful in the rainfilled nothingness as two last year's birdnests" (US, 651; 47-page typescript, pp. 46–47 is almost identical). For a delineation of the various types of stasis in Faulkner's work, see my dissertation, Chapter IV, n. 74. Some of the imagery in this passage of the "scudding and streaming earth" (US, 650; 47-page typescript, p. 44) also recalls "Death Drag" and "Turnabout." This scene also may echo Bellah's "The Cities of the World," *Saturday Evening Post*, 200 (16 June, 1928), 18–19, in which MacAnulty makes a premature transatlantic flight and runs out of petrol with forty-five minutes left on the chronometer. The story romantically but effectively follows the protagonist's fears as he faces the "teeth of death" in the fog and cold gray sea off the British coast — only to be inexplicably saved by a surprise landing in the arctic snows. The descriptions of the planes as huge birds and dramatic stases within vast wastes of space resemble those in "With Caution and Dispatch."

59. Faulkner to Harold Ober, received June 26, 1959. Faulkner himself decided to defer publication of the story in 1959 when Meriwether offered him $500 to publish it in the *Texas Quarterly*. See Blotner, *Faulkner: A Biography*, II, 1736 and n.

"Shot Down Last Spring": The Wounded Aviators of Faulkner's Wasteland

Margaret Yonce*

That Faulkner's poetry is immensely important to an understanding of his accomplished prose style has been noted by many scholars and critics.[1] The numerous drafts and revisions of poems — both published and unpublished — attest to the skill which the young artist was so diligently and painstakingly acquiring and to the seriousness with which he regarded his craft. At present, however, very little has been written about individual Faulkner poems or the relationship of specific poems to themes developed at length in the prose work.

One poem in particular, "The Lilacs," seems especially worthy of study, for it is unusually suggestive in its employment of themes and images which recur in both apprentice and mature work. The most frequent observation about "The Lilacs" by those critics who have commented upon it is that it concerns a wounded pilot and that thematically and tonally it is charged with an atmosphere of death in life.[2] Such an observation is sound, yet it does not explain the whole poem, much of which remains teasingly enigmatic. Besides the death-in-life motif, the poem also touches on other themes such as the pursuit of an immortal woman by mortal man, metamorphosis, and the fragmentation of personality — all of which the young writer employed repeatedly in verse and prose.

"The Lilacs" occupies a special place among Faulkner's poems. With the exception of The Marble Faun, it is Faulkner's longest published poem. It is also the poem most often reprinted during Faulkner's lifetime, first appearing in the Double Dealer in June 1925 and later included in two anthologies: the Anthology of Magazine Verse for 1925 and Salmagundi (1932). More important, Faulkner chose "The Lilacs" as the first poem in A Green Bough (1933), the only collection of his poetry which he was to publish and about whose structure he was very careful. To his publisher Hal Smith he wrote that he had chosen the best manuscripts and "built a volume just like a novel."[3]

As with most of Faulkner's verse, it is difficult to place the exact date when "The Lilacs" was written, but the evidence suggests a composition date much earlier than the first published version. A hand-printed and -bound booklet entitled The Lilacs, which survives only in one partially burned copy, bears a dedication to Phil Stone and that date "Jan. 1 1920."[4] This little gift booklet contains as its first offering a version of "The Lilacs," somewhat different from the later printed texts, as well as some

*Reprinted, with permission, from Mississippi Quarterly, 31, No. 3 (Summer 1978), 359–68.

dozen other poems. If the booklet were given to Stone on January 1, 1920, as the dedication indicates, then obviously the composition occurred before that date, presumably some time in 1919. This would place its writing closer to that of the original composition of *The Marble Faun*, the 1924 published version of which bears the date *April, May, June, 1919* on its final page. Although we cannot be certain that that date marks the actual time of *The Marble Faun's* composition,[5] it seems probable that versions of both *The Marble Faun* and "The Lilacs" were written in the year following the Armistice and that both reflect the post-War malaise and sense of paralysis.

The setting of the poem is a tea party, in a garden, on a spring afternoon. The early drafts place the scene specifically in England; the fifth line, "We are in Blighty" (British slang for *England, home*), has been deleted in published versions. While the deletion perhaps makes the poem more universal, several incidental details—such as the lilacs, the serving of tea, and expressions like "old chap"—strongly suggest a British setting. The time of the poem, though not definitely stated either, appears decidedly post-War. One of the comments overhead by the persona, "Shot down / Last spring," would indicate that the present time of the poem is spring (blooming lilacs) the year after the War's end—1919. The date is significant, both because it places the time of the action of the poem near the time of its probable composition and because that spring of 1919 seems to have had special significance for Faulkner. Not only does *The Marble Faun* conclude with that date; *Soldiers' Pay* takes place in late March to early May 1919 and *Flags in the Dust* begins with the return of young Bayard Sartoris in this same spring. In each of these works, the condition of the protagonist—paralyzed, blinded, or psychically maimed—seems intensified by the vibrant renewal of fecund nature. It is the same chord struck by Eliot in the opening lines of *The Waste Land*—"April is the cruellest month, breeding / Lilacs out of the dead land . . ."—though that poem, published in 1922, could not have influenced the original version of either *The Marble Faun* or "The Lilacs."

After establishing the situation in the first quarter of the poem, in the remaining lines the persona recounts the circumstances of his wounding. Unexpectedly, however, the description is not of aerial combat, a valorous duel with the enemy like that recalled by the dying Donald Mahon or by Bayard Sartoris, but of the pursuit of a woman, a "white wanton," whom he stalks "through the shimmering reaches of the sky" to "the border of a wood: / A cloud forest. . . ."[6] The nymph apparently is Death; he is chided for "going in the far thin sky to stalk / The mouth of death." Faulkner here is dramatizing, as he was to do in many later works, the obvious death wish of so many of the young men, especially the aviators, who eagerly left for the front. The desire to live intensely and die gloriously he himself seems at one time to have shared, though by the time he wrote *Soldiers' Pay* he certainly recognized the fatuousness of the romantic notion of war. His treatment of the theme in "The Lilacs" is more ambivalent: while not a glorification of self-immolation, there is yet a sympathetic attitude toward the aviator's quest for transcendence. The tragedy for the protagonist of "The Lilacs," like that of so many of Faulkner's combat survivors, is that "he didn't die." Though death was his goal, it has somehow eluded him. He says, "I thought that I could find her when I liked, / But now I wonder if I found her, after all."

The "white woman" is a figure which recurs in much of the early material. Usually, she is nymph or naiad, some form of mythological creature associated with nature, and often attendant on death. Typically, she is pursued by a mortal man, whose desire seems to be not merely to possess her, but through her to partake of timelessness. In Faulkner's first published poem, "L'Apres-Midi d'un Faune," the persona follows a nymph "through the singing trees" until at last she pauses and seems momentarily to relent: "Now hand in hand with her I go. . . ."[7] Yet the union is temporary and the persona is left at the poem's end—like Keats's pale knight-at-arms—"alone and palely loitering."

The motif appears again in the early prose piece "Nympholepsy," though here the persona appears to escape with no dire effects. In this expansion of the earlier (1922) sketch "The Hill," the laborer returning to his "casual rooming house" after a day's hard work is attracted by "a little silver flame moving among the trees."[8] Knowing that the figure is a woman, he follows through field and wood, down a hill to a stream, where he is overtaken by fear and a sense that he has trespassed on holy ground. Trying to cross the stream by way of a log, he slips and for a moment knows he is about to die.

> Then the water took him. But here was something more than water. The water ran darkly between his body and his overalls and shirt, he felt his hair lap backward wetly. But here beneath his hand a startled thigh slid like a snake, among dark bubbles he felt a swift leg; and, sinking, the point of a breast scraped his back. Amid a slow commotion of disturbed water he saw death like a woman shining and drowned and waiting, saw a flashing body tortured by water; and his lungs spewing water gulped wet air. (p. 153)

Gaining the stream's bank, she flees and he again pursues, though she outdistances him and he finally loses her.

> She was far ahead, the disturbance of her passage through the wheat had died away ere he reached it. He saw, beyond the spreading ripple of her passage arcing away on either side, her body break briefly against a belt of wood, like a match flame; then he saw her no more.
>   Still running, he crossed the wheat slumbrous along the moony land, and into the trees he went, wearily. But she was gone, and in a recurrent surge of despair he threw himself flat upon the earth. (p. 154)

His disappointment, however, does not last long and he returns to the commonplace matters of food and bed and work. He has touched momentarily something extraordinary which he desires but does not understand, but there is no lasting transformation.

In another early poem, "Naiads' Song," those inhabitants of streams and rivers sing siren-like to all who sorrow to "keep / Tryst with us here in wedded sleep."[9] Their appeal is one of soft and easeful forgetfulness in their depths, yet unmistakably, they lure the hearer to his death. A variation on the theme appears in the little prose romance *Mayday* (1926) written as a gift for Helen Baird. Here Sir Galwyn of Arthgyl embarks upon a quest for the woman whose face he has seen in a stream. Though momentarily distracted by several mortal or mythical maidens, he quickly wearies of each and turns from cloying reality to the pursuit of the ideal. Finally, granted a vision by Saint Francis of Little Sister Death, whose visage is the one he has sought all along, he drowns himself in a river.[10]

The persona of "The Lilacs" encounters the fatal female at dawn in "the shimmering reaches of the sky." Although undoubtedly a sylph, she seems also associated with forest—he finds her "near a brake," "at the border of a wood"—and with water—she seems "A rising whiteness mirrored in a lake." Her presence, like that of other *belles dames sans merci*, is blighting though not fatal. At the moment when the persona feels her arms and her "cool breath," the bullet strikes him "in the left breast." In retrospect, he muses, "One should not die like this / On such a day, / From angry bullet or other modern way." Instead, he longs for metamorphosis: "One should fall, I think, to some Etruscan dart / . . . And, on such a day as this / Become a tall wreathed column: I should like to be / An ilex on an isle in purple seas." Apparently he has in mind some transformation like that recounted in numerous myths of mortal changed into non-human form because he has espied or offended an immortal. Ironically, it is not so much a *death* wish as a desire for immortality, union with the goddess, apotheosis, which drives the persona.

One of the comments often made about "The Lilacs" is that it bears a resemblance to "The Love Song of J. Alfred Prufrock." In particular, the "smooth-shouldered creatures" in sheer scarves concerned about their "tea and cigarettes and books" recall the women whose limbs and gowns and trivial talk enthrall Prufrock.[11] That Faulkner owed a particular debt to Eliot's poem has been well documented; indeed, there are some twenty-nine typescript pages of an unpublished poem which is an obvious imitation of "Prufrock,"[12] and images and phrases echoing Eliot's poem appear frequently throughout Faulkner's work. Yet the most obvious, and perhaps most important, similarity between "The Lilacs" and "The Love Song of J. Alfred Prufrock" has not been noted. That is, both are dramatic *monologues*; there is a single persona in each poem. Just as Prufrock's "Let us go then, you and I" is a directive to the body from a consciousness estranged from its physical being, so the persona in "The Lilacs" has been so fragmented by his war experiences that he manifests multiple personalities. Read in this way, some of the more confusing elements of the poem are easily explicable.

Most readers assume that there are two or three former comrades seated together beneath the lilacs; the speaker plainly says, "And we sit, we three / In diffident contentedness. . . ." Yet the next lines are perplexing: "Lest we let each other guess / How happy we are / Together here. . . ." Why, one wonders, should these maimed veterans be happy? The next section, however, read carefully helps to dispel the confusion. The hostess stops to ask, " — Are you quite all right, sir? . . . / — You are a bit lonely, I fear." A strange comment if there are indeed three friends present! If this is not clue enough, the overheard remarks, " — Who? — shot down / Last spring — Poor chap, his mind / . . . . doctors say. . . hoping rest will bring — " should clarify the situation. There is only one wounded soldier present; the friends with whom he sits "in silent amity" are manifestations of his own fragmented psyche.

Throughout the poem there is a curious shifting of pronouns, especially the alternation between the first person singular and plural pronouns. In the first two stanzas, the first person plural pronoun is employed — with one exception: when the persona speaks, thanking his solicitous hostess, he uses "I"; but when referring to feelings, thoughts, internal matters, he uses the plural pronoun. Perhaps significantly, in early drafts of the poem, Faulkner had used the singular pronoun (". . . and eye *me* strangely as they pass," "one of them, *my* hostess," "To *me* they are . . .")[13] but later changed to the plural. In the apparent dialogue which comprises the middle portion of the poem, the speaker who tells of stalking the "white woman" in his "little pointed-eared machine" refers to himself as "I," and then what seems to be another speaker responds with "you": " — Yes, you are right." The second speaker then tells the story of *his* wounding, of raiding over Mannheim at night, and being drawn down "Out of the bullet-tortured air. . . ." When his account breaks off, he is referred to in the third person: "His voice has dropped and the wind is mouthing his words. . . ." But in the concluding stanzas, the persona once more uses the first person, both singular and plural: "We sit in silent amity. / I am cold, for now the sun is gone. . . ." At the very end, when the lilacs nod their heads and ask, "Old man . . . How did you die?" there is clearly but one unfortunate survivor present. Thus the "conversation" which we hear in the poem is not an exchange of war stories between combat veterans but a single "voice," that of a wounded aviator whose shattered mind attempts to sort among the detritus of war experiences to form a kind of composite memory.

Faulkner developed and extended this concept of the divided psyche still further in subsequent novels. In *Soldiers' Pay* (1926), Donald Mahon — maimed, blind, and amnesic — survives for over a year after being shot down in France until his memory momentarily returns and he can die. All along he has been waiting for something, and that something is the re-integration of mind and body. Bereft of memory at the moment of his wounding, he endures zombie-like until the nerve endings temporarily fuse "sight flickered on again, like a poorly made electrical contact," he relives the events of the day when he was shot down, and finally, mind and body once more intact, he "[puts] calmly out to an immeasurable sea."[14]

Similarly, in *Flags in the Dust* (completed in 1927), Bayard Sartoris searches endlessly for his twin John. When John bails out of his stricken craft without benefit of parachute, Bayard in his own airplane dives through clouds hoping to catch sight of his brother, but he never does. In their somewhat unhealthy twinship, John has always been the "soul" of their being. After John's death, Bayard is like a death-bent demon furiously seeking destruction. Recalling for the thousandth time the scene of his brother's valediction, Bayard thinks,

> Perhaps he [Bayard] was dead, and he recalled that morning, relived it again with strained and intense attention from the time he had seen the first tracer smoke, until from his steep side-slip he watched the flame burst like the gay flapping of an orange pennon from John's Camel and saw his brother's familiar gesture and the sudden awkward sprawl of his plunging body as it lost equilibrium in midair; relived it again as you might run over a printed tale, trying to remember, feel, a bullet going into his body or head that might have slain him at the same instant. That . . . would explain so much: that he too was dead and this was hell, through which he moved forever and ever with an illusion of quickness, seeking his brother who in turn was somewhere seeking him, never the two to meet.[15]

Interestingly, Bayard Sartoris also employs pronouns ambiguously on occasion much as does the persona of "The Lilacs," perhaps likewise indicating psychic division. In a frenzy of self-accusation after the death of his grandfather in the car which he was driving, Bayard thinks:

> Well, dammit, suppose it had: was he to blame? had he insisted that his grandfather ride with him? had he given the old fellow a bum heart? And then, coldly: You were scared to go home. You made a nigger sneak your horse out for you. You, who deliberately do things your judgment tells you may not be successful, even possible, are afraid to face the consequences of your own acts. Then again something bitter and deep and sleepless in him blazed out in vindication and justification and accusation; what, he knew not, blazing out at what, Whom, he did not know: You did it! You caused it all: you killed Johnny. (pp. 306–307)

There are several curious details in the passage quoted. First, we notice the shift from third person to second, which might be explained easily enough as a shift in authorial perspective from omniscient observer to first-person narrator, or as a report of an internal monologue without use of quotation marks. Yet even if one gets past this technical difficulty, he still has to explain why Bayard would refer to himself as "You" rather than "I." A possible explanation is that he recognizes in himself a deep duality, a "self" which is virtually autonomous, over which he has no control. To confuse the issue still further, however, one must decide the implication of the capital letters at the end of the passage. If the "Whom" is directed towards some kind of deity (the "Player" referred to at the end of the novel?), then are the final "You"'s also directed to this Being—or is Bayard addressing himself once more? The matter is not easily resolved.

The development of the concept seems clear. In "The Lilacs" Faulkner had experimented with an aviator whose mind had been fragmented by the war so that he has multiple memories of his wounding. In *Soldiers' Pay*, mind and body are somehow separated at the moment of wounding, and the death-in-life state persists until the two are reunited. In *Flags in the Dust*, the divided psyche is symbolized in terms of twinship, the death of one twin dooming the other. Finally, in *The Sound and the Fury* (1929) Faulkner carries the division of personality to its furthest advance in the Compson brothers, each of whom manifests a portion of the Freudian personality.[16]

"The Lilacs" was certainly an ambitious poem for the young artist, different in form and style from the other verse he was writing. Already he was exhibiting that virtuosity which his mentor Sherwood Anderson would later warn him might, if not disciplined, impede his development. Yet when one examines even the extant typescripts and hand-lettered version of "The Lilacs," as well as those of numerous other poems, one realizes that what may have seemed untrammeled ease of composition to those who saw only the finished products was, in fact, a careful and studied process. In retrospect, we can mark the stages of that artistic growth and see clearly that what perhaps began as "a fumbling in darkness"[17] became very quickly a sure and steady mastery of his craft.

Notes

1. Among the many such notices are George Garrett, "An Examination of the Poetry of William Faulkner," *Princeton University Library Chronicle*, 18 (Spring 1957), 124–135; Cleanth Brooks, "Faulkner as Poet," *Southern Literary Journal*, 1 (December 1968), 5–19, and *William Faulkner: Toward Yoknapatawpha and Beyond* (New Haven: Yale University Press, 1978); and Keen Butterworth, "A Census of Manuscripts and Typescripts of William Faulkner's Poetry," *A Faulkner Miscellany*, ed. James B. Meriwether (Jackson: University Press of Mississippi, 1974), 70–97.

2. See, for example, Joseph Blotner, *Faulkner: A Biography* (New York: Random House, 1974), I, 261.

3. Blotner, p. 790.

4. This booklet is now in the collection of Mr. L. D. Brodsky, to whom I am indebted for permission to examine xerox copies of it.

5. Cleanth Brooks, for example, says, "I am inclined to date the final manuscript of

The Marble Faun later than June 1919 — as late, perhaps, as 1921 or 1922. . . ." *William Faulkner: Toward Yoknapatawpha and Beyond*, p. 12.

6. *A Green Bough*, p. 8, in *The Marble Faun and A Green Bough* (New York: Random House, 1965). All quotations from "The Lilacs" refer to this edition unless otherwise noted.

7. *Early Prose and Poetry*, ed. Carvel Collins (Boston: Little, Brown and Company, 1962), p. 39.

8. *A Faulkner Miscellany*, p. 150. Further references will be cited within the text.

9. *Early Prose and Poetry*, p. 55.

10. *Mayday* (University of Notre Dame Press, 1977).

11. Blotner, notes, I, 48.

12. Butterworth, p. 90.

13. These partially burned typescripts are in The Humanities Research Center, University of Texas.

14. *Soldiers' Pay* (New York: Boni and Liveright, 1926), p. 294.

15. *Flags in the Dust* (New York: Random House, 1973), p. 315. Further references will be cited within the text.

16. Carvel Collins has repeatedly asserted the paralleling of id, ego, and super-ego with Benjy, Quentin, and Jason. See, for example, "The Pairing of *The Sound and the Fury* and *As I Lay Dying*," *Princeton University Library Chronicle*, 18 (Spring 1957), 114-123.

17. Inscription to *Mayday*.

The Sartoris War   John Pikoulis*

The opening story of *The Unvanquished* deals with different points of view within a family, pointing to aspects of the established order that are dying or changing and discriminating between far-from-obvious alliances and animosities. Only by defining these and going on to show them at different times and in different moods could Faulkner hope to describe the impact of the war on the Sartorises. It helps greatly that he did so from the dual perspective of a youthful protagonist, through whose developing consciousness the material unfolds, and of the grandfather he has become who, camouflaged by his younger self, narrates the story, briefly touching on particulars and allowing them to gather emphases of meaning, often in retrospect, as the novel proceeds. To complain of the storybook flavour of the work or to concentrate only on the exposure of the flaws of the family is to overlook such complexities and misread the slight gestures in which the commentary is carried and hence to undermine the whole carefully-developed scale of values of which they are a part. Bayard's youthfulness certainly allows for overmeasures of piety and patriotism but there is the countervailing, if quieter, presence of the narrator to subject these to

*Reprinted, with permission, from *The Art of William Faulkner* (London, 1982), 118–34.

scrutiny and to show how part of the South's experience of war was precisely the element of wish-fulfilment they contain.

As the narrator goes about his work, his mood humorously naive and reflective in turn, he gradually emerges to form a character, one not directly announced but as important as any other we read of. It is that of an aged man who is determined to record the most important events of his life as honestly as he can by imitating the point of view of his childhood self while imperceptibly distancing himself from them. This unhappy, broken man, sincere, loyal, reserved and distinguished by no brilliancies of talent, embarks on a narrative that will rehearse events too disturbing to be more than briefly retold and so perplexing as to have left him with only clues to their meaning. He writes better than he knows.

"Raid" takes for granted the ravages of the Yankee – Confederate war. The Sartorises now live in one of their negro's cabins (ironic shades of the McCaslins), Granny writes with pokeberry juice – and the silver is gone. The mood, despite the energy of Granny and the ever-enthusiastic Ringo, is serious and the view panoramic, taking in the negroes marching to Jordan and the Sartorises forced from theirs, "blind," like their former slaves, "to everything but a hope and a doom." The parallel between the two is reinforced by the grave, laconic episode in which Granny meets a negro woman and her child separated from the main body of marchers. They meet in equality of independence and the certainty of their faiths, though Granny can act contrarily, trying to bribe the woman to stay while disinterestedly abetting her escape.

As Drusilla's embittered speech on the collapse of the South indicates, all is now in a flux, magnificently captured by the marching negroes and the mêlée at the bridge which the Yankees proceed to blow up. Both the negroes and Granny's party are embroiled in the ensuing confusion and the effect is of a single doom embracing them all, negro hopes for freedom and white hopes of rescuing the old order caught up in the same cataclysm. It is against such a background that Granny Millard is to be judged, for the longer she continues to cheat her way to animals and money, the more she endangers herself until, by the time of "Riposte in Tertio," the habit of deception is seen to have done for her; her game, in more senses than one, is up and the turning point to destruction reached. Yet, as ever in this careful novel, a balance has to be struck. A vestigial conscience still nibbles at her mind, even if she has Ringo's zeal and Ab Snopes's support to quell it. More importantly, the proceeds from her mule-trading (and sometimes the mules themselves) are used to keep what remains of society on its feet. An account book is kept; Granny calls out the names of members of the local congregation: "Each time Granny would make them tell what they intended to do with the money, and now she would make them tell her how they had spent it, and she would look at the book to see whether they had lied or not" (pp. 169–70). With those last words, the scales of the balance tilt against her again, for that she who has made a career of lying should affect to be scrupulous about the behaviour of others is a measure of the deception that has overtaken her.

It is the old hierarchical community that Granny strives to resurrect, in which, as so often in Faulkner, only the extremes of aristocrat and peasant or slave have any imaginative substance, "unsoftened," as Roark Bradford notes, "by any appreciable middle ground." (It is this, Mr Bradford thinks, that gives Faulkner 'his feeling for the tragic and for the grisly humor with which he relives' their impact on him.)[1] Once, Doctor Worsham's church was patronised with much ceremony, plantation owners down in the pews, their negroes up in the slave gallery. Now, under Brother Fortinbride, it is in a decrepit state. Some hill-farmers and few bemused negroes are gathered together by one wilful old woman and struggle to survive defeat, poverty and growing despair. They are the "unvanquished" (the original title of "Riposte in Tertio"), those who hold on by the skin of their teeth.

It is before such improbable worshippers that Granny insists on declaring her sins, explaining in her prayer to God that she "did not sin for revenge. I defy You or anyone to say I did. I sinned first for justice" (p. 181), for the profits which she could, in echo of the McCaslins, distribute among the farmers or offer John Sartoris for rebuilding the family fortunes after the war. Her honesty of purpose is not in doubt but the latent charity of her earlier response to the sight of negroes marching away and poor whites huddling for shelter in a charred land is muddled in her prayer, a compound of nobility and arrogance that exposes the defenders of the South as sharply as possible. During the four years of the war, Granny has become "littler and littler and straighter and straighter and more indomitable" (p. 76) and much the same may be said of her supporters, if we allow the words "little" and "straight" full play to suggest a verdict on their diminution through singlemindedness as well as admiration for their resolution in adversity. The latter is nowhere more easily evoked than in the pages devoted to Brother Fortinbride's parishioners. Forlorn as they are and dubiously funded though they may be, the alternative to them is the irregular company that scours the land under the banner of Grumby's Independents.

Unfortunately, Granny tries to play with both and in so doing is infected by a greed differently motivated but nonetheless similar in effect to Ab Snopes's (who is out to line his own pockets) and to the Independents (whose sole means of sustenance is the booty they plunder). She who believes that even Yankees do not harm old women believes she can meddle with scavengers like Grumby with impunity, but she has forgotten that he is simply a pirate feeding off the miseries of war. By compromising herself with him, she has become one of the subverters.

Bayard threatens to go the same way in "Vendee," which is the most sombre of the tales. (The title comes from Balzac's *Les Chouans*, whose first part is called "Ambuscade.") The story looks backwards to Granny's career and forwards to Bayard's attempt — prompted by what he presently experiences — to counter the effects of violence in Yoknapatawpha. Granny is dead, murdered by Grumby. Bayard, accompanied by Ringo and, for a while, Buck McCaslin, determines to punish Ab for his complicity in the crime and then to kill Grumby. That Uncle Buck should play a part in his vendetta is consonant with his earlier appearance as a Sartoris supporter (to the point of adulation) but his role as a thoughtful landowner is not ignored since the posse he joins is a paradigm of Southern society scourging itself of its baser elements, in this instance, Grumby, who is "big and squat, like a bear" (p. 226) and who, like the bear in *Go Down, Moses*, personifies the rankness within. In the circumstances, it is most appropriate that the metaphor of game should once again be raised and that the subject of hunting should call forth some of Faulkner's finest prose: taut, clear, atmospheric writing creating the cold and wet of approaching winter where before the warmth of summer prevailed.

Granted Grumby's character, the pathos of Granny's death and his own youthfulness, Bayard acquits himself much as we should expect, though the moment he cuts off Grumby's hand, like a hunter claiming a trophy, he is forced to consider the consequences of his actions. From what follows, we can deduce that such, precisely, is what he has done, so that when Uncle Buck salutes him as "John Sartoris' boy," narrative tone and strategy combine to make us wince. Knowing what we do of the Colonel and what we have seen happen to Bayard, we can see how the son has again outstripped his father in violence and again foreshadows the latter's corruption, thus rendering the tribute strikingly ironical. Bayard himself senses it as such, for when he is called upon to perform a second act of retribution, this time against his father's killer, not the least of the factors urging him to a pacific decision is his desire to repudiate the cruelty of his treatment of Grumby.

Grumby's murder is a watershed in the drama of Bayard's developing consciousness, the act which finally causes him to recoil from violence. He has been made uncomfortably aware of the faults of his child's view of war and determines to rid the South of its taint — from wherever it might come — in his own way. It is a wholly silent conversion and one which is simultaneous with his revising his estimate of himself as "John Sartoris' boy." Ringo's bare, moving epitaph for Granny gives him the clue: "It wasn't [Grumby] or Ab Snopes either that kilt her. It was them mules. That first batch of mules we got for nothing" (p. 229). Bayard has been pursuing the least important enemy and will have to look closer to home — as close, that is, as he can.

He starts to do so in "Skirmish at Sartoris" which, in one of Faulkner's most brilliant coups, returns the novel to the humour of the opening. There, the comedy, so blithe in appearance yet so oddly sad in effect, was needed to establish the innocent narrator and the controlling metaphor of play, after which the exceptions to the rule and those who pervert its premises steadily darken the mood until, in "Vendee," play itself seems to have been corrupted and Bayard's goodness forfeited. Now, the mood suddenly turns and comedy returns once more to feed off the threatened anarchy of war; catastrophe is averted and the ground laid for Bayard's supreme act of gamesmanship at the end of the novel. When tragedy deals with such subjects, there is a sense of finality about it, of life lived through and seen through. In comedy, finality is made to yield to change and is thereafter seen to work its way through people of mixed virtues. Defeat is recognised but so is resilience, and if there is a major line of development in Faulkner's work, it is from a sense of collapse of the first intensity to a belief in man's capacity to survive the most crushing of defeats, a view given its first prominence in *As I Lay Dying* and now receiving its first major statement.

By the time of "Skirmish at Sartoris" (whose moderated colloquial manner should remind us how varied a thing is Faulkner's "style"), the War is over. Drusilla and John Sartoris are engaged in routing the Burdens at the ballot-box, thus reasserting their command over the South. "Aunt" Louisa, on the other hand, is more interested in getting them married, thus regulating their relations. For her, Drusilla's involvement in the war is no more than a case of "a young woman . . . running about the country with no guard or check of any sort" (p. 252). She must be corrected; neither war nor peace matters where questions of personal conduct are concerned. For Drusilla, however, fighting is all. The campaign waged on the battlefield may be over but another now claims her energies, the one Ringo defines thus: "I ain't a nigger any more. I done been abolished. . . . They ain't no more niggers in Jefferson nor nowhere else. . . . Naw, suh, . . . This war ain't over. Hit just started good." (p. 248) Indeed it has. Accordingly, she insists on retaining the dress of a soldier. When that is denied her, she presses on with the campaign against Reconstruction. As before, though, this fresh battle is only incidentally between Sartoris and Burden-cum-negro. Fundamentally, it is a continuation of the war between Sartoris and Sartoris, in particular for the soul of John Sartoris.

The decisive moment comes when, instead of submitting himself as arranged to a quiet marriage, the Colonel kills the Burdens. In exultant mood, he proclaims his house a polling booth not a wedding hall and Drusilla a voting commissioner not a bride. The cheers of the crowd that greet his announcement are as of nothing compared to Aunt Louisa's shocked reaction:

> "And who are these, pray? Your wedding train of forgetters Your groomsmen of murder and robbery?"
>
> "They came to vote," Drusilla said.
>
> "To vote," Aunt Louisa said. "Ah. To vote. Since you have forced your mother and brother to live under a roof of license and adultery you think you can also force them to live in a polling booth refuge from violence and bloodshed, do you? . . ." (pp. 259–60)

Suddenly, the comedy releases a stirring protest against such an abnegation of morality and the implied elevation of end above means. Private
conduct has been sacrificed to public policy and the crowd incited to cheer
"violence and bloodshed," not the ceremonial of marriage as emblematic
of the communal domain. That is now in tatters with Drusilla as she
stands "in her torn dress and the ruined veil and the twisted wreath
hanging from her hair by a few pins" (p. 260). The busy surface has shifted
to reveal unsuspected depths.

Despite flinging the ballot box away, Aunt Louisa has to admit defeat
and bursts into tears. "So [George Wyatt] made a pack of the ballots and
wrote them against his saddle and fast as he would write them the men
would take them and drop them into the box and Drusilla would call their
names out. We could hear Aunt Louisa still crying inside the cabin . . ."
(p. 261). The reader, too, can still hear her crying while the acclaim of the
Jeffersonians rings on: " 'Yaaaaay, Drusilla!' they hollered. 'Yaaaaaay,
John Sartoris! Yaaaaaaay!' " (p. 262), and it is with the commingling of
these shouts and the tears of an old woman that the episode ends.

Drusilla has won her skirmish with her mother but it is, of course,
John Sartoris who is her real victim, for the implied reminder in his
subsequent conduct of any family life, of the feelings that a marriage
would have sanctioned and the judgement which could order his business,
is a wounding one. Aunt Louisa may be a sentimental old fusspot — we are
meant to feel her limitations — but there is in her a domestic conscience
which will not be stilled. Bayard notices as much. We sense his reserve, his
watchfulness, growing all the while into a composed reflection on "Sartoris." He has shortly before seen Granny go to her death in fending for the
South. He himself has killed a man in vengeance. What he now sees finally
disabuses him of the belief that what Granny and he did is justifiable and
makes him realise that his father is being fatally caught up — as they
were — in public activity, public rhetoric, to the exclusion of all else. More
than that, it makes him realise that Granny's appearance as prime mover
earlier on can now be seen to carry its own meaning. "Her fate is tragic,
having both the moral flaw and the force of circumstance. . . . As
enveloping action she represents the matrix, the core of the doomed South.
It was her part as symbol and person to be protected by the Colonel
Sartorises. That she herself must enter the conflict describes the failure of
manhood in general and the aristocracy in particular."[2] An excellent point,
and one which Bayard is to act upon when he confronts Drusilla in "An
Odour of Verbena."

It is important to note that neither Granny Millard (the Colonel's
mother-in-law) nor Cousin Drusilla (a relative of the Colonel's first wife) is
the genuine article. Granny is a Sartoris by marriage who becomes the
thing itself as no born Sartoris could, the foreigner become more native
than the native. Jenny du Pre, a Sartoris herself, is much more patient.
She can both criticise and tolerate her menfolk but does not involve herself

in action. She behaves as Sartoris women are expected to behave — as "ladies." Sartoris is, in its self-possession, its vanity, its daring and folly, something fitful, iridescently masculine. It is the quality Drusilla Hawk, the foreigner come to assume the native's destiny, absorbs in her passion to keep alive what Granny more circuitously tried to preserve. In "Skirmish at Sartoris" (originally called "Drusilla"), we see her will turn to stone. Just as the Colonel was once involved in light-hearted scenes like the capture of a Yankee troop or the escape from a search party only to become an autocrat who denies negroes their rights, kills people and generally spurns humane considerations, so she suffers under the impact of war nothing less than a transformation, as her manliness of appearance and partly of her manner indicate. The woman has become male has become "priestess of a succinct and formal violence" (p. 273). Like Narcissa in *Sanctuary*, though with infinitely greater emotion, she then devotes herself to defeating all that does not accord with her image of the South, seeking life, the resurrected life of the old country, first in Sartoris' army, then in Sartoris himself and finally, with terrifying singlemindedness, in Sartoris' son. The comic bustle has thus brought to prominence three lives (Granny, Drusilla and the Colonel) decaying under pressure. It is their combined fate which guides Bayard in his attempt to alter not their goal so much as their method of securing it.

His task is made very much harder by the filial devotions he feels and the awesome attractiveness of Drusilla herself. In a strongly wrought passage, he sees her standing "not tall, not slender as a woman is but as a youth, a boy, is motionless, in yellow, the face calm, almost bemused, the head simple and severe, the balancing sprig of verbena above each ear, the two arms bent at the elbows, the two hands shoulder high, the two identical duelling pistols lying upon, not clutched in, one to each . . ." (p. 273). It is a boy's picture of formalised aggression, characterised by a sexual ambivalence we have met before in Joe Christmas and the Bayard of *Sartoris* and which is related to the same crisis of identity they suffered. "An Odour of Verbena" returns to the subject with its repeated references to Drusilla's "boy-hard body" and the obviously sexual imagery of the duelling pistols she gives Bayard. All these form part of the significance of the verbena itself, the smell one can smell above horses, above simple physical activity: glamorous male assertion. The one who best epitomises that quality is undoubtedly John Sartoris, so that there is a sense in which Bayard now approaches his father indirectly through Drusilla after years in which he was more a legend than a living person to the boy. In Drusilla, too, he sees a mightily tempting version of what he might have been, a close companion to the Colonel and combatant in the war untroubled by scruples and loyal only to his own kind. By the same measure, he is reminded of the warmongering boy he was and must now stop being. ". . . and this no poste and riposte of sweat-reeking cavalry which all war-telling is full of, no galloping thunder of guns to wheel up and unlimber and crash and crash into the lurid grime-glare of their own demon-served inferno which even children would recognise, no ragged lines of gaunt and shrill-yelling infantry beneath a tattered flag which is a very part of that child's make-believe" (p. 115). Sartoris and Drusilla have been too busy in the immediate conflict to notice what has been happening to themselves and their country and, despite his adoration of them, Bayard begins to turn from them and the odour of verbena they have come to be identified with, "that quality of outworn violence like a scent, an odor; that fanaticism . . . of some kind of twofisted evangelism which had been one quarter violent conviction and three quarters physical hardihood. (*Light in August*, p. 325, when Doc Hines, of all men, is introduced.)"[3]

Post-bellum Jefferson is an awkward kind of reality. John Sartoris rebuilds his mansion on the site of the previous one and is master of all he surveys, but his formidably attractive qualities have been reduced to the "violent and ruthless dictatorialness" his son first senses in "Skirmish at Sartoris" and which soon becomes apparent in his railroad activities. "I'm for my land," Sutpen tells him when he refuses to join his nightriders' campaign against the carpetbagger. "If every man of you would rehabilitate his own land, the country will take care of itself" (p. 277). It is advice, sound as it is, he cannot follow. Here, we are aware of a masterly obliqueness which reminds us of a scene in "Raid" (another important addition to the original material) in which the Colonel returns home

> afoot like tramps or on crowbait horses, in faded and patched (and at times obviously stolen) clothing, preceded by no flags nor drums and followed not even by two men to keep step with one another, in coats bearing no glitter of golden braid and with scabbards in which no sword reposed, actually almost sneaking home to spend two or three days performing actions not only without glory (ploughing land, repairing fences, killing meat for the smoke house) and in which they had no skill . . . actions in the very clumsy performance of which Father's whole presence seemed . . . to emanate a kind of humility and apology, as if he were saying, "Believe me, boys; take my word for it: there's more to it than this, no matter what it looks like. I can't prove it, so you'll just have to believe me." (pp. 114–15)

We are a long way from the returning warrior of "Ambuscade" riding the impressive Jupiter and armed with a sabre. The glamour of the past has disappeared as Bayard has grown up.

Paradoxically, the effect is to enhance, not to diminish, the Colonel's stature. In becoming more human, he becomes an even more dominant presence and glamour is restored to him in a different way, though it is not he who has changed so much as Bayard. Indeed, a small drama, wholly implicit, inheres in this scene. Just as the sabre-rattler was less a true representation than Bayard's creation at a time when his patriotic blood was up, so the portrait of him in "Raid" is closer to the real man as he tries to warn his son that the cause for which they are fighting is not to be found in ambuscades, ripostes, raids, skirmishes and retreats in "vendee." One is truer to it by mending fences. Having since then yielded to the temptations his father cautioned him against, Bayard recoils in the nick of time and returns to his advice at the end by copying him in another act of "humility and apology," one which derives from "Ambuscade," when the Colonel announces his intention to build a stock pen: "There would be all of us there—Joby and Loosh and Ringo and me on the edge of the bottom and drawn up into a kind or order—an order partaking not of any lusting and sweating for assault or even victory, but rather of that passive yet dynamic affirmation which Napoleon's troops must have felt . . ." (p. 12). Here is the corporate Sartoris ideal, and we realise once again how the early stories deal lightly with matters that are to be revealed as momentous later on. The full meaning of the title of the novel, therefore, includes not only a salute to the Confederacy but also a reference to Bayard's equivocal attempt to deny victory or defeat to his country and aim instead for "passive yet dynamic affirmation," as he does in his meeting with Redmond.

It is John Sartoris' tragedy that he strives throughout the war to make such an affirmation but—the crucial moment is discovered in "Skirmish at Sartoris"—just when he approached reacceptance of the custom and ceremony of the old order, he yielded to his worst impulses. In acting as he then did, no matter the rights and wrongs of the case, his beauty became terrible. It would have been unthinkable for him to surrender without a struggle, yet opposition such as he and Drusilla undertake is eventually as damaging to their cause as inaction. Drusilla confesses as much when she tries to defend him.

"A dream is not a very safe thing to be near, Bayard. . . . But if it's a good dream, it's worth it. There are not many dreams in the world, but there are a lot of human lives. And one human life or two dozen—"
  "Are not worth anything?"
  "No. Not anything— . . ." (p. 278–9)

It is as if the admission were too deadly to come from Sartoris' own lips and must come instead from his alter ego, whom Bayard is thereafter free to oppose. Four years after that exchange, he goes out to confront his father's killer with George Wyatt's elegy in his mind ("I know what's wrong: he's had to kill too many folks, and that's bad for a man" (p. 282) and acts in a way that he hopes will resolve his dilemma by cutting the knot Gavin Stevens refers to in *The Town* when he talks of "that desperate twilight of 1864–5 when more people than men named Snopes had to choose not survival with honour but simply between empty honour and almost as empty survival" (p. 40).

Simon, Sartoris' negro body servant, grieves over his late master's coffin. Contemplating the scene, Bayard realises the meaning of endurance. ". . . this was it—the regret and grief, the despair out of which the tragic mute insensitive bones stand up that can bear anything, anything" (p. 301). Ironically, again, his realisation of what it means to "bear anything" recalls the moment in "Ambuscade" when he smelt his father's "clothes and beard and flesh too which I believed was the smell of powder and glory, the elected victorious but know better now: know now to have been only the will to endure, a sardonic and even humorous declining of self-delusion . . ." (p. 9). The "will to endure" is that solvent which alone can reconcile loyalty to the Sartoris dream with an acknowledgement of the enormities committed in its name. More than that, it allows John Sartoris tragic stature as a man who fought the Civil War magnificently but faltered badly thereafter, who eventually realised the truth about himself and, in the manner of his death — when he refused to defend himself — declined "self-delusion" and did something about it.

This is not to deny that the most important judgement Bayard makes is that his father is the arch-enemy. But this collides with another: that the Colonel is a man to be respected not just because the ties of sentiment insist on it but because he embodies virtues such as Yoknapatawpha is unlikely to see again. Like Sutpen, there is something about the man that will not let go of greatness. Consequently, where before the boy saw "powder and glory," the young man sees "the will to endure," a more principled compulsion to activity which he is to adopt as his own, and realises that his father was indeed heroic in a way he could not have perceived earlier. By adjusting his understanding, Bayard has not so much corrected as deepened his youthful impression and in the novel's developing drama of character he emerges as the Colonel's better self as Drusilla is his worst.

It has not, we know, happened at all easily since his adolescence, coinciding as it does with the war, has led him to associate the gallant life with emulating his father, with sexual potency and the claims of an emergent independence. As a result, the temptations to violence he feels are naturally powerful — when honour and vengeance are invoked, they become almost irresistible. He is therefore intimately involved in the lesson he learns: that if anything is to preserve the South, it is the recovery of true courage, such courage, that is, as is not continually pressed into the service of a series of contingencies, large and small. Granny first tried to teach him that by insisting that moral values — truthfulness, avoidance of foul language, responsibility, courtesy to foe no less than to friend — are *especially* to be sustained in war, though she is no more successful a teacher than the Colonel and both fall victim to the dangers they warn of. It is ironical that the chain of events set off by Bayard's first act of bloodthirstiness should end (via Grumby) with another, the death of his father, calculated to touch him more deeply than any other. It is a further irony that he could emerge as he does from the test only because his father had become corrupted, thereby releasing him from claims he would have found impossibly difficult to discharge. It is the ultimate irony that it should be the Colonel's account of himself in his final hours that finally emboldens him to act for the good.

In his essay, "The Unvanquished—The Restoration of Tradition," William E. Walker notes that the Bayard-Redmond meeting coincides with a preternatural (one might add "poetical") event, a delayed autumnal equinox.[4] By behaving as he does on that occasion, Bayard manages to free the season—but also allows the high summer of Sartoris to pass. Consequently, there is something forlorn about him even in his moment of triumph. He has ensured that the South will survive with honour but he has not reversed its decline so much as arrested it. Worse still, he has crippled himself, for while his treatment of Redmond carries him to manhood, it also ensures the ruin of the wider conditions necessary to his fulfilment. Bayard's achievement is thus no sooner completed than it is called into question. Imaginative diplomacy on the path of compromise assumes certain stabilities and continuities, but these are no longer assured, so that, while the boy's playacting has been transposed into the real world, the real world cannot receive it as it should. It is not for nothing that his adult years should pass in the completest obscurity and that when we next see him, it is as the deaf, disheartened grandfather of *Sartoris*.

At this point, Faulkner's involvement in Bayard, never far from the surface, emerges. As Bayard embraces Drusilla, he realises "the immitigable chasm between all life and all print—that those who can, do, those who cannot and suffer enough because they can't, write about it" (p. 284). The very fact that he has narrated *The Unvanquished* suggests how much he has suffered and how his compromise with Redmond has failed to release him into life. But it is also an astonishing announcement on Faulkner's own behalf, apologising to the shades of Colonel Falkner as Bayard apologises to his father for the failure of his life which has made him into a novelist. The confession is all the more touching when we reflect that part of Faulkner's purpose in writing *The Unvanquished* was to examine the critical years during which the conditions making for his failure were established and to reprove the men who could have prevented it from happening for not doing so.[5]

The fact that John Sartoris has, despite his blunders, managed to retain his stature is thus one more reason why Bayard's attitude towards him should be so ambiguous. It also explains why the Colonel should have left him a relatively colourless figure, although Bayard's passivity (like the indirection of the Colonel's own portrait) is essential to the novel's strategy, as Donald Davie suggests when he describes the kind of figure Sir Walter Scott produced in Edward Waverly.

> . . . the enormous advantage of the Scott method in this particular is that it makes of the central character a sounding-board for historical reverberations, or else, to change the metaphor, a weathervane responding to every shift in the winds of history which blow around it. This

device, and this alone, of a weak hero poised and vacillating between opposites allows the historian to hold the balance absolutely firm and impartial, giving credit everywhere it is due. . . . it is designed to permit judgement of the parties, the ideologies, the alternative societies which contend for his allegiance.[6]

Bayard, of course, is more than weak or vacillating yet, in having become a narrator who contains within himself several competing points of view, he owes allegiance to the Scott tradition. We are all the more inclined to make the connection when we notice that Professor Davie links the weak hero with the theme of the lost father.

We are now in a better position to appreciate the benefit of having The Unvanquished's perspective approximate that of a boy while at the same time being removed from mere youthfulness. It is as if the narrator were the old Bayard casting his younger self as an independent character. (Faulkner employed the strategy to excellent effect again in The Reivers.) This double figure stands inside and outside the novel. Inside it, he mimes the stealthy growth of a conscience and dramatises its development; he structures the events and comments upon them. There is no 'author' to communicate his conclusions to the reader. Only this double strategy could have allowed the narrator of "Ambuscade" to show as intimately as he does that Bayard is no stranger to the behaviour he is later to oppose, having succumbed to it, in fact, long before his relations did. He has such a clear understanding of Sartoris transgressors because he is one himself; he has seen but he is also part of that which is seen.

At the end, two incidents concerned with swearing remind us of those which opened the novel. First, Aunt Jenny tells Bayard of an Englishman she met once, one of the blockade runners at Charleston she idolised not "because they were helping to prolong the Confederacy but heroes in the sense that David Crockett or John Sevier would have been to small boys or fool young women" (pp. 305–6). Or as John Sartoris was to small Bayard and fool young Drusilla. The Englishman's vocabulary was limited to seven words: "I'll have rum, thanks" "No bloody moon." "No bloody moon, Bayard" Aunt Jenny ends, repeating her warning to him to act stealthily for the South, as the blockade runners did under cover of darkness. Bayard then goes to meet Redmond unarmed and allows him to take two shots at him, which Redmond deliberately aims wide. On returning, Aunt Jenny greets him by bursting into tears. "Oh, damn you Sartorises! Damn you! Damn you!" (p. 318). It is a fine art that gives us this mixture of affection and exasperation, gathering all the competing attitudes of the novel into one critical yet compassionate attitude.

The same sure touch prepares for Jenny's outburst with a reference to the contrasting dreams of Sartoris and Sutpen and follows it with Bayard's silent contemplation of Drusilla's parting gift, a sprig of verbena laid on his bed. The flower makes a complicated impression on him. He knows it is designed to reproach him for acting as he has done — indeed, it virtually accuses him of cowardice — but the charge leaves him unrepentant. Nevertheless, he is deeply moved by it and not a little guilty that he should have made it redundant when all he wished to do was restrain it. At the same time, he sees in Drusilla's gift a reluctant (if not unintentional) tribute to himself from his by-now-deranged victim, a token of surrender which recognises him as the new "Sartoris," one worthy of accolade in the Southern way.

It has taken some time for *The Unvanquished* to be regarded as a novel rather than a collection of related stories. It should now be acknowledged as the difficult masterpiece of implication it is, the nearest Faulkner came to writing a novel of sustained and subtle moral enquiry.

Notes

1. Roark Bradford, "The Private World of William Faulkner," *The Magazine of the Year*, 2 (May 1948), 91.

2. Andrew Lytle, "*The Town*: Helen's Last Stand," *The Sewanee Review*, 65 (Summer 1957), 479.

3. The title of "An Odour of Verbena" may derive from Hemingway's "The Short Happy Life of Francis Macomber" as part of an attempt to present a somewhat loftier conception of courage in Bayard.

4. *Reality and Myth*, eds. William E. Walker and Robert L. Welker (Nashville, Tenn., 1964).

5. I am reminded of Evelyn Waugh's involvement in Guy Crouchback's declaration of guilt at the end of *Unconditional Surrender*, a novel which bears comparison with *The Unvanquished* at several points.

6. Donald Davie, *The Heyday of Sir Walter Scott* (London, 1961), p. 41.

V REVISIONS

Introduction to *Flags in the Dust* Douglas Day[*]

In the autumn or winter of 1926, William Faulkner, twenty-nine, began work on the first of his novels about Yoknapatawpha County. Sherwood Anderson had told him some time before that he should write about his native Mississippi, and now Faulkner took that advice: he used his own land, and peopled it with men and women who were partly drawn from real life, and partly depicted as they should have been in some ideal mythopoeic structure. A year later, on September 29, 1927, the new novel was completed. It was 596 pages long in transcript, and he called it *Flags in the Dust*. Full of enthusiasm, Faulkner sent *Flags in the Dust* up to Horace Liveright (who had published his first two novels) in New York. Liveright read it, disliked it, and sent it back with his firm recommendation that Faulkner not try to offer it for publication anywhere else: it was too diffuse, too lacking in plot and structure; and, Liveright felt, no amount of revision would be able to salvage it. Faulkner, crushed, showed *Flags in the Dust* to several of his friends, who shared Liveright's opinion.

But he still believed that this would be the book that would make his name as a writer, and for several months he tried to edit it himself, sitting at his worktable in Oxford. Finally, discouraged, he sent a new typescript off to Ben Wasson, his agent in New York. "Will you please try to sell this for me?" he asked Wasson. "I can't afford all the postage it's costing me." In the meantime, convinced that he would never become a successful novelist, Faulkner began work on a book that he was sure would never mean anything to anyone but himself: *The Sound and the Fury*.

Wasson tried eleven publishers, all of whom rejected *Flags in the Dust*. Finally he gave the typescript to Harrison Smith, then an editor of Harcourt, Brace & Company. Smith liked it, and showed it to Alfred Harcourt, who agreed to publish it, provided that someone other than Faulkner perform the extensive cutting job that Harcourt felt was necessary. For fifty dollars, Wasson agreed to pare down his client's novel. On September 20, 1928, Faulkner received a contract for the book, now to be

[*]Reprinted, with permission, from *Flags in the Dust* (New York: Random House, 1973), pp. vii–xi. © 1973 by Random House, Inc.

called *Sartoris* (no one knows who changed its name), which was to be about 110,000 words long, and which was to be delivered to Harcourt, Brace sixteen days later. Faulkner left immediately for New York, presumably to help Wasson with his revision.

But when he sat down in Wasson's apartment to observe the operation on his novel, Faulkner found himself unable to participate. If it were cut, he felt, it would die. Wasson persisted, however, pointing out that the trouble with *Flags in the Dust* was that it was not one novel, but six, all struggling along simultaneously. This, to Faulkner, was praise: evidence of fecundity and fullness of vision, evidence that the world of Yoknapatawpha was rich enough to last. As he later wrote of his third novel, "I discovered that my own little postage stamp of native soil was worth writing about and that I would never live long enough to exhaust it." Nevertheless, Wasson kept his bargain with Alfred Harcourt. For the next two weeks, while Faulkner sat nearby writing *The Sound and the Fury*, Wasson went through the typescript of *Flags in the Dust*, making cuts of every sort until almost a fourth of the book had been excised. Harcourt, Brace published this truncated version on January 31, 1929, as *Sartoris* (with a dedication: "To Sherwood Anderson through whose kindness I was first published, with the belief that this book will give him no reason to regret that fact"), and the old *Flags in the Dust* was soon forgotten — by everyone but Faulkner.

He had preserved the original holograph manuscript of *Flags in the Dust*, 237 pages in his neat but miniscule and almost illegible hand; and he had bound together with thin wire the 596 pages of a sort of composite typescript of the novel, produced by the combination of three separate but overlapping typescript drafts. The first of these, 447 pages long, seems to have been begun before he completed his manuscript version. The second, 99 pages of which are in the composite typescript, was probably written after he had completed the manuscript and the first typescript. In the third, 146 pages appear to have been a revision of the second typescript. Why Faulkner should have labored over the reconstruction of this text is not clear: perhaps he thought of his composite typescript as a working draft which would allow him ultimately to restore to his novel that which Wasson had carved from it — or perhaps, fastidious man that he was, he simply could not bring himself to throw away all of those typed pages. In any case, the manuscript and typescript both were eventually deposited at the Alderman Library of the University of Virginia, where they lay more or less undisturbed until Mrs. Jill Summers, Faulkner's daughter, remembered that her late father had spoken often of a restoration of *Flags in the Dust*. Mrs. Summers asked this writer and Albert Erskine, editor at Random House, to undertake the task.

The result is, now, *Flags in the Dust*, which aims at being a faithful reproduction of that composite typescript. Certain nonsubstantive alterations in spelling and punctuation have been made, in order to bring this novel into conformity with Faulkner's other books; but wherever possible his many idiosyncrasies, especially those on which he himself insisted during his years of working with editors at Random House, were allowed to stand. The final complete typescript, which must have served as setting copy for the Harcourt, Brace edition of *Sartoris* (and which must have been the draft in which Wasson made his cuts), has not survived. Nor have any galley proofs. All we had to work from, then, was the composite typescript, by any scholar's standards a suspect source. There was no way, finally, to tell which of the many differences between *Flags in the Dust* and *Sartoris* were the result of Faulkner's emendations in the hypothetical setting copy and the galley proofs, and which belonged to Wasson. If there were to be any publication of *Flags in the Dust* at all, then, it had to be what we have here provided.

Whether it is better than *Sartoris*, as Faulkner so firmly believed it to be, is of course a matter of taste. It is tempting to launch into a study of the genesis and development of the novel, from the manuscript version through the typescript of *Flags in the Dust* to the publication of *Sartoris*; but this is not the place to do so. Suffice it here to suggest that whereas *Sartoris* is chiefly about the Sartoris clan, their surly gallantry, and their utter and uncaring inability to adjust to the demands of whatever age they find themselves in, *Flags in the Dust* is far more complicated: primary focus is still on the Sartorises, but Faulkner clearly wished to make of his novel an anatomy of the entire Yoknapatawpha social structure, excluding only the Indians. As foils to the doomed and hawklike Bayard Sartoris, we have not only his dead twin, John, but Horace Benbow, too, as a sort of Delta dilettante; and Buddy MacCallum, the young hillman who possesses all the steady virtues Bayard lacks; Harry Mitchell, as the type of the new southern middle class — and even Byron Snopes, the desperate and reptilian representative of a new class threatening to overthrow the old aristocratic order of the area. All of these are present in *Sartoris*, to be sure; but in *Flags in the Dust* their roles are lengthened and heightened, until we realize that each of them is in his way a commentary not only upon Bayard Sartoris, but also upon the Deep South in the years after the First World War.

Flags in the Dust, then, may or may not be a better work of art than *Sartoris*; but few will dispute that it is a more complete fictional document of a time and place in history — or that it is a better introduction to the grand and complex southern world that William Faulkner was to write about until he died.

[The Text of *Flags in the Dust*: An Interchange]

Thomas L. McHaney
and Albert Erskine*

Flags in the Dust, edited by Douglas Day (Random House, 1973) is apparently a badly edited and unreliable text. Copy-text for this edition of the original form of William Faulkner's third novel is the typescript among the Faulkner papers at the University of Virginia. But this typescript is far from ideal; it is incomplete and filled with difficult editorial problems to which the present editor has not really addressed himself. As the editor notes, this apparently is not the TS that Faulkner sent around to publishers nor the one finally cut by another person to make *Sartoris*. There are missing pages, restored deletions, and various gaps in the text where revisions were not smoothly joined to adjacent passages. In addition, there are revisions between the typescript and the cut version, *Sartoris*, which could be Faulkner's own revisions. The editor of *Flags in the Dust* has dealt with these problems quite insufficiently; though he bandies bibliographical terms in his too-brief introduction, he has worked for the most part silently and unprofessionally. He has not always correctly transcribed revisions in Faulkner's difficult handwriting. He has allowed new errors to appear. And, most regrettably, although he claims to have sought a faithful reproduction of the transcript, he has unaccountably tampered with his copy-text rather badly — moving at least one complete episode, deleting several passages and restoring several deletions, and accepting readings out of the cut version of the novel which was published in 1929, *Sartoris*.

The results of a brief spot check offer sufficient proof that *Flags* is badly edited and deliberately tampered with. The passage on 157.14 beginning "How's Belle . . ." and ending, on 160.37, ". . . leaving no stain," should follow 166.16, ". . . disasters of his days." It has been moved from the end of section 2, Chapter Three, to become the end of section 1. The sentence at 162.29 which begins "At times" actually omits some 60 words of the TS sentence. A few other examples are:

page, line	*Flags*	Typescript
20.20	quietly	quickly
24.32	hut	hurt
33.8	said	added
35.31	hill	hall

*Reprinted, with permission, from the *Faulkner Concordance Newsletter*, No. 2 (November 1973), 7–8 and No. 3 (May 1974), 2–4. McHaney is a scholar of Faulkner's texts; Erskine was at the time this was published Vice President and Editorial Director of Random House who had invited Day to prepare the text under discussion.

| 37.24 | his trains | his two trains |
| 85.26 | restlessly | restively |

Though the editor claims to follow Faulkner's idiosyncratic punctuation, there is wholesale normalization of commas to periods, large numbers of ellipsis points to three points, and large numbers of dashes to 3/m dashes. In some instances dashes have been changed to ellipses and vice versa. These changes affect the texture of Faulkner's work, which was deliberate and consistent throughout his career. The changes are, however, consistent with editorial revision of his work all along. There is a simple irony here. Now *Flags in the Dust* is consistent in form with the great majority of Faulkner's other published works. It exists for the reading public in a corrupt text.

> —Professor Thomas L. McHaney, Georgia State University

The comments in the November 1973 Newsletter concerning *Flags in the Dust* give a reasonably accurate description of the typed draft from which the book was set, but beyond that they are unreliable. Saving for some future date a more detailed reply—when more specific rather than generalized strictures come forth, as they undoubtedly will—I feel it necessary to point out a few things now.

Though Mr. McHaney is not known to me personally, I am familiar with his provenance; and since I was never able to convince his progenitor that Random House is not, should not be and does not intend to be a competitor of the EETS, that we publish novels on behalf of novelists (including Faulkner) and for readers of novels rather than for a small group of intensive proofreaders of them, I can't hope to get through to Mr. McHaney on this point. Nor do I care to: what I wish to do is reach readers who might be fooled by his authoritative tone of voice.

It is true that Mr. McHaney found five printer's errors not caught by our own proofreading process, which in this case was about three times what is normal or commercially feasible. (The 'error' he cites at 20.20 is, I believe, his own.) Having in recent years had scholars offer to sell me lists of printer's errors, I am grateful for having these free, and they and any others forthcoming will be corrected in future printings.

Furthermore, if mistakes other than typographical can be shown to have been committed—errors in judgment on the part of Mr. Day and those of us at Random House who worked with him to prepare the setting copy—we shall try to correct them if we are convinced they are errors.

But the allegations made by Mr. McHaney don't seem to meet this test. For example: "The sentence at 162.29 which begins 'At times' actually omits some 60 words of the TS sentence." It does indeed, actually (the use of "actually" before "omits" should convey a lot to a perceptive reader) omit 59 words from Ts 262. But since nearly all of these words appear, almost verbatim, on Ts 272, it was essential to remove one group or the other, because though this inadvertent repetition might not worry or even be noticed by proofreaders, careful *readers* of the novel might attribute it to *bad editing* (a favorite phrase of Mr. McHaney and his colleagues), and they would be right. Clearly the author did not intend to have these words appear on p. 162 of the printed book and then again on p. 166, where we left them. Perhaps we took out the wrong group, but that is a question on an altogether different level.

As for the passage on 157.14 that "should follow 166.16": It does so follow in the Ts, having come to rest there, apparently, after a number of shifts but there is enough evidence to satisfy us that the author did not regard this position as final and to warrant our shifting it to what is obviously a better place for it.

Mr. McHaney has been taught (perhaps "indoctrinated" is the right word) that certain conventional "normalization" of punctuation marks "affects the texture of Faulkner's work, which was deliberate and consistent throughout his career." Though ambiguous, the statement would seem to imply that Faulkner used different-length dashes and ellipsis dots like some system of musical notation and that he did this consistently throughout his career. This is, of course, demonstrably false, though perhaps readers sufficiently insensitive to the words can have an emotional response to the dashes. (Speaking of dashes: Mr. McHaney who says Mr. Day "bandies bibliographical terms," ought to learn what 3-em dashes are before he bandies them.)

I grow increasingly impatient with those people who, though they did not know William Faulkner, think they know more about what he wanted and intended than those who worked with him. I know that he did not wish to have carried through from typescript to printed book his typing mistakes, misspellings (as opposed to coinages), faulty punctuation and accidental repetition. He depended on my predecessors, and later on me, to point out such errors and correct them; and though we never achieved anything like a perfect performance of these duties we tried. I have no intention now of substituting Mr. McHaney's preferences for what I learned to be Faulkner's.

— Albert Erskine, Editor, Random House

The Introduction to *Flags* states that *it is* an attempt at "a faithful reproduction of that composite typescript" at Virginia with certain "nonsubstantive alterations"; it does not say anything about deleting portions of sentences, for whatever reasons, or moving passages that have come to rest in the typescript.

My note was brief, merely a word of warning to the unwary, and not a full review; it was based on spot checking of some 100 pages of the published text. Maybe there are more errors and more changes; I don't know. As for 20.20, I read *quickly* from Faulkner's handwriting, and it seems to fit the context; I will have to stick by my reading until I see evidence to the contrary.

As for my progenitor, he was an Arkansas lawyer schooled at Ole Miss; he has a high regard for honesty and correctness. My provenance in the textual field begins with study under John G. Kunstmann, a fine old medieval philologist, with whom I took courses when I was a graduate student in German; my first textual study was concerned with a long 19th century German poem, and I did it before I had ever even read much Faulkner. I firmly reject the imputation that I am an "indoctrinated" hatchet man; if arbitration were required, we could direct the question of the text to Mr. Stephen Dennis, who did a textual dissertation on *Sartoris*/ "Flags in the Dust" at Cornell in 1969: the Introduction to *Flags* indicates that the editor is familiar with his work.

I am sympathetic to the problems of the editor-author relationship. I've been struggling with the problems of writing and publishing fiction for going on twenty years now. I've published more than a dozen stories of varied merit, and I've been helped by a good editor more than once. I am interested in the way an author's intentions are translated into print; and especially interested in the way the general reader, the student, and the scholar may be misled about the purity of the process.

—Thomas L. McHaney

William Faulkner's *Flags in the Dust*

George F. Hayhoe*

On 2 August 1973 Random House published Douglas Day's edition of William Faulkner's third novel, *Flags in the Dust*, which had been published in a shorter, much different form as *Sartoris* in 1929. Random House's subsidiary Vintage Books issued a completely reset paperback edition of *Flags* in October 1974. Insofar as both Day and Random House have made the novel available to readers of Faulkner, they are to be commended; yet the texts of both editions are so severely flawed in both intention and execution that they must be used with great care.

The first serious notice of the novel, a brief review by Thomas L. McHaney, challenges Day's claim that his edition is "a faithful reproduction" of the surviving typescript of *Flags in the Dust*. McHaney effectively demonstrates "that *Flags* is badly edited and deliberately tampered with," and that the resulting corrupt text is thus "consistent in form with the great majority of Faulkner's other published works."[1] Random House vice-

*Reprinted, with permission, from *Mississippi Quarterly*, 28, No. 3 (Summer 1975), 370–86, as revised especially for this volume by the author.

president Albert Erskine's response to the charge of editorial negligence and inconsistency is evasive. He acknowledges the fact that there may be typographical errors in the book, or even possibly "errors in judgment on the part of Mr. Day and those of us at Random House who worked with him . . .";[2] but he completely avoids the real issues. Instead, Erskine assumes an offensive, superior attitude toward scholars in general, attacks McHaney personally, and aims a few barbs at those who, "though they did not know William Faulkner, think they know more about what he wanted and intended than those who worked with him."[3]

Aside from McHaney's review and Erskine's response, the publication of *Flags in the Dust* has occasioned very little notice by either Faulkner scholars or textual scholars. The edition appeared too late to receive more than a mention in Melvin R. Roberts' 1974 dissertation, "Faulkner's *Flags in the Dust* and *Sartoris*."[4] The only substantial critical study that the published text of *Flags* has received has been Richard P. Adams' review essay "At Long Last, *Flags in the Dust*."[5]

In order to gauge the shortcomings of the 1973 edition of *Flags* adequately, it is necessary to deal with the history of the novel's composition, the attempts to sell it in 1927–28, and the production of *Sartoris*; to examine the surviving states of the text and draw conclusions regarding their authority, and thus determine the copy-text for such an edition; and finally to analyze Day's edition by comparing it with the copy-text.

I

Probably during the latter part of 1926, Faulkner first began to explore the richness of a fictional county which would eventually become Yoknapatawpha, Mississippi. One project of this period, an early partial draft entitled "Father Abraham" which was eventually to become *The Hamlet*, was soon temporarily abandoned, and Faulkner began to devote his full energies to a novel entitled *Flags in the Dust*. By 29 September 1927 he had completed a manuscript and typescript. He retained both in his files; unfortunately, this typescript is not the one that was to serve as printer's setting copy. It was probably in late October that he submitted the novel to Boni and Liveright, the publishers of *Soldiers' Pay* and *Mosquitoes*.[6] It took less than a month for Horace Liveright to reject the book.

> It is so diffuse and non-integral with neither very much plot develop-
> ment nor character development. . . . The story really doesn't get
> anywhere and has a thousand loose ends. If the book had plot and
> structure, we might suggest shortening and revisions but it is so diffuse
> that I don't think this would be any use. My chief objection is that you
> don't seem to have any story to tell and I contend that a novel should tell
> a story and tell it well.[7]

Liveright also discouraged Faulkner from submitting the book to another publisher.

Such an absolute refusal must have had a considerable impact on Faulkner, since he had described *Flags* as "THE book, of which thoes [*sic*] other things were but foals. I believe it is the damdest best book you'll look at this year, and any other publisher."[8] Though *The Marble Faun* had been published by a vanity press, his first two novels were products of one of the best-known and most successful of American publishers, and, in spite of the fact that they had not sold well, they had attracted a number of favorable notices. But Liveright's response did not shake Faulkner's faith in his work. In his reply to the letter of rejection, Faulkner wrote: "I still believe it is the book which will make my name for me as a writer."[9]

The surviving typescript of *Flags in the Dust* at the University of Virginia suggests that it may have been at this time that Faulkner did a considerable amount of revising, perhaps with the realization that some tightening of this panorama of Yocona County (as it was then called) and its inhabitants was necessary if the book were to be published at all. It is also likely that, after these revisions were made, Faulkner either prepared a new typescript himself, or asked someone else to do it.[10]

Whether Faulkner himself tried to place the novel with other publishers is uncertain, although his remark to Ben Wasson about the postage it was costing him implies that he did.[11] Finally, however, he sent the typescript off to Wasson, who dutifully sent the book to a number of houses. First he submitted it to Holt, where fellow Mississippian Hershell Brickell read it; the novel probably went to about ten other publishers after it was refused there. Finally Wasson gave the typescript to his friend Harrison Smith at Harcourt, Brace. Smith read and liked the novel, but had a difficult time convincing Harcourt to buy it.[12] A compromise was reached, and on 20 September 1928 Harcourt, Brace issued a contract accepting the novel with the provision that it be cut to 110,000 words. Thus, nearly a year after the completion of *Flags in the Dust*, about eighty-five percent of the book was to be published under the title *Sartoris*.[13]

Faulkner probably acquiesced simply in order to get the novel in print in one form or another. He went to New York, where he met his new publishers and worked on *The Sound and the Fury*. Meanwhile Wasson completed the surgery on *Flags in the Dust*, having been paid fifty dollars by Harcourt, Brace, and *Sartoris* was published on 31 January 1929.[14]

Aside from the obvious diminution of length and inclusiveness, *Sartoris* differs from the surviving typescript of *Flags* in several respects. Two passages were repositioned in *Sartoris*, most dramatically Will Falls's first reminiscence of the Old Colonel's Civil War adventures; a number of passages were added; several sections were rewritten (most of the changes being in style). Three hypotheses can be suggested to explain these differences. They may reflect Faulkner's revisions in another typescript which do not appear in the typescript which he kept in his files; they may be the result of changes made by Faulkner in the galley proofs of *Sartoris*; or they may have been the revisions of an editor, a possibility which is not unlikely in view of the liberties taken by Smith as well as by Faulkner's other editors over the years. But no final conclusion can be reached since both the typescript which Wasson cut (and which served as setting copy) and the galleys are no longer extant.

An essay written by Faulkner about two years after *Sartoris* appeared, but only recently published, reveals a great deal about his attitudes at the time Wasson was working on the novel. He "had refused to have anything to do with" the cutting of *Flags* which produced *Sartoris*, and had argued with Wasson that any attempt to shorten the book would effectively kill it. After he had completed the job, Wasson showed the result to Faulkner, who "realised for the first time that I had done better than I knew. . . ."[15] From the context of this remark, it is obvious that, while Wasson's surgery had been successful, for Faulkner it was *Flags in the Dust*, not *Sartoris*, which was the better book. Wasson's editing had simply reinforced Faulkner's conviction about the soundness of his original conception of the novel.

As with *Soldiers' Pay* and *Mosquitoes*, Faulkner bound the original typescript of *Flags*, incorporating the dust jacket of *Sartoris* into his binding. The existence of *Flags in the Dust* remained unknown to all but a handful of people until at the suggestion of Saxe Commins, his editor, Faulkner's manuscripts and typescripts were loaned to Princeton University in order for a graduate student there, James B. Meriwether, to put them in order and catalog them. When Meriwether saw the difference between *Flags in the Dust* and *Sartoris*, he suggested to Commins that Random House acquire the rights to *Sartoris* from Harcourt, Brace and publish the complete text of *Flags*, a project which Faulkner himself had approved. Random House proceeded slowly, but by 1959 the rights to *Sartoris* were transferred to Random House through Harold Ober's agency.[16]

The curiosity of Faulkner's academic readers was stimulated by a brief account of the differences between the typescript and *Sartoris* by Meriwether in 1961[17] and an extended description of the revisions made between the manuscript and typescript, and of the material omitted from *Sartoris*, provided by Michael Millgate in 1966.[18] In the meantime, in 1963, Douglas Day proposed a collaboration with Meriwether on the task of editing *Flags*, and later that year Meriwether agreed to let Day do the job himself. In 1969 Stephen Dennis completed a dissertation, "The Making of *Sartoris*," the first book-length study of a Faulkner text, which attempted to solve the problems posed by the surviving typescript.[19] James E. Kibler's review of the Dennis dissertation in 1971 acknowledged its usefulness, but pointed out the faulty logic of several major conclusions which Dennis drew from the bibliographical evidence.[20]

II

Due to the very nature of the versions in which the text survives, the bibliographical problems posed by *Flags in the Dust* are more difficult than those of any of Faulkner's other novels. The 593 pages of text of the extant typescript contain gaps, overlaps, and repetitions with slight variation of a number of passages, as well as apparently inadvertent cancellations of material necessary to preserve the sense of the narrative. There are numerous manuscript insertions — most by Faulkner, although there is at least one other hand involved — which are very difficult to decipher without a thorough knowledge of Faulkner's handwriting, and there are very few authorial corrections of obvious typing errors.

The text of *Flags in the Dust* is further complicated by the fact that *Sartoris* was published as long ago as 1929. Both Faulkner and Hal Smith are dead, Harcourt's publishing records from the period do not survive, and thus the only source of information and answers to important questions is Ben Wasson. The editor must determine which, if any, of the differences between the typescript and *Sartoris* represent Faulkner's final intentions regarding *Flags*; he must also consider to what degree *Flags in the Dust* (as represented by the typescript) and *Sartoris* are really two quite different books. He might wish that Harcourt, Brace had followed the example of the dozen or so other publishers who refused the novel in 1927-28, or that Faulkner had followed Liveright's advice and not submitted the manuscript to other publishers. Nevertheless, *Sartoris* does exist, and the editor must confront this fact.

The first task should be to collate the typescript and *Sartoris* to discover exactly what the differences are. All of the variants in *Sartoris* for which Faulkner was definitely or probably responsible must be identified. The next step is to decide whether *Sartoris* represents a revision (as well as a shortening) of *Flags*, or whether it is indeed a different though related work.

If the editor decides to reject the authorial revisions of *Sartoris* because he believes it is a different work, he must then produce a text which uses the typescript as copy-text, correcting spelling and punctuation where necessary, eliminating duplicate passages, and supplying from the manuscript any missing sections of the typescript. If he concludes that *Sartoris* is a revision of *Flags in the Dust*, he again uses the typescript as copy-text, since its accidentals are closest to Faulkner's intentions, and emends the substantives of the text with the authorial variants from *Sartoris*. But the editor must be consistent; he cannot use both methods.

No matter whether he is preparing a scholarly edition or a commercial text for a publisher, the editor of *Flags* should provide an introduction containing a general account of the problems which the text poses as well as his method in solving them. A scholarly edition would also contain a textual apparatus recording each of the decisions which the editor has made in emending the copy-text and his reasons for emendation. The result, whether scholarly or commercial, would be an edition which contains a text which has been recovered from the surviving documents in such a way as to present, in the editor's judgment, the closest approximation possible to Faulkner's intentions regarding *Flags in the Dust*. Other textual specialists might disagree with the editor's choice of method, but his execution of that choice should be impeccable.

III

The textual and bibliographical problems connected with *Flags in the Dust* have, then, long been recognized as one of the real nightmares of the Faulkner field. The 1973 Random House publication of *Flags* promised to solve these problems, but does not. Instead, Day's apparent misunderstanding of the nature of the text he was editing resulted in a confusion of the old problems and the creation of new ones. Both are compounded by the copyrighting of a text which, though entitled *Flags in the Dust*, is not really the book which Faulkner wrote. Day's perfunctory four-page introduction to the text provides several clues to the inadequacies of both editor and edition: not only is it riddled with serious errors of fact, but it also misrepresents the method used to establish the text.

Most of the introduction consists of rehashing of previously published information. Day provides a concise account of the novel's composition, of the attempts of Faulkner and Wasson to sell it, and of the production of *Sartoris*. Next he generally describes his editorial methods. Finally, he compares *Flags* and *Sartoris* on a few superficial points and makes several observations concerning the relation of *Flags in the Dust* to the novels of Faulkner's later career. The most important part of the introduction, the discussion of the text, occupies little more than a page.

The most noticeable flaw in the introduction is the absence of documentation for Day's statements. The publisher might argue that scholarly citation of sources would be out of place in an edition intended for the general reader, but that argument can be countered by pointing out that Day's use of technical terms such as "nonsubstantive alterations" and "hypothetical setting copy" (pp. ix–x) might be confusing even to scholars unfamiliar with textual terminology. The presence of an introduction, but one without footnotes, suggests that he has attempted to please the entire spectrum of readers, but the edition which resulted satisfies the needs of neither.

Lack of documentation and a tendency to make absolute statements where qualifications are necessary are the problems which are posed by the first two pages of the introduction, which provide a history of the novel. Day assumes that the book was begun "In the autumn or winter of

1926" (p. vii), despite the lack of firm evidence in dating the genesis of *Flags*. He flatly states that "Wasson tried eleven publishers" (p. viii) after Faulkner sent him the book, although Wasson's own estimation of the number has varied virtually every time he has been interviewed, and it seems likely that he has forgotten the exact number. This point is important because Day did not bother to interview Wasson himself, and Wasson is the only living person who was involved in the process of writing, editing, and publishing *Flags in the Dust*.

Moreover, the description of the cutting of *Flags* is flawed because Day claims that Faulkner "sat down in Wasson's apartment to observe the operation on his novel . . ." (p. viii), while Faulkner stated in his essay on *Sartoris* that he refused to have anything to do with the process. Supporting Faulkner's assertion, Blotner in his biography has stated that Faulkner had rented a flat in Greenwich Village where he lived and worked because Wasson's apartment was too small. Most importantly, while Day quotes extensively from the essay on *Sartoris*, he glosses over the author's dissatisfaction with the necessity for such drastic surgery.

It is only too obvious from the first two pages of the introduction that Day is careless with his sources, but his consideration of the textual problems of the novel is flawed by even more serious errors. He characterizes Faulkner's handwriting as "neat but minuscule and almost illegible" (p. ix) when describing the *Flags* manuscript. This is simply not true. Faulkner's hand at this point of his career (1926–27) is almost always legible to one who has taken the time to study it carefully, even though Faulkner employed a sort of shorthand, especially in writing word endings such as "ing" and "ed." One wonders how much time Day spent working with the manuscript, for he does not seem able to distinguish between unconventional and illegible handwriting.

Day's consideration of the surviving typescript of *Flags in the Dust* relies heavily on the conclusions drawn by Stephen Dennis in his dissertation. Dennis concludes that the typescript is a "composite" made from parts of three separate drafts which were combined. According to Dennis, these three drafts survive in part in the "composite" as follows: 447 pages of the first, 99 pages of the second, and 146 pages of the third.[21] What Day fails to note is that James E. Kibler has demonstrated that this theory is highly unlikely. In his review of the Dennis dissertation, Kibler has suggested that it is far more probable that Faulkner typed one complete draft which was subsequently thoroughly revised, expanded, and rearranged, thus explaining the curious condition of the surviving typescript.

Day has drawn heavily on Dennis, without indicating the source of his information; but he has also confused Dennis' arguments and conclusions. A comparison of both Dennis' and Day's accounts of the typescript demonstrates this error.

Dennis, p. 70	*Day, p. ix*
Faulkner began to type [the first typescript] before he had completed his manuscript. There are 447 pages from this in the composite typescript. . . . There are only 99 pages from this [second typescript] draft in the composite typescript. . . . The third typescript . . . is essentially a revised second typescript. . . . There are 146 pages from this third typescript in the composite. . . .	[The surviving typescript was] produced by the combination of three separate but overlapping typescript drafts. The first of these, 447 pages long, seems to have been begun before he completed his manuscript version. The second, 99 pages of which are in the composite typescript, was probably written after he had completed the manuscript and the first typescript. In the third, 146 pages appear to have been a revision of the second typescript.

Day has adopted the figures which Dennis provides, but has completely dissociated them from the meaning which Dennis attributed to them. Moreover, Day has also borrowed Dennis' mistake in addition. 447, 99, and 146 pages of three underlying typescripts adds up to a total of 692, yet there are only 593 pages in the surviving typescript. It is clear that Day did not understand what Dennis was trying to say, and, as a result, has not even provided an accurate account of Dennis' inaccurate information.

This perhaps explains why Day wonders "Why Faulkner should have labored over the reconstruction of this text . . ." (p. ix). He has drawn all of the wrong conclusions about the typescript. He is unable to see that the surviving typescript is not Faulkner's attempt to reconstruct the text of *Flags in the Dust* after *Sartoris* was published, but a step in the composition and revision of *Flags*. To assume that Faulkner "simply could not bring himself to throw away all of those typed pages" (p. ix) is perfectly ludicrous.

Day's description of his own part in editing *Flags* is more than a little misleading. He states that the manuscript and typescript "lay more or less undisturbed until Mrs. Jill Summers . . . remembered that her late father had spoken often of a restoration of *Flags in the Dust*. Mrs. Summers asked this writer and Albert Erskine . . . to undertake the task" (p. ix). In so doing, Day completely ignores the parts that Meriwether, Commins, Ober, and Faulkner himself played in making his own work possible. And Mrs. Summers has stated that she did not ask Day to edit the book.[22]

While Day's introduction is misleading and often factually incorrect up to this point, his account of his editorial method is even more vague and deceptive.

[This edition] aims at being a faithful reproduction of that composite typescript. Certain nonsubstantive alterations in spelling and punctuation have been made, in order to bring this novel into conformity with Faulkner's other books; but wherever possible his many idiosyncracies, especially those on which he himself insisted during his years at Random House, were allowed to stand. . . . If there were to be any publication of *Flags in the Dust* at all, then, it had to be what we have here provided. (pp. ix–x)

A close scrutiny of this statement suggests that the editor has raised more questions than he has answered. Exactly how many, and what kinds of "nonsubstantive alterations" were involved in reproducing the text of the typescript? Which of Faulkner's idiosyncrasies were retained, and why could they not be retained wherever they occurred, especially if Faulkner himself insisted on their importance during his life? These nagging suspicions cannot be laid to rest, for they result directly from Day's imprecise language in explaining his editorial procedures.

Day's edition could be sound, his text reliable, even if his method is badly described, provided that his statement of editorial procedures were true; unfortunately it is not. A collation of *Flags in the Dust* as Day published it with his copy-text, the surviving typescript, has turned up more than seventeen hundred variants, of which nearly one hundred are substantive. While admittedly a percentage of these variants are demonstrable errors needing emendation, they could not possibly be described as "Certain nonsubstantive alterations."

More seriously, the integrity of the copy-text has been severely violated. Day maintains that "There was no way . . . to tell which of the many differences between *Flags in the Dust* and *Sartoris* were the result of Faulkner's emendations in . . . galley proofs, and which belonged to Wasson" (p. x). In other words, since Day was unable to determine which variants were authorial and which were not, he claims he has ignored *Sartoris* in establishing the text of *Flags in the Dust*. But such a claim is untrue.

Nearly three sentences in Day's text of *Flags* (305.23–29) do not appear in the typescript but are taken from *Sartoris* (310.2–9). In this case there is no question of a need to fill in a gap in the typescript; instead this represents a conscious decision to interpolate material from *Sartoris*, in clear contradiction of Day's stated editorial policy. Furthermore, two passages in the typescript have been rearranged to coincide with the order of the scenes as they occur in *Sartoris*: in Day's *Flags*, 157.14 to 160.37 (" 'How's Belle?' . . . no stain."), which corresponds to *Sartoris* 176.12 to 180.8, should follow 161.2 to 166.16 ("He settled . . . his days."), which corresponds to *Sartoris* 180.10 to 182.19.

There are also two instances in which Day has omitted material which has not been cancelled in the typescript. On page 162, fifty-nine words have been omitted before the paragraph which begins "At times . . ." (l.29); on page 168, the paragraph beginning "But educate them . . ." (ll. 12–14) has been compressed from one hundred and fifty-eight words to only twenty-six words.

Finally, in more than one case, Day has chosen readings from *Sartoris* when he has been unable to decipher Faulkner's marginal additions to the typescript. For example, at 271.17 he has used the *Sartoris* reading "edgeless canopy of ragged stars" (*Sartoris*, 282.29) instead of the manuscript addition which reads "canopy studded with hazy stars." And in at least one case, he has preferred a *Sartoris* variant over a perfectly legible typed reading: 229.12 should read "she hasn't spoken since that day" instead of "she does not speak at all" (as it appears in *Sartoris*, 241.13).[23]

In addition to these serious substantive changes, the accidentals of the typescript have also been tampered with. Dialect forms have been frequently regularized and corrected; in Day's text, for example, "fum" becomes "f'um" (24.3), "shamed" is changed to " 'shamed" (25.2), and "jes" is transformed to "jes' " (25.12). Also, as McHaney pointed out, all of Faulkner's dashes and ellipses are standardized. Whether Faulkner used three or twelve periods to indicate an interruption or break in thought or dialogue, Day has consistently used only three. While it is standard publishing practice to use three periods to indicate an ellipsis, something of Faulkner's meaning—his attempt to evoke the period of time which the ellipsis is supposed to indicate—has been lost in this reduction. Likewise, Day has ignored the fact that Faulkner used dashes of varying lengths; all have been transcribed as one-em dashes, an editorial procedure which is *not* common.

With such a wholesale disregard of seemingly important accidentals, one wonders which of Faulkner's idiosyncrasies were preserved in Day's text. Hyphenated words such as "hawk-like" were combined (38.5); unhyphenated words like "dust filled" were hyphenated (90.23); and occasionally his possessives were changed—"Sartoris's" to "Sartoris' " for example (32.36). In fact, the only obvious departures from conventional style which were retained are the omission of periods after titles (*e.g.* Mr, Mrs, Dr) and of apostrophes in most one-syllable contractions (*e.g.* aint, cant, dont). Yet even here Day was not consistent: "Ain't" appears at 25.6 and "Dr." at 84.34.

Erskine's response to many of these same points when they were raised by McHaney was that "careful *readers* of the novel might attribute" occasional duplications of passages "to *bad editing* . . . and they would be right." That, apparently, is intended to settle the question of cuts made in the typescript. As for the shifting of passages, the fact that Faulkner himself had moved around the passages is for Erskine "enough . . . to satisfy us that the author did not regard this position as final and to warrant our shifting it to what is obviously a better place for it." Also, as far as normalization of punctuation marks is concerned, Erskine maintains that Faulkner did not use "different-length dashes and ellipsis dots like some system of musical notation" nor did he use them the same way throughout his career.[24]

But Faulkner was very much concerned about the transmission of the text of *Flags in the Dust*. In an unusual letter to Horace Liveright, Faulkner speaks of a list of suggestions for the printer which he has prepared, and asks him to "smooth the printer's fur, cajole him, some way. He's been punctuating my stuff to death; giving me gratis quotation marks and premiums of commas that I dont need."[25] I do not think that Faulkner meant that his spelling and punctuation were always to be held sacred. Certainly obvious misspelling and incorrect or ambiguous pointing need emendation, but one would expect that the editor and house-styler, if not the typesetter, would show better and more reasonable judgment, especially when the writer involved is one of Faulkner's stature and importance.

Moreover, publishers like Random House should give the readers of Faulkner credit for realizing that a creative writer need not be bound by the rules of the Chicago *Manual of Style*. Rather than blue-pencil at the mere sight of some grammatical or mechanical eccentricity, copy-editors might consider that such phenomena could be a conscious part of the writer's style. There is no danger that commercial publishers will compete with the services provided by the CEAA or EETS or risk offending their general readers simply by observing this caveat. What they do risk is interfering with the intentions of well-meaning authors like Faulkner who bristle at additions to or deletions from their scripts.

Flags in the Dust presented a special obligation to both Day and Random House because its author was no longer living, as well as because the text involved had so complex a history. Nevertheless, Day and Erskine failed to meet this obligation. They copy-edited, tampered with, and occasionally distorted the text, while maintaining that the result was "a faithful reproduction of that composite typescript" with "Certain nonsubstantive alterations." The resulting corrupted state of the text of *Flags in the Dust* is distressing and reprehensible. There can be no excuse for Day's making such false claims about the edition; indeed, it would have been better to have omitted the introduction altogether than to mislead readers as he has done.

While almost all of the criticism in this review has been aimed at the editor whose name appears on the title page of the book, it is possible that much of the fault may lie elsewhere. An examination of the corrected galley and page proofs of the 1973 edition of *Flags in the Dust* which have been deposited at the University of Virginia Library indicates that much of the tampering with dialect, spelling and punctuation was done in galley and page proof.

It is unlikely that Day's product will soon be replaced with a printed text which will correct its errors. Indeed, the reset Vintage paperback guarantees this bad text a wider, more trusting audience in college classrooms throughout the country. Moreover, the Vintage edition not only contains nearly all of the first edition's mistakes (though a few obvious typographical errors are corrected); it also introduces scores of new misreadings. I give one example only: for the phrase "icy water," the Vintage text reads "city water" (390.8–9).

Douglas Day's 1973 Random House edition of *Flags in the Dust*, then, is not the novel which Faulkner preserved and donated to the Alderman Library at the University of Virginia, but rather a publisher's and editor's opinion of what that novel should have been. It is neither "a faithful reproduction" of the surviving typescript, as it claims to be, nor even a systematic conflation of the typescript with *Sartoris*. It is, instead, a badly edited, copyrighted text which will probably prevent the publication of a sound edition of *Flags in the Dust* for many decades.

Notes

1. "The Text of *Flags in the Dust*" *Faulkner Concordance Newsletter*, No. 2 (November 1973), 7–8.

2. "Commentary on the Text of *Flags in the Dust*," *Faulkner Concordance Newsletter*, No. 3 (May 1974), 2–3.

3. "Commentary," p. 3.

4. "Faulkner's *Flags in the Dust* and *Sartoris*: A Comparative Study of the Typescript and the Originally Published Novel," Univ. of Texas at Austin. Roberts' work points out the major differences between the *Flags* typescript and *Sartoris*, primarily through analysis of differences in treatment of major characters. He also includes a table of significant textual variants (of approximately a sentence or more in length) but, unfortunately, not a complete collation. Because his work had been nearly finished when Day's edition appeared, his discussion of its relation to the typescript and *Sartoris* is necessarily brief.

5. *Southern Review*, 8 (Autumn 1974), 878–88. Adams analyzes the novel's significance to a study of Faulkner's career. His claim that Faulkner learned about revising his writing from Wasson's cutting of *Flags* is questionable in view of Faulkner's essay on *Sartoris*. Adams' statement that the revision of *Flags* was similar to the revision of *Sanctuary* is, I think, demonstrably wrong. There is no evidence that *Flags in the Dust* underwent the degree of rewriting and revision that Faulkner undertook in reworking *Sanctuary* in galley proof.

6. TL carbon, 20 October 1927, Horace Liveright to William Faulkner, 1 p. This letter indicates that Liveright had not yet received the typescript. The carbon is in the Massey-Faulkner Collection at the University of Virginia Library; it is quoted in Joseph Blotner, *Faulkner: A Biography* (New York: Random House, 1974), I, 557.

7. TL carbon, 25 November 1927, Horace Liveright to William Faulkner, 1 p. Massey-Faulkner Collection; quoted in Blotner, p. 560.

8. TLS, 16 [?] October 1927, William Faulkner to Horace Liveright, 1 p. Massey-Faulkner Collection; quoted, with typing error corrected, in Blotner, p. 557.

9. TLS, 30 November 1927, William Faulkner to Horace Liveright, 1 p. Massey-Faulkner Collection; quoted in Blotner, p. 560.

10. Blotner (p. 570) claims, without citing a source, that Faulkner retyped the novel himself. Douglas Day makes the same undocumented assertion in his introduction to *Flags in the Dust* (p. vii).

11. Both Blotner (p. 570) and Day (p. vii) quote from what is apparently a letter from Faulkner to Wasson, or possibly a remark made by Faulkner later. Neither cites a source for the quotation.

12. Interview with Ben Wasson, 30 April 1975.

13. It is not known who retitled the cut version of *Flags in the Dust*. It is likely that, since the title was specified in the contract, either Wasson or Smith may have suggested it.

14. While in New York, Faulkner also painted a watercolor of a proposed dust jacket for *Sartoris*: a black man, a mule, and a plow against a newly plowed field. The design was rejected. Letter from Ben Wasson, 17 June 1975.

15. Joseph Blotner, ed., "William Faulkner's Essay on the Composition of *Sartoris*," *Yale University Library Gazette*, 47 (January 1973), 123–24.

16. Interview with James B. Meriwether, 5 August 1975.

17. *The Literary Career of William Faulkner* (Princeton: Princeton Univ. Library, 1961), pp. 64–65.

18. *The Achievement of William Faulkner* (New York: Random House, 1966), pp. 81–85.

19. "The Making of *Sartoris*: A Description and Discussion of the Manuscript and Composite Typescript of William Faulkner's Third Novel," Cornell Univ.

20. Review of "The Making of *Sartoris*," *Mississippi Quarterly*, 24 (Summer 1971), 315–19.

21. "The Making of *Sartoris*," p. 70.

22. Interview with James B. Meriwether, 14 August 1975.

23. Melvin Roberts points out several of these changes in his dissertation, "Faulkner's *Flags in the Dust* and *Sartoris*," pp. 1–2.

24. "Commentary on the Text of *Flags in the Dust*," p. 3.

25. TLS 16 [?] October 1927, Faulkner to Liveright; quoted in Blotner, p. 557.

VI PRESENT REFLECTIONS

Damned Sartorises! Damned Falkners!

Donald P. Duclos*

At the conclusion of "An Odor of Verbena," Aunt Jenny, the matriarchal "Queen" of the Sartoris family, cradles Bayard Sartoris' head between her hands after he has violated the family code by not killing Ben Redmond for having shot Colonel Sartoris. "Suddenly the tears sprang and streamed down her face. . . . 'Oh, damn you Sartorises!' she said. 'Damn you! Damn you!' "[1]

Almost a decade earlier, William Faulkner had also placed Aunt Jenny as commentator on the Sartoris family in the concluding chapter of *Sartoris*. Visiting the cemetery after the youngest Bayard's death, she inspects the stone monuments that mark the family grave. "Miss Jenny stood for a time, musing, a slender, erect figure in black silk and a small, uncompromising black bonnet. . . . Well, it was the last one at last, gathered in solemn conclave about the dying reverberation beneath the pagan symbols of their vainglory and carven gestures of it in enduring stone."[2]

These negative comments and thoughts about Sartorises — their vainglory and their arrogance — derive from "the virus," Colonel John Sartoris, the sire of his arrogant family who inspired the "game of Sartoris." There was "death in the sound" of the name and "a glamorous fatality."

Juxtaposed against Aunt Jenny's judgments of the family are those of the older Bayard. As a younger man, in "An Odor of Verbena," he had refused to play the game of Sartoris by not avenging his father's death. Nevertheless, in his later years, his reverence for family and tradition is revealed in his recollection of his father's words:

> "In the nineteenth century," John Sartoris said, "genealogy is poppy-cock. Particularly in America, where only what a man takes and keeps has any significance and where all of us have a common ancestry and the only house from which we can claim descent with any assurance is

*For this essay, written especially for this volume, the author has drawn upon his definitive study of the life and works of Colonel W. C. Falkner, "Son of Sorrow: The Life, Works, and Influence of Colonel William C. Falkner, 1825–1889" (Diss., Univ. of Michigan 1961) and applied it to Faulkner's fiction. The essay appears here for the first time, with permission of the author. © 1985 Donald P. Duclos.

the Old Bailey. Yet the man who professes to care nothing about his forebears is only a little less vain than the man who bases all his actions on blood precedent. And I reckon a Sartoris can have a little vanity and poppycock, if he wants it."[3]

Between the conflicting views of Aunt Jenny and old Bayard about John Sartoris lies the concurrent love and hate, fascination and criticism of William Faulkner for his own family, upon which his fictional family is based. In 1953, when William Faulkner could finally confront his conflicting response to his heritage, he wrote in his autobiographical essay, "Mississippi," "Loving all of it while he had to hate some of it because he knows now that you don't love because; you love despite; not for the virtues, but despite the faults."[4]

At the root of this concurrent love and hate for the South and the Sartoris/Falkner family is the fundamental problem of being "a Sartoris . . . in a Snopes world," as Alfred Kazin described it in *On Native Grounds*.[5] Before Faulkner had undertaken the creation of his fictional community and its numerous families, he had struggled to find himself as a writer. Then he decided to follow Sherwood Anderson's advice that a writer "has first got to be what he is, what he was born."[6] Anderson advised Faulkner to return to his home in Mississippi and write about it. Faulkner returned to Oxford and went to work first on *Flags in the Dust*, then on a revised version entitled *Sartoris*, based on his own family history. Recalling his return, Faulkner later wrote, "Now the young man, middle-aged now or anyway middle-aging, is back home. . . . Home again, his native land; he was born of it and his bones will sleep in it; loving it even while hating some of it."[7]

Searching for material for his new work, Faulkner struck upon his great-grandfather, Colonel William C. Falkner. Like Gail Hightower, "all his life he had lived with a ghost,"[8] the ghost of his ancestor who dominated Mississippi history for more than fifty years in the nineteenth century. After his death in 1889, the legend of his life and career had become a part of William's heritage. Like Quentin Compson, absorbing the story of Thomas Sutpen, Faulkner had absorbed the legend of Colonel Falkner:

> It was a part of his twenty years heritage of breathing the same air and hearing his father talk about the man Sutpen; a part of the town's— Jefferson's eighty years heritage of the same air which the man himself had breathed. . . . Quentin had grown up with that; the mere names were interchangeable and almost myriad. His childhood was full of them; his very body was an empty hall echoing with sonorous defeated names; he was not a being, an entity, he was a commonwealth.[9]

In 1938, Faulkner agreed to an interview with Robert Cantwell, in which he talked about "The Old Colonel."

"People at Ripley talk of him as if he were still alive, up in the hills someplace, and might come in at any time. It's a strange thing; there are lots of people who knew him well, and yet no two of them remember him alike or describe him the same way. One will say he was like me, and another will swear he was six feet tall. . . . There's nothing left in the old place, the house is gone and the plantation boundaries, nothing left of his work but a statue. But he rode through the country like a living force. I like it better that way."[10]

This ghostly presence of Colonel Falkner gave William his inspiration for *Sartoris*. In the opening paragraphs of that novel, old Will Falls brings to old Bayard the pipe which John Sartoris was smoking when Bed Redlaw (Redmond) shot him. This pipe, imprinted with "his father's teeth where he had left the very print of his ineradicable bones as though in enduring stone,"[11] is the same one that Colonel Falkner was smoking on the fatal day in 1889 when he was shot by his former business partner, Richard J. Thurmond. William acknowledged owning the pipe, when I met him in 1959, but he did not offer to show it to me.[12]

Sartoris opens with the ghostly presence of Colonel Sartoris, represented by the pipe, and closes with Aunt Jenny's visit to the cemetery and a description of the larger than life-size statue of him that dominates the scene. Between the pipe and the monument is not only the history of Colonel Sartoris and his family, but also that of Colonel Falkner and his. A reconstruction of the first, highlighted by the analogues in the life of the second, will illuminate both.

Although there are several inconsistencies in William's creation of Colonel Sartoris, such as the change of name from Redlaw in *Sartoris* to Redmond in *The Unvanquished*, they are minor. Several events in Colonel Falkner's life seem to be of major importance to William in drawing his fictional counterpart: his Civil War record; his killing of two men; his dream of building the railroad; his partnership with Thurmond; his brutal death; and the central symbol of his arrogance — the statue and monument that tower over the graves of his family. Like Sartoris, his reckless and arrogant spirit repeated itself with "fateful fidelity" in the Falkner family. From a composite biographical sketch of Colonel Sartoris in *Sartoris*, *The Unvanquished*, *Light in August*, *Absalom, Absalom!*, and *Requiem for a Nun* (with incidental details from other works), we learn the following about John Sartoris.

Born in 1823 (two years before Colonel Falkner), Sartoris was one of many who came to Jefferson shortly after that town was named and incorporated. Unlike Falkner, who had walked from St. Genevieve, Missouri, to Tennessee and then south to Mississippi to join maternal relatives, Sartoris had arrived "with slaves and gear and money too like Grenier and Sutpen."[13] By midcentury, Jefferson had grown and progressed beyond its courthouse and jail, and other new buildings had been erected, such as the one that "would be known through all Mississippi and east Tennessee as *the* Academy, the Female Institute."[14] The academy was partly financed by the town, but no one "would . . . ever know how much of the additional cost Sutpen and Sartoris made up."[15]

This academy was in historical fact the Ripley Female Academy. It had been opened in 1849 and was taught by Mary Jane Buchanon, a sister of Elizabeth Houston Vance, Falkner's second wife (usually referred to as "Lizzie"). After the school had been burned to the ground by Federal troops in July 1864, the board of trustees deeded the property to Mrs. Buchanon for a nominal sum. Colonel Falkner, who owned the block of land across the street, deeded the land to his sister-in-law. It is widely accepted that Falkner provided the monetary support for erecting a new school, named Stonewall College, which opened in 1867. For its opening, Falkner wrote and produced a melodramatic and sentimental play, *The Lost Diamond*. While it is customary to identify Jefferson with Oxford, much of the fictional town's history derives from Ripley, the original home of the Falkners.[16]

By the time of the Civil War, John Sartoris was widowed and had one son, Bayard, who was raised by his grandmother. Likewise, Falkner's first wife, Holland Pearce, died in 1850, leaving a son, John Wesley Thompson Falkner I, who was raised by the Thompson family, Falkner's maternal aunt and uncle, as an adopted son.[17] It is through this line that the more prominent Falkners of the twentieth century have descended.

When the time came for Mississippians to take part in the war, Sartoris organized a volunteer regiment, and he "would stand in the first Confederate uniform the town had ever seen, while in the square below the Richmond mustering officer enrolled and swore in the regiment which Sartoris as its Colonel would take to Virginia as part of Bee, to be Jackson's extreme left in front of the Henry house at First Manassas."[18] The infantry, "raised and organized with Jefferson for its headquarters, going to Virginia, numbered Two in the roster of Mississippi regiments," was not yet at its creation even a regiment, "but merely a voluntary association of untried men who knew they were ignorant and hoped they were brave."[19] Sartoris led his group into battle and served creditably under Johnston and Bee at First Manassas; but apparently he was too strict a disciplinarian and "wouldn't be Tom, Dick, and Harry with ever' camprobber that come along with a salvaged muskit and claimed to be a sojer."[20] Later in a regimental election, he was deposed from his colonelcy and was succeeded by Thomas Sutpen.

Colonel Falkner's role in the early days of the war can be traced in detail from his record in the National Archives and other Civil War records. Whether or not he was responsible for organizing a company of volunteers, he was a member of the state militia known as Company F, which, in April 1861 enlisted into Confederate service. Falkner's company, along with ten others from Mississippi, assembled at Corinth in May 1861, and Falkner was elected colonel of the regiment, the Second Mississippi Infantry. They were assigned to Mott's Brigade and were sent to Virginia.

These hastily organized troops were ill equipped, having taken from home whatever arms they possessed — rifles, pistols, or old flint-lock muskets left over from the War of 1812. Their military experience ranged from none to all to some experience in the Mexican War. After their arrival at Harper's Ferry, an inspection report reveals that Falkner's regiment was indeed shabby:

> One of the regiments [the Eleventh], under command of Colonel Moore, is very superior to the other [the Second] under Colonel Falkner. The latter is badly clothed and very careless in its appointments. The officers are entirely without military knowledge of any description and the men have a slovenly and unsoldier-like appearance. . . . In the regiment from Mississippi under Colonel Falkner, almost every necessary is wanting. They seem to have come away from home without making proper preparations in this respect, and, indeed, it would seem that they expected to receive on their arrival in Virginia all the appointments of a soldier.[21]

Stung by this negative report, Falkner became a rigid disciplinarian and earned enmity from many of his troops. Although they served well at First Manassas and Falkner gained recognition from numerous military leaders, their rancor against him would lead to his being deposed. As a military man, however, Falkner was widely praised, even earning from General Beauregard the sobriquet "the knight of the black plume." (William Faulkner later reassigned the black plume to Thomas Sutpen.)

During the later months of 1861 and early 1862, Falkner was influential in recruiting additional men for his regiment, but the personnel had changed and a new election was called for. On 21 April 1862 balloting began to elect a new colonel. On the first ballot, J. M. Stone received 250 votes, Falkner 249, and Captain Hugh R. Miller (of Ripley) 129.[22] Miller withdrew from the race, and, after campaign speeches, a second ballot was taken the next day. Stone was elected by 13 votes. Bitter in his defeat, Falkner returned to Ripley to attempt other ways to gain recognition.

This election is important in *Sartoris*. Young Bayard says, " 'Look at the little two-bit war he went to, . . . a war that was so sorry that grandfather wouldn't even stay up there in Virginia where it was'." With her usual caustic manner, Aunt Jenny replied: " 'And nobody wanted him at it. . . . A man that would get mad just because his men deposed him and elected a better Colonel in his place. Got mad and came back to lead a bunch of red-neck brigands'."[23]

But dates of new conscription and partisan rangers laws coincided with Falkner's being deposed in Virginia; accordingly, he returned to Ripley and in July 1862 he was recruiting a ranger unit, his "red-neck brigands," which he led successfully for the next two years. He probably attracted volunteers by using the "legitimate plunder" inducement; by 28 July his company had grown to "regiment" size of about 600 – a conspicuous achievement.

Although Falkner encountered numerous difficulties with the Confederacy, whose leaders soon discovered that the ranger units were depleting the regular army, he led his regiment successfully and was the bane of Federal forces in northern Mississippi. He recognized, however, that ranger units were in political danger, and, during the closing months of his military service in 1863, he led an active campaign for promotion to brigadier general in the regular army. Enlisting the support of many major military leaders and politicians, Falkner sought official recognition from Jefferson Davis. One such letter, revealing his rank-consciousness, reads in part:

> I see junior officers promoted over me, and men made Brigadiers who remained at home six or eight months after I was in the war. It is exceedingly mortifying for me to be commanded by men, both my juniors in age & office. I am of the opinion, however, that my case has been neglected for want of some friend to take the matter in hand. . . . If you cannot secure the command of a Brigadier for me, try to get the Secretary of War to send me a commission as Col. to date back to the time I was first mustered into the Confederate Service which was 1st May, 1861. This is certainly due me, for I have continuously served the Government from that time to this, in the capacity of Col. I never have received any commission from the Confederate States yet. I am unable to tell why it has never been sent, but such is the case.[24]

But Colonel Falkner never received the desired commission and retired from service. His hopes, ambitions, and attempts to become a glorious hero of the Civil War came to an end with the disbanding of partisan rangers, followed by his resignation from service on 25 October 1863, giving as his reason "ill health," defined as "indigestion and internal hemmorrhoids," certified by W. D. Carter, surgeon with the First Mississippi Partisan Rangers – and Colonel Falkner's future son-in-law.

While he did not gain the recognition he felt he deserved, he was locally idealized, as Colonel Sartoris is. And as Colonel Sartoris rebuilt his house "on the same blackened spot over the same cellar" – "Drusilla said that the house was the aura of Father's dream"[25] – so Colonel Falkner purchased a house from Richard J. Thurmond. Located two blocks from the square, the house and its attendant buildings (including Falkner's office) covered a square block of land. After his visit to Europe in 1883, Falkner had the house extensively remodeled, adding cupolas, spires, balconies, porches, and porthole windows. One of the most expensive and lavish houses in Ripley, the building was razed in 1938 to make way for the United States Post Office and the Tate Clinic; the latter building still contains the staircase and one of the iron balconies from the original structure.[26]

By this time in Sartoris' life, there were carpetbaggers in Jefferson, one of whom was Ben Redmond, "the town's domesticated carpetbagger, symbol of a blind rapacity almost like a biological instinct" who, in his dealings with Sartoris is much like Richard Thurmond with Colonel Falkner. There were others, too, like the Burdens — the abolitionists who attempted to organize the Negroes to vote in the first possible election. In order to keep peace and harmony in the community, Sartoris found it necessary to kill the Burdens.

This killing is loosely connected with Colonel Falkner's killing of two men in 1849 and 1851 — Robert Holt Hindman and Erasmus V. Morris. Early Falkner biographers have connected these two killings, but the latter may have been no more than the result of a monetary disagreement. Although Falkner was acquitted of both killings on grounds of self-defense, he was haunted throughout his life by them. The Hindman case is interesting and is echoed in both *Sartoris* and *Light in August.*

In 1849 Robert Hindman, of a fairly prestigious Ripley family, had applied for membership in an organization to which Falkner belonged. According to legend, Robert was told that Falkner had spoken against his admission. As early as 1849 Falkner had enemies in Ripley, and Robert may have been put up to a confrontation with him, possibly with a faulty gun. When Hindman attempted to shoot Falkner, the pistol failed to fire, and Falkner, defending himself, stabbed and killed Hindman. (Interestingly enough, a similar, faulty gun is in the hands of Joanna Burden in *Light in August*.) Although Falkner was tried and cleared, enmity against him was strong, especially from the Hindman family. They erected a stone over Robert's grave reading "Murdered by W. C. Falkner." Under pressure from Falkner partisans, they were forced to change the inscription to "Killed by W. C. Falkner." This change is reflected in *Sartoris*: "[The] inscription had caused some furor on the part of the slayer's family, and a formal protest had followed. But in complying with popular opinion, old Bayard had had his revenge: he caused the line 'By man's ingratitude he died' to be chiseled crudely out, and added beneath it: 'Fell at the hand of — Redlaw.' "[27]

The killing of Colonel Sartoris by Redmond is another direct link with the joint venture of Colonel Falkner and Richard J. Thurmond in the development of the railroad, the major portion of the Falkner/Sartoris "dream" after the Civil War. In William Faulkner's fictional version, Redmond and General Compson join Sartoris as partners, but they eventually quarrel and Compson withdraws. Finally, Sartoris and Redmond, too, reached the point where they could no longer work together: "They met and agreed to buy or sell, naming a price which, in reference to what they had put into it, was ridiculously low but which each believed the other could not raise — at least Father claimed that Redmond did not believe he could raise it."[28] But Sartoris raised the money, bought out Redmond, and became the railroad's sole owner.

The arrogance of Sartoris gradually began to wear on the community, until "he had no friends; only enemies and frantic admirers" who "began to understand the result of the regimental election in the fall of '62."[29] And Sartoris constantly taunted his former partner, finally running against him for the state legislature in a bitter contest; their feud heightens with Sartoris' premonition of his death by Redmond:

> It showed on John Sartoris' brow, the dark shadow of fatality and doom, that night when he sat beneath the candles in the dining-room and turned a wineglass in his fingers while he talked to his son. The railroad was finished, and that day he had been elected to the state legislature after a hard and bitter fight, and doom lay on his brow, and weariness.
> "And so," he said, "Redlaw'll kill me tomorrow, for I shall be unarmed. I'm tired of killing men."[30]

The next day he was shot by Redmond/Redlaw.

This fictional account of the Falkner/Thurmond relationship parallels both legend and fact. Faulkner inherited the legend that after his great-grandfather's walk from Missouri to Mississippi he had proclaimed that one day he would build a railroad over the route so that no one would ever have to walk again. As early as 1856, plans for a local railroad in northern Mississippi were under way and the Ripley Railroad Company was incorporated by the state; at the time Falkner was not among the incorporators. The earliest evidence of his involvement in the road occurs in 1871 when, in formal legislative action, Mississippi established "An Act to encourage internal improvements in the State of Mississippi" for railroad building and expansion. A few days later, another law reincorporated the Ripley Railroad Company, at which time Falkner was one of about forty incorporators. During that year, Falkner was elected president of the company — a position he held until his death. In 1872, the legislature authorized a change of name for the railroad, the Ship Island, Ripley and Kentucky — an indication that expansion of the road was being contemplated.[31]

By the early 1880s, Falkner, Thurmond, and two other partners named Hines and Harris owned the company; Falkner and Thurmond each held one-third shares, the other two partners one-sixth each. Throughout the 1880s, Falkner was frequently pressed to expand the narrow-gauge road, which originally connected Ripley with Middleton, Tennessee, to New Albany and Pontotoc. Besides drastic differences in the temperaments of Falkner and Thurmond, the expansion of the road seems to have been the major source of disagreement between them — Falkner in favor of expansion, Thurmond not wanting to invest more money.

Early in 1886, their disagreement reached its peak and they agreed to draw lots to settle their future course. The loser of the drawing would sell his one-third interest to the winner and fix a selling price for the $83,000 of first mortgage bonds which he possessed. Thurmond lost and set his price, said to be $19,000 in cash—money he thought Falkner could not raise. One story told by the family is that Thurmond demanded *gold*, more difficult to come by even than cash.[32] Falkner was successful, however, and early in April 1886 he acquired Thurmond's interest. From that time on the men were sworn enemies. Some evidence of the public nature of their feud appears in the Circuit Court records of Tippah County, when on 1 November 1886 Falkner was arraigned and fined $4 and $3 court costs for "swearing and cussing"; on the same day, three cases later, Thurmond was arraigned on the same charge and drew the same fine.[33]

Several revelations of their mismatched personalities appear in letters in my possession about them. In one of her numerous letters to me in the 1950s, his daughter, Bama F. McLean (Mrs. Walter B.), recalled

> Thurmond made his money oppressing the poor, buying mortgages and foreclosing without giving the man an extension or a chance. My Father on the contrary was a benefactor to the poor. When I was in Ripley, after I married, many old negroes sent word to me—calling for the "Cols Baby" as they all called me, to please stop to see those who were too crippled by old age and poor health to reach me—and each one would have a story to tell me—such as "The Col gave me sugar all one winter" or "the Col loaned me money to build my house"— . . . Oh, I could cover pages of such tales of the various kindnesses that my father did.[34]

Andrew Brown, a geologist and engineer by profession, but a northern Mississippi historian by avocation and related to both Falkner supporters (through his mother) and to the Thurmonds (through his father), wrote to me:

> It is about what she honestly believes. However, Thurmond was worth at the time he shot Falkner about half a million dollars—a lot of money now and a lot more then. He could have bought out Falkner several times over, from the best information I can get, though Falkner was no pauper. As to Thurmond's being a robber of widows and orphans, that is the standard accusation in every age and clime against a man who makes his living lending money, and should be disregarded in the absence of specific evidence. I will add that my Uncle Dick was not by any means a soft-hearted individual, but I have no evidence to show that he was any more callous than any money-lender has to be. He was completely self-centered except where his family was concerned, and had a cold personality; Falkner's genuine public spirit was something Thurmond probably could not understand.[35]

Thurmond's name, however, appears numerous times on practically every page of the deed records of Tippah County for the period with notices of foreclosure. By contrast, the same records reveal frequent loans by Colonel Falkner, but relatively few foreclosures. Falkner's public spirit is transferred to Sartoris by Drusilla, who tells Bayard that " 'He is thinking of this whole country which he is trying to raise by its bootstraps, so that all the people in it, not just his kind or his old regiment, but all the people, black and white, the women and children back in the hills who don't even own shoes [can share his dream] — Don't you see?' "[36]

After his formal break with Thurmond in 1886, Falkner did expand the railroad, first to New Albany, then to Pontotoc; in his closing years, he planned to develop the road further by merging with other lines to stretch it from Chicago to the Gulf. To gain legislative support, he became a candidate for state office. Contrary to traditional legend, Thurmond did not oppose him in the race. In the August 1889 primary, he beat three candidates with an overwhelming 400 votes more than their combined tallies — some evidence of the strong support he enjoyed. Going into the November election, he was unopposed.[37]

On 25 October, less than two weeks before he was killed by Thurmond, Falkner drew up his will with his friend and fellow attorney, Captain Thomas Spight, who, on the slightest provocation, according to Andrew Brown, would tell this story: Falkner went to him and told him that he knew Dick Thurmond planned to kill him and that he wanted to make certain his property was well settled. Spight suggested to Falkner that if he really feared Thurmond he should carry a gun; but Falkner, replying that he had already killed enough men in his life, was determined to shed no more blood and refused to arm himself.[38] The will, an interesting document, concludes, "Believing in the boundless mercy of my Great Creator I give my soul back to *Him* hoping and believing that *He* will deal with it in great mercy. *So mote it be. Amen.*"[39] Two weeks later he was dead.

On election day, 5 November 1889, certain of victory, Falkner left his office to go to the square to accept the congratulations of his friends. There he was shot by Thurmond; the ball from his pistol entered Falkner's mouth, breaking his jaw, knocking out two teeth, and lodging in his throat. At first the shot did not seem fatal and the next afternoon he was reported to be "resting comfortably." Later that night, the swelling in his throat caused him to choke to death. Thurmond was charged with manslaughter — a compromise, according to Andrew Brown,[40] between the Falkner supporters who wanted an indictment for murder and the Thurmond faction who sought a verdict of justifiable homicide or self-defense, because neither side had sufficient evidence for the charge it wanted. The trial was delayed until 1891, at which time Thurmond was found not guilty. He was defended by Z. M. Stephens of New Albany, one of the best criminal lawyers in the state and by two others. District Attorney Thomas Spight was the prosecutor, assisted by Falkner's son, J. W. T. I. In addition to the compromise indictment, there are also numerous suggestions that Thurmond's wealth helped to gain his acquittal, for the jury was comprised largely of Thurmond's supporters and county citizens in his debt; after his acquittal, many outstanding notes were canceled. Brown estimates his uncle's trial cost close to $40,000.[41] Shortly after the trial and its results, the editor of the *Grenada Sentinel* called the trial "a mockery of justice," and added, "It is a happy reflection to know that money and corruption have no sway in the world to come."[42] (In later years, Z. M. Stephens purportedly said that he owed Colonel Falkner many kindnesses and "shouldn't have defended the son-of-a-bitch who killed him.")[43]

These stories of events in Colonel Falkner's life were the heritage of William Faulkner, which he used in shaping Colonel Sartoris and his influence on the family and the town. But there are other parallels, demonstrating his familiarity with his great-grandfather. We never know when or how, but Sartoris acquires three daughters, who correspond to Willie, Stephanie, and Alabama ("Aunt Bama"). Sartoris bought a new engine for the railroad, which he named the "Jenny" for his sister, as Falkner purchased an oversized engine, named it the "W. C. Falkner," and rented it to his own company for $50 a month. And just as the Sartoris men are marked by recklessness and violence, so were the Falkner men. When I met the Falkners in 1959, Judge J. W. T. Falkner II (Uncle John) and J. W. T. Falkner III ("Johncy") both delighted in recounting stories about their relatives. Johncy's wife, Lucille, said to me, "The Falkners are all great story-tellers and no two of them tell the same story the same way." Among such stories, the following are illustrative.

Uncle John told me of Henry Falkner, the colonel's son, a shiftless young man who had been sent to the University of Virginia where he was constantly in trouble. One day in a fight or a wrestling contest with a fellow student, the other student fell from a balcony and was killed. Henry was invited to remove himself from the university. Back in Ripley, he became attracted to the pretty young wife of a crippled jeweler. The jeweler went to Colonel Falkner, asking him to do something about Henry. The colonel sent his son to Texas with a bank account which Henry soon gambled away. He returned to Ripley and to the jeweler's wife. One day, the jeweler went to the colonel and said, "I'm sorry to have to tell you this, but I just had to shoot Henry." Judge Falkner said his grandfather replied, "That's all right. I guess I'd have had to shoot him myself one of these days." Henry's grave in the Ripley cemetery is above ground, like his father's, but it reads, simply, "Henry."

Considered a failure in his life, even by his family, Murry Falkner, William's father, once received his Falknerian wound. According to Uncle John, Murry was shot in his attempt to defend the honor of Mary Holland, his sister. Johncy implied that he had been wounded as a result of an extramarital escapade with a druggist's wife in New Albany. ("That was when the Falkners had to move to Oxford," Johncy said.) Jimmy, Johncy's son, told me the incident occurred in a drugstore in Pontotoc, prior to Murry's marriage to "Miss Maud." All three versions agree, however, in the nature of the wound:[44] Murry was shot in the face, the bullet entering his mouth, knocking out the same two teeth that the colonel had lost from Thurmond's bullet, and lodging in his throat. He too might have choked to death had not someone induced vomiting to dislodge the ball. His father attempted to avenge the shooting: when he attacked his son's assailant and tried to wrest the gun from him, he placed his hand over the barrel point just as the gun was discharged and was shot through the hand. Still one more Falkner wound.

On numerous occasions, William Faulkner confessed his admiration for old indomitable Southern women such as Granny Millard, Aunt Jenny, Miss Habersham, and Emily Grierson in his fiction. The Falkner women provided him with models for these strong-willed older ladies. After Colonel Falkner's death, for instance, Willie Falkner Carter commissioned a stained-glass window for the Baptist Church in Ripley to honor her father. The inscription read, "He that giveth to the poor lendeth to the lord," evidence of how she wanted the colonel remembered. The Falkner-Thurmond hostilities persisted, however, and members of the congregation also objected to the window because the colonel was not a churchgoer. Willie was forced to remove the window, but she had it transferred to and installed in the sitting room of her home, directly across the street from the family house.

When Colonel Falkner made his journey to Europe in 1883, he was accompanied by his daughter Effie. Mrs. Falkner did not make the journey because of her deathly fear of water. Although she wanted to be buried after death in a small, quiet cemetery in Memphis which she loved, Willie had her cremated and subsequently deposited her ashes in the ocean off the coast of Baltimore. "I never will forgive her for that," her sister, Aunt Bama, confided to me in telling the story.[45] And Aunt Bama herself, the youngest member of the family, was also strong-willed and determined. When William refused to attend the premiere of *Intruder in the Dust*, his wife Estelle called Aunt Bama, who sent William a telegram, notifying him she would be attending the premiere escorted by him. William attended.[46] Jimmy Falkner, William's nephew, told me of her boldness in demanding entrance to the Marine base in Memphis when he was stationed there. In the Memphis Public Library she was well known for her history of unreturned books and lost umbrellas. Her numerous letters to me during the 1950s were written in a bold "flowing calligraphy" that must have equaled Miss Emily Grierson's. When I met her, she received me at the front door of her home wearing a hat and pulling on gloves. I later learned no proper Southern lady would receive a gentleman guest without hat and gloves. She was a lovable character.

Closer to William in Oxford was Mary Holland, called "Auntee" in the family. The Falkners enjoy telling why Oxford has two Confederate monuments: Auntee was a member of the United Daughters of the Confederacy, responsible for commissioning a monument for the town; but when they had the monument erected at the university campus instead of the town square against Auntee's wishes, she made such a fuss that the family paid for a second monument to place in the square to appease her.[47] Much of Auntee's personality is captured in William Faulkner's portrait of Aunt Jenny.

Comparatively little is known about the colonel's wife, Lizzie. He married her in 1851, just after he had written about her in *The Siege of Monterey*:

> I am in love, too, I must acknowledge,
> I learned the art at beauty's college;
> I am in love clear up to my nose,
> And want to marry so bad I'm nearly froze;
> When I lay down at night my thoughts are busy
> With the phantom of my angelic Lizzie;
> When in Morpheus's embrace I'm sleeping,
> Her image comes round my pillow creeping.[48]

Until a few weeks before his death, Lizzie played the dutiful wife to her more flamboyant husband. (Mrs. Ella S. Brown, a contemporary of Aunt Bama, informed me that the colonel was quite a lady's man and had a mistress; "He was an overbearing man!" she remarked.)[49] In 1889, the Falkners planned to move to Memphis; then the colonel decided to remain in Ripley, run for the legislature, and develop his railroad. We can only speculate on the impact of his decision, coupled with alleged infidelities and the Falkner-Thurmond tensions. On 23 October 1889 the *Ripley Advertiser* reported, "Mrs. Col. W. C. Falkner and her daughter, Mrs. Effie Campbell, left for Memphis this morning. Mrs. Falkner will reside permanently in Memphis." Lizzie had left him. Two days later, Falkner drafted his will, leaving to Lizzie "a child's part of the income" from his estate. After the colonel's death, Lizzie returned to Ripley and the family home.

Frequently, it is impossible to separate the Falkners from the Sartorises—the dominant, arrogant men, the determined women, and, perhaps, the long-suffering wives who occupied inconspicuous positions in life and in fiction. William Faulkner remembered for Cantwell the statue of his great-grandfather. Typical of the colonel, he commissioned an eight-foot statue sometime about 1887, to be given to the town of Ripley and to be erected in the square as a memorial to the town's most distinguished citizen. The statue was designed and cast in plaster by Chancey Joseph Rogers of Grand Junction, Tennessee, then sent to Italy to be carved in Carrara marble. It was returned after the colonel's death. With continuing hostilities with the Thurmond faction, it was kept for several years in the kitchen of the family house (a separate building attached to the main house by a passageway). Later Colonel Falkner's son commissioned a base for it from the same Rogers and moved the statue to the family plot in Ripley cemetery.[50]

The monument still towers over every other grave there. The colonel's right hand (now missing its extended fingers, which were allegedly shot off by a drunken descendant of Thurmond) is extended toward the entrance to the cemetery, in front of which runs his railroad. His left hand is tucked into a pocket, a lifetime habit, to hide the missing fingers he lost in the Mexican War while AWOL from camp, shot by Mexicans while attempting to molest a young Mexican girl. Behind the man is a stack of books, representing his published works. With a few minor changes, this monument appears, vividly described, in the concluding chapter of *Sartoris*: "He stood on a stone pedestal, in his frock coat and bare-headed, one leg slightly advanced and one hand resting on the stone pylon beside him. His head was lifted a little in that gesture of haughty pride which repeated itself generation after generation with a fateful fidelity, his back to the world and his carven eyes gazing out across the valley where his railroad ran."[51]

Although William Faulkner loved and hated the South, he admired his great-grandfather while having no illusions about him. Something about the Colonel's humanitarianism as well as his arrogance is reflected in the epitaph that Faulkner gives to the colonel's fictional counterpart:

> For man's enlightenment he lived
> By man's ingratitude he died
> Pause here, son of sorrow; remember death[52]

If John Sartoris was "the virus" that infected succeeding generations, then William C. Falkner and his descendants are also contagious. Once infected by them, one is tempted to shout, as Aunt Jenny might, "Damn you Falkners! Damn you! Damn you!"

Notes

1. William Faulkner, *The Unvanquished* (New York: New American Library, 1959), p. 160.

2. William Faulkner, *Sartoris* (New York: New American Library, 1953, 1964), pp. 298–99.

3. Ibid., p. 87.

4. William Faulkner, "Mississippi," *Holiday*, April 1954, pp. 35–46.

5. Alfred Kazin, *On Native Grounds* (New York: Doubleday & Co., 1956), p. 351.

6. William Faulkner, "Sherwood Anderson: An Appreciation," *Atlantic Monthly*, June 1953, pp. 27–29.

7. Faulkner, "Mississippi."

8. William Faulkner, *Light in August* (New York: Random House Vintage, 1952); see chapter 20. Throughout the novel, Hightower refers to his Civil War ancestor as "the ghost."

9. William Faulkner, *Absalom, Absalom!* (New York: Random House Modern Library, 1951), pp. 11–12.

10. Robert Cantwell, "The Faulkners: Recollections of a Gifted Family," *New World Writing #2* (New York: New American Library, 1952), pp. 300–15.

11. *Sartoris*, pp. 19–20.

12. Interview with William Faulkner, August 1959.

13. William Faulkner, *Requiem for a Nun* (New York: New American Library, 1954), p. 202.

14. Ibid., p. 203.

15. Ibid.

16. Information provided in letters from Andrew Brown to the author.

17. Though never formally adopted, J. W. T. Falkner I was regarded as an adopted son. Thompson began a family Bible, which he passed on to his "adopted son" and through succeeding generations of elder sons in the Falkner family. The Bible is presently in the possession of James W. Faulkner.

18. *Requiem for a Nun*, p. 203.

19. *Ibid.*

20. *Sartoris*, p. 41.

21. *War of the Rebellion: A Compilation of the Union and Confederate Armies* (Washingon, D.C., 1880–1901), II, 868–69.

22. The record of the election appears in Augustus L. P. Varian's *Old Ord's Journal*, ed. Andrew Brown. Typescript in the Mississippi State Department of Archives and History, Jackson, Mississippi.

23. *Sartoris*, p. 202.

24. Documents relating to Colonel Falkner's Civil War service are located in William C. Falkner Papers, Old Records Section, Adjutant General's Office, National Archives, Washington, D.C.

25. *The Unvanquished*, p. 139.

26. An account of the remodeling of the Falkner home appears in issues of the Ripley, Mississippi, *Southern Sentinel* in 1884 and a detailed description of the house may be found in WPA Project, *Source Material for A History of Tippah County*, State of Mississippi Department of Archives and History, Jackson, Mississippi.

27. *Sartoris*, p. 299.

28. *The Unvanquished*, p. 142.

29. *Requiem for a Nun*, p. 310.

30. *Sartoris*, p. 35.

31. The history of the Falkner railroad is very confused, especially during the early years. The information used here comes from a variety of sources on American railroad history. Some information was provided to the author in letters from Andrew Brown. The full story of Falkner's road is yet to be told. New information is contained in a ledger which L. D. Brodsky will soon release. James M. Faulkner possesses another ledger, which Murry Falkner used as a scrapbook, the pages pasted over with bird pictures! When this new material becomes available, Colonel Falkner's role in railroading may be more accurately assessed.

32. Interview with John W. T. Falkner, Jr., August 1959.

33. *Circuit Records of Tippah County, Issue of the Town of Ripley, 1886*, Cases nos. 282 and 285.

34. Bama F. McLean to author, 25 November 1955.

35. Andrew Brown to author, 11 September 1959.

36. *The Unvanquished*, p. 140.

37. Ripley, Mississippi, *Southern Sentinel*, 17 August 1889.

38. Andrew Brown to author, 23 October 1955. See also, *Chancery Records of Tippah County, Will Book I*, pp. 155–59.

39. Andrew Brown to author, 23 October 1955; *Chancery Records Will Book I*, pp. 155–59.

40. Andrew Brown to author, 7 August 1957.

41. Andrew Brown to author, 2 March 1962.

42. Quoted in *Biographical and Historical Memories of Mississippi* (1891), pp. 713–14.

43. Recounted to author by William H. Anderson, August 1959.

44. These stories were recounted in visits with the Falkner family in August 1959, and updated in an interview with James M. Faulkner in August 1983.

45. Some of the stories about the Falkner women are recounted in letters from Andrew Brown to the author and from meetings with the Falkner family in 1959.

46. This incident is recorded in Robert Coughlan, *The Private World of William Faulkner* (New York: Harper & Brothers, 1954).

47. A more detailed account of this story appears in James M. Faulkner's "Auntee Owned Two," *Southern Review*, 8 (October 1972), 836–44.

48. *The Siege of Monterey* was Colonel Falkner's first book, a long epic poem about the Mexican War and a sentimental love story, interlaced with numerous autobiographical comments. In the same year, he also produced a short sentimental novel, *The Spanish Heroine*. In 1881, he returned to writing and produced his most famous novel, *The White Rose of Memphis*, followed in 1882 by *The Little Brick Church* and in 1884 by *Rapid Ramblings in Europe*. The story is frequently told that when William Faulkner was a boy and his teacher asked what he wanted to be when he grew up, he responded that he wanted to be a writer like his great-granddaddy.

49. Interview with Ella S. Brown, August 1959.

50. The history of the statue is a composite of information gained in personal interviews in 1959 and from letters to the author from Beulah Mae Price of Corinth, Mississippi.

51. *Sartoris*, p. 299.

52. Ibid.

On the Roots of the Sartoris Family

Franklin E. Moak*

"Genealogy is poppycock. Particularly in America, where only what a man takes and keeps has any significance and where all of us have a common ancestry and the only house from which we can claim descent with any assurance is the Old Bailey. . . . And I reckon a Sartoris can have a little vanity and poppycock, if he wants it." As if he were quoting from the scriptures, John Sartoris, William Faulkner's fictional head of the Sartoris family, says these words. The phrasing of his epigraph and the description of his monument in the last chapter of *Sartoris* leave little doubt that Colonel John Sartoris (1823–76) is based largely upon Colonel

*This essay was written for this volume and is published here for the first time by permission of the author. Former Dean Franklin E. Moak has been researching the genealogy of William Faulkner's family for more than twenty years; this is the first account of his results. Like Faulkner, he is a citizen of Oxford, Mississippi.

William C. Falkner (1825–89). His brother, James Word Falkner (1832–?), moreover, was apparently the prototype for his fictional brother, the Carolina Bayard.

James Word Falkner was about ten years old when his father died in St. Genevieve County, Missouri. He and William were part of a large family left to their widowed mother, but little is known of the other children except for Caroline who married John W. Perringer and moved to Kansas and later to Oregon. Much earlier, before the Civil War, James moved with his mother to Ripley, Mississippi. Shortly afterward, he probably became the first in his family to attend college, graduating with a law degree from the University of Mississippi in 1860 after studying with one of America's best legal minds, Professor William F. Stearns. James Word Falkner married Helen Hancock of Memphis in 1861 and established himself in law practice with his brother William in Ripley. When war broke out, he joined his brother's unit, ultimately rising to the rank of lieutenant-colonel. If he enjoyed much less glamor in his military pursuits than his older brother William, James nevertheless was in several serious engagements, including the Battle of Seven Pines on 31 May–1 June 1862.

James Word Falkner's first assignment was as a first lieutenant in Captain Storey's company in the 2nd Regiment of the Mississippi Volunteers. He was left sick at Staunton, Virginia, on 18 June 1862, and again at Richmond on 9 August 1862, before being furloughed for thirty days. When his commission expired on 25 September 1862, he was dropped from the rolls and classified as a "deserter" on 1 October. During November and December of 1862 he was marked "absent without leave." But at some later point, he became captain of Company L, 1st Regiment of the Mississippi Cavalry and was captured at Holly Springs on 16 May 1863. He subsequently appeared on the roll of prisoners of war at Johnson's Island. On 3 May 1864 he was transferred to Hammond U.S.A. General Depot with a diagnosis of chronic diarrhea. According to Civil War records in Washington, he was five feet, eight inches tall, had hazel eyes, dark hair, and dark skin. He returned to Ripley after the war, practiced law there for a number of years, and then moved to Belen in Quitman County where he was still living when his son James, Jr., enrolled at the University of Mississippi in the 1890s. James, Jr., became a judge in the Indian Territory of Oklahoma and later practiced law in Los Angeles where he is believed to have died. He was the father of Brown and Eugene Falkner who, as children, visited for lengthy periods of time in Oxford and were not only cousins but also playmates and friends of William Faulkner and his two brothers.

There is little in James Word Falkner's life to suggest Carolina Bayard except his appearance, perhaps, and his role in the early years of the Civil War; but there are these general ways in which Faulkner seems to have acknowledged him in developing the Sartoris family. The same is true for Old Bayard, the son of John Sartoris, who is loosely based on J. W. T.

Falkner, the son of Colonel William C. Falkner. Again there is at least one broad allusion — it is the encounter that Old Bayard has with an automobile, not unlike what J. W. T. experienced often. And in the next generation, John Sartoris has the kind of obscurity which seems to suggest generally that assigned to Murry Falkner, William Faulkner's father; while in the fourth generation, William Faulkner's failure to achieve in World War I what he wished in action and reputation is echoed in Young Bayard Sartoris, while his dreams are projected onto Lieutenant John Sartoris (1898–1918).

These are general similarities between the Sartoris and Falkner families. They may remain general because there is also a decisive difference between the two family lines. While in *Sartoris* the fictional family is viewed as aristocracy which, through the generations, decays, the story of the Falkner family is one of success. J. W. T. Falkner, for example, the Young Colonel, far exceeded his father: he was a bank president, railroad president, sometime university professor, university trustee, and legislator. Murry Falkner served as business manager and financial secretary of the University of Mississippi and lived in what was probably the best faculty house on campus. His son, William, won the Nobel Prize for Literature.

Still, the decadence which is portrayed in *Sartoris* is not unlike what the Falkners in Oxford certainly observed from day to day and year to year. It is only natural that as some of the Snopeses began to strive for and achieve upward mobility, their values, particularly the negative ones, became more visible, thus giving the illusion of increasing decadence among the older families, when, in fact, that decadence had been for generations built into that stratum of society. A case could be made for the decadence, as William Faulkner viewed it through the Sartoris family, that existed in the early part of the twentieth century being merely the residue of an earlier period when the social and economic structure of the Old South was undergoing radical changes. The alternative to decay would be a kind of ruthless ambition or a kind of shoddiness that Faulkner portrays in the Snopes family. It is just possible, in fact, that the other side of Colonel Falkner would be the making of a Snopes tradition, but this is something that William Faulkner did not live long enough to pursue: his postage stamp was too large and inexhaustible for him to cover during his own lifetime.

"Anything but Earth": The Disastrous and Necessary Sartoris Game

François L. Pitavy*

I

House painter or power plant keeper, shrimper or bootlegger, farmer and horse breeder or landlord in a brothel, dandy and bohemian poet, or one of the "dead" pilots, parading in his Royal Air Force uniform and officer's stick, even limping — Faulkner devised and sometimes flaunted an impressive range of self-images as so many masks by which he managed to project and protect himself, through his life. The ambiguous terms of his recognition, so as to remain free for the work to come, helped to retain what in the 1933 preface to *The Sound and the Fury* he superbly called "that ecstasy, that eager and joyous faith and anticipation of surprise which the yet unmarred sheet beneath my hand held inviolate and unfailing, waiting for release."[1] Feistily defending his privacy (as in the 1953 essay by this name) and thus his creative power, Faulkner indeed never ceased to reassert that "the writer's only responsibility is to his art."[2]

Some of those (im)*persona*(tions) may admittedly have been temporary masks, deadpan mystifications, even verging on the tall tale. But the different possible "biographies" they made up (never pure fantasy, as they always originated in some experience, however limited and transient) were ultimately for private more than public use, experience and fiction in Faulkner being the obverse and reverse of a one and same project. It then appears that the two more *representative* masks in his work are that of the *poet* — that is, etymologically, the maker, the creator — and that of the *hero*.

Significantly, the latter seems to have preceded the former. In 1918 Faulkner finally managed to sign up with the Royal Air Force and went to Toronto to begin training as a pilot. But, like Cadet Lowe, he remained only an "embryonic ace": "they had stopped the war on him."[3] Faulkner never met the lightning death in the sky of France he may have dreamed of like many of his contemporaries; he never even made the crash "landing in luck" of his first printed short story; he probably never even flew. The "giant in him"[4] had to pit himself against more vital risks and find another path to immortality: he became a poet and took up literature. Whence the recurrence of heroes and *poets* in his work: representing the two major dimensions of his desire and what appear to be the two major clusters of his phantasmic images (especially in his early work), these two sets of figures rest beyond any pose or juvenile mystification — indeed too close to be explored and *ex-pressed* in any significant way other than fictitious.

*This essay has been written for this volume and is published here for the first time with permission of the author.

In their achieved expressions, the two figures are structurally and thematically interrelated and stand as inverted mirrors of each other (vide Hightower and his grandfather, Darl and Jewel), or are even fused, as in the "up-palm" and pontific horseman Sutpen, hero and (would-be) demiurge.

The very defects—or the imbalance—in Faulkner's third novel, *Sartoris*, make it of special interest here. At the time when Faulkner discovers the *locus* of his work, when the "little postage stamp of native soil" is "sublimated" into the Yoknapatawpha "cosmos,"[5] not only do the heroic figures still predominate (as was already the case in his first novel, *Soldiers' Pay*), but the interrelationship of the hero and the poet remains unrealized.

Horace Benbow is a *persona* of the poet, who has "produced one almost perfect vase of clear amber, . . . richly and chastely serene, which he kept always on his night table and called by his sister's name in the intervals of apostrophizing both of them impartially in his moments of rhapsody over the realization of the meaning of peace and the unblemished attainment of it, as 'Thou still unravished bride of quietness.' "[6] The "air of fine and delicate futility" (161) and the incestuous attachment to a sister who must remain chaste, unblemished, designate him as an older brother to Quentin Compson. More profoundly, effete poet and creator though he be, Horace Benbow clearly maintains the same libidinal relationship with a "thing of beauty" as Quentin Compson with his sister and as Faulkner with the act of writing, when he decided, after he had "shut a door between [himself] and all publishers' addresses and book lists," to create for his private use and ecstatic enjoyment what would become *The Sound and the Fury*: "I said to myself, Now I can write. Now I can make myself a vase like that which the old Roman kept at his bedside and wore the rim slowly away with kissing it. So I, who had never had a sister and was fated to lose my daughter in infancy, set out to make myself a beautiful and tragic little girl."[7] The overdetermination of meaning in the vase/urn image renders almost redundant the reference to Keats—in Faulkner's eyes the paragon and paradigm of poets.

But Horace Benbow does not stand in any precise relation to the Sartoris myth; he does not appear as an inverted mirror image of the heroic figures in the novel. Such lack of perfected and meaningful structure may have been the profound reason that Faulkner complied with his publisher's request that he discard part of the Benbow material of *Flags in the Dust* and even contributed with Ben Wasson (as a comparison of texts demonstrates beyond doubt) to the final making of a novel clearly dominated by heroes.

Sartoris is peopled with ancestors-at-arms, gallant and glamorous cavalrymen, daredevil horsemen and pilots—all heroic doubles, that is, ideal, inaccessible figures of being. Thus the novel is at once overshadowed by the silhouette of the eponymous hero, Colonel Sartoris, a shadow all the more "palpable" (the word recurs three times in the first paragraph), in the room given over to the reminiscing of two old men, as death has rendered his presence — his bones — ineradicable:

> Freed as he was of time and flesh, he was a far more palpable presence than either of the two old men who sat shouting periodically into one another's deafness. . . . John Sartoris seemed to loom still in the room, above and about his son, with his bearded, hawklike face. . . .
>
> The bowl of the pipe was ornately carved, and it was charred with much usage, and on the bit were the prints of his father's teeth, where they had left the very print of his ineradicable bones as though in enduring stone, like the creatures of that prehistoric day that they were too grandly conceived and executed either to exist very long or to vanish utterly when dead from an earth shaped and furnished for punier things. (1–2)[8]

At the close of the novel, the trip to the cemetery — an almost obliged topos of the literature, and of the experience, of the South — ends with a description of the monument to the colonel, "Soldier, Statesman, Citizen of the World," frozen in "that gesture of haughty pride which repeated itself generation after generation with a fateful fidelity" (375): a confirmation of the prestige of the founding (great-grand) father, a recognition that such prestige bears a generic name — Sartoris (without a first name, as is at once told by the title) — a name which is also a destiny.

Thus the Sartoris myth does not merely feed upon constant reminiscing, as in the beginning of the novel. The fascination exerted by the hero immobilized in death fashions its own code, ordering the behavior of the succeeding generations: this is the Sartoris game, in which the players' — the pawns' — movements have become the necessary figures defining the game itself; they can exercise no freedom in the conduct of the game, but keep replaying the first round (yet with a difference and degradation):

> the dusk was peopled with ghosts of glamorous and old disastrous things. And if they were just glamorous enough, there was sure to be a Sartoris in them, and then they were sure to be disastrous. Pawns. But the Player, and the game He plays. . . . He must have a name for His pawns, though. But perhaps Sartoris is the game itself — a game outmoded and played with pawns shaped too late and to an old dead pattern, and of which the Player Himself is a little wearied. (380)

The first player of the Sartoris game is the eponymous hero's brother, Bayard, a daredevil who "had been rather a handful even for Sartorises" (9). Despite the "mellow splendor" cast over the tale by Miss Jenny's recounting, Bayard's last gesture is no more than the "hare-brained prank" of a "heedless and reckless" boy (9): in a vain attempt to retrieve anchovies forgotten in the commissary tent of General Pope, he gets himself shot in the back by a cook hidden under the mess. Three generations and another war later, the great-grandnephew Johnny, bearing the dead ancestor's first name, literally thumbs his nose at death when he jumps out of his plane set on fire by a German plane he had deliberately dared, even though he knew that he stood no chance before it. John's twin brother, Bayard (the compulsion to repeat the game seems written into his first name), obsessed by the death of his brother whom he failed to pick up and save with his own plane, plays with death in his turn, riding a wild stallion and a no less wild automobile (but he also plays with the death of others, as he indirectly brings about that of his grandfather in an automobile accident), and ends mimicking the death of John, getting himself killed testing a new plane which he knew to be unsafe. Only in death can he coincide with his ideal being, that twin part of himself. But unlike his great-granduncle, he cannot claim the alibi of a war: the reenacting of the game is also a degradation. That is why the Sartoris game seems "outmoded" and a little wearisome: "there is death in the sound of it, and a glamorous fatality, like silver pennons downrushing at sunset, or a dying fall of horns along the road to Roncevaux."[9]

II

Beyond its sheer recurrence, what does the Sartoris death signify? The ways to that manner of death, the images applied to the heroes and the elements connected with them reveal the desire, or the dream, behind or beyond the game.

The first instrument (or vehicle) of the game is of course the horse, so intimately a part of the heroic dream that man and beast can even appear as a single centaur (13). As everywhere in Faulkner, horse and horseman are clearly connected with the two most unsubstantial elements, air and fire, indicating surge and flight, freedom of vision, inspiration, dream.[10] When General Stuart (whom the first Bayard follows and emulates) is seen in full gallop, "his long tawny locks, tossing to the rhythm of his speed, appeared as gallant flames smoking with the wild and self-consuming splendor of his daring" (14). Bayard and Stuart significantly emerge from Miss Jenny's retelling as "two *angels* valiantly fallen" (9; my italics) — an image occurring again in connection with young Bayard telling of the war (while swilling almost raw liquor with MacCallum): "he fell to talking of the war. Not of combat, but rather of a life peopled by young men like fallen *angels*, and of a *meteoric* violence like that of fallen *angels*, beyond heaven or hell and partaking of both: doomed immortality and immortal doom" (126; my italics). Bayard and Stuart are also "sudden as meteors" in the "military sky," or seem "like two flaming stars garlanded with Fame's burgeoning laurel" (10).[11] The wild, saddleless stallion that young Bayard manages to ride briefly becomes an almost obtrusive Pegasus: "The beast burst like bronze unfolding wings" (133). And when young Bayard courts death in his headlong races in the country, the automobile again and again shoots "upward" (150).

Horse riders, automobile racers, or daredevil pilots, the Sartorises all appear as (would-be) conquerors of the sky, tempted by one impossible, oxymoronic dream: *crashing upward.* The first Bayard rides up a knoll to General Pope's commissary tent and "jump[s] his horse over the breakfast table" (17), when he is shot to death. John, too, senses that his destiny must be met upward. As a young man, he makes a poor attempt in a balloon (71–73), then soon carries on his (death) wish: despite his twin brother's frantic efforts "to keep him from going up there" (43, 45, 127), he disappears in the sky, significantly leaving no corpse ("no body to be returned clumsily to the earth" [74]). Like a shooting star, he is entirely consumed on his brief orbit: a sublime conflagration leaving no scoria, the dream operating without any remainder — or remains. Thus in the eyes of his twin brother — his earthbound other half — John appears to have achieved what Bayard vainly pursues, his unrealizable wish: "If . . . you could only crash upward, burst; anything but earth" (203).

For such is Bayard's tragedy: to him, any "normal," down-to-earth activity must be only temporary respite or forgetfulness: "he had become submerged in a monotony of days, had been snared by a rhythm of activities repeated and repeated until his muscles grew so familiar with them as to get his body through the days without assistance from him at all. He had been so neatly tricked by earth, that ancient Delilah, that he was not aware that his locks were shorn" (204).[12] Then, "coming dazed out of sleep," he realizes that the "sunny valleys" (that is, the two "horizontal" elements, earth and water, as opposed to the "verticality" of air and fire, to his great-granduncle's horse and to his brother's plane) are not for him,[13] and he yearns again for the "cold *peaks* of savage despair . . . , among black and savage *stars*" (205; my italics).

Just after his car accident, Bayard symbolically reenacts the death of John (before he tries to *realize* his imitation, and fails in the attempt, as he crashes *down*): gathering up John's mementos (including a photograph) from a chest in the attic, he burns them all while Elnora's mellow crooning is heard "along the sunny reaches of the air" (215). While he masochistically fuels his sense of guilt by "killing" John anew, he also *sublimates* the figure of John and thus satisfies at once his brother's, and his own, desire, by severing John's ties with this puny earth and refining him into pure light.

Later, temporarily immobilized by his accident, he does recognize the two irreconcilable dimensions of his destiny: "Far above him now the peaks among the black and savage stars, and about him the valleys of tranquillity and of peace" (254). But Sartorises are made for peaks alone. No more than the earth will Narcissa succeed in ensaring him: he deserts her and dies at the time his son is born.[14]

Thus the Sartorises achieve nothing, and the sound of their name is no more than "a dying fall of horns." Paradoxically, it is not that with them the dream remains unrealized: on the contrary, they try too literally to realize it and so burn themselves to death in the attempt. Yet death remains the only way the hero has to justify or verify the beauty of his dreams — dissolving in the illuminating coincidence with it, like a shooting star or a "furious meteor."[15] The trouble with the Sartoris hero is that he has "not waited for Time and its furniture to teach him that the end of wisdom is to dream high enough not to lose the dream in the seeking of it" (74). Contrary to appearances, he has not dreamed high enough or, rather, long enough, preferring the "now now now" of the impatient idealist to the "tomorrow and tomorrow and tomorrow" of the patient, biding, and enduring man who has not forgotten "the dark and tragic figure of the Earth, his mother" (the concluding words of "Carcassonne").

The Sartoris game may be disastrous, but in the last analysis it is not outmoded. Rather, it stands as an inevitable reminder that the pride of man is not just to be capable of endurance, but also to have "the courage, the recklessness" to rise to "the flash, the instant of sublimation." The aim of the *poet* is precisely to try to "preserve" and "prolong" that flash,[16] to conjoin the endurance and the dream, to harness together the two irreconcilable dimensions of man's desire — horizontality and verticality or, as Addie Bundren puts it, "doing" and "words": "I would think how words go straight up in a thin line, quick and harmless, and how terribly doing goes along the earth, clinging to it, so that after a while the two lines are too far apart for the same person to straddle from one to the other."[17]

The Sartoris hero has disastrously lost touch with the enduring earth, but he has in him the courage and the recklessness of the poet (which Horace Benbow does not have). Thumbing his nose at death, John Sartoris may even know the ultimate vanity, or contingency, of the poet's attempt, as is suggested in the conclusion of "All the Dead Pilots": "[the flash] can be preserved and prolonged only on paper: a picture, a few written words that any match, a minute and harmless flame that any child can engender, can obliterate in an instant. A one-inch sliver of sulphur-tipped wood is longer than memory or grief; a flame no longer than a sixpence is fiercer than courage or despair." But "the basest of all things" would be "to be afraid," as Faulkner said in Stockholm. The necessary attempt at the impossible is "worth the agony and the sweat."

Notes

1. "An Introduction for *The Sound and the Fury*," ed. James B. Meriwether, *Southern Review*, 8 (October 1972), 709.

2. *Lion in the Garden: Interviews with William Faulkner, 1926–1962*, ed. James B. Meriwether and Michael Millgate (New York: Random House, 1968), p. 239.

3. *Soldiers' Pay* (New York: Boni and Liveright, 1926), p. 7.

4. "And Now What's To Do," *A Faulkner Miscellany*, ed. James B. Meriwether (Jackson: Univ. Press of Mississippi, 1974), p. 146.

5. *Lion in the Garden*, p. 255.

6. *Sartoris* (New York: Harcourt, Brace and Company, 1929), p. 182; hereafter cited in the text.

7. "An Introduction for *The Sound and the Fury*," p. 710.

8. These two paragraphs do not appear in *Flags in the Dust*; moreover, the novel then opened with the actual conversation between old man Falls and old Bayard. So the reordering and the addition of material at once set *Sartoris* in the palpable and enduring shadow of the dead hero and more clearly announce the "dying fall" of the ending.

9. The last four paragraphs on the Sartoris game are adapted from my article, "Le héros, la guerre et le rêve: L'idéalisme faulknérien revisité," *L'Arc* (Editions Le Jas), 84–85 (3rd trimester 1983), 93–108.

10. That the soaring horse is a figure of air and fire and comes to symbolize the poet's dream is evident in the *vision* of Jewel's horse by Darl, in the relationship of Hightower to his galloping grandfather, in the idealization of the horseman Sutpen by Wash Jones, and of course in the poet's identification, in "Carcasonne," with the *"buckskin pony with eyes like blue electricity and a mane of tangled fire, galloping up the hill and right off into the high heaven of the world"* (*Collected Stories* [New York: Random House, 1950], p. 895.

11. Images of "shooting star," "orbit" or "rocket" also occur on pp. 18, 358, 375.

12. The sense of submersion, oppression, and choking under a "sagging" sky prevails through Bayard's first night at the MacCallums' (pp. 320–22).

13. The earth is one of the temptations to which the Marshall submits the Corporal in *A Fable*.

14. In "Bayard Sartoris: Suicidal or Foolhardy?" (*Southern Literary Journal*, 15 [Fall 1982], 54–60), Arthur H. Blair argues that the addition of the "suicidal temptation" in the transformation of *Flags in the Dust* into *Sartoris* (p. 322) proves that Bayard is more foolhardy than suicidal. This seems to me a superficial reading of Bayard's actions: if he refuses to kill himself with a *shotgun*, it is because he must, even though unconsciously, reenact the manner of his brother's death, so as to assuage his own sense of guilt in having failed to save him and also, more profoundly, to identify with the admired and *sublimated* (hence inaccessible) brother. Thus the anguish over the brother's death experienced during the night at the MacCallums' cannot end in death by shotgun. All of Bayard's actions demonstrate that his behavior is suicidal, but he does refuse such *deliberate* suicide as would invert and mock John's own reckless and laughing manner of meeting his death.

15. This phrase is taken up from the end of the Faulkner's review of *Test Pilot*, by Jimmy Collins, in *Essays, Speeches, and Public Letters*, ed. James B. Meriwether (New York: Random House, 1965), p. 192.

16. "All the Dead Pilots," in *Collected Stories*, p. 531.

17. *As I Lay Dying* (New York: Random House, 1964), p. 165.

War Birds and the Politics of Refusal

Bruce Kawin*

I

At the end of "Ad Astra" (1930), someone asks Bayard Sartoris what time it is. He insists that it's "Twelfth" November 1918, even though it must be after midnight and into the thirteenth of November, the second full day of peace. What Bayard is refusing here is to enter the continuity of the calendar of peace, the world of the living; he prefers instead — or is doomed — to remain a ghost, one who is as good as dead because whether or not he recognizes that part of him has already died, his authentic life — or, better, his authenticity — is based in the time of death and the region of war. Although the war can end, the time of war cannot; although the countries can find peace, this kind of soldier cannot — not because he needs to be in some war but because in the center of this particular war he has found his own center which is also his fate, and in the case of Bayard as Faulkner has imagined him here, both center and fate are the energy of self-destruction, of refusal to live, refusal to go on. Somehow he has been ruined; he can no longer be good for anything but death.

In *A Fable* (1954), an old porter tells a runner " 'that all we ever needed to do was just to say, Enough of this — us, not even the sergeants and corporals, but just us, Germans and Colonials and Frenchmen and all the other foreigners in the mud here, saying together: Enough. Let them that's already dead and maimed and missing be enough of this — a thing so easy and simple that even human man, as full of evil and sin and folly as he is, can understand and believe it this time'."[1] And the runner, putting this in his own terms sometime later, tells a sentry: " 'For six thousand years we labored under the delusion that the only way to stop a war was to get together more regiments and battalions than the enemy could, or vice versa, and hurl them upon each other until one lot was destroyed and, the one having nothing left to fight with, the other would stop fighting. We were wrong, because yesterday morning, by simply declining to make an attack, one single French regiment stopped us all'."[2] What is being refused here, in a politics of passive resistance influenced not only by Thoreau and Gandhi but also by whatever Faulkner himself had learned between the time he desperately wanted to fight in World War I and the time he contemplated the Korean War from the perspective of the Atomic Age — is killing.

Where Bayard refuses to go on with life, the soldiers in *A Fable* refuse

*This essay was written for this volume and is published here for the first time by permission of the author. At one point this essay draws upon material originally appearing in *Faulkner's MGM Screenplays*, by Bruce F. Kawin (Knoxville: University of Tennessee Press, 1982), pp. 258–60.

to go on with death. Their strategies are very similar — both are what psychologists would identify as passive-aggressive stances; that is, a strategy of winning by not doing what the opponent wants to be done, for instance, not moving off a train track, nor reacting to a stimulus — and appeal not only to a politics of refusal but also to something that Faulkner seems always to have found attractive: the power of passivity, a moving without motion that signaled eternity to him when he admired it in Keats's "Ode on a Grecian Urn," connected somehow with female sexuality when he described some of his heroines in terms of that ode (especially in *Flags in the Dust* and *Sanctuary*) or when, as in the case of Eula Varner, he dropped the ode and rhapsodized on the irresistibly sexual magnetism of indolence, and was further connected with his lifelong investigation of what it means to endure and to prevail. All these things are examples of passive-aggressive behavior, often expressed oxymorons and "un"-words, as in this example from *A Fable*: "it would not matter whether Authority knew about it or not, since even ruthless and all-powerful and unchallengeable Authority would be impotent before that massed unresisting undemanding passivity."[3] But this is not simply a question of indolence or nonaction; to endure and prevail involves winning, and not by default. It involves power and choice, integrity and vision. And it is a phenomenally effective strategy, for just as no one can make Bayard live when he does not want to, no one can make *A Fable*'s Corporal betray his vision or become a hired killer.

Both these stories are set in 1918; both are about the end of the war; both are, of course, by Faulkner. If the strategies of refusal are common, the ends are entirely different, for "Ad Astra" is a story of not being able to live outside the limbo of war, and *A Fable* is about life's decision to let war die. What happened between the writing of these two works? Hitler, who made war necessary; Gandhi, who made nonviolent resistance an effective political program; the A-Bomb and H-Bomb, which made war impossible; the Nobel Prize, which may on a more personal level have given Faulkner the impression that what he said about the state of the world might be listened to; time and chance. What also happened were two important fictions, one of them a filmscript, in which Faulkner and his characters discovered the positive choice for life that can transform the politics of refusal from the path of morose narcissism to that of peace and vision. Those works are "An Odor of Verbena" (1937) from *The Unvanquished*, and *War Birds* (1933).

Before addressing *War Birds* in depth, however, it seems important to offer a few more general remarks on Faulkner's work and on the relations among the themes of fatherhood, tradition, and war. Just as it is a mistake to approach Faulkner simply in terms of local color — the Balzac of Yoknapatawpha — or simply in terms of metaphysics — the latter-day Melville/Conrad — it is misleading to ignore the importance of his filmscripts and of his work on World War I. As I have argued elsewhere,[4] there are many examples of Faulkner's having tried out in treatments and screenplays some of the themes that he would later work into his fiction (of which the chain from *War Birds* to "An Odor of Verbena" to *A Fable* is one of the more obvious), or of his having resolved in a screenplay a problem that he had not been able to resolve in fiction (for instance, the resolution in *Turn About* of the sublimated incest problem in *The Sound and the Fury*). When the scripts are figured into the catalog of Faulkner's work, one pattern that emerges is that of a career-long preoccupation with war — and not only because he was employed at the Warner Brothers propaganda mill during World War II, for many of his best war scripts were written during peacetime, in the 1930s, notably *Turn About*, *War Birds*, and *The Road to Glory*. He wrote more about World War I than he did about any other secondary subject. It was his Wasteland as Quentin Compson's dorm room could never be; it was the place to evaluate the nature of hope, the prospects for humanity, and the value of tradition — rivaled in that role only by the hunter's dream of woods. And the central characters in that landscape were Sartorian if not the doomed twin themselves, John and Bayard, because they were the best way to dramatize the differences between the Civil War and global wars, since they were anchored by tradition in the world of romance and glamor and honor, of homeland and home — values that gave the Civil War its moral fervor and idealistic center, making it a valid symbol for the premodernist world — and since they were also inhabitants of the modernist wreckage, the early twentieth century, trying to live out their glorious heritage in the context of something that was less a war than a bureaucratic morass that smelled of the slaughterhouse and had no more moral center than that which was brought to it by the young men who decided that it ought to have had one.

To struggle with tradition, as Bayard does, is to bring all of these matters forward. Simply to repeat tradition is to fall into patterns of doom; to repeat it while making it new is to endure and prevail. Much of what disturbs the Bayard of "Ad Astra" is that he cannot find a good theater in which to repeat, without adequate revision or renewal, the Sartorian tradition, and this is one — fairly cheap — way of discussing the modernist crisis, a sort of "poor me" attitude that would later be whipped into a frenzy by Ezra Pound in his lament for the lost Roman Empire and that had already found its best parodistic slant in *Ulysses*, if not in *Don Quixote*. In the early Faulkner this tone of self-pity is not as absent as one might wish, but there are moments when he approaches that fire of reinvention that distinguishes, for instance, Wallace Stevens from the rest of the modernists, and where that starts in Faulkner is in *War Birds*, where Bayard learns that the only successful way to repeat the Sartorian tradition is to reinvent it, to go back to its ethical center and find a way to extend its authenticity, without compromise, into the fallen world. And the theater for that *is* World War I, perhaps the last time Faulkner felt one had a choice set in the proper terms, or perhaps the best metaphor, even as late as *A Fable*, for the enhanced modernist crisis brought on by the prospect of nuclear war.

Where this all comes together, oddly enough, is in two similar passages in "Ad Astra" and *A Fable*, where the question of tradition is linked to the problem of fatherhood. In *A Fable* the group commander explains to the division commander that the soldiers must not become aware of how much power they actually have: "They may even stop the wars, as they have done before and will again; ours merely to guard them from the knowledge that it was actually they who accomplished that act. Let the whole vast moil and seethe of man confederate in stopping wars if they wish, so long as we can prevent them learning that they have done so. A moment ago you said that we must enforce our rules, or die. It's no abrogation of a rule that will destroy us. It's less. The simple effacement from man's memory of a single word will be enough. But we are safe. Do you know what that word is? . . . Fatherland."[5] In "Ad Astra" the captured German pilot who had been a baron but has renounced that role — his name in *War Birds* is Dorn — says, "I return home; I say to my father, in the University I haf learned it iss not good; baron I will not be. He cannot believe. He talks of Germany, the fatherland; I say to him, It iss there; so. You say fatherland, I, brotherland, I say, the word *father* iss that barbarism which will be first swept away; it iss the symbol of that hierarchy which hass stained the history of man with injustice of arbitrary instead of moral; force instead of love."[6]

In that passage Dorn has many of the ideas that will become real for Bayard in *War Birds*, but they do not yet have the efficacy to renew the moral landscape of "Ad Astra"; if anything, this is like one of the more helpful remarks that pops up as a pipe dream in *The Iceman Cometh*; nevertheless, it is on target, and Faulkner will let this insight have progressively more weight as his career continues. It is the power of the father as a political force, the notion of the fatherland, that can doom the sons to repetition or prompt them to renewal (which I have sometimes referred to, in such a context, as "repetition in reverse").[7] *A Fable* is explicitly a father/son conflict; "An Odor of Verbena," where old Bayard learns from his father the route to the end of killing, is implicitly a father/son collaboration. *A Fable* is the story of what happens when the men of the warring nations join together in a common goal — the abolition of war, the discovery of their true power; "Ad Astra" is, among other things, the story of how young Bayard is part of, or symbol for, the inability of men to join together and the inhibiting power of the tradition of the fathers:

> "There should never have been an alliance between Frenchmen and Englishmen," the subadar said. He spoke without effort; invisible, his effortless voice had an organ quality, out of all proportion to his size. "Different nations should never join forces to fight for the same object. Let each fight for something different; ends that do not conflict, each in his own way." Sartoris passed us, returning from the fountain, carrying

his bulging cap carefully before him, bottom-up. We could hear the water dripping from it between his footsteps. He became one of the blob of thicker shadow where the bandage gleamed and where Monaghan cursed steadily and quietly. "And each after his own tradition," the subadar said.[8]

Here the subadar is prompted by the sight of Bayard into an approving remark about the importance of observing family and cultural tradition, the way of the fathers which is also the way of isolation: not just of isolationism, which is probably what the subadar is getting at, but also of the absence of solidarity and shared goals. This is a good way to deflate the Great War's pretensions of having represented a group effort for the general welfare, because the goals that were announced as shared were false fronts for more particular greeds and failures, but it is also an unfortunate argument against viable collective action and the sort of broad ethical perspective that the German and *A Fable* are each pointing at.

On the whole, what "Ad Astra" does is to set the terms of Bayard's dead-end depression, to clarify his suicidal dilemma and — despite the later date of composition — to leave him more or less as he was in *Flags in the Dust* (1926–27), much as *Absalom, Absalom!* clarified the suicidal dilemma of Quentin Compson in the earlier *The Sound and the Fury*. Dorn may have a bright idea, but Bayard cannot see his way into the next day, and drunkenness and delusion carry the story to its conclusion. But two seeds of the coming work have been planted: Dorn's character and insights are one, and the other is buried in Monaghan's jest that he will bring Dorn home with him to America after the war.[9] Investigated and given moral force, this joke is central to *War Birds* and to the renewal of the Sartorian tradition that the Bayard of "Ad Astra" is unable to imagine.

II

War Birds was Faulkner's second full-length filmscript, written for MGM — and more particularly for Howard Hawks — in Oxford between late November 1932 and early January 1933. In typescript it was called *A Ghost Story*, which may have been the title Faulkner or Hawks preferred, but *War Birds* was the name of the property on which MGM had been working for several years and the name under which *A Ghost Story* was reproduced and distributed by the Script Department on or before 12 January 1933.[10] It exists in only one draft, despite the two extant titles, and that draft is emphatically a rough one. Whatever it is, *War Birds* is no finished masterpiece. It is too long, often ludicrously melodramatic, full of hysterical dialogue and inefficient subplots. The briefest accurate description of it, I think, would identify it as an adaptation of "All the Dead Pilots" followed by an adaptation of "Ad Astra," but with a happy ending — all of this told by John Sartoris' widow to her son, with the aid of a diary kept by John during the war but actually adapted by Faulkner from the property MGM had assigned him to adapt in the first place, *The Diary of the Aviator*.

In 1926, *Liberty* magazine published serially *The Diary of the Unknown Aviator* under the title of *War Birds*. This anonymous diary, which broke off at the point of the author's death, was largely authentic. It had been written by John McGavock Grider, a young Southerner whose grandfather had served as a captain in the Confederate Army and later became a banker. Major Elliot White Springs, who had served with Grider, rewrote the diary and sold it to *Liberty*, to a publishing house, and to MGM.[11] There is some evidence that Faulkner read the diary when it appeared in *Liberty*.[12] An MGM reader said of it:

> Honestly, this is the best account of a man's part in the war that I have read, it is the most thrilling. It is almost a work of unconscious art. Who touches it touches a man! The air battles are positively unequaled in war literature. I make no bones about detailing a few [i.e., in his synopsis] as he writes them; it was the only way to do the MS justice. What this boy writes makes me, who had such a comparatively feeble part in the war, feel simply toadish — it is epical, romantic, oh, incomparably romantic, on a heroic scale! A picture, and those 3 incomparable young Americans, I should say so![13]

This reader was responding to the diary, however, and not to a treatment by Springs and Merlin Taylor (May 1926) that had been bought by MGM along with the screen rights — a treatment, focused on a ludicrous love triangle, whose only relation to the Faulkner script was some business about pursuing a German aviator who had shot down one of the heroes and who turned out, on his deathbed, to be a relatively sympathetic figure; it had little or no relation to the original diary. (It is, however, quite possible that this treatment gave Faulkner the idea of linking *War Birds* with the story of John Sartoris's death, via the figure of Dorn.) It appears that no other treatments were written until Faulkner submitted a (lost) outline, "Faulkner Story No. 2," which apparently interested Hawks and led to Faulkner's being put back on the MGM payroll despite the fact that he had returned to Oxford after completing the third draft of *Turn About*.

There may be some significance in the fact that the lost treatment or story outline is "Faulkner Story No. 2." Since Faulkner had already written several treatments and had seen *Turn About* nearly to completion (it was filmed as *Today We Live*, 1933), this was not his second story for MGM; it is much more likely that it was the second version of *War Birds* that he had submitted for consideration by Hawks and/or the Story Department and/or the executives in a position to give final approval to the project. There is no record of his first proposal, but it appears to have been rejected. The point of going through all this is to suggest that Faulkner's original plans for adapting the story of the twins may have been very different from what finally became *War Birds*; in Hollywood it is extremely common to have a story kicked around by a number of writers and executives before it comes back for expansion into a screenplay. There is little point in generalizing about Faulkner's decision to make Bayard and John more positive figures, then, because that is just the kind of decision that could have been expected to come from Hawks or—less predictably—from Irving Thalberg; Hawks hated "losers" and said so, and the Bayard of *Flags* is the type that would have irritated Hawks in the extreme. The thing to follow is this: assuming that Faulkner received an instruction to make Bayard a more positive figure and to give the film a happy ending, how did he go about imagining that new story and what did he find out about his characters and about the issues brought up by the story in the process of fulfilling that demand? These questions are not always worth asking, since the suggestions and follow-through may not always be interesting in their own right—but in the case of *War Birds* they are, because what appears as new in *War Birds* continues as an extremely important presence in the fiction written later on. The important issue is not where the idea came from, but that once it showed up, it stuck around. And a number of good ideas came from the *Diary*. One thing that we know for sure was Faulkner's idea was to adapt that diary by way of a revision of the story of the Sartoris brothers, and we know this simply because—as will be discussed later—the studio protested Faulkner's request to be paid for the rights to "Ad Astra" and "All the Dead Pilots," which would certainly not have been the case if they had assigned him to work with that material.

There are many aspects of the diary that might have interested Faulkner and prompted his revision, in *War Birds*, of the story of John and Bayard Sartoris. Grider had left Memphis to join the Royal Flying Corps, had been trained in England, and had fought in France—a course of action similar to that which Faulkner had attempted. Grider's grandfather shared professions with "old Bayard" Sartoris (a banker) and had served in the same war as Colonel John Sartoris (who was modeled on Faulkner's great-grandfather, Colonel William Clark Falkner). Grider began as an enthusiastic romantic, attracted to the war partly because "it's the North and South over again"[14]—his point being that the Germans had better equipment but that the cause of the Allies was just. By 1918, he was capable of writing:

> I have never been serious about anything in my life and now I know I'll never be otherwise again. But my seriousness will be a burlesque for no one will recognize it. Here I am, twenty-four years old, I look forty and I feel ninety. I've lost all interest in life beyond the next patrol. . . . Oh, for a parachute! The Huns are using them now. I haven't a chance, I know, and it's this eternal waiting around that's killing me. I've even lost my taste for likker. It doesn't seem to do me any good now. I guess I'm stale. Last week I actually got frightened in the air and lost my head.

Then I found ten Huns and took them all on and I got one of them down out of control. I got my nerve back by that time and came back home and slept like a baby for the first time in two months. What a blessing sleep is! I know now why men go out and take such long chances and pull off such wild stunts. No discipline in the world could make them do what they do of their own accord. I know now what a brave man is. I know now how men laugh at death and welcome it. I know now why Ball went over and sat above a Hun airdrome and dared them to come up and fight with him. It takes a brave man to even experience real fear. A coward couldn't last long enough at the job to get to that stage.[15]

Much of this is similar to Faulkner's treatment, in many of his works, of the questions of fear and courage and is implicit in the reckless exploits of his overstressed pilots, especially John Sartoris. In the final, undated entry, Grider wrote of the futility of the war effort in terms that not only are politically astute — in fact prophetic — but also return to the question of the legacy of the Civil War.

War is a horrible thing, a grotesque comedy. And it is so useless. This war won't prove anything. All we'll do when we win is to substitute one sort of Dictator for another. In the meantime we have destroyed our best resources. Human life, the most precious thing in the world has become the cheapest. After we've won this war by drowning the Hun in our own blood, in five years time the sentimental fools at home will be taking up a collection for these same Huns that are killing us now and our fool politicians will be cooking up another good war. Why shouldn't they? They have to keep the public stirred up to keep their jobs. . . . The worst thing about this war is that it takes the best. . . . Even those that live thru it will never be fit for anything else. Look at what the Civil War did for the South. It wasn't the defeat that wrecked us. It was the loss of half our manhood and the demoralization of the other half. . . . My grandfather was a Captain in the Confederate Army and served thruout the war. He became a banker, a merchant, a farmer and a good citizen, but he was always a little different from other men and now I know where the difference lay. At the age of seventy he still hadn't gotten over those four years of misery and spiritual damnation. My father used to explain to me that he wasn't himself. But he was himself, that was just the trouble with him. The rest were just out of step.[16]

A few pages later, Grider indirectly suggested what would become one of the major tropes of Faulkner's wartime and postwar ghost story: "I saw a man in Boulogne the other day that I had dreamed I saw killed and I thought I was seeing a ghost. I can't realize that any of them are gone. Surely human life is not a candle to be snuffed out. The English have all turned spiritualistic since the war. I used to think that was sort of far fetched but now it's hard for me to believe that a man ever becomes even a ghost. I have sort of a feeling that he stays just as he is and simply jumps behind a cloud or steps thru a mirror."[17]

Whether or not Faulkner read this diary in 1926 — when he might have drawn on it for some of the details of air combat in *Flags in the Dust* — it is certain that he read it carefully while writing *War Birds*, and more than likely that he respected it. The task he set himself, then, was to adapt this diary while also revising and incorporating the story of John and Bayard. As suggested above, the principal way he accomplished this was by having Caroline Sartoris (here married not to Bayard but to John, and allowed to survive) explain to her son Johnny the circumstances of his father's death by reading to him from the wartime diary she had asked John to keep, and by having some of its passages echo Grider's. Before discussing the climax and resolution of *War Birds*, however, it might be valuable to offer brief summaries of the previous fictions that concerned the twins.

Flags in the Dust (1926–27), like the abbreviated *Sartoris* (1929), tells how the heritage of glorious recklessness begun by John and Bayard Sartoris during the Civil War is ironically fulfilled in the self-destructive exploits of their namesakes during and after World War I. John jumps to his death after his Camel has been mercilessly barraged, before Bayard's eyes, by a German pilot with a "skull and bones" on his plane. Bayard returns to Jefferson overwhelmed by the guilt of having survived. Bayard's wife Caroline has died the year before, and eventually he marries Narcissa Benbow. When he causes the death of old Bayard in an automobile accident, Bayard runs away and finally gets himself killed while testing a plane he has been warned is unsafe. Narcissa refuses to carry on the namesake tradition and gives her and Bayard's son the name of Benbow Sartoris, as if hopeful that that would bring an end to the related tradition of glamorous disaster.

"Ad Astra," set the night after Armistice, features Bayard; a German pilot who was not the one who shot John but who will become the foundation for that character in *War Birds*; Monaghan, who captured the German and jokes about taking him home to America; and several other soldiers who get drunk and come to terms with the possibility that they are all as good as dead but have simply not realized it. No longer soldiers but exhausted beyond the point of returning to civilian innocence, watching their commitments dissolve into anachronisms and illusions (the last image is of one man's crying over his imaginary wife), the men discover that they are in limbo. " 'This life is nothing'," says the German who will not become a baron; Bayard, who is cut off from the viable aspects of the Sartoris tradition, believes that time has stopped; and the subadar who, like the German, is prepared for a life of exile and who will renounce his own title in India, sums it up by saying that " 'All this generation which fought in the war are dead tonight. But we do not yet know it.' "[18]

"All the Dead Pilots" (1931) fills in the story of John Sartoris' death and his rivalry with Captain Spoomer for the favors of a French woman, Antoinette. John makes a bitter game out of releasing Spoomer's dog — who will track Spoomer to Amiens and Antoinette, or else simply grub in the refuse from the enlisted men's mess hall should Spoomer not be in Amiens. Finally John finds his rival with Antoinette, steals his clothes (putting them on an unconscious ambulance driver), and sees Spoomer disgraced when he shows up at the base in the dress of a peasant woman; in revenge, Spoomer has John transferred to a night-flying Camel squadron, indirectly causing his death.

A third story, "With Caution and Dispatch," begun just after *War Birds*, details John's uncautious and interrupted attempts to fly a Camel across the English channel to join his outfit. The only use Faulkner made of this story in *War Birds* was to emphasize John's difficulty in flying Camels. But the other stories posed a serious challenge, as did Grider ("Even those that live thru it will never be fit for anything else"). For although some of the changes Faulkner wrought in this material in the course of writing *War Birds* may have resulted from a desire to give Hawks or the front office what they wanted, and some of them from the sheer practical difficulty or reconciling the *Diary* with the Sartoris storyline, some of them evidently came from Faulkner's own decision to take a new look at the ironic and negative elements of the earlier fictions. The logical twist that makes Johnny Sartoris understand the makeup of the extended family his uncle Bayard has created, for example, is peculiarly Faulkner's and is far more involuted than anything in Hawks's work.

Some of the minor changes Faulkner made may help to clarify the major ones. In "All the Dead Pilots" John is described as having a vocabulary of perhaps two hundred words, and a letter he sends home bears this out. As the author of the diary in *War Birds* he is necessarily more articulate and thoughtful. So that it would be John's son rather than nephew who would have to deal with the question of hating or forgiving Dorn and Antoinette, Bayard is childless while Caroline is married to John. These changes also make the diary a more natural focal point for the unfolding of John's story, as a document Caroline had initially hoped would strengthen the sense of closeness between herself and John but which comes at last to clarify and validate the bonds among the surviving family unit, however unconventionally constituted that family first appears. So that the twins John and Bayard can accumulate to one good man rather than one dead man, Bayard is made more articulate, effective, and concerned than he is in *Flags* or "Ad Astra," and he is led from concerns of revenge on Spoomer and Dorn to an experience of forgiveness—a shift in which Faulkner reinforces, or makes more than a pipe dream, the insight in "Ad Astra" that love and moral force are superior to notions of any "fatherland" or the history of any feud. Monaghan's jest about taking the German home with him is reworked into Bayard's bizarre but elevated gesture of ethical renewal, as he brings home to Caroline the woman who loved John and the man who killed him—a gesture not of morbid attachment to the dark past but of acknowledgment and going onward. When reading over a synopsis of *War Birds* to decide how much of it was new and how much supported Faulkner's demand to be paid for the rights to "Ad Astra" and "All the Dead Pilots," an MGM employee wrote that "There is nothing unusual in this thought because the majority of Americans going overseas were promising to bring back Germans as presents to their friends, etc." It is possible, ironically, that the use of this joke in "Ad Astra" was no more than a reference to this common remark, but by the time the idea was played out in *War Birds*, it should have been clear that something new was going on and that the motives behind Bayard's action were quite obviously "unusual"; one could argue that financial motives led the studio to miss this point, but it remains clear that *War Birds* both proceeded from "Ad Astra" and was something new on its own. It was this disagreement over the rights to the previous stories, by the way, that appears to have stopped the studio from going ahead with the picture. It was never filmed.

What Faulkner did, in terms of the previous fictions, was to revise the outcome of *Flags* while retaining/renewing the theme of the Sartoris tradition, to incorporate most of "All the Dead Pilots," and to augment or reverse many of the most significant aspects of "Ad Astra." To understand what he did that was new, it is necessary to take a look at the climax of the script, a scene in which Bayard does not shoot Dorn.

Up until this point, the story has been fairly simple. Johnny has been told by some kids that the German who helped to raise him, who took him fishing and hunting and taught him about honor — Dorn — was the man who killed his father John during the war. He confronts Dorn, who does not deny it. Caroline gets out John's diary and reads it to Johnny (Faulkner dissolves back and forth between the entries and dramatized re-creations of the events, some of which occur after John's death but are narrated by Caroline as the book remains open). "All the Dead Pilots" plays out, and then "Ad Astra," with the difference that it is Bayard who has shot down Dorn. During the bar scene, there is a fight with Spoomer. A bayonet is aimed at Bayard, but Dorn saves him, taking the thrust of the blade in his own left arm. Dorn wakes up on a cot with Bayard and Antoinette present, and overhears Bayard's telling a departing soldier that, Armistice or not, he intends to avenge his brother ("I'm the same man now I was before eleven this morning. So is he. My brother didn't come back to life at eleven this morning, like in a game for children").[19] Dorn then tells Bayard the story of his life, his decision not to inherit the family title, the loss of his wife and son. Then:

> Bayard: What are you getting at? What's the matter with you?
> Dorn: Still, please. Listen. I will try to tell you.
> (*At the foot of the bed, also unmoving, Antoinette is puzzled, looking from one to the other*)
>> Listen, then. Your brother was slain. Jumped from his burning machine and fell to death.

(CLOCK *to Dorn's hand moving quietly beneath the flap of Bayard's pocket*)

Ha. He fell a long time, that morning, waiting to die. Yes?

Bayard's Voice: (*He draws a long shuddering breath*) Yes.

Dorn's Voice: (*His hand is now inside the pocket; it can be seen to grasp something inside the cloth*)

A long while, alone, looking back at the man who killed him and the brother who could not save him, waiting to die — so?

(*Bayard moves, his tunic pocket jerks away. Dorn's hand moves too. It comes clear, holding Bayard's pistol. Antoinette screams.*)

CUT TO:

(*Bayard standing crouched, tense, still, Dorn on the bed, his eyes open, the pistol in his hand, covering Bayard. Antoinette standing, her hands to her face.*)

Dorn: Do not move. And since that day you hunted the man who slew your brother. And when you found him, the man was not dead. The man lay on a bed and bored you with the history of his life. Do you know why?

(*Bayard does not move nor speak*)

This is why. You have that man who did not die in your power and at your mercy. But unfortunately the circumstances in which that man became the slayer of your brother and the object of your vengeance have passed away, ceased. And worse than that, that man was enabled to do you a small service in the matter of an ill-directed bayonet. That man believed that perhaps this favor might counter balance his debt to you, thinking you were perhaps that sort of man. So he told you what he did in order to remove that counter balance, to free your hand.

Bayard: Free my hand?

Dorn: Free your hand.

(*They look at one another. Suddenly Dorn flips the pistol, catches it by the barrel, the butt extended to Bayard*)

Here.

Bayard: Here?

Dorn: Your pistol, Captain.

(*Bayard puts his hand out slowly. It touches the pistol. They look at one another. Suddenly Bayard grasps the pistol, springs back. Again Antoinette screams. Dorn looks at her.*)

Dorn: Perhaps mademoiselle would like to retire now?

Antoinette: Bayard! Bayard!

Bayard: (*Crouching, glaring at Dorn*) To me? To me?

Dorn: Yes. I thought you were the sort of man whom that accidental favor of the bayonet might incommode. But you are not that sort of man, are you?

Bayard: No.

Dorn: Then send mademoiselle from the room.

Antoinette: Bayard! Bayard!

(*Her hands to her face, she runs forward a step, pauses again in horror. They do not look at her*)

Dorn: Well? Why do you wait? Your brother is slain, but my country is slain; fallen from a greater height than any Camel has ever reached. Shoot, Captain.

(Antoinette watches Bayard, her hands to her face, poised as though to run. Bayard looks down at Dorn, his face wrung, terrible. Slowly the pistol rises, covers Dorn's chest, steadies. They look at one another. Tableau. Then Bayard flings the pistol through window. The fractured glass is in the shape of a star. Antoinette runs forward, falls at Bayard's feet, clutching his knees.)

Antoinette: Thank God! Thank God!

(Bayard stands, his head bent. As DISSOLVE *begins, the star shaped fracture in the glass begins to glow faintly as daylight begins behind it. It is brightest at the instant of complete dissolve, then it begins also to fade.)*[20]

Shortly after this, Caroline tells Johnny of her outrage when she learned that Bayard intended to bring Antoinette and Dorn home with him, as if to "turn your house into a mausoleum of your brother's infidelity and a memorial to his murderer!" She tells how they all came to accept one another. Johnny then goes downstairs to make peace with Dorn, now that he knows the whole truth, and the script ends with Johnny, Dorn, and Antoinette watching Bayard ride home. Bayard jumps the fence, and "IN DISSOLVE there passes behind Bayard the ghost of John's ship, John looking down at them, his face bright, peaceful. The ship goes on in dissolve; sound of an engine dies away."[21]

This is a very different Bayard from the one in *Flags* who returned from the war destroyed by guilt and looking only for a way to atone for surviving his brother. Rather than leave him, as in "Ad Astra," vomiting on the streets of the Wasteland with a metaphysically stopped watch, Faulkner here makes Bayard a strong figure and lets him discover a way to keep John alive (in memory, much like the ending of *The Wild Palms*, 1939) and to bring his family into a renewed future, even retaining some of the old Sartorian splendor as he jumps his horse at the finish and released the ghost of his brother into a serene and satisfying peace. For all these reasons, there is no need in *War Birds* to name the latest offspring Benbow; he can be Johnny and can learn, like the adults around him, to forgive and endure. The curse of repetition that dogged the Johns and Bayards for nearly a hundred years has, then, been broken; doom has been neutralized and released. It is almost as if Faulkner understood the Freudian "repetition compulsion" and its relation to the "death instinct" as formalized in *Beyond the Pleasure Principle*—that that was what was behind the doom that pursued the Johns and Bayards, the relation between their names and their deaths, and more particularly Bayard's search for oblivion in *Flags*—and furthermore that Faulkner saw that Bayard had a choice: to fulfill the drive to death or to resolve the trauma and reconcile the loss that led to the compulsion in the first place. He takes the first option in *Flags*, the second in *War Birds*, and thus discovers personal and social health in a way that is not at all forced, not a matter of a Hollywood happy ending but a resolution that comes directly and appropriately from the dynamics of the original material.

III

Dorn gives Bayard every opportunity for revenge, and that is what makes Bayard's renunciation of revenge ethically significant and dramatically powerful. He makes sure that Bayard knows what he would be abandoning—his hold on the image of his brother's death—and makes that real for him rather than attempt to cash in on the favor of the bayonet. Bayard makes the decision to honor his anger and loss, to fulfill his revenge—then he changes his mind. In that gesture of throwing the pistol through the window, what he implies is that Dorn's death would not resolve the loss of John; he rejects futility, then, rather than let it be his master as it is in the previous fictions. And by what he goes on to do (creating the extended family), Bayard discovers a positive action (as revenge would be negative) that does make up for the loss, that in a sense brings John home from the war—though it is undeniable that at first this gesture appears perverse, and Faulkner lets Caroline voice that judgment for the audience. Bayard does more good, in this context, than the war did harm, not only finding a way to love his enemy but letting that enemy save himself by giving him a chance to fulfill the role John would have if that enemy had not killed him—or if not to fulfill that role, since Dorn could never be Johnny's father and Caroline's husband, at least to honor it, in the dignified and loving way Dorn helps to rear Johnny (and by the same token, the way Antoinette becomes a comfort and companion to Caroline).

The question is, then, what all of this positive action has to do with the dynamics of passive aggression, and to clarify that it is necessary to take a brief look at "An Odor of Verbena" (which was, before the discovery of *War Birds*, considered the first instance of Faulkner's mature vision of the ethics of peace). What is essential to remember, in making this connection, is that Bayard's primary act is a nonaction: his decision *not* to shoot Dorn and to let those who have already died be enough dead. The corresponding line from *A Fable*, quoted at the beginning of this essay, is: " 'Enough. Let them that's already dead and maimed and missing be enough of this,' " and it will be remembered that *A Fable* is, among other things, the story of Christ. The key is in the *active* aspect of *not* fulfilling an expectation, of going instead into one's own moral center and doing what is right, even if that can best be expressed only by not doing something that is wrong, because whether the result be action or nonaction, what it will do is shine with the light of that star in the broken window — whether or not that leads to victory, whether or not that light begins to fade.

In "An Odor of Verbena," Bayard (the old Bayard in *Flags*, grandfather of John and Bayard) finds that his father, Colonel John Sartoris, does not intend to defend himself against his former partner, Ben Redmond, although Redmond intends to kill him. The colonel speaks of " 'men who have killed too much, who have killed so much that never again as long as they live will they ever be alone. . . . Yes, I have accomplished my aim, and now I shall do a little moral house-cleaning. I am tired of killing men, no matter what the necessity nor the end. Tomorrow, when I go to town and meet Ben Redmond, I shall be unarmed `.'"[22] This is much like what happened to Colonel Falkner, but his son was simply persuaded not to continue the feud and to renounce vengeance.[23] That might be analogous to a *War Birds* in which Bayard simply did not shoot Dorn but did not go on to bring Dorn and Antoinette home. In the story Faulkner wrote, however, Bayard is pressured to shoot the man who shot his father, and what he does instead is to let Redmond fire at him, thus not simply abandoning the feud but rising above it in a demonstration of charity and moral courage.

Although this story concerns not young but old Bayard, it is clearly related to the same tangle of moral issues and fatality that the earlier Sartoris stories — but not *War Birds* — had presented in a more hopeless light. "An Odor of Verbena" is a story of man's ability to rise above the compulsive fixations and destructive inheritance that so regularly (at least in Faulkner's early work) force him into tragic repetitions and hopeless quests for oblivion; it is a story of how to find peace — in fact, how to create it. It is in *War Birds* that this level of hope, of ethics, is first approached. It is in *A Fable* that it finds its most categorically political and religious expression. In the course of these writings Faulkner moved from the passive-aggressive refusal to live (the Bayard of *Flags*) to the discovery of the moral power of active refusal (the old Bayard of "Verbena" and the mutinous soldiers of *A Fable*), and in that process he moved from a literature of passivity and defeat that stretched back to *Mayday* and in which there was no possible way to renew the Sartorian or any other tradition save to write stories about the earlier history of the family, to a literature of qualified victory — a victory qualified not by the depressed pessimism of a young romantic but by the conditions of the real world, seen accurately and seen through.

Notes

1. William Faulkner, *A Fable* (New York: New American Library, Signet Classics, 1968), p. 77.

2. Ibid., p. 83.

3. Ibid., p. 78.

4. Bruce Kawin, *Faulkner and Film* (New York: Frederick Ungar Publishing Co., 1977), and *Faulkner's MGM Screenplays* (Knoxville: Univ. of Tennessee Press, 1982).

5. *A Fable*, pp. 66–67.

6. William Faulkner, *Collected Stories* (New York: Random House, Vintage edition, 1977), p. 417.

7. Kawin, *Telling It Again and Again: Repetition in Literature and Film* (Ithaca: Cornell Univ. Press, 1972), pp. 66–67, 70, 72–84, 101, 158, 160; see also pp. 16–18 on repetition compulsion.

8. *Collected Stories*, p. 424.

9. Ibid., p. 412. I am calling him Dorn for convenience; in "Ad Astra" he is an unnamed German.

10. The Script Department version is reproduced in full in *Faulkner's MGM Screenplays*, pp. 275–420; *War Birds* has never been published anywhere else. Much of what follows in this section is a revised version of the introduction to *War Birds* in that volume, pp. 257–64.

11. Joseph Blotner, *Faulkner: A Biography* (New York: Random House, 1974), p. *113* note to p. 792, 35.

12. Ibid., p. 648.

13. R. B. Wills, 30 September 1926.

14. "Diary of the Unknown Aviator," MGM typescript (vault copy), p. 25.

15. Ibid., pp. 293–95. In *Flags* and *War Birds*, John jumps to his death without a parachute.

16. Ibid., pp. 295–97.

17. Ibid., p. 299. A note indicates that shortly after writing this, Grider was killed in action.

18. *Collected Stories*, p. 421.

19. *Faulkner's MGM Screenplays*, p. 404. All excerpts from *War Birds* are copyright © 1982 by Metro-Goldwyn-Mayer Film Co.

20. Ibid., pp. 406–09.

21. Ibid., p. 420.

22. William Faulkner, *The Unvanquished* (New York: New American Library, Signet Classics, 1960), p. 175.

23. *Faulkner: A Biography*, pp. 44–51.

Two Sartoris Women: Faulkner, Femininity, and Changing Times   Sherrill Harbison*

I

Devastation is a curious thing. By instinct we try, as fiercely as though it were death, to prevent the experience of loss. Loss does not mean death — only starting over. But starting over means losing control, being

*This essay was written for this volume and is published here for the first time by permission of the author.

cast adrift from the familiar people, patterns, and responses on which we have learned to rely for our sense of place and esteem in the world. Bound as we are by ties of affection and anxiety, loss leaves us desolate, even when we grieve for times or persons never wholly satisfactory. We mourn their potential—the dreams we have built up around them—as much as the extent to which those dreams have been realized.

But in a real and sobering sense the only way we can truly start over, truly be reborn, is when we have endured the pain of loss. And once in a while, when the energy of grief is translated into anger and given immediate outlet, it results in an exhilarating release quite as unfamiliar and unexpected as the loss itself. This happened to Drusilla Hawk Sartoris, one of the most compelling and tragic of William Faulkner's characters.

Drusilla's star rises in Alabama, when she is twenty-two and the Civil War has stripped her of Dennison Hawk, her father, Gavin Breckbridge, her fiancé, and Hawkhurst, her home. It falls ten years later when she leaves the Sartoris compound forever. Drusilla appears only in *The Unvanquished*, but her example haunts every other Faulkner novel in which a female character feels dissatisfied and out of place, and whose efforts to transcend her situation—though usually less glorious—also meet with defeat.

Her role in *The Unvanquished* begins when, in the midst of the war, young Bayard Sartoris travels with his slave companion Ringo and his Grandmother Millard to Hawkhurst, home of Granny's sister Louisa Hawk. They find that like theirs, the Hawks' home has been burned down, and like them, the family is living in the slave quarters. Drusilla and ten-year-old Denny have also witnessed the Yankees' destruction of the new Atlanta-Chattanooga railroad and the passage in the night of bands of Negroes traveling toward promises of freedom in Yankee territory, the new political Jerusalem.

When Cousin Bayard meets her, he sees she is feverish—haggard, but excited. " 'I've quit sleeping,' " she confesses. " 'Quit sleeping?' I said. 'Why?' "

> She was looking at me. "Why not stay awake now? Who wants to sleep now, with so much happening, so much to see? Living used to be dull, you see. Stupid. You lived in the same house your father was born in, and your father's sons and daughters had the sons and daughters of the same Negro slaves to nurse and coddle; and then you grew up and you fell in love with your acceptable young man, and in time you would marry him, in your mother's wedding gown, perhaps, and with the same silver for presents she had received; and then you settled down forevermore while you got children to feed and bathe and dress until they grew up, too; and then you and your husband died quietly and were buried together maybe on a summer afternoon just before supper-time. Stupid, you see. But now you can see for yourself how fine it is; it's fine now; you don't have to worry about the house and the silver,

because they get burned up and carried away; and you don't have to worry about the Negroes, because they tramp the roads all night waiting for a chance to drown in homemade Jordan; and you don't have to worry about getting children to bathe and feed and change, because the young men can ride away and get killed in the fine battles; and you don't even have to sleep alone, you don't even have to sleep at all; and so, all you have to do is show the stick to the dog now and then and say, 'Thank God for nothing.' You see?"[1]

"Listen," she continued.

"When you go back home and see Uncle John, ask him to let me come there and ride with his troop. Tell him I can ride, and maybe I can learn to shoot. Will you?"

"Yes," I said, "I'll tell him you are not afraid too."

"Aren't I?" she said. "I hadn't thought about it. It doesn't matter anyway. Just tell him I can ride and that I don't get tired." (*Un*, 115–16)

During the invasion of their land Drusilla, "the best woman rider in the country," had saved her horse Bobolink (a gift from her late fiance) from abduction by the Yankees, but at a dreadful cost.

"Yawl sho must 'a' had this horse hid good when the Yankees come" Ringo said.

"This horse?" Cousin Denny said. "Ain't no damn Yankee going to fool with Dru's horse no more." He didn't holler now, but pretty soon he began again: "When they come to burn the house, Dru grabbed the pistol and run out here — she had on her Sunday dress — and them right behind her. She run in here and she jumped on Bobolink bareback, without even waiting for the bridle, and one of them right there in the door hollering 'Stop,' and Dru said, 'Get away, or I'll ride you down,' and him hollering 'Stop! Stop!' with his pistol out too" — Cousin Denny was hollering good now — "and Dru leaned down to Bobolink's ear and said 'Kill him, Bob,' and the Yankee jumped back just in time. The lot was full of them, too, and Dru stopped Bobolink and jumped down in her Sunday dress and put the pistol to Bobolink's ear and said, 'I can't shoot you all, because I haven't enough bullets, and it wouldn't do any good anyway; but I won't need but one shot for the horse, and which shall it be?' So they burned the house and went away!" (*Un*, 102–03)

Her arousal to passion and rage — and the punishment of that passion with destruction — was repeated when the Yankees destroyed the railroad after the dramatic escape of a Rebel locomotive from the Yankee one in pursuit: " 'The other one, the Yankee one, was right behind it,' Drusilla said. 'But they never caught it. Then the next day they came and tore the track up. They tore the track up but they couldn't take away the fact that we had done it. They couldn't take that from us' " (*Un*, 112). Whatever capacity she may have had for resignation must have snapped at that moment; Drusilla was radically changed. She gave up dresses for men's clothes, and cropped her hair short. And she no longer had time for sleep.

In all of Faulkner's writing questions about male and female roles reverberate. The story told in *The Unvanquished* is startling for its bold acts of outrageous, compassionate courage — committed mostly by the women — and reckless, self-aggrandizing bravado, committed mostly by the men. In the characters of Drusilla and her cousin Bayard we have a reversal of the behaviors typical of other members of their sex, and the consummation of that travesty in ironic, moving tragedy. For Bayard, adopting the more "womanly" attitude toward violence and retribution served to restore his family to good graces with the community. For Drusilla, adopting the masculine, chivalric code of honor, demanding satisfaction for injuries by retaliation, led to the loss of all she had.

The Unvanquished is rich with humor and love, elements missing in much of Faulkner's writing. Therein lies much of its appeal. The balance is provided by its function as restorative mythology — perhaps its major function, like so much of Southern writing for generations. For it was necessary to create a legend of glory for the warriors who had fought for the Southern Cause, even if it were a cause they never fully understood. ("Will," asks seventy-two-year-old Bayard Sartoris many years later, " 'What the devil were you folks fighting about, anyhow?' 'Bayard,' old man Falls answered, 'Damned if I ever did know.' ")[2]

It was perhaps the greatest weakness of the South's campaign that it was not for them a holy war, that it had no moral edge to compare with that for which the North had raised its banner. Southerners fought to fend off loss — to protect life as they knew it. And they saw the defense of women and property through a veil of romanticism nurtured by European literary and artistic trends. Restorative mythology — built on themes incorporated in the Jim Crow laws and the Ku Klux Klan — was necessary for the vanquished, who found the Reconstruction era otherwise unendurable. Distilled in the twilight zone between memory and recorded history, stories of the glory of Johnny Reb served as moral pabulum for generations of white Southern children after the war was concluded. They flowered and grew, as myths do, because without them the vanquished would have been not just defeated but destroyed.

Faulkner understood that defeat curiously carries within it the seed of a different kind of victory. (As the German prisoner observes in his World War I story, "Ad Astra," " 'Defeat will be good for us. Defeat iss good for art, victory, it iss not good.' ")[3] It was thus that hyperbole — the favorite device of those who fear insignificance — became in the South a highly developed art form, a romantic fiction designed to accommodate unacceptable fact.

Drusilla Hawk Sartoris is an unusual character for Faulkner in several ways. In most cases his female characters are "hard," "cold," "savage," "blank-eyed," "bloodless," "ruthless" (his words) — finally, unsympathetic. Like most of his generation his bias in sexual thinking was strongly Freudian. Role reversal, when desired (and it often is) by his characters, is desired by females, not by males. Even when initially appealing, when push comes to shove his most interesting women tend to sift down to caricatures of what Freudians most fear: a voracious, all-consuming, crazed nymphomaniac like Joanna Burden in *Light in August*, or a bitchy, heartless, manipulating, castrating intellectual-achiever, like Charlotte Rittenmeyer in *The Wild Palms*. They manage neither to gratify nor to challenge the male without destroying him. There are few satisfactory alternatives for Faulkner in the pre-Freudian social archives either: he shows little patience with women who, like Caroline Compson, spin ever-smaller circles around their concept of duty to the family name — duty defined by their own self-sacrifice and guilt.

By welcome contrast, when dealing with his own family history (fictionalized as the Sartorises) Faulkner is full of admiration for the women. In his two Sartoris novels, *The Unvanquished* from 1937 and *Flags in the Dust* (first published as *Sartoris* in 1929), his preoccupation with the pattern of male aggressiveness and female nurturing sings out like a litany, repeatedly stated, challenged, and defended until its answers, like its questions, face each other on the combat field exhausted and perspiring, redefined but not resolved.

It is interesting to realize that there is only one Sartoris-blooded woman who is a developed character, and when we meet her her name is no longer Sartoris, but DuPre. Virginia Sartoris DuPre (Aunt Jenny), widowed by the war at twenty-two, appears first in the last chapter of *The Unvanquished* arriving in Mississippi from her home state of Carolina to live with her brother John, her last surviving kin. She is eighty in *Flags in the Dust*; ninety at her death (in "There Was a Queen," a short story designed as a postlude to *Flags*). By straddling the gap between all Sartoris generations Jenny provides a link for the other women — Rosa (Granny) Millard, Cousin Drusilla Hawk, and Narcissa Benbow — whom we think of as Sartorises because of their marital ties to Sartoris men.

Even though Faulkner drew on his own family history in fleshing out his Sartoris portraits, Civil War days were not part of his personal memory; they were rather the subject of tales told and retold by an older generation who (like Aunt Jenny) straddled both worlds. Aunt Jenny's chief task and obligation to those who had suffered loss was to create and propagate a redeeming story, and in that function she serves as something of a Faulkner alter ego.

"The highest destiny of a Southern woman," according to Drusilla's mother Louisa Hawk, was "to be the bride-widow of a lost cause" (*Un*, 219). That destiny was prevailingly popular in the postwar South, not only because for so many it required (like the Virgin Birth) only acceptance to be accomplished. Most genteel, educated Southern women of the time — drenched in the self-effacing aspects of Christian theology and steeped in neo-medieval romances of writers like Sir Walter Scott — were disinclined to consider other choices. While Aunt Jenny filled this Sartoris-nun role to perfection, Drusilla — Jenny's exact contemporary — rejected it utterly.

And Faulkner never deprived her of dignity, as he did so many others of his spirited women. He clearly adored her.

When we meet Drusilla next after her "thank God for nothing" credo, seven months have passed. Louisa writes her sister that "after trying to unsex herself by refusing to feel any natural grief" (*Un*, 217) for her father and fiance, Drusilla had disappeared, leaving no trace. Shortly afterward another letter came reporting the shocking news: Drusilla had one night

> walked into the cabin where Aunt Louisa and Denny were (and now it had a line drawn under it, like this:) *in the garments not alone of a man but of a common private soldier* and told them how she had been a member of Father's troop for six months, bivouacking at night surrounded by sleeping men and not even bothering to put up the tent for her and Father except when the weather was bad, and how Drusilla not only showed neither shame nor remorse but actually pretended she did not even know what Aunt Louisa was talking about; how when Aunt Louisa told her that she and Father must marry at once, Drusilla said, "Can't you understand that I am tired of burying husbands in this war? that I am riding in Cousin John's troop not to find a man but to hurt Yankees?" (*Un*, 220)

Aunt Louisa was correct that Drusilla had "unsexed herself" in a sense critical to Faulkner's world, which held that the instinct to preserve justice and peace was (literally) mother to the instinct to fight for it. Males engaged in conflict to establish and protect that which was then entrusted to females, who nurtured and preserved it for their sons, who protected it, and their daughters, who preserved it. But Drusilla realized that she had nothing left to preserve. And she discovered that living on the edge of existence — fighting tooth and nail in a perfect fury — was exhilarating both in its peril and its profundity. But like Joan of Arc before her, she paid a price for her martial prowess: not death; merely convention.

Drusilla returned to the Sartoris compound at the end of the fighting to help rebuild the house, while John and other members of his regiment dedicated themselves to vigilante politics, frustrating the activities of carpetbaggers. Aunt Louisa, convinced that Drusilla was not only living in sin but corrupting young Bayard in the bargain, arrived to tidy up domestic arrangements. (" 'I have come to appeal to them once more with a mother's tears though I don't think it will do any good though I had prayed until the very last that this boy's innocence might be spared and preserved but what must be must be and at least we can all three bear our burden together' " [*Un*, 230]). Drusilla was working in the mill lot, cutting timber, a thin sun-burned girl "in the muddy brogans and the sweaty shirt and overalls and her hair sunburned and full of sawdust, and Aunt Louisa looked at her once and began to cry again, saying, 'Lost, lost. Thank God in his mercy that Dennison Hawk was taken before he lived to see what I see' " (*Un*, 231). Drusilla, who could ride all day and not get tired, was out of her element now.

She was already beaten. Aunt Louisa made her put on a dress that night we watched her run out of the cabin in it and run down the hill toward the spring while we were waiting for Father. . . . Father came out too and we went down to the spring and found Drusilla hiding behind the big beech, crouched down like she was trying to hide the skirt from Father even while he raised her up. "What's a dress?" he said. "It don't matter. Come. Get up, soldier."

But she was beaten, like as soon as she let them put the dress on her she was whipped; like in the dress she could neither fight back nor run away. (*Un*, 231)

Women are prey to many symbols of defeat, especially when they battle on unfamiliar terrain and do not know how to use the artillery. Dresses, children, husbands, social conventions — any or all of these can and do interfere with the pursuit of a dream or a goal.

"Colonel Sartoris," Aunt Louisa said, "I am a woman; I must request what the husband whom I have lost and the man son which I have not would demand, perhaps at the point of a pistol. — Will you marry my daughter?" . . .

I heard the light sharp sound when Drusilla's head went down between her flungout arms on the table, and the sound the bench made when Father got up too; I passed him standing beside Drusilla with his hand on her head. "They have beat you, Drusilla," he said. (*Un*, 233–34)

Drusilla's tragedy was that though she was robbed of her innocence she was too innocent to understand what she had lost. Before arriving at a maturity that could have helped her transform her energy into something transcendent, she succumbed to pressure and bridled her passion, bequeathing her fighting spirit to the Sartoris men to be used in pursuit of their common goals. Stripped thus of her power, dressed in helpless ball gowns, she was left to employ the avenue of satisfaction more traditional for women — that vicarious pleasure derived from living through (and manipulating) the men to whom the larger tasks are assigned. As constant reminder of this change she wore in her cropped hair sprigs of verbena, which had, she said, "the only scent you could smell above the scent of horses and courage and so the only one worth the wearing" (*Un*, 253–54).

But the legacy that blood-vengeance — the kind she had tasted — often leaves is an addiction to violence as the solution to difficulties. Every generation of Sartoris women — everyone but Drusilla — saw and loathed the postwar carryover of violence by Sartoris men into civilian life. None but Drusilla understood it. Of all of them, only she faced the same challenge the men faced.

To find outlets for aggression on a scale approaching that of war, men like John Sartoris ruthlessly built commercial empires. In doing so they were perfectly amenable to disrupting civil order, even to killing, if it served their larger aim and kept the blood running high. Drusilla was convinced that John Sartoris had " 'a dream' " in which he was " 'thinking of this whole country' " which he was " 'trying to raise by its bootstraps, so that all the people in it — not just his kind nor his old regiment, but all the people, black and white, the women and the children back in the hills who don't even own shoes' " could be restored to dignity (*Un*, 256). When Cousin Bayard, now reading law and looking for an escape from the chain of violence of which he too was part, asks her

> "But how can they get any good from what he wants to do for them if they are — after he has — "
> "Killed some of them? I suppose you include those two carpetbaggers he had to kill to hold that first election, don't you?"
> "They were men. Human beings."
> "They were Northerners, foreigners who had no business here. They were pirates." (*Un*, 257)

In spite of her humiliating and needless marriage to him, as long as John Sartoris lived Drusilla successfully rechanneled her impulse to fight for what mattered to her. But, though her courage was precocious, her heart matured late.

Drusilla was thirty-two ten years after the war had ended, when John prepared to abdicate his commercial and political empire. By now he had destroyed his credit with most of his neighbors, including his business partner Ben Redmond. The bravado and cunning which made him admired and feared in wartime had had a different effect in civilian life. To those nonmembers of his old troop who did not revere him as a god, John Sartoris was a braggart, a snob, and a menace. As Bayard watched his father continue to goad Redmond, he listened to their friend George Wyatt's warning: " 'He ought to leave Redmond alone. I know what's wrong: he's had to kill too many folks, and that's bad for a man. We all know Colonel's brave as a lion, but Redmond ain't no coward either and there ain't no use in making a brave man that made one mistake eat crow all the time. Can't you talk to him?' " (*Un*, 260). Bayard agreed. But Drusilla defended John.

> "A dream is not a very safe thing to be near, Bayard, I know; I had one once. It's like a loaded pistol with a hair trigger: if it stays alive long enough, somebody is going to be hurt. But if it's a good dream, it's worth it. There are not many dreams in the world, but there are a lot of human lives. And one human life or two dozen — "
> "Are not worth anything?"
> "No. Not anything." (*Un*, 257)

John is finally challenged to a duel by Redmond. Suddenly weary, and concluding that he had achieved everything he could by brute force and leftover charisma, he takes an uncharacteristic step, signaling a changing of the guard.

It was his idea to have Bayard study law, planning that his son would then be equipped to follow his business lead, in " 'the matters of consolidation, of pettifogging and doubtless chicanery in which I would be a babe in arms but you, trained in the law, can hold your own — our own. Yes,' " he concluded, " 'I have accomplished my aim, and now I shall do a little moral housecleaning. Tomorrow, when I go to meet Ben Redmond, I shall be unarmed' " (*Un*, 266).

But as John prepares for his come-uppance and Drusilla prepares for love, Bayard prepares for his initiation to manhood and the burdens of his name. (" 'At least this will be my chance to find out if I am what I think I am or if I just hope; if I am going to do what I have taught myself is right or if I am just going to wish I were' " [*Un*, 248]). Bayard has learned more from the law than "pettifogging and chicanery." He was struggling with the cycle of violence-breeding-violence himself: when but a child of fourteen he had killed the outlaw Grumby in revenge for the murder of Granny Millard. Now his preparation for coming of age grew diametrically away from Drusilla's dreams for him — and through him, for herself.

> Drusilla and I walked out in the garden in the twilight and I said something about what George Wyatt had told me and she released my arm and turned me to face her and said, "This from you? You? Have you forgotten Grumby?"
>
> "No," I said. "I never will forget him."
>
> "You never will. I wouldn't let you. There are worse things than killing men, Bayard. There are worse things than being killed. Sometimes I think the finest thing that can happen to a man is to love something, a woman preferably, well, hard hard hard, then to die young because he believed what he could not help but believe and was what he could not (could not? would not) help but be." (*Un*, 261)

Drusilla's fervor, in its celebration of tempestuous emotion, fanatical devotion, libertarian impulses, and early death, is straight from the by-laws of romanticism. By contrast, in Bayard rational, self-reserving instincts were stronger. He saw the need to emerge from that emotional spiral as from the grip of a typhoon: otherwise he would have begun to die at fourteen, and, already battered and spent, would never reach his adult potential. But he was as naive about love as Drusilla had been before.

Drusilla had locked herself into a feminine behavioral role with John that appeared to be ending, and she was beginning to cast about for some hold on the future.

> Now she was looking at me in a way she never had before. . . . the scent of the verbena in her hair seemed to have increased a hundred times, to have got a hundred times stronger, to be everywhere in the dusk in which something was about to happen which I had never dreamed of. Then she spoke. "Kiss me, Bayard."
>
> "No. You are Father's wife."
>
> "And eight years older than you are. And your fourth cousin, too. And I have black hair. Kiss me, Bayard."
>
> "No."

> "Kiss me, Bayard." So I leaned my face down to her. But she didn't move, standing so, bent lightly back from me from the waist, looking at me; now it was she who said, "No." So I put my arms around her. Then she came to me, melted as women will and can, the arms with the wrist- and elbow-power to control horses about my shoulders, using the wrists to hold my face to hers until there was no need for the wrists. (*Un*, 261–62)

And then, in the chivalric custom of a lady bestowing her favor, Drusilla marked Bayard as the knight of her choice: "I watched her arms rise with almost the exact gesture with which she had put them around me as if she were repeating the empty and formal gesture of all promise so that I should never forget it . . . as she removed the verbena sprig and put it into my lapel" (*Un*, 263).

Probably Drusilla sensed that John would allow—would even approve—this liaison; like Bayard's training in the law, it would be one more guarantee of the perpetuation of his empire. But Drusilla's feelings were far more complicated than John's; more complicated than she knew. She had only now discovered that the heights of feeling she had once reached through vengeance could be matched by the transports of eros:

> "Now I must tell Father," I said.
> "Yes," she said. "You must tell him. Kiss me." So again it was like it had been before. No. Twice, a thousand times and never like . . . ; the skill without weariness, the knowledge virginal to surfeit, the cunning secret muscles to guide and control just as within the wrists and elbows lay slumbering the mastery of horses: she stood back, already turning, not looking at me when she spoke, never having looked at me, already moving swiftly on in the dusk: "Tell John. Tell him tonight." (*Un*, 263–64)

John's inevitable violent death, when it came, brought Drusilla to a feverish pitch of exaltation. Charged again with the same thirst for holy vengeance she used to know, escalated to a peak of ardent rapture, in an intricate dance-step of the heart she again surrendered her drive for action and assumed the archetypal passive role, charging her true knight to slay the dragon for her sake. It was a gamble, and she was playing for the highest stakes.

Bayard knew, then, when the news of his father's death arrived, what was awaiting him at home:

> Drusilla would be waiting for me beneath all the festive glitter of the chandeliers, in the yellow ball gown and the sprig of verbena in her hair, holding the two loaded pistols. . . . The face calm, almost bemused, the head simple and severe, the balancing sprig of verbena above each ear, the two arms bent at the elbows, the two hands shoulder high, the two identical duelling pistols lying upon, not clutched in, one to each: the Greek amphora priestess of a succinct and formal violence. (*Un*, 252)

Again on the edge of existence as when she was young, Drusilla has no time for sleep. Enraptured by the imminence of danger and trembling with desire, she cast her lot into the wheel of fortune, and then stood back to prepare for certain triumph.

"Bayard." She faced me, she was quite near; again the scent of the verbena in her hair seemed to have increased a hundred times as she stood holding out to me, one in either hand, the two duelling pistols. "Take them, Bayard," she said, in the same tone in which she had said "Kiss me" last summer, already pressing them into my hands, watching me with that passionate and voracious exaltation, speaking in a voice fainting and passionate with promise: "Take them. I have kept them for you. I give them to you. Oh you will thank me, you will remember me who put into your hands what they say is an attribute only of God's, who took what belongs to heaven and gave it to you. Do you feel them? the long true barrels true as justice, the triggers (you have fired them) quick as retribution, the two of them slender and invincible and fatal as the physical shape of love?" Again I watched her arms angle out and upward as she removed the two verbena sprigs from her hair in two motions faster than the eye could follow, already putting one of them into my lapel and crushing the other in her other hand while she still spoke in that rapid passionate voice not much louder than a whisper: "There. One I give to you to wear tomorrow (it will not fade), the other I cast away, like this—" dropping the crushed bloom at her feet. "I abjure it. I abjure verbena forever more; I have smelt it above the odor of courage; that was all I wanted. Now let me look at you." She stood back, staring at me—the face tearless and exalted, the feverish eyes brilliant and voracious. "How beautiful you are: do you know it? How beautiful: young, to be permitted to kill, to be permitted vengeance, to take into your bare hands the fire of heaven that cast down Lucifer. No: I. I gave it to you; I put it into your hands; Oh you will thank me, you will remember me when I am dead and you are an old man saying to himself, 'I have tasted all things,'—It will be the right hand, won't it?" (*Un*, 273–74)

And she kissed his hand.

But alas, Drusilla—and not alone of all her sex—mistook the bargain she had made, forfeiting the free agency that gave her life its savor for the intoxication of carnal passion. Because she (like John) had been corrupted by the taste of blood, when Bayard renounced revenge, she lost in one stroke her authority, her love, and her lucidity.

Then she stopped dead still, still stooping in that attitude of fierce exultant humility, her hot lips and her hot hands still touching my flesh, light on my flesh as dead leaves yet communicating to it that battery charge dark, passionate and damned forever of all peace. Because they are wise, women are—a touch, lips or fingers, and the knowledge, even clairvoyance, goes straight to the heart without bothering the laggard brain at all. She stood erect now, staring at me with intolerable and amazed incredulity which occupied her face alone for a whole minute while her eyes were completely empty. . . . Then her eyes filled with an expression of bitter and passionate betrayal. "Why, he's not—" she said. "He's not—And I kissed his hand," she said in an aghast whisper; "*I kissed his hand!*" beginning to laugh, the laughter rising, becoming a scream yet still remaining laughter, screaming with laughter, trying herself to deaden the sound by putting her hand over her mouth, the laughter spilling out between her fingers like vomit, the incredulous betrayed eyes still watching me across the hand. (*Un*, 274–75)

So this time it was Drusilla who knew what to expect at the end of the day. Bayard declined the dueling advantage. Redmond, spooked by this reversal, fired to miss; then walked out of town never to return. Drusilla elected not to witness her betrayal, and at the same time as Redmond went away forever. Behind her she left the last symbol of her feminity, her surrender, her memories, her loss: on Bayard's pillow lay a single sprig of verbena, "filling the room, the dusk, the evening with that odor which she had said you could smell alone above the smell of horses" (*Un* 293).

II

Faulkner's sympathy with Drusilla is complete, even as it conflicts with his (complete) sympathy with Bayard and with Jenny, who had supported Bayard's decision not to perpetuate the primitive cycle of vengeance. This conflict is Faulkner's own. And when he reaches his own generation in *Flags in the Dust*, the same issues prevail and the tension peaks. Rather than being resolved, the subject is injected with a new element—the absurd—by the dubious victories of World War I. In the wake of that tragedy, pointless violence spreads like a stain over the complexion of society.

In *Flags*, seventy-two-year-old Bayard—the very one Drusilla had pinned her hopes on—now spends his time either asleep or reflecting on the past, and having his health fussed over by eighty-year-old Jenny. Bayard's grandson and namesake comes back from the war shorn of his twin brother John, full of frustration, guilt, and anger. Jenny, concerned about the continuation of the family line, sets about to tame young Bayard just long enough to get from him an heir. She makes it her business to select for him a sensible match in Narcissa Benbow, a serious, sheltered local girl in whose "face was the serene repose of lilies" (*FD*, 31).

The said Narcissa bears little resemblance to Drusilla. The opposite of driven, she protects her image of serene impeccability with all of her energy. Young Bayard's brutality, his compulsive self-destructiveness are continual assaults on her repose, assaults she cannot escape; but in spite of her loathing the violence also fascinates her. The fascination becomes a challenge when, while he is recovering from the injuries of an automobile accident, she gets Bayard's promise that he will mend his reckless ways. On that basis — that she can influence and control him — she agrees to marry him.

Here Narcissa shares an error with Drusilla: both try to control men in exchange for sexual privileges. Both fail. But the influence they try to wield is of opposite nature. Drusilla favored violence if it protected principle; Narcissa shrank from it (and any unpleasantness that might ruffle her serenity), yet she had no higher principle. Repelled by the "dirtiness" of her lawyer brother Horace's already-married paramour, Narcissa cuts herself off from him. After her husband succeeds in destroying himself, crashing a plane on the same day their son is born, Narcissa rejects Jenny's urgings that she remarry. She becomes instead another Sartoris nun, dressing always in virginal white. As she ages her narrowness and self-satisfaction increase. She fights Horace's efforts to help the wife of a bootlegger client (*Sanctuary*) on the grounds that the association will damage her "reputation" in town. Horace, though defiant, feels shabby beside her "perfection."

But beneath this antiseptic persona Narcissa still harbors her private fascination with the lurid, the violent, the seamy side of life. Before her marriage to Bayard she had received several dozen desperate, titillating pornographic letters from a peeping-Tom, bank-robbing Snopes in old Bayard's employ. Rather than turning them over to the police for tracing, as Jenny had urged, or destroying them, as she insisted to Jenny she would do, she kept them in her lingerie drawer, rereading them at her pleasure. On the night that Snopes robbed the Sartoris bank her bedroom was also entered and ransacked, and the letters disappeared.

It was about 1930 — contemporary time for Faulkner — that Narcissa exposed the underbelly of her character, and sold her chastity to protect not her honor, but her vanity ("There Was a Queen").[4] The letters had been dropped, then found in the wake of the robbery. Twelve years later she was contacted by the FBI agent who retained them, the only remaining evidence in the still-unsolved case. Narcissa's "reputation" again looms larger to her than truth or justice: she is frantic that no one else should learn that someone "had ever had those thoughts" about her. " 'They were out in the world,' " she explained to Aunt Jenny: " 'They were somewhere. I was crazy for a while. I thought of people, men, reading them, seeing not only my name on them, but the marks of my eyes where I had read them again and again. I was wild. When Bayard and I were on our honeymoon, I was wild. I couldn't even think about him alone. It was like having to sleep with all the men in the world at the same time' " (*CS*, 739–40). When the smooth-talking federal agent visits her in hopes of gaining information about Snopes, she ascertains how she can assure protection of her secret. She makes a "sudden and mysterious trip to Memphis and stayed two nights, who had never before been separated from her son since he was born" (*CS*, 737). " 'That man had my letters,' " she explained to Aunt Jenny on her return. " 'He had had them for twelve years.' "

> "*Had* had?" the old woman said. "*Had* had?"
>
> "Yes. I have them now. He hadn't sent them to Washington yet, so no one had read them except him. And now nobody will ever read them." She ceased; she breathed quietly, tranquil. "You don't understand yet, do you? He had all the information the letters could give him, but he would have to turn them in to the Department anyway and I asked him for them but he said he would have to turn them in and I asked him if he would make his final decision in Memphis and he said why Memphis and I told him why. I knew I couldn't buy them with money, you see. That's why I had to go to Memphis. I had that much regard for Bory and you, to go somewhere else. And that's all. Men are all about the same, with their ideas of good and bad. Fools." (CS, 740–41)

By not destroying the letters in the first place Narcissa had laid claim to the character suggested by her baptismal name; when she added the insult of an assignation with a stranger (and even worse to Aunt Jenny, one who was both a Yankee and a Jew), she for all intents and purposes lost her inheritance to the Sartoris one. For at that news Aunt Jenny (alias Faulkner) quit her job — gave up the ghost. And, in a moment ominous with Faulkner's prophecy of doom for the white South (" 'I think that in time . . . I who regard you will also have sprung from the loins of African kings' " — [AA, 398], Elnora, the mulatto family retainer whose veins run with as much Sartoris blood as those of Bory, the family heir, quietly disinherits the mother, assuming that Sartoris "quality" to herself. " 'I nigger and she white. But my black children got more blood than she got. More behavior' " (C, 732).

Faulkner's ambivalence about sexual roles continues throughout his writing, as surely it did in his life. Like the race issue, which for white Southern males it resembled, the refusal of women to keep to their "proper place" was galling and humiliating; but as a modern artist there was no way Faulkner could not embrace the change, whether distasteful or not. Through these Sartoris women as much as through the men, Faulkner closes the family chapter on life in the Old South at his own doorstep, firmly knotting the tie to the past, but letting the line drop as it tugs toward the future, about which he — at this point in his life — claims no clairvoyance and feels but little hope.

Notes

1. *The Unvanquished* (New York: Random House, 1966), pp. 114–15; hereafter cited in the text as *Un*.

2. *Flags in the Dust* (New York: Random House, 1974), p. 252; hereafter cited in the text as *FD*.

3. *Absalom, Absalom!* (New York: Random House Modern Library, 1964), p. 413; hereafter cited in the text as *AA*.

4. *Collected Stories* (New York: Random House, 1977), pp. 727–44; hereafter cited in the text as *CS*.

For "blood and kin and home": Black Characterization in William Faulkner's Sartoris Saga

Esther Alexander Terry*

Many writers have discussed the impact of the Civil War and its aftermath on the soul of the Southern White.[1] And this, most of them agree, not only because a young nation, so recently pledged to indivisibility had publicly to suspend that pledge for four years while uniforms and ammunition made fratricide acceptable, legal, and even honorable; but also because, part way through the war, what lay in the balance for the victorious North was the right — even the obligation — to declare that the vanquished South had engaged in a way of life that was not merely impractical or uneconomical, but depraved, unchristian, and immoral at its very core because of the role it had assigned to human beings of African descent. "You believe in Providence," a frustrated Abraham Lincoln is reputed to have asked, "will you tell me why He allowed the African to be made a slave in this country?"[2] Lincoln is further reputed to have said: "I have on more than one occasion in this room, when beset by extremists [on the question of slavery] been compelled to appear very mad. I think none of you will ever dispose of this question without getting mad."[3]

The element of prophecy inherent in the president's statement is surely not to be gainsaid; for what to do with and for the slaves of Lincoln's day and their descendants — even to our time of school integration, civil rights, and affirmative action — has continued so to trouble and confound the moral conscience of the reunited nation that attempts at disposition and resolution have brought it close to his predicted "madness." And this madness — this uneasy preoccupation with blackness — has been no more visible with the nation's statesmen than with its artists: "What has cast such a shadow upon you?" Captain Delano asks the subdued Don Benito of Herman Melville's *Benito Cereno.* His reply is as prophetic for the nation's artists as Lincoln's was for its statesmen. It ended all conversation for that day: "The negro."[4]

And from no other region in the nation has the artist so relentlessly

*This essay was written for this volume, and is published here for the first time with the permission of the author.

worked to give meaning to and explanation of the role of the American Black as in the South. The Civil War had been for the Southerners a war of integrity — and they had lost. With homeland vanquished, the Southern advocates had to find a way to explain and defend not its secession, not its economy, but its treatment of those whom they had insisted were simultaneously their property and their brothers. No justification of, no discussion of, indeed, no yearning for and memory of the past Southern tradition could be begun without a consideration of Blacks. Thus "the Negro" becomes the center, the core, of any traditional Southern mythmaking, whether such mythmaking is personal or universal.[5]

William Faulkner stands as chief among the Southern artists. This is not to say simply that he was born in the South and grew up to become its ranking artist — but more than this, his very Southernness forms the source of his creative genius and for him, like other Southern advocates, the Negro question, with all its implications of good and evil, morality and immorality, is ever present in his work. A moralist, Faulkner clearly recognized the evils inherent in slavery. When asked to identify "the curse upon the South" by a student at the University of Virginia, he did not hesitate in his answer: "The curse is slavery, which is an intolerable condition — no man shall be enslaved — and the South has got to work that curse out and it will, if it's let alone."[6] A Southerner, Faulkner seems unable to break with his fellow kinsmen's need to find at least a *qualified* moral justification for the system that provided the cornerposts upholding the tradition that he believed produced his ancestors and his home.

What does this dilemma mean for Faulkner the artist? A continuous "working it out." Throughout his work, he returns again and again to his Southern past and the role of the slave and the ex-slave. Over and over he reassembles it, reexamines it — so much so that one is convinced that his efforts are as much to fix the Negro's place in that tradition so extolled for its codes of honor, courage, and gentility as for any other reason. Always when Faulkner contemplates the South, the Negro is there; but despite the artist, it is a contradictory presence: at one moment it comforts, at another it accuses.

The world of William Faulkner is, then, as Irving Howe writes, "neither social photography nor historical record";[7] Howe continues to make the important point that behind the telling and retelling of the Faulkner story "there is always a desperate search for order, not merely as strategy in narrative but also as an actual motive for composition."[8] Is it possible that, for Faulkner, "motive for composition" becomes so important that strategy (and logic) in narrative is sometimes sacrificed? A look at the black characters in the Sartoris stories illustrates the point.

These black characters represent one of the artist's most clearly delineated attempts at re-creation of a past time in which Blacks and Whites lived together in unstrained harmony. In "Ambuscade" Bayard Sartoris remembers that as a young boy he and Ringo were playmates.

Given the fact that Bayard is white and the future plantation owner while Ringer is a black slave, Bayard's future property, Faulkner must employ an unusual language to describe their youthful equality:

> Ringo and I had been born in the same month and had both fed at the same breast and had slept together and eaten together for so long that Ringo called Granny "Granny" just like I did, until maybe he wasn't a nigger anymore or maybe I wasn't a white boy anymore, the two of us neither, not even people any longer: the two supreme undefeated like two moths, two feathers riding above a hurricane.[9]

Both race (black and white) and condition (owner and owned) must be removed immediately from this simple description of human kinship between the two young boys if this youthful idyll is to be not only sustained, but *begun*. But the result of such a removal produces an image that is strained, forced, and troubled. After all, Bayard merely sets out to tell us that two boys who feed at the same breast[10] and hide under Granny Millard's skirts from Union soldiers, thwart Union soldiers, and proclaim the rebel South together feel like brothers toward each other. But do they? Or, more particularly, are we convinced by Bayard's self-conscious elimination of race and his substitution of "moths" and "feathers"? On the contrary, the sensitive reader is made doubly conscious that Bayard's type of brotherhood can be achieved only in the absence of the recognition of one's station in life.

But no shibboleth, no peculiarity of phrase, no moths and feathers can prevail against the inevitable. Slave and master can never be equal. By the time Bayard and Ringo are twenty-four, "feathers" and "moths" are replaced by white "man" and black "boy." When Bayard's father, Colonel John, is shot, Ringo rides forty miles to bring him the news. " 'Your boy is downstairs in the kitchen,' " Judge Wilkins announces, establishing forever Ringo's place in society. And Bayard's acceptance of Ringo's place comes too easily for one who has declared a felt brotherhood: " 'A fresh horse for my boy,' " he tells the judge. " 'He will want to go back with me.' "[11]

The idyll gone forever, we are left to consider why it is that Bayard insists upon it. Irving Howe, recognizing the problems inherent in such a memory, makes this explanation:

> The white man is repeatedly tempted by a memory playing on the rim of his consciousness: a memory of boyhood, when he could live as a brother with his Ringo or Lucas Beauchamp—his Nigger Jim or Queequeg—and not yet wince under the needle of self-consciousness. The memory—is it a longing in the guise of memory?—can be downed by the will and blunted by convention, but it is too lovely and in some final sense too real to be discarded entirely.[12]

Howe might well have added that such a memory, steeped as it is in the denial of humanity of which Ralph Ellison speaks,[13] is necessary for the expiation of white Southern guilt. So necessary, in fact, that it must be preserved at all costs. He might further have remarked (and he did allude to the fact that nobody bothered to ask the Negroes how they felt) that such a memory could never be evoked except by a white slave owner; for it is supported by an arrogance so deadly and inhumane that it turns on itself and makes impossible the end to which Howe says such mythmaking reaches: that end being, of course, an honest rendering of a past time that may be recognized and shared by the Ringos and Lucas Beauchamps and Nigger Jims and Queequegs whom it mourns.

"Shared" is the key word here, it seems to me — not "owned." Shared: that word the concept of which all children learn with difficulty and reluctance as it is always easier to accept the place of privileged position; but a circumstance that makes itself painfully understood when one is on the short end of a bounty that pretends equality. Surely, one as bright as Ringo ("Father always said that Ringo was a little smarter than I was, but that didn't count with us any more than the difference in the color of our skins counted")[14] must have recognized and wondered at the fact that his place of sleep was a pallet while Bayard's was the bed above his pallet; and he must surely have noticed that when the boys were told, " 'Look who coming up the big road!,' " they "ran as one" to meet him, but Colonel John rode them back on his fine horse Jupiter with this difference: Bayard is "standing in one stirrup with Father's arm around me and Ringo holding to the other stirrup and running beside the horse."[15] And the time they did not run to meet him out of an unexplained sense that he came not out of victory but out of danger and waited at the front yard: Bayard "mounted the steps and stood beside Granny, and with Ringo and Loosh on the ground below the gallery we watched the claybank stallion enter the gate which was never closed now, and come up the drive."[16]

As Faulkner presents the story, then, Ringo shares no believable childhood equality with Bayard Sartoris — shared feeding breasts or not: a wet nurse does not a brother make. Instead, he is merely in training to become Bayard's "boy" and as such is given every opportunity to understand and love his future master. He knows this; and Bayard knows it; and the reader knows it. If there is any bond to be boasted here, it is that Ringo accepts his "nigger" status with a humanity that allows him to love his future master *despite* the inequality of their lives (a tactic that may be his only salvation). Ellison speaks for many when he says that Ringo's abject loyalty to Bayard, "given where one's humanity is unrecognized seems a bit obscene."[17] And this is precisely the point: the mindless creature that Ringo becomes can be accomplished only by the most elaborate (and unbelievable) scheme to train him out of himself. And if we are to believe Faulkner's characterizations, the elaborate training works. When Ringo is no longer a slave (" 'I ain't a nigger anymore. I done been abolished' "),[18] he continues to be faithful to the one who is no longer, by law, his master. He does so without guilt and incrimination ("because niggers know, they know things,"[19] Bayard says). And what does one say about that unique training which makes Ringo possible? Lee Jenkins makes this important point:

> It is certainly the case that their [Faulkner's "positive" Negro characters] ability to survive in a caste society requires that they possess humor, sanity, imagination, and moral courage; but it is also the case, in Faulkner's presentation of the situation, that the manner in which they employ these virtues to achieve dignity and self-respect nevertheless involves a conception of self-limitation, in which they do not recognize their right to *absolute* equality with the whites, as human beings. I am not speaking of the denial of this right through social sanctions, but of the *belief* in it on the part of the blacks, no matter how many times it is denied. Such a belief is the essence of humanity, and it ensures the survival of the sense of inherent human worth and spiritual freedom against great and profound opposition, even as was demonstrated to be the case in the Nazi death camps. The lack of such a belief makes the behavior of a Louvinia or a Ringo possible, and even a Lucas Beauchamp, whose sense of worth derives not from respect for himself as a black person—he even views other blacks with contempt—but from identification with his white ancestors.[20]

When one witnesses Ringo's indifference to his Uncle Loosh's aspirations for freedom, or hears his response to the question as to whether he would like to hear about the migration of his people to the North (" 'I been having to hear about niggers all my life. I got to hear about that railroad' "),[21] and finally, one witnesses his seemingly deliberate dehumanization, one knows that Faulkner has played the ultimate hoax on him; and one is forced to remark, as Jenkins does, at Faulkner's "distorting addition in the working out of his conceptual scheme."[22] And one further concurs with him that even "the most extreme instance of Uncle Tomism is a more complex thing"[23] than what Faulkner gives us. So it is not for Ringo, then, and in many ways it is not even *about* him that we read such a strained description of boyhood chums that requires "moths" and "feathers" for the telling; it is all for Bayard Sartoris and justification of the Southern tradition. Objective art gives way, indeed, to a "comforting sense of confederate self-gratification."[24]

Faulkner's contrived presentation of pastoral (past-oral) love between Bayard and Ringo during the height of slavery, and Irving Howe's keen observation that the slave's side of the story is left untold, bring to mind an instance where the black man does speak. Consider the stories found in Charles Chesnutt's *The Conjure Woman*, a collection of stories that makes use of the motif of conjure—a device that some fortunate (desperate) slaves used in order to transform themselves from humans into nonhuman objects in order to escape the harshness of slavery. In one story, "Sis' Becky's Pickaninny," Becky's husband is sold from a neighboring plantation and she comforts herself with their baby, little Mose. When, as slavery ordained, Becky is exchanged for a horse to a new master and thus separated from her child, both mother and child become ill of heartbreak. A sympathetic slave woman, Nancy, turns the child into a hummingbird for a day and

> "So little Mose flewed, en flewed, en flewed away, 'til bimeby he got ter de place whar Sis' Becky b'longed. He seed his mammy walkin' roun' de ya'd, en he could tell from lookin' at her dat she wuz trouble in min' 'bout sump'n, en feeling kin'er po'ly. Sis' Becky heared sum'n hummin' roun' en roun' her, sweet en low. Fus' she 'lowed it wuz a 'hummin' bird; den she thought it sounded lack her little Mose croonin' on her bres' way back yander on de plantation. En she des 'magine it wuz her little Mose, en it made her feel bettah, en she went on 'bout her wuk peartner'n she'd done sence she'd b'en down dere."[25]

Uncle Julius McAdoo's memory of slavery and Bayard Sartoris' are poles apart in more ways than one, of course, but one cannot overlook the fact (and the obvious irony) that the white writer resorts, however stiltedly, to the images of moths and feathers to convince us that the tradition provided a space for black and white brotherhood while the black writer insists that the tradition was so harsh that it compelled the Blacks to seek transformation into nonhuman objects as the only way they could maintain their humanity. One wonders what Ringo might say if Faulkner had allowed him to speak on the matter.

Such muteness is not reserved for Ringo alone. Throughout Faulkner's works, Blacks who do not voice the Southern position are allowed to open their mouths only to have them closed, and oftentimes with violence. And while I do not agree in the main with Charles H. Nilon's thesis, I do agree that "as a rule Faulkner does not develop character. He reveals it."[26] Where his black characters are concerned, this most often means that white characters are left to do the revealing. For instance, in *The Sound and the Fury*, Quentin Compson, aboard a train one morning in Virginia, raises the shade of his compartment to see "a nigger on a mule in the middle of the stiff ruts, waiting for the train to move. How long he had been there I didn't know, but he sat straddle of the mule, his head wrapped in a piece of blanket, as if they had been built there with the fence and the road, or with the hill, carved out of the hill itself, like a sign put there saying You are home again."[27] Clearly, the black man is there, like the hill and the road, *for Quentin*. Quentin imposes his own "Christmas gift" greetings upon the Negro and gets the appropriate response. But we learn nothing of what the Negro feels or thinks.[28]

The fact that Faulkner does not allow his black characters to reveal themselves to us through their development, but "grows" them all, like Topsy, from a Southern white psyche, deserves serious consideration before one turns to him for meaningful depiction of the Southern Black. An assessment of their full humanity demands more than that they "endure." Nor can, in the case of his treatment of Ringo, Faulkner's actions be explained away as Nilon suggests: "In many ways Ringo illustrates

Faulkner's ideas that the main question is what 'quality' *does* rather than *is*. Ringo's attitudes toward the South, a means that Faulkner employs to show his quality, is reflected in the things he does and says. Speech is an aspect of action."[29]

The black character closest to Ringo in the Sartoris saga is old Simon.[30] Indeed, in *The Unvanquished* we see Simon in a cameo that portends Ringo's future. As he sits beside the bier of Colonel John, Bayard fixes the faithful retainer in his mind and ours:

> Simon had been his body servant during the War and when they came home Simon had a uniform too — a Confederate private's coat with a Yankee brigadier's star on it and he had put it on now too, like they had dressed Father, squatting on the stool beside him, not crying, not weeping the facile tears which are the white man's futile trait and which Negroes know nothing about but just sitting there, motionless his lower lip slacked down a little; he raised his hand and touched the coffin, the black hand rigid and fragile-looking as a clutch of dead twigs, then dropped the hand; once he turned his head and I saw his eyes roll red and unwinking in his skull like those of a cornered fox.[31]

One need not ask *who* Simon is, but rather *what* he is. One of the Colonel's faithful dogs might just as well be seated beside the bier. Despite the unkindness of the image Bayard draws for us, however, it is in perfect harmony with the *tradition* that demanded of the Negro that he be a perpetual child on the one hand and a fount of wisdom, love, strength (the old verities), and loyalty on the other. If the image is strained and incredulous it is no more so than the tradition. When wisdom, love, strength, and loyalty are forced onto the image of a simpleton (a Confederate private's coat with a Yankee brigadier's star pinned on it?), logic runs amok; and under such weight, language again falters, giving us a picture more reminiscent of an inhabitant of a bestiary than of the human race. A "cornered fox" is what Bayard finally sees beside the colonel's bier. And the fact that he does see a fox and not a human being betrays him, makes a lie of his entire image of love and affection — exploding it forever from the realm of believability. The fox is cornered, scared, trapped; and Simon is there out of something more?

Not necessarily; but yes. The system made necessary the contradiction and justified it. Sterling Brown has pointed out that when slavery was being attacked, "southern authors countered with the contented slave; when cruelties were mentioned, they dragged forward the comical and happy-hearted Negro. Admittedly wrong for white people, slavery was represented as a boon for Negroes on theological, biological, psychological warrant. Since Negroes were of 'peculiar endowment,' slavery could not hurt them."[32] Simon (and Ringo; for Simon is merely an aged Ringo) at the colonel's death is consistent with his portrayal throughout the Sartoris saga. More animal than human, more child than grown-up, more simple-minded than alert, he is that particular species of humanity that is not only content to be a slave but for whom freedom would be a burden and a mockery. Thus, Simon mourns the past as much 'as old Bayard. Hear him speaking to his long dead master:

> "you jes got ter lay down da law ter 'um, Marse John; wid all dese foreign wars en sich de young folks is growed away fum de correck behavier; dey don't know how ter conduck deyselfs in de gent'man way. What you reckon folks gwine think when de sees yo' own folks ridin' in de same kine o' rig trash rides in? You jes got ter resert yo'self, Marse John. Ain't Sartorises sot de quality in dis country since befo' de War? And now jes' look at 'um."[33]

And finally, he makes the ultimate apology for the System: " 'Whut us niggers want ter be free fer anyhow? Ain't we got ez many white folks ez we kin suppo't?' "[34] One is left to wonder who is supporting whom? And at what human expense? Simon and old Bayard's system of mutual exploitation make them dependent upon each other: Simon spends money that the black church has entrusted to his keeping, and despite old Bayard's protestations to the contrary, he replaces it — exacting, of course, his pound of comedy:

> "Get it back. Haven't you got collateral for it?"
>
> "Is I got which?"
>
> "Something worth the money, to keep until the money is paid back."
>
> "Yessuh, I got dat." Simon chuckled again, unctuously a satyrish chuckle rich with complacent innuendo. "Yessuh, I got dat, all right. Only I never heard hit called collateral befo'. Naw suh, not dat."
>
> "Did you give that money to some nigger wench?" old Bayard demanded.
>
> "Well, suh, hit's like dis — " Simon began. But the other interrupted him.
>
> "Ah, the devil. And now you expect me to pay it back, do you? How much was it?"
>
> "I don't rightly ricollick. Dem niggers claims hit wuz seventy er ninety dollars er somethin'. But don't you pay 'um no mind; you jes' give 'um whutever you think is right: dey'll take it."
>
> "I'm damned if I will. They can take it out of your worthless hide, or send you to jail — whichever they want to, but I'm damned if I'll pay one cent of it."
>
> "Now, Cunnel," Simon said, "you ain't gwine let dem town niggers 'cuse a member of yo' family of stealin', is you?"[35]

Simon dies, predictably, in a whore's apartment; he is, also predictably, murdered. Too old to work when we first meet him (although we are told that he has gone to war with Colonel John Sartoris as his retainer), he is Bayard's fool and Miss Jenny's whipping boy:

> Hers was a forceful clarity and a colorful simplicity and a bold use of metaphor that Demosthenes would have envied and which even mules comprehended and of whose intent the most obtuse persons remained,

not long in doubt; and beneath it Simon's head bobbed lower and lower and the fine assumption of detached preoccupation moulted like feathers from about him, until he caught up the tray and ducked from the room. Miss Jenny's voice followed him, descending easily with a sweeping comprehensiveness that included a warning and a suggestion for future conduct for Simon and Elnora and all their descendants, actual and problematical, for some years.[36]

Neither Miss Jenny nor Bayard (and, by extension, the Southern tradition) can provide any opportunity for Simon to be anything *but* what he is; for as is, he is *essential* to their way of life. Is his performance, then, at the bier of Colonel John to be marveled at?

Having reviewed the role assigned to black men and young black boys in the Sartoris legend of the great Old South, we turn to the role assigned to black women. In *Sartoris*, Elnora, the house servant and cook, is soon described—with what can now be seen as description bent on establishing the *specialness* of the Negro: "Her faded blue garment was pinned up about her knees and it was darkly and irregularly blotched with moisture. Beneath it her shanks were straight and lean as the legs of a tall bird, and her bare feet pale coffee splashes on the dark polished floor."[37] She is more form than substance, going to and from the kitchen on "sibilant"[38] bare feet; steadfast and Christian, she does her work and, not yet fully matured in the tradition, she reminds us of nothing so much as a young Dilsey of other Faulkner stories. In "There Was a Queen,"[39] however, she emerges as the full-blown black slave matriarch in the flesh; she is high priestess and keeper of the Sartoris flame:

> So the quiet now was the quiet of womenfolks. As Elnora crossed the backyard toward the kitchen door she remembered how ten years ago at this hour old Bayard, who was her half-brother (though possibly but not probably neither of them knew it, including Bayard's father), would be tramping up and down the back porch, shouting stableward for the Negro men and for his saddle mare. But he was dead now, and his grandson Bayard was also dead at twenty-six years old, and the Negro men were gone: Simon, Elnora's mother's husband in the graveyard too, and Caspey, Elnora's husband,[40] in the penitentiary for stealing, and Joby, her son, gone to Memphis to wear fine clothes on Beale Street. So there were left in the house only the first John Sartoris' sister, Virginia, who was ninety years old and who lived in a wheel chair beside a window above the flower garden, and Narcissa, young Bayard's widow, and her son.[41]

Her past loves, her children, her enslavement, nothing is more important to Elnora than that she keep the Sartoris faith and bear witness to Sartoris importance through her care for Miss Jenny. She must do this lest the world forget the Sartorises. Such is her special privilege: " 'I can take care of her,' Elnora thought, crossing the backyard. 'I don't need no help,' she said aloud, to no one—a tall, coffee-colored woman with a small high fine head. " 'Because it's a Sartoris job. Cunnel knowed that when he died and tole me to take care of her. Tole me. Not no outsiders from town.' "[42] One need say no more about Elnora and her proscribed destiny except that she does not disappoint our expectations of the Southern tradition in literature. With the exception of age, she is not unlike Louvinia of *The Unvanquished*. Louvinia is devastated when she realizes that her son Loosh has shown Yankee soldiers where the Sartoris silver was buried before he and his wife had run to the Yankees and freedom. When Granny Millard, Ringo, and Bayard leave to find and retrieve the silver, Louvinia's parting words are: " 'You tell them niggers to send Loosh to you, and you tell him to get that chest and them mules, and then you whup him!' "[43] In a sense, nothing more need be said about any of the black women characters in the entire Sartoris saga beyond what Lee Jenkins has already explained: "These women do not object to their subjugate status; on the contrary, they are presented as defenders of it as they pursue their functions and submit to a destiny which they seem to accept."[44] (Meloney, the prostitute, is what she is and nothing more.) Jenkins makes the further point that "It is no wonder that the blacks are loved [?] and respected [?] by the whites they serve. How else could the whites live with them at all unless the blacks are presented as accepting and submissive — which in the final analysis only means that they are forgiving? By being presented as accepting the burden and the evils of servitude, the blacks absolve the whites of guilt, and allow for the continued enactment of inequality in white relations with the blacks."[45]

What *does* Faulkner intend, then, that we make of the Ringos, Simons, Elnoras, and Louvinias? I certainly cannot agree with Charles Peavy that he "was in no way intending to sentimentalize the slavery system."[46] On the contrary, when one considers that of all the black types represented in the Sartoris saga, the author, like a biased parent, reserves his most careful attention for the Ringos and Simons and Elnoras (he hardly masks his impatience with those who do not allow themselves to be woven into the tapestry of the great Old South), one is hard put to find any other rationale for their existence.

Early in this essay, I declared my feeling that William Faulkner stands as the South's ranking artist. Nothing convinces me more of that fact than that, keen observer of human nature that he is, he cannot completely ignore the fact that other Blacks people his idyllic Southern land. What he does with such "others" bears testimony, I believe, to his commitment to (and identification with) his Southern tradition. Loosh, his wife Philadelphy, Caspey, and that sea of black humanity which moves blindly toward freedom represent such characters.

When Caspey returns to the Sartoris plantation after serving in World War I, he is firm in his conviction that " 'War showed de white folks dey can't git along widout de cullud man. Tromple him in de dus', but when de trouble bust loose, hit's " 'Please, suh, Mr. Cullud Man; right dis way

whar de bugle blowin', Mr. Cullud Man; you is de savior of de country."
And now de cullud race gwine reap de benefits of de war, and dat soon.' "[47]
His militant talk does not impress old Bayard, however, and he shows
himself capable of quieting it. Boastful Caspey entertains his family
(Simon, his father; Elnora, his sister; and Isom, Elnora's son), with his
exploits in France when Bayard orders him to " 'Get up from there and
saddle my horse.' "[48] When Caspey moves too slowly, "old Bayard reached a
stick of stove wood from the box at his hand and knocked Caspey through
the opening door and down the steps at his father's feet."[49] Neither Bayard
Sartoris nor William Faulkner seems to be disturbed by this different black
voice in the plantation choir. In fact, by the time Bayard hits Caspey,
Faulkner has already warned the reader of his uselessness. During the war,
we are told, Caspey (whatever boastful stories he might tell his family)
was merely "working a little and trifling with continental life in its martial
phases rather to his future detriment."[50] He has returned home, we are
further told, "a total loss, sociologically speaking, with a definite disincli-
nation toward labor, honest or otherwise, and two honorable wounds
incurred in a razor-hedged crap game."[51] Thadious M. Davis makes the
point that Faulkner's comic treatment of Blacks sometimes seems inappropriate. She chides the artist:

> Faulkner does not pursue his development of Caspey's rebellion and
> changed attitudes, instead he lapses into ridiculing the youth's militancy
> by having the aged white patriarch, Bayard Sartoris, best him into
> submission to his former status. In spite of the brief delineation and the
> reversion to type, Caspey's loss of faith in the old mores and his desire for
> change are harbingers not only of Faulkner's increased awareness that
> the tensions between past and present affect blacks as well as whites, but
> also of his inability to portray the sensibilities of modern blacks.[52]

My reading of the Sartoris saga leads one to disagree only partly with
Davis. Where Davis feels that Faulkner is unable to portray modern black
sensibility, I remain convinced that Faulkner *refused* to portray such
sensibilities (with swift and sure judgment he dismisses them) because to
do so would compromise his original intention of shoring up the Southern
tradition.

Loosh and Philadelphy fare no better than Caspey. Like Caspey, too,
however, they are not easily dispensed with. It is Loosh who watches the
movement of the Civil War with a heart that affects his physical being.
When he comes upon young Bayard and Ringo playing their war game,
mapping the progress of the Confederate soldiers with celebration, he
brings a knowledge of the progression of the Union soldiers that so delights
him that he can barely contain himself. Even Faulkner's bent for establishing the past Southern tradition is not strong enough to deny the artist this
picture. Given it, should Davis speak of Faulkner's "inabilities to portray
the sensibilities of modern blacks?"

Then suddenly Loosh was standing there, watching us. He was Joby's son and Ringo's uncle; he stood there (we did not know where he had come from; we had not seen him appear, emerge) in the fierce dull early afternoon sunlight, bareheaded, his head slanted a little, tilted a little yet firm and not askew, like a cannonball (which it resembled) bedded hurriedly and carelessly in concrete, his eyes a little red at the inner corners as Negroes' eyes get when they have been drinking, looking down at what Ringo and I called Vicksburg. Then I saw Philadelphy, his wife, over at the woodpile, stooped, with an armful of wood already gathered into the crook of her elbow, watching Loosh's back.

"What's that?" Loosh said.

"Vicksburg," I said.

Loosh laughed. He stood there laughing, not loud, looking at the chips.

"Come on here, Loosh," Philadelphy said from the woodpile. There was something curious in her voice too — urgent, perhaps frightened. "If you wants any supper, you better tote me some wood." But I didn't know which, urgency or fright; I didn't have time to wonder or speculate, because suddenly Loosh squatted, looking at me with that expression on his face. I was just twelve then; I didn't know triumph; I didn't even know the word.

"And I tell you nother un you ain't know," he said. "Corinth."

"Corinth?" I said. Philadelphy had dropped the wood and she was coming fast toward us. "That's in Mississippi too. That's not far. I've been there."

"Far don't matter," Loosh said. Now he sounded as if he were about to chant, to sing; squatting there with the fierce dull sun on his iron skull and the flattening slant of his nose, he was not looking at me or Ringo either; it was as if the red-cornered eyes had reversed in his skull and it was the blank flat obverses of the balls which we saw. "Far don't matter. Case hit's on the way!"[53]

Long after the Sartoris celebration is ended, Loosh (and Philadelphy, of whom I will speak shortly) will disturb our minds not unlike the ghosts of Faulkner's past must have disturbed his — demanding explanation, justification, and, most importantly, remembrance. It is they who disturb the otherwise easily tranquil (and dismissable) Sartoris legend with a sound so powerful in its discordance that its carefully laid foundation is shaken forever. Childhood idylls, mutual dependencies — nothing can secure the Southern tradition against the force of Loosh's declaration: " 'I done been freed. God's own angel proclamated me free and gonter general me to to Jordan. I don't belong to John Sartoris now; I belongs to me and God.' "[54] Who in the presence of such a statement can defend the peculiar institution of slavery or celebrate its past?

Carefully reading Faulkner's description of Loosh's reaction to his impending freedom, it is hard for me to understand Nilon's suggestion that "Loosh's position is essentially tragic because he has no preparation for his freedom; he has no place to go."[55] It is much easier to say, with Nancy Tischler, that Loosh "has every right to turn against his Southern owners during the Civil War. And we come to admire honest disloyalty as we once admired unthinking loyalty."[56] *Where* one goes is inconsequential; that one is able to go is the testimony to freedom. Loosh and Philadelphy may yet be seen as the only unvanquished characters in the entire saga; for she matches his eloquence with her own courage. Against Granny's threats of misery and starvation, this woman, obviously afraid, weighs creature comfort against the call to freedom and makes a choice that is the first and only recognition of black manhood that Faulkner provides:

> "Don't go, Philadelphy," Granny said. "Don't you know he's leading you into misery and starvation."
> Philadelphy began to cry. "I knows it. I knows what they tole him can't be true. But he my husband. I reckon I got to go with him."[57]

They go; and though we do not hear from them again, the lesson they teach us remains: there is no fear, no uncertainty, no ignorance that will make an entire people opt for slavery; and as long as there is one voice of discontent, a system that seeks to enslave is in peril.

What one can say of the great sea of black humanity's push for freedom is little beyond the fact that Faulkner presents it only as a backdrop to Granny Millard's unreal foray into Union territory. All's the pity; for despite his downplaying of that event, it remains one of the few instances where the artist might have connected a main artery of his anemic (and dying) time and tradition directly into the healthy heart of the modern world. Why, then, if not to connect a dying world with the living, the Sartoris legend? Why the illogical and unashamed support of certain black characters and the total rejection of others? How can the traditional Southerner ever come to terms with—or share an affinity with—the descendants of slaves?

Perhaps Faulkner himself is a source from which to seek answers. Hear him on the question of modern black/white relations in 1956 when Blacks were demanding nothing less than full citizenship: "This problem is far beyond a mere legal one. It is even far beyond the moral one it is and still was a hundred years ago in 1860, when many Southerners, including Robert E. Lee, recognized it as a moral one at the very instant when they in turn elected to champion that underdog because that underdog was blood and kin and home."[58] It is understandable that William Faulkner recognizes and admires the tribalism of Robert E. Lee. In many ways they are alike; for just as Lee, that brilliant strategist of war—one whose brilliance the North recognized and tried to woo—chose to put aside personal morality and stay with his kin, so, too, it appears, did William Faulkner. And this leaves but one further question to be asked: what does it mean to be a great general in a wrong cause? Or a great writer in a wrong cause? Is it not time, and do we not need, as a nation (for the nation's sake), to demand of our great writers and generals that their efforts support what we hold to be morally correct?

Notes

1. Cf. Irving Howe, "William Faulkner and the Negroes: A Vision of Lost Fraternity" in *Commentary*, 12 (October 1951), 359.

2. Carl Sandburg, *Abraham Lincoln: The War Years* (New York, 1939), I, 569.

3. Ibid., 1: 555.

4. Herman Melville, "Benito Cereno," in *The Shorter Novels of Herman Melville* (New York: Liveright Publishing Corp., 1942), p. 114.

5. Ralph Ellison, *Shadow and Act* (New York, 1953), pp. 39–41.

6. *Faulkner in the University*, ed. Frederick L. Gwynn and Joseph L. Blotner (Charlottesville: Univ. Press of Virginia, 1959), p. 79. It is interesting to note that Faulkner is speaking in 1958 as if slavery were only just abolished. He suggests that the South/he is still "working out" a system that has been outlawed for nearly a hundred years.

7. Howe, "William Faulkner," p. 359.

8. Ibid.

9. *The Unvanquished* (New York, 1959), p. 16.

10. Although in other Faulkner stories this childhood friendship is evoked (Miss Worsham of *Go Down, Moses* states that she and Mollie Beauchamp "grew up together as sisters would"), this is the most detailed and descriptive of the actual experience in Faulkner's works. It is in this actual detailing that language becomes revealing.

11. *The Unvanquished*, p. 162.

12. Howe, "William Faulkner," p. 360.

13. Ellison, "Twentieth-Century Fiction and the Black Mask of Humanity," in *Shadow and Act*, pp. 24–44.

14. *The Unvanquished*, p. 67.

15. Ibid., p. 16.

16. Ibid., pp. 16–17.

17. Ellison, *Shadow and Act*, p. 43.

18. *The Unvanquished*, p. 152.

19. Ibid., p. 15.

20. Lee Jenkins, *Faulkner and Black-White Relations: A Psychoanalytic Approach* (New York: Columbia Univ. Press, 1981), p. 121.

21. *The Unvanquished*, p. 103.

22. Jenkins, *Faulkner*, p. 120.

23. Ibid.

24. Ibid., p. 107.

25. Charles Chesnutt, *The Conjure Woman* (Ann Arbor, 1969), p. 147. See Eugene Terry, "A Critical Analysis of Charles Waddell Chesnutt's 'The Conjure Woman' and 'The Wife of his Youth' and 'Other Stories of the Color Line' " (diss. Univ. of Massachusetts 1974).

26. Charles H. Nilon, *Faulkner and the Negro* (New York, 1965), p. 2.

27. *The Sound and the Fury* (New York, 1955), p. 106.

28. Perhaps for that point of view we must turn to Nate Shaw in Theodore Rosengarten's *All God's Dangers*.

29. Nilon, *Faulkner*, p. 62.

30. I have not chosen to treat all the black characters found in the Sartoris saga, but the typical types. I have also not followed the stories in any particular sequence.

31. *The Unvanquished*, p. 182.

32. Sterling Brown, *The Negro in American Fiction* (Washington, D.C., 1937), p. 2.

33. *Sartoris* (New York, 1953), p. 113.

34. Ibid., p. 89.

35. Ibid., pp. 204–05.

36. Ibid., p. 55.

37. Ibid., p. 32.

38. Ibid.

39. "There Was a Queen" in *Collected Stories of William Faulkner* (New York, 1950), pp. 727–44.

40. In *Sartoris* Caspey is Elnora's brother. I do not, however, see that this makes a difference to my discussion of the black types in the Sartoris saga as the character remains unchanged.

41. "There Was a Queen," pp. 727–28.

42. Ibid., p. 728.

43. *The Unvanquished*, pp. 66–67.

44. Jenkins, *Faulkner*, p. 120.

45. Ibid.

46. Charles D. Peavy, *"Go Slow Now": Faulkner and the Race Question* (Eugene, Ore.: Univ. of Oregon Press, 1971), p. 31.

47. *Sartoris*, p. 76.

48. Ibid., p. 83.

49. Ibid., p. 89.

50. Ibid., p. 73.

51. Ibid.

52. Thadious M. Davis, *Faulkner's "Negro"* (Baton Rouge, La.: Louisiana State Univ. Press, 1983), p. 67.

53. *The Unvanquished*, pp. 14–15.

54. Ibid., p. 64.

55. Nilon, *Faulkner*, p. 62.

56. Nancy M. Tischler, *"Black Masks": Negro Characters in Modern Southern Fiction* (University Park, Penn.: Pennsylvania State Univ. Press, 1969), p. 184.

57. *The Unvanquished*, p. 64.

58. "Letter to the North," *Life*, 5 March 1956, p. 52.

A Coda to *Sartoris*: Faulkner's "My Grandmother Millard and General Nathan Bedford Forrest and the Battle of Harrykin Creek"

M. E. Bradford*

The imaginative energy that produced the Sartoris family — in *Sartoris*, "There Was a Queen," and *The Unvanquished* — was not quite expended in these works. During the years of World War II, in the midst of Faulkner's consciously patriotic phase, he returned once more to "the matter of Sartoris" and made a memorable addition to his chronicle of that worthy family. This addition, "Grandmother Millard,"[1] links the indomitable, gallant Sartoris spirit and the Sartoris' deeds of former days with the American military and political enterprise of the early 1940s.

The closest analogue to "My Grandmother Millard" is *The Unvanquished*. The story is almost like an extra chapter of the novel. But not really. For though the central character here, as in *The Unvanquished*, is the corporate spirit of the Sartoris family and the principles of order which it comprehends, particularly in the person of its matriarch, Granny Rosa Millard, and though the Sartoris clan is brought forward as an epitome of the regime of the Old South, that order in its successful struggle to survive is remembered in this context not as a comment on the South's place in the dialectic of American culture but rather as a prescription or example to strengthen and propel forward the entire nation — the Union it had almost broken — in the great global trial of an international war for survival.[2]

Colonel John Sartoris, in words remembered by the narrator, his son, is the one responsible for objectifying this larger envelope of American history which frames and deepens the story proper, the "courtship" and marriage of Cousin Melisandre (from Memphis) to Lieutenant Philip St-Just Backus (Backhouse) of Tennessee, with a little special help from General Bedford Forrest and Colonel Sartoris' mother-in-law. Speaking with a high heart, he tells his son Bayard and Bayard's companion, the Negro boy Ringo, " 'I won't see it, but you will. You will see it in the next war, and in all the wars Americans will have to fight from then on. There will be men from the South in the forefront of all the battles, even leading some of them, helping those who conquered us defend that same freedom which they believed they had taken from us' " (672–73). In other words, that temper which was conquered but not "vanquished" with Appomattox, that "uncomplex will for freedom engaged with a tyrannous machine," could lose battles but "could not be defeated" because "they just

---

*This essay was written for this volume, and appears here for the first time by permission of the author.

willed that freedom strongly and completely enough to sacrifice all else for it" (672).

The freedom of which he speaks is, to be sure, the liberty of a culture or a community to be itself, a self-determination of structured "families" of independent people, not a freedom from the social bond.[3] Granny plays off the feckless idea of "freedom from" in her remarks to her household after one of the black men on the place begins to talk about what the tide of emancipation will mean, once it reaches Yoknapatawpha. During her ritual practice of burying family silver, she declares, " 'I want all of you free folks to watch what the rest of us that aint free have to do to keep that way' " (669).[4] "Freedom from" here means to be cut off, adrift, beyond the shelter of interdependence. When she invites the restive Lucius to think of himself in that way and points to the road, "he went back to the garden" (670). But defense of the patriarchal (or matriarchal) order is the struggle for the freedom of the possibility of the human community, the association of real persons who are individually fulfilled in their support of each other, and so alive. And even preserving that possibility is worth whatever it costs.

However, though duty and responsibility (the positive names for what Granny calls "not free") are major motifs in "My Grandmother Millard" and though the story ends in a marriage, comedy's traditional image for the promise that civilization will continue, excessive emphasis on these sober concerns exposes us to the danger that we will distort the story's flavor and attribute to the author a heaviness of touch not, in this instance, to be proved against him. The tone here is light. No real "dangers" obtrude upon the course of events. Only foolish complications— like Yankees bent upon victory in a war they cannot really win, and the exaggerated delicacy of young Southern girls. Or the foolish notions that some men have—that war is what war is really about. Or if not war, then honor, instead of home and family and the safety of those we love. Rosa Millard's role in correcting these misconceptions is high comedy surrounding a moment of low farce. But it suffuses the entire narrative, giving considerable unity to its casual flow. And it is to her performance that we must look in order to read the work.

The story opens with Bayard's account of how his maternal grandmother made all the inhabitants of the Sartoris plantation periodically practice the burying of the family silver and other valuables. She is almost a military figure in her timed rehearsals of this operation. Knowing that Memphis has fallen to Federal control and that Vicksburg is under siege, she anticipates the arrival of marauding enemy troops. Yet she proposes to allow them to do no more than interrupt the orderly flow of life in her dominion. Part of the labor of preservation is preventing the enemy from changing the way people react and how they can be expected to behave. Another part is restricting the amount of external damage he can do, given the limits of his own moral code. Mrs. Millard is mindful of both of these components of resistance in a fashion that is summarized in the regular burial and unearthing of the precious trunk.[5] Something of what Sartoris means is, of necessity, put by during the turmoil of war. But we can expect it to reappear as soon as the war is done—and even during the war, whenever possible.

For the chatelaine of Sartoris will not completely suspend the order of civility even to protect properties and ways. It is her view that war, even at its worst, must accommodate itself to the central business of life: that the priorities which she represents have precedence over the routines of clash and maneuver and the imperatives of military pride. And for this reason she interrupts the principal Confederate hero for her part of the South and summons him into her parlor from the midst of his campaigns. Asserting her antecedent claims upon his courtesy, she calls him (as *Mr.* Forrest) from the defense of northern Mississippi to help her briefly in some *really important* work. As we learn in *The Unvanquished*, Granny finds it difficult to regard the War as anything more than an outburst of interacting male vanities, complicated somewhat by the influence of conflicting ideologies, such as the notions which almost infect Lucius.[6] Therefore, when the conjunction of Melisandre's misadventure in the outhouse and the name of the gallant Confederate officer who rescues her from its destruction produce a verbal and situational irony which obstructs the romance that begins when they first set eyes on one another, the matriarch turns for the instruments of solution to the male authority who is supposed to command the powers she requires.

Bedford Forrest is that figure. He can spell the names of his officers however he wishes. As long as the young lieutenant who has found his "beautiful girl" sitting with the silver chest in the ruins of the Sartoris privy is called Philip St—Just *Backhouse*, Melisandre can only scream in his presence and flee when he is announced. But the officers and men of General Forrest's command are officially what and who he says they are. And they can be made into whatever he needs them to be—including husbands. Forrest had known "Miss Rosie" in her Memphis years and had been a regular guest in her husband's house (688). It might be argued that she presumes upon that relation, upon her station and upon his. Yet her ability to ask this much of Forrest, like his response to her message, is a measure of the health and soundness of the regime they both represent.

And he does honor her request, coming in all his dusty grandeur to receive his marching orders. At her bidding (and in keeping with the suggestion of an uncomplicated child, plus Philip's announced willingness to surrender his name in death), Forrest lists Lieutenant *Backhouse* as officially dead—after first appointing him an honorary brevet major general (696). Then he "re-creates" the young man as Lieutenant *Backus*.[7] To finish his work at Sartoris, he makes up a report of the "action" at Harrykin Creek and writes a furlough pass to bring John Sartoris home for the wedding (690). This metamorphosis is a fragile thing—clearly resting upon the general's emergency powers as military commander of the Confederate States of America in north Mississippi. But it is strong enough to pacify the affected sensibilities of Cousin Melisandre and thus put a check on the troublesome vainglory of the fine boy who is soon to be Cousin Philip as well as arrange for a military wedding which will allow the elders to go about their ordinary business without emotional intimidation from young love.

Granny's trouble was clear to her from the moment when, already recognizing that both boy and girl were incurably "smitten," she hears someone speak Philip's name. The lieutenant's behavior, even when only reported to her, seems to Granny the perfect male equivalent of Melisandre's distraction once he rides away: "she could look at one of them and know all the other Cousin Melisandres and Cousin Philips both without having to see them" (679). From past experience with the species, "she knew more about Cousin Philip than even Ringo could find out by looking at him" (680). But when first invited to take breakfast at Sartoris and consider the problem created by his charge and Granny's charge, Forrest's polite answer includes " 'why boy' " (689). There has been in his world a brief delay in the unfolding of consequences from the impasse at Sartoris. But it lasts only until the general attempts to give battle to Yankees under "Sookey" Smith.[8] At this point the desire of Philip St-Just Backhouse to lose his name in glorious death proves to be a time bomb that was just waiting to explode the well-laid plans of the Wizard of the Saddle. Cousin Philip takes a small force given him to demonstrate in the enemy's front, visits (at dawn) Granny's front yard (and flowerbed) for one more "long, lingering goodbye," and so frightens the Federal forces by his wild charges through their picket that Smith throws out all his cavalry and begins a cautious retreat (692). Then Forrest knows what boy Mrs. Millard expected him to bring along for breakfast — the most gallant and the politically best connected junior officer in his command, and, so long as he believes his love is hopeless, the most dangerous officer to any future plan of entrapping General Smith.

Both Philip and Melisandre are acting out roles in a conventional romantic melodrama: the young officer with his gestures of bravado and exaggerated chivalry, the girl with peculiar mooning patterns for sleep and eating and the composition of wistful poetry and song. And though the girl knows that Backhouse's old and honorable name is not finally going to keep them apart, she and her love together insist on the importance of certain words that belong to and inform the ritual of fated, hopeless courtly love (683). Their language on this theme, as in Melisandre's flowery speech to General Forrest (695) and in Cousin Philip's wooden recitation of the Backhouse heritage (682), remind us of the distance between concept and fact, language and life, as in Lucius' original understanding of "free," Ab Snopes' idea of the "spoils of war," or even the notion of "General" as sometimes entertained by Bedford Forrest (688,

684, 694). Each, in his own way, is thus brought back to a simpler reality: the truth that the only proper reason for war is to defend civilization, and that the relations of men to women (and of both to children) define what civilization means—that people, not abstractions, confederate and "cohere."

A sensible woman like Rosa Millard will not be controlled by these "mere counters" because she is a woman intent upon the care and management of real people, existing and living within the orbit of her influence. She represents, as Cleanth Brooks has written, "the nurturing and sustaining force on which a society rests."[9] In her familial vision the being of people is logically prior to their meaning. It is true that portions of the story seem to lack an organic connection to its central thrust—particularly Faulkner's brief glance backward to the account of Granny as a collector of Yankee livestock in *The Unvanquished*.[10] At times the narrative focus appears to wander too far away from Mrs. Millard. And her problems in this embroglio are no full test of her mettle. She is surrounded by patently comic figures whose "actions . . . grow out of some image of the self which is carried to the point of affectation."[11] They detract from our sense of her magnificence. And the element of low comedy, linked to a mere verbal irony at the heart of this work, prevents her triumph from being anything half so impressive as the victory of Sartoris in the antecedent novel.[12] Yet it is the same *kind* of triumph. Moreover, the stature of her performance in this upbeat "afterthought" to *The Unvanquished* is not so much diminished by its ease or its context as might at first appear.[13] For Faulkner was correct in the point which he was making in most of the fiction which he wrote in the 1940s. To survive in war, a society must preserve its character, its system of values, in private things—even while it engages the enemy without. It must remember why and by whom it was made and not become what it fights against. Granny personifies the determination of her entire culture to honor the imperatives that Faulkner hopes will be the case with the larger American of World War II.[14] For these reasons the story ends as it begins—with the Sartoris household practicing the burial and recovery of the silver chest. The exercise, as a trope, is a summary of everything else that occurs as a result of the "battle" at Harrykin Creek (699).

Notes

1. "My Grandmother Millard and General Bedford Forrest and the Battle of Harrykin Creek" was first published in *Story*, 30 (March–April 1943), 68–88, and reprinted in *Collected Stories of William Faulkner* (New York, 1950), pp. 667–99.

2. Related evidence appears in "The Tall Men," "Two Soldiers," and "Shall Not Perish" in *Collected Stories*, pp. 45–61, 61–99, 101–15.

3. Liberty to the South meant "the rights and autonomy of communities." See Charles G. Sellers, Jr., ed., *The Southerner as American* (Chapel Hill, 1960), p. 42; Eugene D. Genovese, *Roll, Jordan, Roll: The World the Slaves Made* (New York, 1974), pp. 118–20.

4. "Free" is frequently an ironic term in Faulkner. See below on "Mountain Victory" and in the fourth section of "The Bear" in *Go Down, Moses* (New York, 1942), where Isaac McCaslin claims "Sam Fathers set me free" (p. 300).

5. For the importance of this theme in *The Unvanquished* (1938), see my essay, "Faulkner's *The Unvanquished*: The High Costs of Survival," *Southern Review*, 14 (Summer 1978), 428–37. I concur with James B. Meriwether that if this story were part of that novel it would appear as the first episode, but I cannot agree that the story has no connection with the whole meaning of the novel. See Meriwether, "The Place of *The Unvanquished* in William Faulkner's Yoknapatawpha Series," (Diss. Princeton 1958), pp. 136, 139. The story too is about coming out of conflict unvanquished and presents the same virtues as necessary for survival; the difference is in tone and stature.

6. In *The Unvanquished*, Lucius is less easily corrected; there he is intoxicated by the idea of freedom, betrays Granny, and leaves with the other slaves. But events confirm what Granny tells him in the short story. The change of name to "Lucius" here is in keeping with the positive temper of most Faulkner fiction after *Go Down, Moses*.

7. The Backhouse genealogy (and the original spelling) is not implausible; the name was well known in South Carolina in the eighteenth century, though Backus is, of course, a much more common spelling. See Robert D. Bass's *The Green Dragoon* (Columbia, S.C., 1973), pp. 12, 292.

8. Despite the date of the dispatches Granny writes for Forrest (28 April 1862), the appearance of General Smith would date the story in February 1863 — when Forrest enjoyed his victory at West Point. A second General Smith (A. J.) came against Forrest in June 1864. Faulkner appears to be relying here on folk memories. See Meriwether, p. 136; on Forrest's career, see Andrew Lytle, *Bedford Forrest and His Critter Country* (New York, 1960).

9. Cleanth Brooks, *William Faulkner: The Yoknapatawpha Country* (New Haven, 1963), p. 99.

10. *The Unvanquished*, pp. 127–75.

11. I quote John Lewis Longley, Jr., *The Tragic Mask: A Study of Faulkner's Heroes* (Chapel Hill, 1963), p. 113, the best previous treatment of this story.

12. Longley appropriately calls the story a "comedy of manners" (p. 113), although the low comic elements do not fit this pattern. Melisandre's name may come from the puppet-play in *Don Quixote*, I, 26, where she is saved by Don Quixote interrupting the puppet show, violently destroying most of the puppets in the name of chivalry. If this is the source, we have further evidence this is not all romantic or high comedy.

13. Meriwether, "The Place of *The Unvanquished*," p. 136.

14. See Faulkner to Harold Ober, *Selected Letters of William Faulkner*, ed. Joseph Blotner (New York, 1977), p. 150.

Vision and Re-Vision: Bayard Sartoris

Judith Bryant Wittenberg*

Bayard Sartoris, whom a critic called one of Faulkner's "sick heroes,"[1] was a haunting and significant figure in the author's imagination. He dominated the 1929 novel *Sartoris*, a shortened version of *Flags in the*

*This essay has been written for this volume, and is published here for the first time with permission of the author.

Dust and a work that Faulkner said contained "the germ of my apoch-rypha,"[2] serving as the immediate precursor of Faulkner's most famous protagonist, Quentin Compson, and he and his twin brother John appeared in several other works Faulkner wrote during the period 1927–1933, including the short stories "Ad Astra," "With Caution and Dispatch," and "All the Dead Pilots" and the screen play *War Birds*. Until 1973, however, when *Flags in the Dust* was published, our vision of Bayard was based solely on *Sartoris* and two of the short stories.[3] As a result, the question almost inevitably arises as to how our sense of the tormented young veteran of World War I has been amplified or altered with the availability of the full-length version of the novel.

Virtually none of the material which treats Bayard directly was excised when Ben Wasson performed his now-notorious surgery on *Flags in the Dust* after it had been rejected by several publishers and accepted by Harcourt, Brace only on the condition that it be cut by several thousand words; instead, Wasson eliminated passages depicting Horace Benbow, his sister Narcissa, and Byron Snopes, the bank clerk who spies on Narcissa and sends her lascivious letters. The result, as the new title *Sartoris* suggests, is a novel much more tightly focused on Bayard and other members of his family, on Bayard's futile efforts, after World War I and the death of his twin, to find some pattern by which he can live, and on his series of self-destructive actions and ultimate death. Yet Faulkner was unhappy with the revision, expressing his displeasure in his essay on the composition of *Sartoris* in which he compared the original version of the novel to a living plant that is brutally trimmed and dies in the process.[4] Because *Flags in the Dust* is a rich and expansive work, more appropriate as the cornerstone of the Yoknapatawpha saga than the streamlined work actually published in 1929, one can sympathize with Faulkner's dismay at the situation. Still, one needs to ask, how does the restoration of the material from the original version, none of it pertaining directly to Bayard, affect our vision of him?

Many of the passages excised by Wasson in 1928 and thus unavailable to us until 1973 merit consideration, because they help us, albeit rather obliquely, to understand Bayard better and to assess more properly the place of the novel in which he appears in Faulkner's development as a novelist. Critics, for example, have often commented on the inadequacy of the Bayard of *Sartoris* as a tragic hero, on the problems created by thrusting the weight of meaning on a central character who is inarticulate and unreflective and whose very motives seem confused. They have also discussed the way in which very little in Faulkner's previous work prepares us for the greatness of the Yoknapatawpha novels published during the period bracketed by *The Sound and the Fury* and *Absalom, Absalom!* Yet many of the passages eliminated from the typescript of *Flags in the Dust* serve, to some degree, to rebut these critical positions.

Admittedly, these passages do little to alter our direct experience of

Bayard as guilty and doom-ridden, obsessed with his twin brother to the exclusion of much else, regressively given to childish behavior that harms both others and himself, and unable either to make the sort of affectionate connections that would offer him succor or to find a vocation that would provide him psychic sustenance. They do, however, develop other characters who serve as crucial foils to Bayard, illuminating his problems by means of parallelism or contrast and thus making him seem less singular in his destructive behavior and attitudes. An early passage in the novel suggests the motif of mimicry when it describes the faces of Stuart's men as "like mirrors reflecting their leader's constant consuming flame" (18),[5] and such mimicry, whether in the form of literal mirroring or in the more extreme guise of parody, contributes in important ways to our understanding of Bayard's plight.

Much has already been written about the ways in which Horace Benbow functions as a figure whose difficulties are similar to those of Bayard—his problems of readjusting to life in Jefferson after being overseas, his entanglements with women that provide complications but no satisfaction, and his self-destructiveness. What becomes even more striking upon looking at the passages in question is how pointedly Faulkner intended him to be, despite some personality differences from Bayard, almost a mirror image of him in significant ways. The men are together only once, in the Thanksgiving scene, and they never interact, but—and in this they are akin to Quentin and Benjy in *The Sound and the Fury*—crucial aspects of their experiences are much alike.

Such parallels between the men are made even clearer by the restoration of original material. The important scene in which Bayard lies in an actual jail cell, after a binge engendered by his desperate efforts to assuage his grief for his dead twin, musing despairingly about the fact that there is "nothing to be seen" in his life, is followed some pages later in the original version by a long section in which Horace thinks about the fact that he is in a "solitary cage" and ponders the way in which his life has been a "golden and purposeless dream" filled with lost hopes and futile actions (*Flags*, 143–44, 162–63); the essential parallels are striking. A passage detailing Horace's vision of himself and his sister as "two children" and his own state of mind as "adolescent," eliminated from *Sartoris* (190), underscores, in pointed fashion, the fact that much about Bayard, too, is childish. Another such passage mentions Horace's tacit struggles with Narcissa over the subject of Belle and augurs the overt quarrels in the Sartoris household that occur some pages later, while a scene in which Horace confesses feeling that he has "exchanged" his sister for his future wife nicely serves as a reminder of an early scene in which Bayard's efforts at physical and psychic union with his wife Caroline are rapidly superseded by his yearning for his lost sibling; the scene is followed by another one in which Horace feels "revulsion" at having had another woman in the house he shared with his sister. Horace's excised affair with Belle's sister,

Joan Heppleton, presages Bayard's otherwise rather shocking infidelity to Narcissa. Because these subtle parallels and recapitulations are missing from *Sartoris*, Bayard's plight seems more singular and thus more puzzling.

The restoration of the material depicting Narcissa Benbow has many of the same effects. Not only is the Narcissa we see in *Flags in the Dust* a more richly developed character with greater claims to the reader's sympathy, but her responses to Bayard tell us a good deal both about her problematic psychological state and about his ambiguous relationship with his twin brother. Some pages excised from the original version of the novel show her musing about the Sartoris twins in a comparative way — "Bayard's was a cold, arrogant sort of leashed violence, while in John it was a warmer thing, spontaneous and merry and wild" (*Flags*, 64) — and contrasting the "cruel skill" of Bayard's leap from a rope into a swimming pool with John's insouciant ascent in a balloon; in the same moment she displays the "shrinking and fearful curiosity" which marks her responses to Bayard in other excised passages, revealing that she is, psychosexually, far from healthy. In this she is like both Bayard and Horace, who seem virtually unable to have mature and fulfilling relationships with members of the opposite sex; she is like them also in manifesting a self-centered response to events that is often so extreme as to seem almost comical — "to her the war had been brought about for the sole purpose of removing [the Sartoris twins] from her life" (65–66). Narcissa's situation has further similarities to those of Horace and Bayard; experiencing the premature loss of her parents, she was virtually forced into a certain role and compelled to undertake her quest for maturity without appropriate guidance. All three are essentially victims of crucial deprivations in their family lives; learning that the situation of the Benbow brother and sister parallels that of Bayard increases our understanding of all three. Bayard's postmarital ambivalence to Narcissa is made all too explicit in either version of the novel by his broken promises to her, his heedless behavior, and his ultimate desertion and infidelity; what is explicit only in *Flags in the Dust* is the way in which Narcissa, too, struggles with and against her marriage, caught between pity and distaste in one moment, between shrinking and fascination the next. The late passage describing the way in which Bayard's presence had been "a violation of the very depths of her nature" and her feeling of being with him that of "a lily in a gale" (*Flags*, 368), serves as a reminder both of the way in which he has been a harsh and turbulent visitant in her world. She is thus at once his double and his victim, a fact we can understand fully only by reading the complete version of the novel.

Although Byron Snopes is far more pathological than any of the other main characters, we need the full delineation of him available in *Flags in the Dust* in order to see clearly the way in which he provides a parodically extreme version of their plights in both his attitudes and his behavior. To be sure, parody is a useful device in either version of the novel; the romantic ghosts of the Sartoris world "in crinoline and hooped muslin and silk" are ironically mimicked by those in the world of Snopes, "ghosts of discouraged weeds, of food in the shape of empty tins, broken boxes and barrels," while the problems in the black Strothers family either echo or parody those in the white world. Yet only in the depiction of Byron available in *Flags in the Dust* do we see Faulkner using the device to its fullest extent. An excised sentence presents him as "a silent man who performed his duties with tedious slow care and who watched Bayard constantly and covertly all the while he was in view" (7), and a deleted passage depicts him writing one of his obscene letters to Narcissa while "the clock ticked on like a measured dropping of small shot" during a long and tedious day (95).

While both Byron's voyeurism and his anonymous letters to Narcissa, like his later theft, mark his criminal bent, aspects of his desperation and his actions provide crucial reminders of problems also troubling the central characters. He is behind "a grille" in the bank and later expresses a sense of being a "cornered rat"; we thus see him as entrapped, like Bayard in his jail cell and Horace in his "solitary cage," all of them either literally or metaphorically incarcerated. He is also like them in feeling guilty and restless and unable to find any sort of truly rewarding outlet; hence he resorts to peeping and writing, demonstrating an ineffectualness like that of Horace and a propensity for actions destructive to himself and others like that of both Horace and Bayard. His isolation, like his lasciviousness, is extreme, but in both he reveals affinities with the other main characters, and his defeated sexual assault on his fiancée, Minnie Sue Turpin, depicted in yet another excised passage, leaves him in a state of "helpless rage and thwarted desire" (260) which is a parodic version of the frustrations experienced by his male counterparts, though theirs is rather less object-oriented.

Byron's writing of his final letter to Narcissa before his bank theft and flight is described in another excised passage as one in which "the language was the obscenity which his jealousy and desire had hoarded away in his temporarily half-crazed mind and which the past night and day had liberated" (253). Here Faulkner invokes one of the central motifs of the novel, what one might call the problematics of authorship. Byron is misusing language, or employing it for pathological ends, but his compulsion to express himself verbally which has, in a way, replaced his capacity to live in any sort of meaningful fashion links him with several other characters. As he admits in an earlier letter to Narcissa. " 'I could touch you. . . . But I can not I must pore out on paper must talk' " (244). Byron's obsessive letter-writing, like his compulsive voyeurism, has supplanted any rewarding direct involvement in the world around him.

In this respect, Byron is virtually a parody of the artist figure, much like Horace Benbow, whose earnest and futile efforts to create one perfect vase, along with his endless verbal effusions, also make him an extreme of the type. Yet Horace's description of "lying" as a creative act definable as a "struggle for survival," "little puny man's way of dragging circumstance about to fit his preconception of himself as a figure in the world" (*Flags*, 189), reveals that such efforts at "artistry," however doomed and however estranging, are psychically necessary. "Authorship" may be problematic, but it is in some sense sustaining.

In these ways the novel, particularly in its original version, serves as a harbinger of Faulkner's greatest work, *Absalom, Absalom!*, which is at one level essentially about the quest to find meaning in and through narrative. *Flags in the Dust*, too, depicts the search for sustaining forms; these are predominantly linguistic, making many of the characters incipient "authors" in a metaphoric sense, but they can be otherwise, such as Aunt Sally Wyatt's bag of scraps, "containing odds and ends of colored fabric in all possible shapes," which she "shifted and fitted . . . like pieces of a puzzle picture, trying to fit them to a pattern or to create a pattern about them" (*Flags*, 136), or Belle Mitchell's pretentious domestic rituals which become a form of theatrics in which she is "the principal actor. . . . preening and petulant" and the scene seems to onlookers a sort of "moving picture" (*Flags*, 167).

Like Aunt Sally's efforts to shape her fabric to a pattern and Belle's attempts to make her life a ritualized drama, the many tale-tellers and letter-writers of the novel are also struggling to impose shape on the chaos of experience and, implicitly, to "author" themselves into being and find some sort of meaning in the process. Faulkner may have intended to make this clear from the outset of *Flags in the Dust*, because he began it with old man Falls's story about Colonel John Sartoris's clever escape from a Yankee patrol. The presence of the teller in the tale is obvious; Falls uses the vernacular of his ordinary speech and reveals his admiration for the Colonel's resourcefulness in the shape of his narrative and his delight in the Colonel's sangfroid with his closing line, " 'And then he tole you to tell yo' aunt he wouldn't be home fer supper' " (*Flags*, 5). Ironically, Falls was not even present at the event he describes, but it is clear that his regular reiterations of the tale satisfy some need he has to apotheosize a local Civil War hero and thus implicitly to endow his own past with meaning. Caspey's tall tales about the exploits of the black forces in Europe serve a similar function; his assertions that " 'black regiments kilt mo' Germans dan all de white armies put together' " and that the enemy soldiers were " 'sort of pink lookin' and 'bout eight foot tall' " and could be handled only by fighters of his race reveal his newly acquired sense of racial self-esteem and act as a prologue to his vow that " 'I don't take nothin' offen no white man' " (*Flags*, 53–56). Of course the exaggerations in the tales also reveal Caspey's somewhat self-destructive affinity for statements that are incongruous with the realities of his situation, a propensity that later badly angers Old Bayard and causes him to knock Caspey down with a piece of stove-wood.

A rather more complicated role in the novel is played by Aunt Jenny's storytelling. She is the repository of much of the family lore and also verbally quite expressive, but her love of the more colorful stories of human foibles that she reads in the daily press makes her a less than fully reliable narrator, and the process by which, telling stories about the first Bayard, she transmutes fact into legend "until what had been a hair-brained prank of two heedless and reckless boys wild with their own youth had become a gallant and finely tragical focal point to which the history of the race had been raised from out the old miasmic swamps of spiritual sloth by two angels valiantly and glamorously fallen and strayed" (*Flags*, 12), serves as a key to what has been seen by many as a flaw in the book as a whole, its tendency to romanticize what is essentially sophomoric behavior. At other points, however, Aunt Jenny's commentary plays the sort of role occupied by Shreve McCannon's responses to Quentin Compson's anguished outpourings in *Absalom, Absalom!*, serving to deflate or bring into ironic perspective the excesses of another "narrator." Jenny's ambivalence toward her material is clearly a result of her conflicting feelings toward the family itself; on the one hand, she is proud of their derring-do, while on the other she is forced to recognize how much it is a product of a highly masculine ethos in which as a woman she cannot participate, and this recognition engenders the irony that is often precipitated by the status of "outsider."

The letters of Horace and Byron to Narcissa are one form of verbal artistry, while the somewhat exaggerated tales of old man Falls, Caspey, and Aunt Jenny are another; yet another is evident in the recital of actual memories either to oneself or to another listener. So many of these either deal directly with Bayard and his brother or parallel his own situation that they do much to illuminate his ongoing and anguished struggle with the memory of his brother's wasteful and yet faintly glamorous death. Narcissa's memories of the exploits of the Sartoris twins as youths reveal the way in which they were both foolhardy and yet compellingly theatrical, while her later recurrent mental pictures of Bayard's mad rush on the wild horse and his swerving it "with an utter disregard of consequences to himself onto a wet sidewalk in order to avoid a frightened child" (*Flags*, 135) indicate simultaneously the insane excesses of his behavior and the fact that he is not totally insensitive to other human beings, something his later behavior toward Narcissa and his unborn child would seem to belie.

The memories of Bayard's brother John repeated to Bayard on various occasions by members of the MacCallum family, who are otherwise a salutary, if temporary, force in his life, serve as painful reminders of the ways in which other people found his dead brother more attractive than himself and thus increase his sense of worthlessness, impelling him farther along the path of self-destruction. Rafe's memory of the time John was floating along on a log "singing that fool song as loud as he could yell" (*Flags*, 113) is followed by other MacCallum brothers' praise for John's thoughtfulness—" 'he never come out hyer withouten he brung Mandy and the boys a little sto-bought somethin' " (324)—his stalwartness on a hunt, "no matter how cold and wet it was," and his unfailing cheerfulness, and all of it painfully underscores our sense of Bayard's insufficiency and his own sense of guilt and loss. Even V. K. Suratt's seemingly neutral memory of being taught to chop cotton by his older brother, " 'and ever' time my hoe chopped once I could year his'n chop twice' " (*Flags*, 126), reintroduces the theme of a sibling feeling comparative inadequacy.

All of these excursions into the recollections of others shed light on the values of those who are doing the recalling as well as on the relationship of the Sartoris brothers, thus revealing how consistently the narrator is a significant presence in anything being narrated, a concept obviously central to the multiple visions of Thomas Sutpen offered in *Absalom, Absalom!* At the same time, if the narrative, whether it is a letter, a tall tale, or a memory, gives a certain shape and meaning to experience, it also serves to imprison the narrator in some mysterious fashion; although the process of authorship is a liberating one in crucial ways, the artifact, once produced, serves to define and constrict its producer. This seeming paradox is evident in a primitive way in the actions of a neurotic suffering from a repetition compulsion—his acts at once sustain and entrap him—but it also informs in more subtle ways some of Faulkner's major fiction, much of which is about the process of arriving at order-giving visions, a process which simultaneously frees and restricts and is analogous on the whole to authorship itself.

As the central character of the novel in either of its forms, Bayard Sartoris offers a vivid example of this process in all of its problematic aspects. Essentially a taciturn and unreflective man, he is in no sense a type of the "author," a type of which the verbose and "literary" Horace Benbow seems a more obvious representative. Yet Bayard's expression of, and his virtual imprisonment by, the haunting memories of his brother's death provides a parallel to Horace's—and others'—difficulties with the same process and ends more tragically than any of theirs.

Bayard's first version of his brother's death is terse and angry, filled with incomplete sentences and expletives; both the opening and closing sentences of his account are the same—" 'I tried to keep him from going up there on that goddam little popgun' " (*Flags*, 38, 40)—suggesting in their implication of circularity that he is somehow enclosed in and by the tale. Subsequent accounts, a very brief one to Rafe MacCallum and a longer one to Narcissa, appear when he is in a twilight state psychologically, either having drunk a good deal of whiskey or awakened from a nightmare, and each is "a brutal tale, without beginning, and crassly and uselessly violent and at times profane and gross" (238), a self-absorbed presentation which takes no heed of the listener and his or her desires. His final accounts are all inward, and they appear eruptively; the first is his irrational self-accusation, after his grandfather's death, that " 'You caused it all: you killed Johnny' " (*Flags*, 307), the second occurs during his insomniac night at the MacCallums as he "relived it again as you might run over a printed, oft-read tale" and is able only to articulate his awareness that he is in a "hell" of perpetually "seeking his brother" (315). Bayard's experience with the circularity and reiterativeness of grief-stricken and guilty memory entraps him; it is a circle from which the only exit is death. Bayard's capacity for "authorship," though it exists, is limited and finally counterproductive, for the only verbal form he can discover for his anguished thoughts proves both solipsistic and destructive. He is thus like Horace in the fact of somehow being " 'ordered by words,' " as Horace puts it in the phrase that hints at the paradoxical problematics of authorship which Faulkner explores in the novel.

Thus the restored text of *Flags in the Dust* provides us with a portrait of young Bayard Sartoris and his difficulties that is greatly enriched by its development of characters with problems parallel to his, problems that are either psychological or linguistic in nature. It reveals that Faulkner saw Bayard as symptomatic of a general dis-ease affecting members of his community and as one element in an expansive and variegated work. Moreover, it is a work whose consideration of such issues as the utility yet constriction of verbal forms imposed upon the chaos of experience — its implicit self-reflexity — anticipates aspects of his later great novels. The revision offered by the publication of the complete version of *Flags in the Dust* after so many years is consequently twofold, clarifying the novel's relationship to major works in the Yoknapatawpha saga even as it vividly amplifies the Bayard depicted in *Sartoris*.

Notes

1. Melvin Backman, "Faulkner's Sick Heroes: Bayard Sartoris and Quentin Compson," *Modern Fiction Studies*, 2, No. 3 (Autumn 1956), 95–108.

2. *Faulkner in the University*, ed. Frederick L. Gwynn and Joseph L. Blotner (Charlottesville, 1959), p. 285.

3. "With Caution and Dispatch" was published in *Uncollected Stories of William Faulkner*, ed. Joseph Blotner (New York, 1979), pp. 642–64, and *War Birds* was published in *Faulkner's MGM Screenplays*, ed. Bruce Kawin (Knoxville, 1982), pp. 275–420. For a more detailed analysis of *War Birds*, see Kawin's new essay.

4. "William Faulkner's Essay on the Composition of *Sartoris*," *Yale University Library Gazette*, 47 (January 1973), 124. The entire text appears in this volume.

5. All page references are to the 1973 Random House edition of the novel as edited by Douglas Day. A paperback version appeared under the Vintage imprint in 1974. Both texts have been severely criticized by Faulkner scholars; see Part V of this volume.

The Dream of the Present:
Time, Creativity, and
the Sartoris Family

Andrea Dimino*

Faulkner's writing of *Flags in the Dust* in 1926–27 marks not only his appropriation of his "little postage stamp of native soil" as his fictional territory, but also the beginning of a more intense engagement with the problem of human time.[1] From the vantage point of Faulkner's major period, from *The Sound and the Fury* in 1929 to *Go Down, Moses* in 1942, we can discern in the earlier novel a remarkable probing of the nature of time that informs every aspect of the work. In *Flags in the Dust* Faulkner develops, for example, a precise vocabulary to describe the inner dynamics of his characters' experience of time, and he links this terminology to a network of temporal images; of particular interest in *Flags in the Dust* is Faulkner's effort to create a fruitful image of the present moment. Faulkner's depiction of time also has important ramifications for his narrative structure, techniques of characterization, and psychology.

In the theme of creativity in *Flags in the Dust* Faulkner's fascination with the human experience of time meshes with his personal interest in the art and craft of the novelist. Throughout Faulkner's career creativity remains one of the central values in his novels: though Faulkner seldom chooses writers, artists, or musicians as characters, he uses artistic creation as a crucial metaphor for all creativity, and often shows people engaged in creative processes, as they tell stories in order to come to terms with the past or with the present or as they conceive of projects for the future. Inherent in this depiction is an essential doubleness that corresponds to the doubleness of Faulkner's own creative imagination: David Minter has described Faulkner's creativity as the "happy conjunction" of "conservative" and "radical" tendencies.[2] Faulkner's "conserving or preserving" imagination commits him, like his characters, to "following, copying, and repeating," which also manifests itself in narrative as "extension, elaboration, and rearrangement"; his "radically innovative" imagination commits him to "playing, improvising, and inventing," to "transgressions," to "ignoring boundaries and breaking rules"—and to depicting characters who do the same.[3]

Ideally, Faulkner's characters should be moved to create out of a desire to go beyond the limits of their past selves, to keep "on trying endlessly to express" themselves, "and to make contact with other human beings."[4] But Faulkner's depictions of creativity usually reveal deeply problematic elements, especially in regard to time. For one thing, Faulkner regards longevity as an imperative of creation: someone "can

---

*This essay has been written for this volume, and is published here for the first time by permission of the author.

build a bridge and will be remembered for a day or two, a monument, for a day or two, but somehow the picture, the poem — that lasts a long time, a very long time, longer than anything."[5] Faulkner's characters, however, often employ in their creations materials that decay too quickly or that even work against the very aim of their creation. Moreover, Faulkner's novels contain endless examples of characters whose creation stems from a hatred or fear of time: Thomas Sutpen's "design" of founding a dynasty is an act of revenge against a past insult, and the Old Frenchman's audacious straightening of a riverbed in *The Hamlet* reflects his need to leave a lasting mark on the future. Often a character's most significant creation will be a mode of time itself: for example, Miss Rosa Coldfield in *Absalom, Absalom!* chooses to remain in the temporal mode of "fury," looking toward the past, because she will not forget Sutpen's insult.

Faulkner's description of the actual nature of time helps to explain why his characters find time problematic. It is important to note that Faulkner's memories of writing *Flags in the Dust* evoked, during an interview, his most detailed explanation of his "theory" of time: "time is a fluid condition which has no existence except in the momentary avatars of individual people. There is no such thing as *was* — only *is*."[6] Thus all creative projects are based on characters' prior creations of a sense of their temporal existence. Faulkner's characters must synthesize two different, paradoxical, aspects of the present: a sense of the fluidity of the self in time and a sense of being re-created anew in each succeeding moment. The vertigo of momentariness drives Faulkner's characters to overemphasize the continuity associated with the fluid aspect of the present. In reaction against the unstable momentariness of time and the prospect of death, Faulkner's characters may want to reify temporal continuity in their creations — in their children, or in an inanimate object like a mansion that they can pass on to their heirs; or they may seize upon an abstract idea of the eternal in order to escape altogether from the tensions of human time. This reaction against time involves a concomitant movement toward space, which many of Faulkner's characters find a more congenial field of action, more tangible, easier to understand, more malleable to their efforts. Faulkner's characters may even treat temporal phenomena as if they were spatial. I shall use the term "spatialized time" in referring to characters' creation of such modes of time, which Faulkner often describes with spatial metaphors or similes; in *Flags in the Dust* John Sartoris is a prime example of a character who attempts to turn time into space.

Within *Flags in the Dust*, as I shall show, the relation between time and creativity is rendered by means of a complex structure of repetition; not only does young Bayard Sartoris repeat certain actions obsessively, but a number of characters function as doubles for him, repeating temporal patterns that shed light on his struggle to be creative. If we use *Flags in the Dust* as a vantage point from which to assess Faulkner's depiction of time and creativity later in his career, a larger structure of repetition emerges.

In its extreme spatialization, and in other important aspects, the Sartoris experience of time serves as one essential pole in Faulkner's overall depiction of time. Because of his deep predilection for antithesis, which Walter Slatoff calls his "polar imagination," Faulkner returns to the Sartoris family at a critical point roughly midway in his major period, as he tries to conceive of new characters who can experience the present moment in a mode of time that is freer of the encroachments of the past and of the future.[7]

Faulkner's return to the Sartorises in *The Unvanquished* marks an essential transition in his portrayal of time and creativity. On the one hand *The Unvanquished* serves as a critique of the temporal experiences of such characters as Quentin Compson, Joe Christmas, and Thomas Sutpen in the first half of Faulkner's major period, experiences of spatialized time that have their root in *Flags in the Dust*. On the other, *The Unvanquished* represents an early formulation of new possibilities of living in the present, inaugurating a movement that will culminate in Faulkner's creation of Ike McCaslin in *Go Down, Moses*.

SARTORIS: TIME'S DEADLY GAME

In *Flags in the Dust* Faulkner conceives of "Sartoris" not merely as the name of a flamboyant dynasty emerging at a crucial formative period in the South, but also as a way of experiencing one's existence. The most important component of Faulkner's idea of "Sartoris" is a temporal one. As old Bayard Sartoris looks at the family Bible, in which he is about to enter the deaths of his grandson, his granddaughter, and his great-grandson, he muses that "Sartorises had derided Time, but Time was not vindictive, because it was longer than Sartorises. And probably unaware of them. But it was a good gesture anyway."[8] The Bible's list of births and deaths becomes for old Bayard the "stark dissolving apotheosis of his name," made more troubling by the fact that the family is now threatened with extinction: of the younger generation, only his widowed grandson, young Bayard, remains.

John Sartoris, old Bayard's father and the founder of the dynasty, has tried to mold his own existence and that of his family by substituting genealogy, his family line, for a fuller and more dynamic conception of time. John exalts genealogy over time even though he recognizes the irony of his act: in the acquisitive, mobile society of nineteenth-century America, where all people have in common the same dubious origins, a concern with genealogy is "poppycock" (96). More seriously, John Sartoris' declaring himself the point of origin of a patriarchal genealogy has wide-ranging ramifications for the structuring of thought and experience: in *Time and the Novel* Patricia Drechsel Tobin discusses the relation in Western thought between the line of generations and the linearity of our conceptions of logic, causality, history, and language, a linearity that informs the

traditional novel as well. In responding to what Tobin calls the "genealogical imperative," John Sartoris chooses vanity and arrogance, a choice that
old Bayard is still Sartoris enough to consider a "good gesture."[9]

Fundamentally, then, to be a Sartoris means to live arrogantly, both
with respect to time and with respect to other people. These two aspects of
Sartoris arrogance cannot, in fact, be separated, for in depicting his vision
of time Faulkner insists on the crucial importance of the relation of the self
to another; without a certain kind of relation one cannot live fully in time,
and one cannot attain full adulthood. John Sartoris' arrogance toward
time denies the integrity of the other, since he imposes a diminution or
fragmentation of self not only on his contemporaries but also on those who
come later in his genealogy. His domination of other people is reflected in
the genealogy itself, in his heading of a regiment during the Civil War, in
his opposition to the carpetbaggers, in his election to the state legislature,
and in his murder of other men in order to further his own ends. Old Man
Falls reenacts the process of gaining domination in miniature, and in a
comic way, when he impersonates John Sartoris opposing the carpetbaggers in 1872: "He crossed his arms on his breast, his hands in sight, and for
a moment old Bayard saw, as through a cloudy glass, that arrogant and
familiar shape which the old man in shabby overalls had contrived in some
way to immolate and preserve in the vacuum of his own abnegated self"
(263). The external symbol of Sartoris domination is the hawklike nose
that even Miss Jenny possesses, a nose curiously similar to that of Faulkner
himself, the literary parent of the Sartorises. When young Bayard first
appears in the novel, he symbolically repeats his taking on of this Sartoris
legacy of arrogance at birth: at first a formless "tall shape" emerging from
the garden, "he came on and mounted the steps and stood with the
moonlight bringing the hawklike planes of his face into high relief" (44).
Young Bayard's paradoxical "abnegation" of self in becoming an arrogant
Sartoris has made him bleak and cold, whereas his dead brother's "merry
wild spirit" helped him to "laugh away so much of his heritage of
humorless and fustian vainglory" (426).

Only one aspect of John Sartoris' experience of time offers a potential
alternative to his genealogical arrogance. In his desire to project himself
into the future he creates not only his genealogy but his "dream," which
Faulkner describes in elevated but vague terms. The word "dream" is an
important one in Faulkner's temporal vocabulary, for it represents one of
the primary ways in which people can orient themselves toward the
future. Characters who dream will concentrate on people or on concrete
things or on ideas that will in some way complete them, give them a
fullness of existence lacking in what Faulkner calls the "momentary
avatar" of their present selves. Unlike John Sartoris' will to genealogy, the
dream does not impose a completely rigid pattern on future generations.
In fact, in its very essence the dream appears to transcend his individual
existence: John's "stubborn dream, flouting him so deviously and cun-

ningly while the dream was impure," seems to have "shaped itself fine and clear now that the dreamer was purged of the grossness of pride with that of the flesh" (120). Ironically, his death in some way arrests the decay of his dream in the concrete world of passing time: "Freed as he was of time," John Sartoris "was a far more definite presence in the room" than Old Man Falls or old Bayard, "the two of them cemented by deafness to a dead time and drawn thin by the slow attenuation of days" (5).

Like Sutpen in *Absalom, Absalom!*, whose dream of a fuller existence is reduced to a genealogical "design," John Sartoris channels much of his dream of creativity into the domination of space — his ironic stance toward his genealogy reveals that he hardly dares hope to dominate time. This domination of space is reflected in his railroad, in his house, and in his land. His domination over other people has an essential spatial element as well, as we see in the image of Sartoris women being drawn, generation after generation, into their husbands' "orbits," and in Old Man Falls's remark that someone who kills you is more "kin" to you than your wife, forcing you to become an irrevocable part of your murderer's linear genealogy (427, 264).

John Sartoris' railroad represents the boldest and most promising part of his dream, since it involves a less rigid relation between Sartorises and other people. Sitting on his veranda, as his son Bayard is to sit nearly fifty years later, John Sartoris perceives the trains noisily entering his valley and then departing. The railroad thus projects Sartoris' dream beyond his immediate surroundings, and even into the future: after his death the railroad will project itself across the whole nation, "from Chicago to the Gulf, completing his dream" (44). If history will complete John Sartoris' dream of spatial expansion, his house will continue to preserve something of its first master in a more problematic way. Faulkner's description of the ghosts in the Sartoris house marks the beginning of his long fascination with ghostliness, with the ways in which people can leave their imprint on space and on later generations. Though old Bayard's struggle with his father's heritage has changed the character of the Sartoris parlor to some extent, the room still preserves something of John Sartoris' "jovial and stately masculinity"; behind the "dun bulks" of "shrouded furniture" one can perceive the ghosts of his former guests, "as actors stand within the wings beside the waiting stage" (60–61).

Sartoris' land, however, opposes his domination. Although he has named his land "Sartoris," after himself, the land preserves almost nothing of his existence; in spite of cultivation, it exists in its own immemorial rhythms, molding the people who work it more than it allows itself to be molded by them. At the beginning of the novel, the "familiar changeful monotony of the land" gives old Bayard a "drowsing peace" that is inimical to his father's restless spirit, the same feeling that old Bayard gets from roaming the "peaceful woodlands in their dreaming seasonal mutations" (9, 36). As in the novels of his major period, Faulkner here uses the word "peace" to describe an existence in which a person has given up the struggle of human time, reverting to a quiescent state that Faulkner often compares to the existence of a plant. In appropriating the "dreaming" land to serve his own dream, John Sartoris has therefore had to use something whose very nature undermines his hopes of dominating time and space.

The resistance of the temporality of the land to John Sartoris' dream helps to underscore our perception that the secret dream of dominating time is, at its core, a longing for the absolute that can only be frustrated by the actual conditions of human existence. Gary Stonum has shown how Faulkner's career as a novelist hinged on his ability to move beyond the fascination with the absolute reflected in the "visionary poetics" of his early works; in *Flags in the Dust* we learn the sobering lesson that the impossibility of John Sartoris' dream of dominating time will inevitably transform it into a dream of death.[10] Since his ultimate enemy is time, his only truly creative act can be the creation of the moment of his death: this moment, alone of all the moments of his existence, can put a stop to time. Yet after this one absolute moment, old Bayard imagines eternal frustration; Sartorises will be "denied that Sartoris heaven in which they could spend eternity dying deaths of needless and magnificent violence while spectators doomed to immortality looked eternally on" (94). This Sartoris Valhalla, which John Sartoris has seen in the "chaste and fragile bubble" of his wine glass the night before Redlaw kills him, is another futile dream; the perfect spherical form of the bubble stands in striking contrast to Faulkner's images of the fixed, irrevocable elements of the actual human condition (94). As in such novels as *The Hamlet* and *Light in August*, Faulkner uses the image of a game to evoke these fixed elements, in this case the game of chess. Within the clearly marked space of the chessboard, John Sartoris has created his own role as time's enemy. But the chess game has an added temporal dimension as well. At the end of the novel Faulkner characterizes the Sartoris style of battle with time as a historical anomaly:

> The dusk was peopled with ghosts of glamorous and old disastrous things. And if they were just glamorous enough, there would be a Sartoris in them, and then they were sure to be disastrous. Pawns. But the Player and the game He plays — who knows? He must have a name for his pawns, though, but perhaps Sartoris is the name of the game itself — a game outmoded and played with pawns shaped too late and to an old dead pattern, and of which the Player Himself is a little wearied. For there is death in the sound of it, and a glamorous fatality, like silver pennons downrushing at sunset, or the dying fall of horns along the road to Roncevaux. (432–33)

This historical conception of the game of Sartoris gives added urgency to young Bayard's existential struggle throughout the novel to live in a creative present rather than within the fixed space of "Sartoris." Faulkner sets his novel in the historical present, as in his first two novels, *Soldiers'*

Pay and *Mosquitos*, and makes young Bayard his contemporary — Bayard was born in 1893, Faulkner in 1897. It is only after the accretion of dozens of episodes, however, that the historical dimensions of Bayard's problem can come to the foreground on the last page of the novel. Within the world of *Flags in the Dust*, "Sartoris" is more often regarded as an essence, an ahistorical absolute, and the core of Bayard's struggle is a searing sense of alienation that stems from his Sartoris arrogance.

BAYARDS STRUGGLE FOR THE PRESENT:
SELF, TWIN, DOUBLE

Young Bayard Sartoris erupts into the well-established world of Jefferson in Part I of *Flags in the Dust* in much the same way that Thomas Sutpen erupts onto the scene in *Absalom, Absalom!*: he descends on the town unexpectedly, having gone through an experience — in Bayard's case, World War I — that the town finds alien to its familiar routine, and possessing an arrogant personality that the town finds alien as well. Bayard's dilemma can, however, be seen as the opposite of Sutpen's: the townspeople regard Sutpen as something radically new and cannot understand him, whereas they regard Bayard as something completely known, a "Sartoris," and cannot understand him. The fragmentation of self that young Bayard's "Sartoris" identity entails is reflected in the proliferation of doubles in the novel, some of whom bear the same name. If Faulkner's conception of a creative life in time involves the meaningful confrontation of the self with another, then the Sartoris distortion of self emerges as one key aspect of Bayard's temporal problem.

The first Sartoris double we meet in the novel is young Bayard's namesake, the Bayard from Carolina who was killed in the Civil War, the brother of John Sartoris, and Miss Jenny. Although the actual Carolina Bayard was a reckless young man who died needlessly in an absurd bravura attempt to capture anchovies from the Yankees, Miss Jenny's impassioned Sartoris storytelling has transformed him into a flame or a shooting star, and has shaped his death into "a gallant and finely tragic focal point to which the history of the race had been raised from out the old miasmic swamp of spiritual sloth by two angels valiantly and glamorously fallen and strayed, altering the course of human events and purging the souls of men" (14). When young Bayard returns to Sartoris after World War I, this doubling relation is superseded by young Bayard's anguished obsession with the death of his twin, John; ironically, John resembled Carolina Bayard much more than his brother did. But young Bayard's tale of "violence and speed and death" seems incongruous when juxtaposed to the current historical situation in Jefferson, and also jars with the tranquil and mysterious natural world that surrounds him as he tells it (46).

Though Faulkner envelops the Sartoris house with haunting music, the rhythmic sounds of crickets and frogs, the "musical rain" of the moon, and the "deep timbrous . . . measured respirations" of the water pump, within the house young Bayard finds himself trapped in the enclosure of the room he shared with John:

> He was thinking of his dead brother; the spirit of their violent complementing days lay like a dust everywhere in the room, obliterating the scent of that other presence [the presence of Bayard's dead wife], stopping his breathing, and he went to the window and flung the sash crashing upward and leaned there, gulping air into his lungs like a man who has been submerged and who still cannot believe that he has reached the surface again. (49)

Like the genealogical "game" of John Sartoris, then, the twinship of Bayard and John has transformed Bayard's time into an airless, sinister space that threatens to crush his existence.

Though the nature of the twinship remains somewhat mysterious, Bayard reveals early in the novel that his merry, laughing brother actually shot at him when Bayard tried to deflect him from his suicidal mission. It is a measure of the absurd unresponsiveness of Bayard's world that not one character even mentions John's fratricidal act; instead, most people seem to regret that John died instead of Bayard. Left to brood alone on his brother's surrender to Sartoris fatality, Bayard reverses the actual situation: during his visit to the MacCallums he blames himself for John's death. The episode of his return home, which closes Part I of the novel, ends with Miss Jenny giving Bayard milk and telling him to hush and go to sleep, indicating that people use his childhood self as a double for the present Bayard.

Bayard's grandfather, old Bayard, another Sartoris namesake, also serves as a double in the sense that young Bayard could perceive him as a possible projection of his own self into the future: young Bayard could conceivably take over his grandfather's position at the bank and could also choose to combat the temporal curse of the Sartorises in his grandfather's way. However, Faulkner depicts old Bayard as a man exhausted by his opposition to John Sartoris' will to genealogy; at the moment of his death he suddenly slumps "as though the very fibre of him, knit so erect and firm for so long by pride and by his unflagging and hopeless struggling against the curse of his name, had given way all at once, letting his skeleton rest at last" (360). Old Bayard's transformation of the Sartoris parlor from a scene of jovial hospitality to a mausoleum for "shrouded furniture" reveals that he has primarily worked to negate the past, to oppose his father's sensuousness and energy with emptiness. Old Bayard's memory of seeing his skull reflected in a spring during the Civil War suggests that a realization of his own mortality has made him abjure much of the Sartoris dream of a victory over time. Although he has managed to become the only male Sartoris ever to live past sixty, this capacity for endurance rings hollow: as Dr. Loosh Peabody says, " 'You'd be about as well off dead, anyhow. I don't know anybody that gets less fun out of living than you seem to' " (104).

Old Bayard's choice of "peace" over a creative life in time is reflected in the spatialized universe of his deafness, the "walled serene tower" that he uses as a convenient excuse to ignore other people (37). Since he no longer lives in time, he reacts violently to evidence of historical change, striking Caspey with a piece of stove wood when he realizes that his black servant, after fighting in World War I, now dares to talk back to him. A man of Spartan habits following an absolutely rigid schedule, old Bayard is powerless to affect his grandson's despair; when young Bayard silently touches him on the arm, he finds no satisfying response. It is not clear to what extent old Bayard's insistence on accompanying his grandson in the speeding car is an actual attempt to "touch" young Bayard in time, and to what extent it is simply another Sartoris suicide, as Miss Jenny claims it is. Even though old Bayard dies of natural causes, much to Miss Jenny's disgust, young Bayard's shame after his grandfather's death triggers his final surrender to violent Sartoris annihilation.

Throughout *Flags in the Dust* Faulkner depicts young Bayard as a man divided within himself, caught up in the "dark and stubborn struggling of his heart" (46). Although we sense that Bayard's relation to his twin lies at the core of his struggle, Faulkner's method of characterization prevents the reader from having an immediate emotional response to Bayard. At times the reader will draw conclusions about Bayard because of the proximity of two statements in the text: the phrase "dark and stubborn struggling," for example, occurs for the first time just before Bayard recounts John's death in Part I. At times Faulkner's images may serve as harbingers of psychological insights: the image of the "twinned" rose and wistaria, the rose slowly killing the other vine trained on the same frame, occurs before we even know of the existence of Bayard and John. In general, then, we gain knowledge of Bayard's struggle by responding to Faulkner's techniques of juxtaposition and symbolic substitution. A juxtaposed episode may have an ironic relation to an episode recounting Bayard's struggle, or may reenact in some symbolic way an aspect of that struggle.

Since Bayard is relatively inarticulate, and the people who know him have little insight into his problem, material objects and animals often serve as projections of his psyche, in addition to his human doubles: we come to perceive the wild stallion he rides, the sleek automobile he buys in Memphis, and the airplane he dies in as doubles as well. The automobile, for example, helps to crystallize several issues linked to Bayard's temporal problem. In one sense Bayard's purchase of the automobile, the "gleaming long thing," is an historical act of self-affirmation, a declaration that he is in the vanguard of Jefferson society in 1919 (122). But this straightforward action is overwhelmed by a welter of counterimages that link Bayard's car to John Sartoris' yearning for the absolute, the sinister spatialization of time, and the fatal violence of war. Potentially the car may be a counterpart of John Sartoris' future-oriented dream of a railroad, since it stands "dynamic as a motionless locomotive," but the actual motion of the car recalls the hysterical deaths of the "fallen angels," Carolina Bayard and John, since it flattens space into a frightening enclosure: "they shot forward on a roar of sound like blurred thunderous wings. Earth, the unbelievable ribbon of the road, crashed beneath them and away behind into dust convulvulae: a dun moiling nausea of speed, and the roadside greenery was a tunnel rigid and streaming and unbroken" (122–23). In a limited way the car does enable Bayard to rebel against Miss Jenny and old Bayard to escape from the place called "Sartoris," but as long as Bayard moves only in space the car remains a futile symbol of rebellion, an impotent gesture that anticipates Jason's car in *The Sound and the Fury*. The car as double imprisons Bayard in space, and the novel's action from Part II onward will revolve around Bayard's attempt to transcend the car and enter time.[11]

Among Bayard's contemporaries, who could offer him alternative models of a creative life directed toward the future, only Horace Benbow is depicted in much detail. Horace and Bayard never even meet in the novel, however, except figuratively in the sense that Narcissa Benbow mediates between them as Horace's sister and Bayard's wife. Like old Bayard, then, Horace is juxtaposed to young Bayard in space — reflected in the juxtaposition of their respective strands of narrative — but does not "touch" him in time.

Nevertheless, Horace's temporal experience serves as a mirroring double to Bayard's in a significant, often ironic way. Horace enters the novel at a crucial point, directly after Bayard's long "symbolic day" at the end of Part II, which I shall discuss later in this essay; Horace's return from World War I opens Part III. Like Bayard, who has lived in the prison of Sartoris genealogy, Horace has existed in "a region remote from time," surrounded by the peaceful "Arcadian drowse" of his old home in Jefferson; in England he had lived a "golden and purposeless dream" described as spatialized within the college walls of Oxford (191, 177, 192). He excels at tennis because the game is enclosed within a clearly marked space, unlike the woods where Bayard goes to hunt. Horace's estrangement from time appears in his work as well; in deference to family tradition, another example of the "genealogical imperative," he resigns himself to the "polite interminable litigation" of his law practice, a process that will never be consummated (194).

Thus it is not surprising that the form of art that fascinates Horace is an art removed from time, the tragic beauty of the glass vases that he blows, "preserved flowers" that reflect the same chaste, timeless beauty that he loves in his sister (180). Altering Keats, he apostrophizes both the vase and Narcissa as "Thou still unravished bride of quietude" (190). Fundamentally, Horace's visionary art, where imagery closely resembles that of Faulkner's own early poetry, exists in space rather than time, in fantastic lonely regions "beyond the moon" that he hopes to reach on "flaming verbal wings" (187, 180). Horace appears, then, as an aesthetic version of the Sartorises, the violent fallen angels who also strive to fly to the realms of the absolute.

Horace's existence seems to crystallize in space as a "winged and solitary cage," a "topless cage" in which "his spirit might wing on short excursions into the blue, but far afield his spirit did not desire to go: its direction was always upward plummeting, for a plummeting fall" (191). The idyllic period he spends with Narcissa after returning from the war marks only a "neap tide in his affairs," however; time will intrude on Horace's refined but futile existence in the form of the descent of his doom. In Faulkner's temporal vocabulary, "doom" is a catalyst between two different modes of time, and divides people's lives in two; doom is always associated with the death of one's dream and of creativity, and thus signals that one's life is no longer oriented toward the future. For Horace, as for many other male characters in Faulkner's novels, doom takes the form of a woman: here it is sensuous, overripe Belle Mitchell. Moreover, the woman he is doomed to marry is not a virgin, a situation that has important temporal ramifications for Faulkner. In such novels as *The Sound and the Fury*, *Absalom, Absalom!* and *The Hamlet*, Faulkner's characters seize on the idea of female virginity in order to express their desire to live in a pristine present moment rather than a moment that is polluted by the past. Once Horace surrenders to Belle, the mechanism of Faulknerian doom will spatialize the remainder of Horace's life in a straight line analogous to linear Sartoris genealogy, so that the future will be wholly determined by the past: the days "to come seemed as undeviating and logical as mathematical formulae behind an incurious golden veil" (191). Faulkner's description of Horace and Narcissa traveling on two parallel roads, never to meet, repeats this image of spatialized doom.

Though Horace is more conscious of the onset of his doom than Bayard is, and can articulate the shape of his doom in carefully wrought, feverish phrases, he is equally powerless to make the transition from a spatialized old self to a new self that could be creative in time. Horace's impossible solution to the problem anticipates the episode in which Bayard and Buddy MacCallum sleep in the same room, with Buddy serving as an image of the new self that Bayard is trying to give birth to. Horace wants not a concrete temporal transition to a new self, but a totally different self created magically out of nothing: " 'If you could just be translated every so often,' " he says to Narcissa, " 'given a blank, fresh start with nothing to remember. Dipped in Lethe every decade or so . . . ' " (339–40). This longing for temporal absolutes — a virginal wife, the virginal newness of a present moment without a past, a virginal self — prevents Horace from working toward transcendence in actual time, forging a dream that could be realized in some concrete, albeit imperfect, way.

The crude new town where Horace settles with Belle mocks his dream of virginity, since his home and the town itself are not really new but are cheap imitations of something else. The town smells of the foulness of new money, which Horace finds only somewhat less repulsive than the foulness of the body; yet the money is creative, possessing a "rank fecundity" (411). The town thus mirrors Belle herself, whose spirit proves closer after all to that of her ex-husband, Harry Mitchell. And indeed, the "family" relation between Horace and young Bayard comes to the foreground toward the end of the novel through the mediation of Harry himself, Bayard's " 'wife's brother's husband-in-law,' " whom Bayard sees in a Chicago nightclub (415). Harry, an ugly, crude, but likeable representative of new Southern wealth, can at least endure in the raw chaos of modern America; Bayard can only return to the Sartoris graveyard, and, as we surmise from our last view of Horace in the novel, Horace's future will take the rigid form of a straight line, an endless street down which he will carry, every week, the dripping shrimp that Belle craves. Thus Horace's experience does not simply mirror in a passive way Bayard's struggle to live in time and to avoid his doom: Faulkner's use of Horace as Bayard's double extends the implications of Bayard's temporal problem into the realm of the artist and into modern American society as a whole. If the Sartoris "genealogical imperative" aims to trap time within the family, Faulkner's technique of doubling—playing off Sartoris doubles of Bayard against other doubles who are not kin and against inanimate doubles—works, somewhat paradoxically, both toward an expansion of the family to include all of America, and toward a radical questioning of a family-centered conception of time.[12]

THE MUSIC OF THE PRESENT

Given the domination of Sartoris genealogical time in young Bayard's strangely claustrophobic world, one of Faulkner's greatest challenges in *Flags in the Dust* was to find a vivid, suggestive way of depicting the potentially creative present moment that Bayard finds so elusive. Bayard's struggle to live in time crystallizes at the end of Part II in Faulkner's depiction of a long, eventful day. Faulkner inaugurates here a practice that he is to develop in some of his major novels: he traces the rhythms of one crucial symbolic day, juxtaposing changes in human consciousness to changes in the natural world. In *The Hamlet*, for example, Ike Snopes enjoys his outrageous idyll with the cow during such a day, and the idiot's exalted procession through the hours with the object of his love reflects his achievement of a creative, poised existence in time. Faulkner also uses this technique to depict people's flight from time; Quentin Compson's long day in *The Sound and the Fury* is the last day of his life.

Young Bayard's symbolic day in *Flags in the Dust* plays out all the major aspects of his temporal struggle, reifying for the reader not only compressed, sometimes dreamlike images of his internal dilemma but also images of his relation to the world, to nature, and to society. Essentially Faulkner conveys to us a creative cycle that reflects Bayard's effort to transcend his spatialized Sartoris existence, so that during this day we must distinguish between impulses toward space and impulses toward time. In a sense Faulkner's imagery establishes a symbolic topography of space and time, a topography mirrored by Bayard's actual journey in space during the day, from Sartoris to Jefferson to the countryside, back to Jefferson, to the college town, and finally to Jefferson again. This symbolic topography helps to discern which actions and events are allied with spatialized time and which impel Bayard toward a fuller temporal existence. Faulkner's description of Bayard's car helps to identify the journey as an exploration of Bayard's time: "The car swept onward, borne on the sustained hiss of its huge muffled intake like a dry sibilance of sand in a huge hour glass" (154).

The day begins with several images of John Sartoris' influence over the present, including Bayard's arrogant terrorizing of Simon, the Sartorises' old black servant, and his vision of the effigy of John Sartoris in the cemetery overlooking the valley. Once in Jefferson, however, Bayard can find no responsive image of his own struggle. The townspeople appear to have surrendered their battle with time, creating instead a spatialized world of "shady streets like green tunnels along which tight lives accomplished their peaceful tragedies . . ." (126). Bayard finds the black townspeople incomprehensible, "slow and aimless as figures of a dark placid dream," and the awkward country people are clearly doomed to narrow lives of toil (127). In the blind black beggar he sees a tantalizing but elusive temporal image. The beggar's guitar playing "patterned" the disorderly scene, but not in a truly creative way: he can produce only a "plaintive reiteration of rich monotonous chords, rhythmic as a mathematical formula but without music" (127). Wearing castoff military clothing, the beggar creates music in a diminished present moment of monotony, "patient resignation," and loss.

Around noon, an hour of the day that Faulkner often associates with creativity—it is the hour of Ike McCaslin's transcendent vision of Old Ben in the glade in "The Bear"—Bayard begins to grope tentatively toward a life in time. His friend Rafe MacCallum serves as an important catalyst in Bayard's day, for this yeoman who dwells in the hills recalls Bayard and John's boyhood hunts with his family; the temporal meaning of these hunts will be developed later in the novel. The whiskey that Rafe has brought to town enables Bayard to break out of the constricting routine at the Sartoris place and to try to communicate once again the trauma of the war, the ghostly, hysterical tale of fallen angels, meteors, and "immortal doom" (133).[13] In his drunkenness Bayard claims that his dead brother only helped relieve life's monotony, monotony that we have seen imaged in the blind beggar's music; John did not help his twin to be creative. Bayard also reveals that John shot at him during his suicidal mission, but Rafe only responds by taking him out of the restaurant.

Bayard's problem of creativity is strikingly dramatized when Bayard rides the magnificent stallion that Rafe has taken him to see, a stallion that evokes the whole complex network of images of Sartoris pride and violence: "The stallion stood against the yawning cavern of the livery stable door like a motionless bronze flame, and along its burnished coat ran at intervals little tremors of nervousness and pride. But its eye was quiet and arrogant, and occasionally and with a kingly air its gaze swept along the group at the gate with a fine disdain . . ." (137). The horsetrader's remark, " 'I wouldn't no more walk up to that animal than I'd fly,' " explicitly links the dangerous motion of the stallion with the aviators of World War I and with John Sartoris' dream of escaping the rigid conditions of the concrete, to "fly" like a hawk above the temporal world. The stallion also represents an early stage in Faulkner's development of the concept of "male" time. In such novels as *Light in August*, *Absalom, Absalom!*, and *The Hamlet*, Faulkner associates "male" time with horses, with air and fire, and with linear spatialized time like the Sartoris genealogy. Male time does involve the urge to make a mark on time as an individual, but Faulkner often portrays this mode of time as merely destructive or futile unless linked to the fluid continuity of female time.

Though to a certain extent Bayard's participation in the stallion's rampage stems from a desire to repudiate the human condition, to spurn the earth on "unfolding bronze wings," the rampage also conveys some suggestion of an impulse toward a creative life in the temporal world (140). In this context the motion of the horse, its "fluid desperation," is analogous to the headlong, uncontrollable rush of time itself, and Bayard's attempted mastery of the stallion becomes a first, clumsy effort toward creative work in time: "The stallion moved beneath him like a tremendous mad music, uncontrolled, splendidly uncontrollable. The rope seemed only to curb its direction, not its speed . . ." (140). Faulkner's choice of the "mad music" of the stallion as a metaphor for the fluid momentariness of the present reflects a complex conception of the nature of time. In part this mad music evokes the immaterial, the ineffable, and the ideal. It is this aspect of music that Samuel Beckett celebrates in discussing the temporal meaning of the music of Vinteuil in Proust; Proust regards music as "the idea itself, unaware of the world of phenomena, existing ideally outside the universe, apprehended not in Space but in Time only. . . ."[14] Faulkner's "mad music" of the stallion, however, marries this ideal music to the material animal, thereby giving more value than Proust does to the actual experience of what Beckett calls the "impure subject" — Proust's Swann, who, unlike Proust's narrator, "spatialises what is extra-spatial. . . ."[15] In *Flags in the Dust* Faulkner has already underscored the impurity of the subject in the creative present in describing John Sartoris' dream being purged of the " 'grossness of pride' " and " 'flesh' " after his death (120).

Bayard's more direct experience of the present during the stallion's rampage proves too much for him to handle; the "mad music" stops only with his loss of consciousness. In reaction against the speed and unpredictable momentariness of the rampage, later in the afternoon Bayard regards the "mad music" as a descent into a circular chaos or vortex; in his memory only the chance vision of Narcissa passing in her car holds out a promise of relief from the senselessness of the onrushing present. As in *Absalom, Absalom!*, the vortex is an image of the "maelstrom" of unpredictable reality that sometimes foils people's efforts to be creative, and which threatens to become spatialized into cycles or convolutions.[16]

If the vision of Narcissa cannot help Bayard keep a grasp on the creative potential of the onrushing present, Bayard must search for someone who can play a more helpful role in the crucial temporal dialogue between self and other. In the early evening images of new possibilities for the enlargement of Bayard's self unfold, as he overcomes the social barriers between Sartorises and the rest of humanity and develops a heightened sensitivity to the natural world. The commandeering of V. K. Suratt's car to take the wounded Bayard to the doctor has brought Bayard the company of two country people, Suratt and Hub. Unlike most of the characters in the novel, the shrewd and affable Suratt, who will be renamed Ratliff in *The Hamlet*, offers Bayard a model of a man at home in time.

In order to break through to a mood of fellowship, the three men must first undergo a kind of initiation, walking through sinister reminders of the futility of farm labor and the decaying power of time, the skeletal farm tools and the skull of the old Ford car. Their companion in this initiation is Hub's jug of liquor, which they bring into the shadows where the three stand like "mottled ghosts" next to a spring. With a peaceful fluidity that transcends the "fluid desperation" of the stallion, the spring presides over a transformation of both people and objects. This episode presents us with a positive but fragile vision of human poised in time, within the "small bowl of peacefulness" by the spring, "remote from the world and its rumors" (146).[17] Time is now marked by the steady forward movement of Suratt's voice, which "seemed to fit easily into the still scene, speaking of earthy things" and of his congenial work (148). At the same time that he represents a progressive temporal model and also serves as a suggestive image of Faulkner himself, creating a homespun new voice in his fiction, Suratt reminds us that no one has mentioned work in connection with Bayard so far. We can now identify Bayard's lack of meaningful work as one aspect of his inability to create a self that can live in time.

His contact with Suratt and with the calming fluidity of the spring allows Bayard to undertake an action more creative than his earlier ones. This new movement toward time is reflected in the slower pace of the narrative, which becomes a lyrical evocation of passing moments in the natural world around sunset. When Bayard reclaims his car in town he conceives of a project that will harness and integrate in a socially acceptable way the quiet music of the bowl of peacefulness and the mad music of the stallion; with Hub, Mitch, and three black musicians he will drive to a college town to serenade the coeds. Bayard is no longer alone in his car, but carries people belonging to several of the main classes of his society—a farmer from the hills, a middle-class townsman, and three black men. The instrument of Sartoris arrogance—Bayard has used the car to terrorize black and white alike—has become a microcosm of the South in the historical present, and as such strongly evokes Faulkner's own discovery of the "gold mine" of his creativity in writing *Flags in the Dust*: "I created a cosmos of my own. I can move these people around like God, not only in space but in time too."[18] Bayard, however, feels disoriented in this new mode of existence, as images of treacherous moonlit formlessness and the liquid, flutelike music of birds play off against each other.

The description of the college town suggests that Bayard's new movement toward time has transformed his everyday world, just as the spring has transformed social relations and homely objects: "Through streets identical with those at home they moved smoothly, toward an identical square" (155). The college town—another double of Faulkner's Oxford—thus serves also as a heightened double of Jefferson, Jefferson infused with the possibility of a creative musical present. Appropriately, Bayard has come to town to create music, but as in a dream the old tunes are out of harmony with the treacherous moonlit surroundings, dying and fading in the air. Faulkner's stiffer language in this episode and his use of clichés like the "college Cerberus" also signals the inadequacy of this old-fashioned action and conventional music to express the new existence that Bayard is groping toward. A movement toward a young woman would be an important part of Bayard's life in time, but the need to create music that will be pleasing to conventional young ladies makes it impossible to incorporate the "mad music" of the horse into his serenade.

Since the music is flawed art, it loses its hold on time, deteriorating into the "fading magic of the lost moment" (156). The evanescence of Bayard's creative moment relates directly to the theme of the temporality of art associated with Horace. Faulkner's own conception of art centers on the artist's ability to capture the "fading magic": "The aim of every artist is to arrest motion, which is life, by artificial means and hold it fixed so that 100 years later when a stranger looks at it, it moves again since it is life."[19] As Gary Stonum has shown, the concept of arrested motion is of crucial importance throughout Faulkner's career, giving us not only "the most significant image for the overall coherence of Faulkner's writings" but also "an explicit paradigm for his art" insofar as it "implies specifications of method, form, theme, and purpose."[20] Behind Faulkner's creation of doubles for Bayard there now seems to be an initial creation of Bayard as a double for Faulkner himself, not merely in the sense that Bayard's family background is the closest of all Faulkner's characters to Faulkner's own family, but also in the deeper sense that Bayard's temporal struggle relates to particular choices that an artist like Faulkner must make in harnessing and directing the "mad music" of his imagination. In the distinction between the "mad music" of the stallion and the conventional college serenade, for example, we can discern the tension between the "radical" and "conservative" aspects of Faulkner's imagination. Though Faulkner's depiction of Bayard's groping toward creativity in terms of music anticipates Faulkner's identification of music as the primal mode of all artistic creativity, Faulkner has denied Bayard that one crucial tool of his own creativity: the discovery of the word.[21]

Bayard reacts to his own failure to arrest motion by surrendering once again to sheer motion and to the old madness of racing his car. This countermovement away from an existence in the musical present is accompanied by increasingly spatialized images. The height on which Bayard stops prefigures the more rigid spatialization of Bayard's existence later in the novel into the heights of despair and the valley of peace; moreover, Faulkner links this spatialization with Bayard's movement toward Narcissa, for it is on this height that Bayard finally realizes that the serene head that he saw in the stallion's vortex was hers. This movement from time to space is mirrored by a break in the narrative, for the next short section reflects, for the first time in this symbolic day, Narcissa's point of view rather than Bayard's. This juxtaposition of a new point of view reveals an underlying structural principle of Faulkner's narrative, in that the internal divisions of a narrative have a precise correspondence to the characters' inability to touch each other in time. Since Narcissa appears as an atemporal essence whose very "being" is antipathetic to Bayard's, she is ultimately attracted to him as a fixed form in space rather than as a person existing in time (158). She remembers "the pallid, suddenly dreaming calm of his bloody face from which violence had been temporarily wiped as with a damp cloth, leaving it still with that fine bold austerity of Roman statuary, beautiful as a flame shaped in bronze and cooled: the outward form of its energy but without its heat" (159). The vision of Bayard as statue rather than as creator, which recalls the effigy of John Sartoris in the cemetery, becomes yet another double for Bayard. Narcissa aligns herself with an overly rigid arresting of motion that robs the bronze flame associated with the stallion of its heat and its life, thus killing the music of the present.

Before the serenaders reach Narcissa's house, however, they are able to participate in a tipsy ritual of human connection. Formerly the white men in Bayard's car insisted that the blacks drink home brew out of the automobile's breather cap, but now "all six of them drank fraternally from the jug, turn and turn about" (165). Nevertheless, the visit to Narcissa occurs under a "coldly wearied" moon, and Bayard's creative cycle ends with an anguished return into the spatialized time of the Sartorises. Miss Jenny has ordered the town marshal to take Bayard into custody, so that Bayard winds up literally and figuratively in jail. As if to replace his lost twin, Bayard becomes divided within himself, into a remote impersonal head and a bleak tortured body. Bayard now conceives of the remainder of his life as an infernal enclosure in spatialized time: "Three score and ten years to drag a stubborn body about the world and cozen its insistent demands. Three score and ten, the Bible said. Seventy years. And he was only twenty-six. Not much more than a third through it. Hell" (169).

FROM TIME TO SPACE:
THE SHAPE OF BAYARD'S DOOM

Bayard's movement during his symbolic day from Sartoris spatialized time to the music of the present to the "jail" of spatialized time represents a temporal cycle that Faulkner will continue to use consistently in later novels: characters will alternate between the actual present and spatialized time until the descent of their "doom" brings about the irrevocable substitution of spatialized time for the fluid, momentary present. Thus Faulkner's creative characters must be capable of transcending spatialized time repeatedly in order to live in the actual present, in spite of knowing that at the end of the creative cycle they will sink back into spatialized time again; such a cycle is clearly depicted in Quentin's narrative collaboration with his roommate, Shreve, in *Absalom, Absalom!*.[22] The onset of doom marks the end of a character's creativity; he or she may be able to "endure," but not to move beyond old selves or to establish meaningful contacts with others.

We can identify the pattern of Bayard's creative cycles as half of the basic temporal structure of the novel; the other half, as David Minter notes, is the "temporal framework" provided by the "ineluctable procession of the seasons," from the early spring of 1919 to the spring and early summer of 1920.[23] At times the two halves of the novel's temporal structure are juxtaposed in an ironic way; at times events in one half will influence events in the other. For example, when Bayard reappears in Part III after a long absence in the narrative, he returns at a point when the cycle of the seasons enables him to live in a particular kind of time again, a "smoldering hiatus" in the process of doom (228). This hiatus occurs because of the conjunction between his desire to live in time and a particular stage in the time of the earth, the planting season. Bayard's body becomes submerged in the earth's "sober rhythms," the monotonous repetition of his work on the plantation: "He had been so neatly tricked by earth, that ancient Delilah, that he was not aware that his locks were shorn" (229–30). The hiatus cannot, however, alter Bayard's doom: just as the appearance of

Horace Benbow in the novel after Bayard's symbolic day reflects an accelerated process of doubling associated with doom, so does the deeper splitting of Bayard's existence into body and mind during the hiatus mark the weakening of his life in time.

This splitting becomes even more serious when the subsequent car crash deprives Bayard of the use of his body, thus condemning him to an added measure of passivity. Lying in the black man's wagon on the way to town, Bayard feels "caught in a ceaseless and senseless treadmill, a motion without progress, forever and to no escape" (237). His desperate effort to reenter time first takes the form of burning souvenirs of his dead twin. In Faulkner's imagery of the four elements, fire is often associated with the temporal mode of "fury," a mode of time in which a character is oriented toward the past, endlessly duplicating a moment of extreme anger because the object of the anger seems more meaningful than the phenomena of the actual present. But Faulkner also uses fire in portraying the creative/ destructive doubleness of time, and even his most creative characters must destroy something in order to create something new: Sutpen's French architect in *Absalom, Absalom!*, a memorable minor character who serves as a model of creativity, must destroy part of Sutpen's "dream of grim and castlelike magnificence" in order to build the actual house, thus creating "of Sutpen's very defeat the victory which, in conquering, Sutpen himself would have failed to gain."[24] Thus if Bayard could transcend the fury of the fire, he could enter a new stage of the creative cycle and live in the present; Faulkner dramatizes this process in *The Hamlet* in the powerful image of Ike Snopes bursting through the flames to reach his beloved cow.

The image of fire also suggests a basic problem associated with the Sartoris experience of time. In "All the Dead Pilots," a story that recounts the death of Bayard's twin in 1918, fire is linked to the momentariness of John's "courage" and "recklessness": "And so, being momentary, it can be preserved and prolonged only on paper: a picture, a few written words that any match, a minute and harmless flame that any child can engender, can obliterate in an instant. A one-inch sliver of sulphur-tipped wood is longer than memory or grief: a flame no larger than a sixpence is fiercer than courage or despair."[25] Thus in setting fire to John's belongings, Bayard not only "kills" his twin in a symbolic revenge for John's shooting at him, but also attests to the flawed nature of his twin's experience of time: John's momentariness is not integrated with the other aspect of the present, fluidity. The aim of creativity, then, is to preserve or prolong such momentary qualities by marrying them to the fluid continuity of the present. In seeking an "other" to replace his twin, Bayard must choose someone who can help him make contact with this aspect of the present.

As the burning episode suggests, Bayard's particular doom involves not only his inner "Sartoris" spatialization but also the failure of other people to offer points of connection with his impulses toward a life in time. As we trace Bayard's creative cycles in Parts III and IV of the novel, charting his impulses toward time and toward space, we find that Bayard's relation to Narcissa plays an important role in bringing about his doom. Though Bayard's future wife pities the stiff "long shape" lying in bed, ironically Bayard is actually becoming the rigid statue she wants him to be (278). Reaching out to Narcissa, for the third time in the novel Bayard tries to tell the story of John's death, but as before the story's lack of a beginning or ending reflects Bayard's lack of control over time. Bayard binds himself to Narcissa in space rather than in time, in the "valleys of tranquility and peace" (282). Moreover, Bayard's attraction to Narcissa traps him in yet another spatialized definition: space here takes the form of an abstract conceptual polarization, for Miss Jenny and Narcissa now think of Bayard as a "man" rather than as a "Sartoris," as a member of the other half of a humankind polarized by gender. The absurd diminishment or warping of the self involved in this gender polarization is reflected in the sudden prominence of Byron Snopes. A grotesque double for Bayard, Byron works in the Sartoris bank and is a shadowy "rival" for Narcissa; he and Bayard even have the same initials. Whereas the endings of the previous two parts of the novel focus on Bayard, Part III ends with the defeat of the furious, lustful Byron.

Like Part III, Part IV repeats once again the symbolic structure of the creative cycle — the movement from spatialized time to the actual present and back — but now, since Bayard's doom is nearer, in a darker key. Narcissa is pregnant with the next Sartoris in the year's Indian summer; assuming that the child will be a boy, Miss Jenny wants to continue the endless line of Sartoris genealogy by naming the child John, after her dead brother and Bayard's dead twin. Not only is Bayard likely to feel that his son is replacing him, but he knows that his son will bear the name of the powerful patriarch and of the twin whom everyone, including Narcissa, preferred to Bayard. He is confronted both with the spatializing doom of "Sartoris" and with Narcissa's persistent fluid spatialization, which is meant to protect him: "her spirit went out in serene and steady waves, surrounding him unawares" (315).

In opposition to this movement toward space, Faulkner creates a strange, outrageously comic double for Bayard, a creature who lives solely in time: a mule. In such novels as *The Sound and the Fury* and *The Hamlet*, Faulkner depicts the temporal existence of idiots in order to isolate certain basic elements of human time, in particular the sense of the present moment; in *Flags in the Dust* Faulkner gives us a new perspective on the human tendency to spatialize time by celebrating the temporality of the mule. Trapped in an endless round of toil, the mule can nevertheless endure the outrages of history, "steadfast to the land when all else faltered before the hopeless juggernaut of circumstance, impervious to conditions that broke men's hearts because of his venomous and patient preoccupation with the immediate present" (313–14). If Bayard is burdened with the Sartoris doom, the mule exists outside of the "genealogical imperative":

"Father and mother he does not resemble, sons and daughters he will never have. . . ." The celibate mule will never be tempted by sexual desire, and will have no "dreams" or "visions" of the future. The mule suffers, as Bayard does, from the unresponsiveness of the world, for he performs "alien actions among alien surroundings," but at death he will receive no arrogant Sartoris monument, serving instead as food for buzzards. This tour de force, which seems intrusive unless related to Bayard's temporal struggle, thus celebrates the bedrock of time, the present moment. Though not necessarily creative in itself, the present moment is the sine qua non of all creativity, and it is highly fitting that Faulkner's encomium to the mule calls forth some of the most energized writing in the novel, an innovative liberation of his style.

Representing a new impulse toward time, this encomium modulates into an action that has important ramifications for artistic creativity: Bayard's possum hunt with Narcissa and his black servants Caspey and Isom. Though the possum hunt is a failure, and the subsequent death of old Bayard in the car accident brings young Bayard closer to despair, Faulkner will return to the theme of the hunt when Bayard flees to the MacCallum place in the hills after the accident. As I have mentioned earlier, Faulkner's temporal paradigm of the hunt will, as his career develops, come to hold a special place in his imagination. Paradoxically creative even though its purpose is to kill a living creature, the hunt represents for Faulkner a symbolic ritual of human beings moving progressively toward the future in the timeless space of the wilderness, thus mirroring the "radical" and "conservative" aspects of the creative act. The movement of the hunt takes on a special meaning in relation to the artist's activity in arresting motion: the motion is "killed" in its transformation into art, but paradoxically it will live again in art, just as the wilderness will in some sense restore life to creatures that have died in the hunt.[26]

In *Flags in the Dust* Faulkner thus experiments with a fruitful new temporal configuration that will culminate at the end of his major period in Ike McCaslin's wilderness experience in "The Bear." The tighter structure of juxtaposition in "The Bear" makes it clearer that Faulkner conceives of the wilderness as a counterweight to the internal psychic pressures and external pressures of family, society, and history that threaten to rob people like Bayard of the chance to live in the actual present. Ike McCaslin's wilderness exists in an ageless creative present in which death is impossible, constituting a world in which the exalted ritual of the hunt will allow human beings to pursue their dreams. For the hunter who has undergone a novitiate to the wilderness, as Ike has, the future-directed hunt has as its goal not merely killing but the communion with the prey as well, a communion that represents for Faulkner the transcendence of the old self through a meaningful confrontation of self and other.

Though these themes are not as forcefully developed in young

Bayard's approach to the wilderness, Faulkner's creation of Buddy Mac-Callum as another double for Bayard does evoke a new possibility of freedom and potential creativity in the present; in a sense, Buddy is a significant forerunner of Ike McCaslin. Like Bayard, Buddy has experienced the spatialized nightmare of World War I, in which "creatures without initiation or background or future" are "caught timelessly in a maze of conflicting preoccupations" (367). But the wilderness to which he returns offers Buddy a congenial solitude and the opportunity to grow, so that he alone of the five MacCallum sons — named for his father, but bearing a different nickname — has the possibility of marrying some day, transcending the strange patriarchal world that old Virginius MacCallum has created. Hunting the elusive fox with Buddy and his family, Bayard can hear another version of the music of the present, a more coherent version than the "mad music" of the stallion during Bayard's symbolic day and a more exalted version than the old-fashioned college serenade: "Long ringing cries fading, falling with a quavering suspense, like touched bells or strings, repeated and sustained by bell-like echoes repeated and dying among the dark hills beneath the stars, lingering upon the the ears crystal-clear, mournful and valiant and a little sad" (378). Old Mr. MacCallum exclaims, " 'Aint that music fer a man, now?' "

The symbolic psychology of such images in this episode conveys much more powerfully than the overt psychological analysis of Bayard the dimensions of his temporal struggle. This symbolic psychology anchors Bayard's feelings of guilt over the deaths of his grandfather and his brother in a wider context of a temporal problem embracing nature, the family, society, and history. For example, as a harbinger of the issues to be confronted at the MacCallum place, Bayard's entrance into their world is marked by the sight of a fox that is astonishingly unafraid of humans or dogs. The fox, Ethel, has become the MacCallums' pet, and serves as an example of a creature that has been able to transform itself, to go against its own biological nature. Thus Ethel images for Bayard the tantalizing possibility of surmounting his Sartoris blood, of forging a new, creative self.

The masculine preserve of the MacCallums, in which Mandy the cook is the only woman, also plays an important role in Faulkner's symbolic psychology, since it provides Bayard with an image of the diminished, spatialized world of patriarchy. Though patriarchal or genealogical creation is in some ways analogous to artistic creation — especially since it imposes continuity on time, arresting motion in the sense of decreasing random influences — the art it creates remains a lower, imitative form of art: like the Sartorises with their hawklike noses, the MacCallums "sat without word or movement, their grave acquiline faces as though carved by the firelight out of the shadowy darkness, shaped by a single thought and smoothed and colored by the same hand" (365).

In spite of the flawed art of patriarchy, the Sartorises' and the

MacCallums' obsession with genealogy remains a powerful force, and the mating of Ethel the fox with the MacCallums' hound, General, reveals why this is so. Jackson MacCallum had hoped to combine the best qualities of fox and hound, but his mixing of species has resulted in a litter of Frankenstein's monster puppies that can't smell, bark, or see. Similarly, when people dare to break taboos, or even transgress social norms, in the sinister laboratory of history, they risk degradation and chaos; in "Father Abraham," part of a projected novel that Faulkner was working on during the same period that he wrote *Flags in the Dust*, Faulkner conceives of such a grotesque human creation in the new tribe of Snopeses. An analogous possibility exists for creative artists who allow their "radical" imaginations to outstrip their "conservative" imaginations: a modernist's bold innovation may be merely grotesque, a creative dead end.

The MacCallum episode also crystallizes in a striking way the significance of Bayard's doubles in Faulkner's depiction of Bayard's creative cycles. Like Bayard and his twin in the past, Bayard and Buddy sleep together in a small, cold room that reflects Bayard's claustrophobic world. The memories of his relation to his brother plunge Bayard into a crisis of selfhood, since his feelings of guilt, longing, and hatred leave no room for a creative existence in the present: "Bayard could hear his own breathing also, but above it, all around it, surrounding hum, that other breathing. As though he were one thing breathing with restrained laboring, within himself breathing with Buddy's breathing; using up all the air so that the lesser thing must pant for it. Meanwhile the greater thing breathed peacefully and steadily and unawares, asleep, remote; ay, perhaps dead" (368–69).

Only an inner change in time can provide an alternative to Bayard's subsequent vision of a spatialized hell in which he seeks his brother endlessly. Faulkner depicts in this episode Bayard's struggle to enter time by giving birth to himself, an effort that will be the explicit goal of Ike McCaslin's novitiate to the wilderness in "The Bear" and the implicit goal of Quentin Compson's creative collaboration with Shreve in *Absalom, Absalom!* Faulkner even anticipates some specific images of Quentin's collaboration: like Quentin at Harvard, in the cold bed Bayard's flesh "jerked and jerked as though something within the dead envelope of him strove to free itself" (370). It is this freer new self, this yet uncreated "double," that Bayard must bring to birth if he is to cease searching futilely for his twin. Ultimately Bayard can solve his problem only by forging a self that can confront another person in time, "striving for . . . comprehension, a hand, no matter whose, to touch him out of his black chaos" (370). But since it is the nature of the Sartoris curse to abort this very process, Bayard's arrogance would make him "spurn" such a hand, settling for a solipsistic "cold sufficiency."

Even if Bayard were to remain in time, he could have as his goal only the diminished spatialized form of time that Faulkner calls "peace." Part

IV closes with an image of the end of Bayard's creative cycle and a return to death-in-life, as "drop by drop the rain wore the night away, wore time away" (371). The next day he takes the road that leads him to exile from Sartoris and to a spectacular death: he chooses to fly a flawed experimental plane, another man's failed dream of creativity, and actually becomes at the moment of his death the creature of the hysterical Sartoris myth, the fallen angel or Icarus who loses his wings. The historical image of the airplane as a symbol of Bayard's existence in the modern world is joined, perhaps superseded, by the mythic image of the Sartoris flight into the absolute.

BAYARD'S HUNT FOR THE OTHER: BLACK TIME

As my analysis of Bayard's creative cycles has demonstrated, Bayard's effort to come in contact with an "other" plays a crucial role in his struggle to live in time. Whereas the male characters who serve as Bayard's doubles are trapped in similar temporal mechanisms, both women and black people hold out meaningful but elusive possibilities of a creative new time that Bayard could "touch" in his attempt to transcend the Sartoris curse. Faulkner's depiction of black characters in *Flags in the Dust* anticipates the importance of blacks in creating a temporal dialectic in such novels as *The Sound and the Fury, Light in August, Absalom, Absalom!, Go Down, Moses,* and *Intruder in the Dust.*

By associating black people with music in *Flags in the Dust* Faulkner suggests that they may in fact be able to create the "music of the present" that Bayard is seeking. In the Sartoris household the "endless crooning song" of the Sartoris cook, Elnora, flows constantly beneath the daily sound and fury, and during Bayard's symbolic day several black characters help to suggest new temporal possibilities (120). Faulkner also depicts black characters as actors seizing the present, as when Simon communicates to the horses the "histrionic moment" when they are to create together a majestic drama of old Bayard's routine departure from the bank (8). Blacks like Simon are able to live as artists even with homely materials like horses because they love what they are creating: "beneath his hands the sorriest beast bloomed and acquired comeliness like a caressed woman, temperament like an opera star" (8). Simon's creativity and power reach comic heights of magnificence at the Sartoris Thanksgiving feast, where he stands "overlooking the field somewhat as Caesar must have stood looking down into Gaul, once he had it well in hand, or the Lord God himself when he looked down upon His latest chemical experiment and said It is well" (329). Unlike Bayard, Simon can be a soldier and a creator — almost a Creator — at the same time.

For much of the novel, however, the experience of blacks serves simply as comic juxtaposition to that of the whites. Blacks may also function as background, meaningful but so ambiguous that Bayard cannot understand how their existences could enlarge his own. At one point Bayard even seems to regard black people as abstractions. When he spends Christmas with a poor black family after fleeing the MacCallums, Faulkner describes their tenuous temporary communion in a cerebral way that works against the communion's emotional impact: they drink together as "two opposed concepts antipathetic by race, blood, nature, and environment, touching for a moment and fused within the illusion of a contradiction — humankind forgetting its lust and cowardice and greed for a day" (393).

But in reacting against this overabstraction, which militates against the concrete "touch" of time, Faulkner resorts to racist stereotypes and associates black people with animals, such as the celebrated mule who lives in the present. This association makes it more plausible to regard the "miscegenation" of Ethel the fox and the hound as a foreshadowing of Faulkner's grappling with the idea of human miscegenation in his later works; early in his career the idea was apparently so disturbing that it was deflected onto animals. The catastrophic mating of fox and hound reinforces our sense in *Flags in the Dust* that black time and white time will remain separate; only later will such mixed-blood characters as Joe Christmas, Charles Bon, and Sam Fathers image forth the need for a fuller experience of time.

BAYARD'S HUNT FOR THE OTHER: IN THE GARDEN OF WOMEN

If blacks cannot serve as the "other" for Bayard to touch primarily because of what appears to be an excessive dreamlike fluidity in their experience of time, Faulkner's women are problematic "others" because of their overriding tendency to spatialize time into cycles. We first see Narcissa Benbow in Miss Jenny's garden, a carefully tended space in which creation is governed by the cyclical order of the seasons. Though this spatial creation can at its best be golden and harmonious, it does tend to prevent the self from venturing beyond certain known boundaries, interposing between the self and the world "all the impalpable veil of the immediate, the familiar" (56). Women's spatialized time thus corresponds to the "conservative" imagination, in both the positive and the negative senses, for it works to preserve things of value at the same time that it fosters inertia and discourages creative innovation.

Narcissa dwells not in the changing historical world but in an "aura of grave and serene repose," an inner garden where the pain of World War I hardly touches her except to evoke a "pointless pity" (31, 78). Incapable of responding effectively to the needs of those around her, particularly Bayard and Horace, Narcissa possesses the inert fluidity of a pool or a "tideless summer sea," a fluidity more static than that of the moving present moment (189). Narcissa's very name echoes the self-love that makes this "chaste vase" admire in Bayard the rigid timeless beauty of a statue. When Bayard is in motion she tends to regard him as an animal, and the sober music of her piano remains only potentially the music of the present.

In contrast to Narcissa, Miss Jenny experiences time in a paradoxical way, since she is both a woman and a Sartoris, and the essence of "Sartoris" is maleness. The spatialized "orbit" of her will links her with Sartorises, as does her fatalistic prediction, as a Sartoris sibyl, that eventually Bayard will discard his car for a deadly airplane. Miss Jenny also wants to name Narcissa's baby John, upholding the rigid genealogical recapitulation of Johns and Bayards in the family. By insisting on the overriding value of reproduction over the individual's life in the present — she claims not to care whether Bayard kills himself as long as he has a son — Miss Jenny acts both as a Sartoris who exalts the linear "genealogical imperative" and as a woman who exalts the eternal cyclical process of physical creation. Neverthelsss she is open to the historical present, unlike old Bayard, and a ride in young Bayard's car revivifies her; though her myth of Carolina Bayard moves toward the absolute, as an artistic creation it mellows in time like wine (14).

As in many other novels, Faulkner seems to admire women's courageous ability to endure in time. If we can respond to Bayard's doom, we can also respond to Narcissa's uncharacteristically forceful meditation on the passive doom of women, which is "waiting"; some, like Miss Jenny, wait and endure with an "indomitable spirit" as their familiar world disintegrates (410). Yet insofar as we are most closely engaged in *Flags in the Dust* with Bayard's absorbing struggle, we attempt to create as we read an image of a woman who could "touch" Bayard in time. Faulkner gives us only a glimpse of Bayard's dead first wife, Caroline, whose qualities are opposed to Narcissa's: "a girl with a bronze skirling of hair and a small, supple body in a constant epicene unrepose, a dynamic fixation like that of carven sexless figures caught in moments of action, striving, a mechanism all of whose members must move in performing the most trivial action, her wild hands not accusing but passionate . . ." (56). Faulkner's image points to an imaginative failure, conceivably Bayard's failure to find a good wife but more likely an inability of Faulkner himself to move beyond old polarized images of men and women. Unlike the rather inert Narcissa, Bayard's ideal wife would have to be in motion in order to have a creative existence in time, yet Faulkner describes only a paradoxical opposite of Narcissa's organic repose, Caroline's mechanical, fixated "unrepose." Faulkner cannot imagine a truly modern woman except as the sexless negation of a "real" woman, and thus Narcissa's superseding of Caroline signals a regression to an ahistorical view of women as timeless essences.

Ultimately Faulkner's view of women's time crystallizes in his basic image of the creativity of women, the creation of a child. Since temporally this creation is part of an infinite cycle of birth and death, Faulkner depicts Narcissa's activity as circular in a spatial sense: just as she has surrounded Bayard with her serenity, so does she now surround her unborn child with her strength so that he can escape the Sartoris doom. In terms of the individual woman, Faulkner sees the nurturing of a child as a surrender of self, depicting Narcissa, Miss Jenny, and the nurse in a "choral debauch of abnegation" that recalls Old Man Falls's abengation of self in imitating John Sartoris (423). If we think of the Faulknerian relation of self and other as a continuum, women's abnegation is at one pole and Sartoris arrogance is at the other: in the center of the continuum is the creative relation between self and other that brings the self into time. Seen as one extreme, then, the garden of women is a graveyard for one who wants a creative relation in the present; as Horace finds out, Belle Mitchell's bed has " 'ghosts,' " and Miss Jenny's visit to the cemetery with its wilting flowers at the end of the novel carries Faulkner's imagery to its logical conclusion (406).

The polarization of Faulkner's imagery of gender can be so extreme that it sometimes seems as if he regards the mating of a man and a woman as a kind of miscegenation, or even a mingling of distinct species. In this context the mating of the fox and the hound takes on an added meaning. In Narcissa's new name for her child, Benbow Sartoris, which replaces Miss Jenny's "John," Faulkner evokes a vision of a human being composed of two separate halves, and Dr. Peabody and his son duly speculate on the outcome of the internal war in the child between Benbow and Sartoris blood. Though we see Ethel's grotesque puppies, the novel does not show us what this new Benbow-Sartoris creation will become: ontologically it remains a potential, historically it looms in the future.

We do know, however, that Faulkner regarded a change in name as an emblem of creativity, since his addition of a *u* to his family name heralded his birth as a writer. We also know that a writer must practice the self-abnegation that Faulkner associates with women to a certain extent: " 'I listen to the voices,' " Faulkner told Malcolm Cowley, " 'and when I put down what the voices say, it's right. Sometimes I don't like what they say, but I don't change it.' "[27] And when Faulkner describes Bayard struggling at the MacCallum place to give birth to a new self, he evokes a vision of women's creativity as the fundamental creative mode. Faulkner discussed art in similar terms: " 'The most important thing is that man continues to create, just as woman continues to give birth.' "[28] In creating the temporal structure of his novel, as I have mentioned, he plays off two complementary temporal frameworks against each other, Bayard's "male" striving to transcend the past in his creative cycles, and the "female" cycle of the seasons.

In the very fabric of *Flags in the Dust*, then, Faulkner may have tried to embody the union of Narcissa's creativity and Bayard's, the visionary symbolistic technique that we can associate with Narcissa's garden and Bayard's existential struggle to take his place in the contemporary world. Another image of women's creativity has intriguing ramifications in this context. For fifteen years Narcissa's querulous old neighbor Aunt Sally has carried around with her an "interminable" piece of fancy work, stitching together "odds and ends of colored fabric in all possible shapes. She could never bring herself to trim any of them to any pattern, so she shifted and fitted and mused and shifted them like pieces of a picture puzzle, trying to fit them to a pattern or to create a pattern about them without cutting them, smoothing her colored scraps on a card table with flaccid, patient putty-colored fingers, shifting and shifting them" (160). Aunt Sally's patchwork can serve as a provocative comic image of what Eugene Goodheart has called "decentered" art: "The fate of modernist literature has been a 'decentering' of the imagination and intelligence — a deliberate loss of poise amidst the variety of experience, so that no point of view, no position is privileged."[29]   Insofar as Faulkner has written a novel with a relatively episodic structure and has included random glimpses of his characters' consciousnesses and of the world in which they live, he has created such a decentered patchwork art; in *Absalom, Absalom!* Faulkner will depict this aspect of artistic creation in Quentin and Shreve's "creating between them, out of the rag-tag and bob-ends of old tales and talking, people who perhaps had never existed at all anywhere. . . ."[30]

Like the timeless symbolic essences of Faulkner's imagery, this patchwork art of the moment militates against the oppressive linearity of genealogical creation. But as I have shown in discussing the novel's preoccupation with doubling, Bayard's creative cycles, and Bayard's hunt for the "other," *Flags in the Dust* is far more than patchwork art. As Arthur F. Kinney notes, in novels like *Flags in the Dust* Faulkner relies on the reader's creative work of cognition, on the "constitutive" and "structural" capacities of consciousness that enable the reader to maintain a sense of the parts of the book in the ongoing process of putting them together, and to form a sense of the book as a whole. Thus, if the separate episodes of the novel are a force of disjunction, the recurrence of motifs and analogous experiences works as a unifying force.[31] Moreover, Faulkner's fascination with the hunt in particular reflects a strong need to balance the patchwork with an element of progressive form rather than the cyclical form of recurrence. In crafting the story of young Bayard's "dream of the present," Faulkner attempts to trace a dynamic history of a man's struggle to live in time, and in this context Faulkner's ultimate view of "Sartoris" as a historical anachronism, a deadly "outmoded" game, is a deeply significant one (433).

Notes

1. Faulkner to Jean Stein vanden Heuvel, in *Lion in the Garden: Interviews with William Faulkner, 1926–1962*, ed. James B. Meriwether and Michael Millgate (New York: Random House, 1968), p. 255.

2. David Minter, "Notes on Faulkner and Creativity," in *Faulkner and the Southern Renaissance*, ed. Doreen Fowler and Ann J. Abadie (Jackson: Univ. Press of Mississippi, 1982), pp. 264, 247.

3. Ibid., pp. 248, 257, 258, 251, 254.

4. Faulkner to Loïc Bouvard, in *Lion in the Garden*, pp. 70–71.

5. Faulkner to Nagano Seminar, in ibid., p. 103.

6. Faulkner to Jean Stein vanden Heuvel, in ibid., p. 255.

7. Walter J. Slatoff, *Quest for Failure: A Study of William Faulkner* (Ithaca: Cornell Univ. Press, 1960), p. 4. Faulkner wrote the first six stories in *The Unvanquished* in 1934, during the same period he was working on *Absalom, Absalom!*; he wrote the seventh in 1937.

8. *Flags in the Dust* (New York: Random House, Vintage Books, 1973), p. 96; hereafter cited in the text.

9. Patricia Drechsel Tobin, *Time and the Novel: The Genealogical Imperative* (Princeton: Princeton University Press, 1978), p. 5.

10. See Gary Lee Stonum, *Faulkner's Career: An Internal Literary History* (Ithaca: Cornell Univ. Press, 1979), pp. 41–60.

11. Bayard's fascination with the dynamism of cars and planes suggests a rebellious modernist urge similar to that of the Italian futurists. In his "Futuristic Manifesto," the poet F. T. Marinetti declared, "We want to sing the love of danger. . . . the beauty of speed. . . . a roaring car . . . is more beautiful than the *Victory of Samothrace*" ("The Joy of Mechanical Force," from "The Foundation of Futurism/Manifesto of Futurism, 1909," reprinted in *The Modern Tradition: Backgrounds of Modern Literature*, ed. Richard Ellmann and Charles Feidelson, Jr. [New York: Oxford Univ. Press, 1965], p. 433). Marinetti would have admired John Sartoris's arrogance and the part of his dream that yearned toward the absolute: "Time and Space died yesterday. We live already in the absolute, since we have already created the eternal omnipresent speed" (p. 433). Futurist creativity denied the past, exhorting young people to throw their "sensitiveness . . . forward by violent casts of creation and action," to view art as "violence, cruelty, and injustice," the displacing of the old by the young, the weak by the strong (p. 434). Like Bayard, the futurists resented the domination of the past in their country. But Bayard's "futurism" can only be of a residual, diminished sort: he is cut off from the urban industrial society that fueled the futurists' visions, and he cannot, after his nightmarish experience of World War I, accept the futurist glorification of war and destruction.

12. Doubling appears in *Flags in the Dust* primarily as a thematic and formal element with little of the deep psychic content of such novels as *Absalom, Absalom!* and *The Sound and the Fury*, in which doubling is also an important part of the novels' structure. Though it seems significant that Bayard has lost both his parents, that his memories of his twin are so highly charged, and that he marries a woman whose brother cherishes strong, perhaps incestuous, feelings for her, we do not have enough concrete evidence for a psychological interpretation of doubling. This aspect of the novel prompted Jean-Paul Sartre's identification of Bayard as one of Faulkner's "men who have secrets and keep quiet" ("William Faulkner's 'Sartoris,' " reprinted in this volume). There is much more psychological evidence for Sartoris doubling in *The Unvanquished*; using psychoanalytic concepts, John Irwin refers briefly to doubling in *Sartoris* and analyzes *The Unvanquished* in more detail. See *Doubling and Incest/Repetition and Revenge: A Speculative Reading of Faulkner* (Baltimore: Johns Hopkins Univ. Press, 1975), pp. 55–59.

13. This episode anticipates "The Bear," in which whiskey will play an important role in the hunters' ritual of confronting the immemorial time of the wilderness. It seems to Ike McCaslin that the "fine fierce instants" of the hunt and the "wild immortal spirit" of the prey are concentrated in the liquor; see *Go Down, Moses* (New York: Random House, 1942), p. 192.

14. Samuel Beckett, *Proust* (New York: Grove Press, 1957), p. 71.

15. Ibid., pp. 71–72.

16. *Absalom, Absalom!* (New York: Random House, 1936), p. 275.

17. In *The Hamlet* Faulkner will return to the spring as a temporal image, making Ike Snopes' "well of days" the repository of all time, which "holds in tranquil paradox of suspended precipitation dawn, noon, and sunset; yesterday, today, and tomorrow . . ." ([New York: Random House, 1964] p. 186).

18. Faulkner to Jean Stein vanden Heuvel, in *Lion in the Garden*, p. 255.

19. Faulkner to Jean Stein vanden Heuvel, in ibid., p. 253.

20. Stonum, *Faulkner's Career*, p. 33.

21. See Faulkner's interview with Jean Stein vanden Heuvel, in *Lion in the Garden*.

22. From the spatialized time of Chapters VI and VII, Quentin moves to the actual present in Chapter VIII, and returns to spatialized time in Chapter IX.

23. David Minter, *William Faulkner: His Life and Work* (Baltimore: Johns Hopkins Univ. Press, 1980), p. 83.

24. *Absalom, Absalom!*, pp. 38–39.

25. In *Collected Stories of William Faulkner* (New York: Random House, 1950), p. 531.

26. See Faulkner's depiction of the deathless unified "myriad" creativity of the wilderness in "The Bear" (in *Go Down, Moses*, pp. 326–29).

27. Malcolm Cowley, *The Faulkner-Cowley File: Letters and Memories, 1944–1962* (New York: Viking Press, 1966), p. 144.

28. Faulkner to Loïc Bouvard, in *Lion in the Garden*, p. 73.

29. Eugene Goodheart, *The Failure of Criticism* (Cambridge, Mass.: Harvard Univ. Press, 1978), p. 2.

30. *Absalom, Absalom!*, p. 313.

31. Arthur F. Kinney, *Faulkner's Narrative Poetics: Style as Vision* (Amherst: Univ. of Massachusetts Press, 1978), p. 9.

Index

Only substantial references are indexed. Works and characters appear under the author's name except in the case of Faulkner where they are listed separately *in italics*. Only notes of substance or of important bibliographical concern are included.